International Perspectives on Aging

Volume 31

Series Editors
Jason L. Powell
Department of Social and Political Science
University of Chester
Chester, UK

Sheying Chen
Department of Public Administration
Pace University
New York, NY, USA

The study of aging is continuing to increase rapidly across multiple disciplines. This wide-ranging series on International Perspectives on Aging provides readers with much-needed comprehensive texts and critical perspectives on the latest research, policy, and practical developments. Both aging and globalization have become a reality of our times, yet a systematic effort of a global magnitude to address aging is yet to be seen. The series bridges the gaps in the literature and provides cutting-edge debate on new and traditional areas of comparative aging, all from an international perspective. More specifically, this book series on International Perspectives on Aging puts the spotlight on international and comparative studies of aging.

More information about this series at https://link.springer.com/bookseries/8818

Hanna Falk Erhag
Ulrika Lagerlöf Nilsson
Therese Rydberg Sterner • Ingmar Skoog
Editors

A Multidisciplinary Approach to Capability in Age and Ageing

Springer

Editors
Hanna Falk Erhag
Neuropsychiatric Epidemiology Unit,
Department of Psychiatry and Neurochemistry,
Institute of Neuroscience and Physiology
Sahlgrenska Academy at the University of Gothenburg, Gothenburg, Sweden

Centre for Ageing and Health – AgeCap
University of Gothenburg
Gothenburg, Sweden

Institute of Health and Care Sciences
Sahlgrenska Academy at the University of Gothenburg, Gothenburg, Sweden

Therese Rydberg Sterner
Neuropsychiatric Epidemiology Unit,
Department of Psychiatry and Neurochemistry,
Institute of Neuroscience and Physiology
Sahlgrenska Academy at the University of Gothenburg, Gothenburg, Sweden

Centre for Ageing and Health – AgeCap
University of Gothenburg
Gothenburg, Sweden

Ulrika Lagerlöf Nilsson
Department of Historical Studies
University of Gothenburg
Gothenburg, Sweden

Centre for Ageing and Health – AgeCap
University of Gothenburg
Gothenburg, Sweden

Ingmar Skoog
Neuropsychiatric Epidemiology Unit,
Department of Psychiatry and Neurochemistry,
Institute of Neuroscience and Physiology
Sahlgrenska Academy at the University of Gothenburg, Gothenburg, Sweden

Centre for Ageing and Health – AgeCap
University of Gothenburg
Gothenburg, Sweden

Region Västra Götaland, Sahlgrenska University Hospital
Psychiatry, Cognition and Old Age Psychiatry Clinic
Gothenburg, Sweden

ISSN 2197-5841 ISSN 2197-585X (electronic)
International Perspectives on Aging
ISBN 978-3-030-78062-3 ISBN 978-3-030-78063-0 (eBook)
https://doi.org/10.1007/978-3-030-78063-0

This Springer imprint is published by the registered company Springer Nature Switzerland AG
The registered company address is: Gewerbestrasse 11, 6330 Cham, Switzerland

This book is dedicated to all those older adults contributing in various ways to increase our knowledge about capability in ageing.

Foreword

'Capability' is one of those concepts that is risky to think about for too long. Like 'social class', it seems straightforward enough to begin with, but then the more you delve into it the more it threatens to slip through your fingers. It is therefore very gratifying to see the challenge taken on in this book, and everyone involved should feel proud of their achievements. 'Multidisciplinarity' is the key, of course: capability underpins so much of what we know or seek to know about ageing, but it has to be understood from a range of perspectives. People from my (healthcare) academic background are tempted to think in a very reductive way about diseases and disability, possibly dipping our toes in the waters of underpinning biology/physiology or those of social and societal impacts. This risks missing the point without the wider perspectives of policy, history, law, geography, design, etc. And we need to draw together expertise in these fields with genuine collaboration and mutual understanding, rather than hope that one discipline alone can make a difference.

It has been a pleasure to serve on the external advisory board for the truly innovative AgeCap, Centre for Ageing and Health, which has supported this book and the collaborations underlying its creation. The breadth and depth of knowledge distilled in its chapters will go a long way to achieving genuine progress in ageing and capability research, and not just in direct advances in understanding. For a book on ageing, publication longevity is a more-than-usually pertinent consideration. With luck in any rapidly advancing research field, findings will end up outmoded and replaced by more recent discoveries. However, there is something much longer-lasting here. Time will tell, but I think the collaborative, multidisciplinary principle will endure, and examples like this of its successful application will remain relevant to every generation whose attention drifts into silos and hyper-specialism. I believe this book will remain inspiring and eminently 'capable' for many years to come.

King's College London, London, UK
Robert Stewart

South London and Maudsley NHS
Foundation Trust, London, UK

Foreword

Ageing is an extremely complex and multifaceted process. Studying ageing, therefore, requires a variety of perspectives and methods and, above all, open-minded researchers willing to engage in meaningful multidisciplinary dialogues and debates. While promising in terms of its scholarly outcomes and often inspiring also on a personal level, working across disciplines can be extremely demanding. Yet, the Center for Aging and Health (AgeCap) has found a brilliant way of tackling this challenge: using capability as a common denominator and theoretical lens through which to approach ageing and the life course has proven to be a fantastic and fruitful idea. Capability lends itself very well as a boundary concept that allows for multi- and interdisciplinary collaboration on age and ageing, enabling researchers to do focused and rigorous research within and across their fields. Most importantly, however, the framework's focus on conversion factors means always acknowledging that age and ageing are not only biologically but also socially and culturally constructed. As a researcher from the humanities, I cannot emphasize this aspect enough.

AgeCap's approach can be seen as a model of good practice in the field of Ageing Studies that has already had a tremendous impact both in Sweden and internationally. I am delighted to say that AgeCap's work – which is now documented in this fantastic and timely publication – has also had a ripple effect on a structural level: its researchers have helped to facilitate the founding of a new research center at the University of Graz, the 'Center for Interdisciplinary Research on Aging and Care (CIRAC)', started 2020. This book documents the efforts, vision and leadership and will also guide future generations of researchers.

Center for Interdisciplinary Research on Ageing and Care
University of Graz, Graz, Australia

Ulla Kriebernegg

Acknowledgment

We want to thank the Swedish Research Council for Health, Working Life and Welfare (FORTE) and UGOT Challenges at the University of Gothenburg.

Contents

Chapter 1
Introduction

Hanna Falk Erhag, Ulrika Lagerlöf Nilsson, Therese Rydberg Sterner, and Ingmar Skoog

In 2020, for the first time in history, there were more people in the world aged **60 years and over** than there were children below the age of 5 years. The population aged over 65 years is projected to increase from one billion in 2019 to more than two billion in 2050, and those aged over 80 years are projected to increase from 143 to 426 million, with the largest increase occurring in the developing world (UN World Population Prospects, 2019). This demographic trend constitutes the largest global health challenge, according to the World Health Organisation (WHO). The European Union has set it as one of the major challenges in Horizon 2020 and it has important societal implications (European Commission, 2020). The proportion of

H. Falk Erhag (✉)
Neuropsychiatric Epidemiology Unit, Department of Psychiatry and Neurochemistry, Institute of Neuroscience and Physiology, Sahlgrenska Academy at the University of Gothenburg, Gothenburg, Sweden

Centre for Ageing and Health – AgeCap, University of Gothenburg, Gothenburg, Sweden

Institute of Health and Care Sciences, Sahlgrenska Academy at the University of Gothenburg, Gothenburg, Sweden
e-mail: hanna.falk@gu.se

U. Lagerlöf Nilsson
Department of Historical Studies, University of Gothenburg, Gothenburg, Sweden

Centre for Ageing and Health – AgeCap, University of Gothenburg, Gothenburg, Sweden
e-mail: ulrika.lagerlof.nilsson@history.gu.se

T. Rydberg Sterner
Neuropsychiatric Epidemiology Unit, Department of Psychiatry and Neurochemistry, Institute of Neuroscience and Physiology, Sahlgrenska Academy at the University of Gothenburg, Gothenburg, Sweden

Centre for Ageing and Health – AgeCap, University of Gothenburg, Gothenburg, Sweden
e-mail: therese.rydberg.sterner@neuro.gu.se

H. Falk Erhag et al. (eds.), *A Multidisciplinary Approach to Capability in Age and Ageing*, International Perspectives on Aging 31,
https://doi.org/10.1007/978-3-030-78063-0_1

retired individuals will increase, leading to an increased ratio between those who have exited the workforce and those still active in the labour market. Thus, ageing represents a global societal and scientific challenge requiring integrated efforts, multidisciplinary translational research approaches and social innovations that build on ideas of potentials and capabilities, emphasising the value of old age.

Ageing as a process is neither linear nor consistent and is only loosely associated with a person's chronological age (i.e. years since birth). Ageing also includes biological, social and psychological aspects. Biological age refers to 'an age-associated decline of physiological and cognitive functions, and de-tuning of adaptive responses, followed by an increase in age-specific mortality' (Rydberg Sterner et al., 2019; Flatt, 2012). Social age refers to age as defined by laws and regulations and by the societal norms and beliefs reflected in particular geographical areas and historical times. Psychological age includes the subjective experience of ageing as well as wisdom, life experiences and personal development (Higgs & Gilleard, 2015). As such, no single scientific discipline can fully address the many dimensions of ageing. Although we focus on later life in this book, we are fully aware of the need to adopt a life-course perspective. Hence, we apply a perspective that views inequalities and diversities at older ages as being the result of accumulated inequalities and diversities across the entire life course.

The Centre for Ageing and Health (AgeCap) at the University of Gothenburg, Sweden, was founded in 2013 with funding from the Swedish Research Council for Health, Working Life and Welfare (FORTE). In 2016, AgeCap was included in the UGOT Challenge, a unique research initiative in which the University of Gothenburg invested 300 million SEK in six multidisciplinary research centres. The research fields span a large number of areas. Some have clear cross-disciplinary elements. Some initiatives are new, while others are based on previous research structures that have been expanded as a consequence of the changing perspectives on challenges in our society. Thanks to the UGOT Challenge, AgeCap now comprises researchers from five faculties, 15 institutions, and 24 disciplines, with the primary objective of generating knowledge that can improve our understanding of capability in ageing across all societal levels.

The common denominator of all the research projects at AgeCap is *capability*, which can be used as a guiding concept or an approach, depending on the purpose or perspective of the project. Building on the seminal work by Amartya Sen (2005, 2009), capability can be viewed as the individual's ability to perform the actions required to reach goals that he or she has reason to value. At any given time, what a

I. Skoog
Neuropsychiatric Epidemiology Unit, Department of Psychiatry and Neurochemistry, Institute of Neuroscience and Physiology, Sahlgrenska Academy at the University of Gothenburg, Gothenburg, Sweden

Centre for Ageing and Health – AgeCap, University of Gothenburg, Gothenburg, Sweden

Region Västra Götaland, Sahlgrenska University Hospital, Psychiatry, Cognition and Old Age Psychiatry Clinic, Gothenburg, Sweden
e-mail: ingmar.skoog@neuro.gu.se

person can or cannot do is limited by the available resources to which she has access and her ability to convert these resources into the desired goal, for example enjoying good health, being able to socially integrate and participate or maintaining independence. Individuals are characterised by different conversion factors, meaning that, even where two people have access to the same resources, they may not have the capability to enjoy the same functions. Many of the current discussions and policies concerning the challenge of ageing at the individual and societal levels can be related to capabilities. For example, via elderly care, we add resources to secure older people the capability to maintain an independent life, assuming that this is what they value; and in order to provide older workers with the capability to remain in the workforce, we need to invest in age management and anti-discriminatory practices. However, resources, capabilities and goals of value form a complex and dynamic pattern that needs to be researched using cross-disciplinary approaches. Most people, regardless of age, value their health, but the capability to live healthy lives varies substantially because it is influenced by multiple factors occurring from before birth to late life, including genetics and other hereditary factors, personality, mental and somatic health, cognitive, functional and physical ability, biological factors, socioeconomic gradient, social environment, family, working life, gender and ethnicity, as well as policies, laws, regulations and access to services and care. To complicate things even further, health is not only a valued goal but also a central resource that, in combination with other factors, determines capability in ageing. The digital revolution and the rise of home computers, along with the invention of the World Wide Web, social media and smartphones, has led to digital skills being considered a vital aspect of a person's capabilities. This illustrates how numerous factors are interrelated in complex interactions, not merely in the format of simple cause-and-effect, and are also embedded in the historical period.

To add to the complexity, factors that were previously thought of as relatively stable, such as genes and personality, are now found to be modified by the external environment. For example, personality has been shown not only to change over the life course but also to be shaped by environmental factors. The same goes for our genes, with large epigenetic studies demonstrating that gene expression can be influenced by the environment. Another important aspect of capability is that it includes preferences, wishes and desires, which brings the focus to subjective experience, which is only accessible by the human being herself, and only she can determine what she has reason to value in order to maintain a good life. This is a vital aspect if we want to understand individual actions and factors that promote wellbeing.

Ageism is embedded in all layers of society. To achieve health equality and maintain good health in later life, we need to focus on the potential to increase capability in ageing worldwide, at both the societal and individual levels, taking into account the intersections of diversity, such as age, sex, gender, disability, social gradient, civil status, migration and belonging to ethnic minorities. I*t also needs to be emphasised that 'ageing'* and '*older people'* are relative concepts, which vary over historical time and geographical areas, affecting both society's view and treatment of older people, and the self-images of older people themselves. The capability of the person depends on three levels and defines the core concepts used in the capability approach. The combination of macro-, meso- and micro-circumstances form the basis for an individual capability set – that is, what an individual actually can or cannot do. The macro-level refers to laws and regulations that affect aspects such as retirement systems, social security, the labour market, home-care and healthcare. It could also include factors such as ageism, historical period, the media and political decisions. Changes at this level are often guided by explicit goals to change incentives, such as changes in the retirement system and taxation, making it more profitable to work for longer, or constraining available exit options through changes to early retirement options. The meso-level refers to the configurations in which daily life is embedded within the family, relations, social networks, caring facilities, caring obligations, healthcare services and, for the young-old, the workplace. The micro-level includes a range of accumulated features that either enable or limit the ageing person's capability, such as genetic predisposition, personality, somatic and mental health, functional ability, lifestyle, cognitive functioning, neurobiology, physical activity, psychosocial and socioeconomic factors. So-called 'human capital factors', such as educational attainment, acquired work skills, earning capacity and social capital, are examples of important factors influencing the capability of each person at the micro-level.

1.1 The Purpose of This Book

This book aims to provide its readers with diverse accounts of how capability as a concept or an approach can be used in research on age and ageing. In the AgeCap seminars and discussions, it became evident that a plethora of different views, taken together, could form the basis for something new – a book that could contribute to knowledge development by using a multidisciplinary approach to describe capability in ageing from different angles in order to generate novel insights. As a starting point, we asked the authors three questions: how do you define capability in your field of research, how do you make use of it in your research, and how do you relate your research to the micro-, meso- and macro-levels? In parallel, AgeCap hosted seminars inviting scholars to discuss capability from different perspectives that later also included reading and editing each other's drafts for this book. This back-and-forth process was not intended to reach a consensus on how to define capability in ageing, but rather the opposite – enabling scholars from a variety of different research fields to elaborate on how they define capability and how they use their concept or approach in their research.

In this book, different ontological and epistemological perspectives are presented. There are also examples of how knowledge acquisition can be deductive, value-free and generalisable, or inductive, value-laden and contextually unique. The chapters describe different research approaches in studies of capability in ageing that aim to predict, understand, emancipate or deconstruct, or a combination of all these approaches. Regardless of the multitude of views, definitions and applications, we have a common goal of raising questions and doing research to focus on older people's capability to live a life they value as meaningful and good.

1.2 Outline of the Book

This anthology comprises 16 chapters, spanning disciplines from the humanities to neuroscience, and discussing health, cognition, epidemiology, diagnostics, healthcare for frail older people, participation in society, representations in the media, time-trends, design, self-determination and health literacy, social work, work and retirement, and cumulative disadvantages/advantages in old age using the capability framework.

To set the stage, the chapter by Rydberg Sterner and colleagues provides a brief description of the capability approach and its core concepts. This framework is based on the work of Amartya Sen, Martha Nussbaum and Ingrid Robeyns, which has been adapted for the multidisciplinary ageing context of AgeCap. The conceptual framework of capability introduced in this chapter was developed as an endeavour to meet the pronounced need for a shared platform related to capability in ageing within AgeCap and to make our theoretical framework more accessible to the general public. However, as the reader will discover while exploring the different chapters in this anthology, building a shared platform related to capability in ageing within AgeCap is challenging. Thus, the conceptual framework merely serves as a launchpad for researchers to use in any way they find relevant from their own research perspective.

In the chapter by Gustafsson and Hörder, the ICECAP-O instrument is described. This is a questionnaire especially targeting the capability level of older individuals, which can be used in evaluations of interventions and longitudinal studies, where older people's capabilities are a focus. The ICECAP-O is one of the few research measures of wellbeing that taps into the concept of capability, i.e. the opportunities to 'do' and 'be' the things that a person regards as important in life.

The chapter by Skoog and colleagues describes how capability can be used in epidemiological studies, with special emphasis on population epidemiology. It is suggested that the capability approach is an ideal framework for epidemiological studies, because it captures the dynamic multiplicity of processes involved in these types of studies, in relation to both time and space, and socioeconomic, psychological and biological factors. It thus captures the complex interactions that arise from a multitude of factors acting between and within macro-, meso- and micro-levels during the life course of an individual. The authors give examples relating to specific conditions, such as cognitive function and dementia, depression, multimorbidity and functional ability, and non-modifiable and modifiable risk factors, such as genetics and nutrition.

In the chapter by Falk Erhag, the author argues that self-rated health can be used as an indicator of a person's capability to master the gains and losses of late life. Although a person's capabilities are dependent upon a wide variety of factors at the individual level, symptom experience, chronic illnesses and functional disability are paramount. By operationalising personal capability into self-rated health, the many dimensions that make up the complex concept of health and wellbeing in old age can be studied in large and representative population-based samples using epidemiological methods, which have the potential to generate new evidence to solve nursing problems and expand nursing knowledge.

In the chapter by Johansson and colleagues, the capability approach is described in relation to cognitive ageing and subjective well-being, including a discussion of how intact cognition is a core component for generating, achieving and prioritising personally valued goals. Ageing trajectories are embedded in a historical and sociocultural context in which societal systems regulate brain-behaviour relationships according to the age of their members. The authors conclude that the capability approach can be used to improve our understanding of the factors and mechanisms involved in shaping age-related developmental and psychological processes across the life course, especially in late life.

The chapter by Blennow and Zetterberg focuses in on the absolute micro-level, the chemistry of the brain, and how different chemical biomarkers relate to ageing and dementia, and thus extend into and affect the meso- and macro-levels. Alzheimer's disease (AD) is the most common form of dementia and a major cause of capability impairment in older adults. In recent years, there has been a successful development of blood biomarkers for AD pathophysiologies. This opens up new ways of diagnosing AD and predicting future cognitive decline.

In the chapter by Dahlin-Ivanoff and colleagues, the capability approach is used as a theoretical framework in research with and for frail older people, focusing in particular on their opportunities to realise their goals in relation to contextual influencing factors. The concept of frailty is developed and the authors stress that the capability approach can contribute to an understanding of the process of becoming frail, because this approach focuses on the real opportunities of the frail person in relation to the resources that they have, or do not have, to hand.

In his chapter, Kokkinakis outlines his thoughts on capability in relation to the incorporation of eHealth into social and healthcare services for older people living alone, enabling them to choose the best way to manage their needs and demands for health and medical care. The author points out several important dimensions in this context, namely eHealth literacy, and its relation to health-promoting behaviours, taking into account the exceptional circumstances caused by the Covid-19 pandemic.

In their chapter, Frisk and Svengren Holm discuss how caregiving needs to be transformed and based on old people's real needs and what they perceive as important. Taking Design Thinking (DT) as a starting point, the authors discuss how DT could improve people's capabilities and help to provide tools and processes for supporting innovations and new ways of thinking about solving problems. The results show that DT can provide valuable knowledge about users' needs in a resource-efficient way, as well as balancing the economic and human perspectives when developing new services, thereby also increasing people's capabilities.

In the chapter by Kjellberg, the author presents the results of a scoping review focusing on how the use of the capability approach is linked to policies, practices and social justice approaches in social work research. The capability approach was framed as congruent with the aims of social work, and applicable in relation to social well-being and social inequality. The author concludes that the capability approach has attracted some attention in social work with older people, and that the number of studies elaborating on the capability approach in social work, in general, is growing.

In their chapter, Lagerlöf Nilsson and Castenbrandt discuss the value of a capability approach in historical research on older people, and how it can be used as an analytical tool for visualising historical patterns to add another perspective to this theoretical framework. In this context, the authors use historical examples to argue that historical change alters how we value certain capabilities and that the meanings of functions differ over time.

In the chapter by Svensson and colleagues, the authors describe the tension between self-determination and human dignity in the Swedish legal system relating to social care for older people, and how the capability approach can be used as an analytical tool in studies of legal scholarship. A person's capability to make decisions is highlighted, as well as the supportive societal system that enables the realisation of self-determination, specifically for individuals who are not fully capable of making arrangements for themselves.

In their chapter, Bergström and Edström argue that the core human rights to freedom of expression and freedom of information connect the concept of capability with the role of the media in society. The media can be a tool for enhancing a person's voice and capabilities, but it can also be seen as hindering a good life if media technologies are perceived as inaccessible and if certain groups are marginalised by the media. The authors also discuss how the media has the potential to increase capability in older age groups, and who should be held accountable when the media reinforces ageist stereotypes.

In the chapter by Dellve and colleagues, the authors combine the capability approach with system theory to provide an understanding of the multi-component key resources supporting the capability of older workers. The authors describe central working-life conditions and conversion factors relevant to capability *to* work and capability *through* work. Having a reasonable degree of control and influence (freedom of choice) at work, as well as opportunities to make individual deals and adjustments that match one's competence and experience, is important for an individual's decisions leading to a long working life.

In the chapter by Wikström and colleagues, the focus is on the organisational capability approach. The workplace conditions and practices that may inhibit or promote the retention of workers beyond the previous norm for the age of retirement are highlighted and discussed. Workplace resources, capabilities and functions form a dynamic pattern. Factors that influence the work abilities of older workers are related to complex interactions and do not merely follow the format of simple cause and effect. Since organisational capability makes it possible to focus on the interactions between an individual's resources and preferences, and the opportunity structure existing in the workplace (meso-level) and embodied in the retirement system (macro-level), much of the discussion and many of the policies and practices concerning older people can be related to the concept of capabilities.

In the chapter by Solevid and Scheiber Gyllenspetz, the focus is on political participation and non-participation among seniors. The authors conducted long interviews with eight individuals aged 80 years or older, both voters and non-voters. The empirical results show that the concepts of internal and combined capabilities are fruitful when understanding conceptions of and reasons for non-voting. The chapter ends with a discussion about the importance of continuing to integrate explanations at different levels in order to understand political (in)activity among older individuals.

The authors in this anthology represent different research areas, including medical science, political science, the social sciences, psychology, business administration, law, history, the media, linguistics and design. This anthology includes a remarkable array of contributions that present state-of-the-art, innovative, interdisciplinary and intra-disciplinary theorising about the use of the capability approach in the study of ageing. It represents the abundance of innovative research projects and ideas that can be said to characterise AgeCap as a research centre. Multidisciplinary collaboration is a challenging task and crucially important to the cumulative construction of knowledge. We hope that this anthology will inspire researchers to address the capability approach and to use its theoretical gaze when pursuing explanations that extend beyond specific empirical findings.

References

European Commission. (2020). https://ec.europa.eu/.

Flatt, T. (2012). A new definition of aging? *Frontiers in Genetics, 2012*(3), 148.

Higgs, P., & Gilleard, C. (2015). *Rethinking old age: Theorising the fourth age*. Macmillan International Higher Education.

Rydberg Sterner, T., Ahlner, F., Blennow, K., Dahlin-Ivanoff, S., Falk, H., Havstam Johansson, L., & Skoog, I. (2019). The Gothenburg H70 birth cohort study 2014–16: design, methods and study population. *European Journal of Epidemiology, 34*(2), 191–209.

Sen, A. (2005). Human rights and capabilities. *Journal of Human Development, 6*(2), 151–166.

Sen, A. (2009). *The idea of justice*. Belknap Press of Harvard University Press.

UN World Population Prospects. (2019). https://population.un.org/wpp/.

Chapter 2
The AgeCap Conceptual Framework for Research on Capability in Ageing

Therese Rydberg Sterner, Greta Häggblom-Kronlöf, and Pia Gudmundsson

2.1 Theoretical Framework in Brief

The overall vision of AgeCap is a society in which ageing is valued for its potential and older adults are respected – a society in which older people are viewed as resources. The research within our Centre originates from the perception that today's society is not optimal for promoting the health of older people. Our aim is to investigate and understand capability in ageing and related factors in order to fulfil our common goal of increasing the quality of life and societal participation of older people. While there are several ways to meet this challenge, AgeCap has chosen the capability approach in order to focus on a more health- and ability-related perspective, rather than on disease or disabilities.

The understanding of capability used within the centre is based on the work of the philosopher and economist Amartya Sen, described as the individual's ability to perform actions in order to reach goals he or she has reason to value (Sen, 2009). The capability approach focuses on what people are able to do and to be – their

T. Rydberg Sterner (✉) · P. Gudmundsson
Neuropsychiatric Epidemiology Unit, Department of Psychiatry and Neurochemistry, Institute of Neuroscience and Physiology, Sahlgrenska Academy at the University of Gothenburg, Gothenburg, Sweden

Centre for Ageing and Health – AgeCap, University of Gothenburg, Gothenburg, Sweden
e-mail: therese.rydberg.sterner@gu.se; pia.gudmundsson@neuro.gu.se

G. Häggblom-Kronlöf
Institute of Neuroscience and Physiology, Department of Health and Rehabilitation, Sahlgrenska Academy at the University if Gothenburg, Gothenburg, Sweden

Centre for Ageing and Health – AgeCap, University of Gothenburg, Gothenburg, Sweden
e-mail: greta.haggblom-hronlof@neuro.gu.se

H. Falk Erhag et al. (eds.), *A Multidisciplinary Approach to Capability in Age and Ageing*, International Perspectives on Aging 31,
https://doi.org/10.1007/978-3-030-78063-0_2

capabilities – and on their freedom of choice to perform those actions. The capability approach has been further developed by philosopher Martha Nussbaum, who focuses on justice and human rights in her theory and defends the importance of the capability approach in the context of welfare and quality of life (Nussbaum, 1997). Both Nussbaum and Sen argue that the capability approach needs to be combined with a human rights perspective. As such, every older person has the right to be able to perform actions in order to reach their own goals of value. In the model and graphic illustration of the conceptual framework of capability outlined in this chapter (see Figs. 2.1 and 2.2), justice is therefore the platform upon which the approach rests. The graphic illustration is also inspired by the work of Ingrid Robeyns, who has focused on how to apply the capability approach in practice in research settings (Robeyns, 2005).

2.2 Why a Theoretical Framework?

AgeCap's multidisciplinary setting was an opportunity to adopt the capability approach within our research. Nevertheless, this multidisciplinary approach also created challenges in establishing a common definition of capability, and how to apply the concept in collaborations across several different research fields. When AgeCap was formed in 2013, the need for a common conceptual foundation quickly became evident. It was also proposed during the first meeting with our Advisory Board in the autumn of 2014 that a conceptual framework laying out our shared view of capability in ageing needed to be developed. Thus, the purpose of having a common conceptual framework and graphic illustration was to facilitate the implementation of the capability approach in our research setting.

Based on the above-described circumstances, 'capability seminars' involving researchers from all the collaborations within AgeCap were initiated during 2014. In addition, each research group organised internal discussions about the concept of capability based on pre-selected literature from different perspectives, which were summarised and utilised as a foundation for developing the framework. After approval from the AgeCap Steering Committee, members of the Communication Group became responsible for leading this process, with continuing discussions with the Steering Committee, Principal Investigators and other researchers within AgeCap. The final version of the capability framework was completed in March 2016 and communicated to all members of AgeCap.

2.3 Central Concepts in the AgeCap Capability Framework

The content and core characteristics of the AgeCap capability framework are based on the work of Amartya Sen (2009), Martha Nussbaum (1997) and, primarily, the theoretical model published by Ingrid Robeyns (2005). The core characteristics are

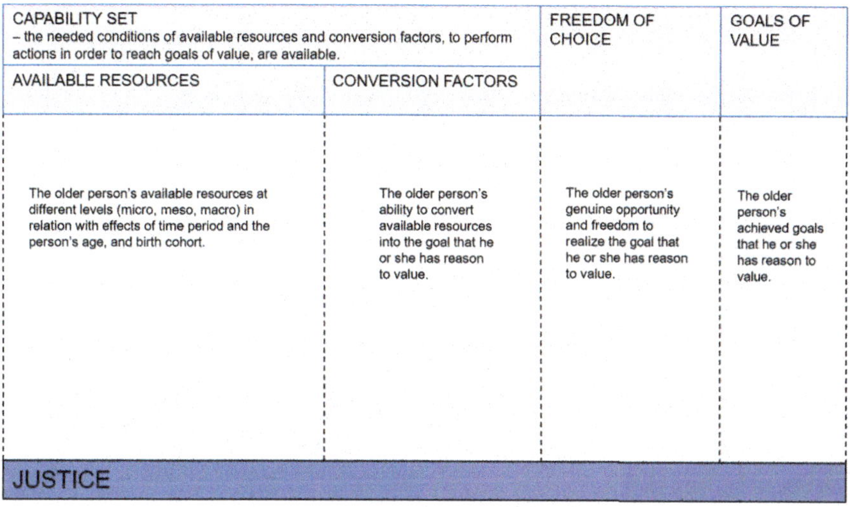

Fig. 2.1 A conceptual model of the capability framework in AgeCap

presented below. All concepts in the framework are related to each other by dynamic and complex interactions, and various factors can be classified as different concepts in the graphical illustration below, depending on each specific situation. Furthermore, although the description and examples below focus on an older person, the capability approach may also be applied to groups of people, organisations or systems, depending on the field of research.

2.3.1 *Capability Set*

What an individual can do and prefers to do is dependent on actual available resources and existing constraints. The combination of macro-, meso- and micro-levels, as well as time-trend circumstances, constitute the basis for an individual's capability set, i.e., what a person actually can or cannot do (a combination of available resources and conversion factors). Having a full capability set entails that the necessary conditions for reaching the valued goal are available. There is an overlap between available resources and conversion factors, which generates a challenge to separate them. For example, health literacy (the degree to which individuals have the capacity to obtain, process and understand the basic health information and services needed to make appropriate health decisions) could be both a resource (e.g. being able to understand the information) and a conversion factor (e.g. being able to make appropriate health decisions).

2.3.2 Available Resources

A person's resources throughout the life course are available at several societal levels (i.e. the macro-, meso- and micro-levels). Resources at the macro-level refer to laws and regulations that affect pensions, social security, norms about ageing, the labour market, healthcare and its related organisations and costs. At the meso-level, we find the configurations within which daily life is embedded, e.g. family life, relationships, social networks, meetings with caring facilities, caring obligations and, for the young-old, the workplace. The micro-level contains a whole range of accumulated features that may enable or limit a person's capability. Resources at the micro-level include factors such as genetic predispositions, personality, physical, mental and social health, lifestyle, cognitive functioning, neurobiology, psychosocial and socioeconomic factors, preferences and education. The balance and relative importance of the resources at each societal level vary between individuals, and are affected by our age, within which birth cohort we were born and during which time period we live.

2.3.3 Conversion Factors

A person's conversion factors consist of their ability to actually convert available resources into a goal that he or she has reason to value. The ability to use and adapt the available resources exists in everyday life and is divided into three levels: personal, social and environmental. Personal conversion factors include, for instance, metabolism, health literacy, physical health status etc. The social conversion factors include societal mechanisms such as discriminatory circumstances like social class, hierarchies or power structures between the sexes etc. Environmental conversion factors include climate or geographical location etc. In order to reach a goal of value, a person must first be able to recognise the necessary resources and then have the ability to use them.

2.3.4 Freedom of Choice

Freedom of choice refers to a person's everyday choices when performing actions in order to reach their goal of value. Martha Nussbaum explained this by saying 'once the stage is set, the choice is up to them' (Nussbaum, 1997: 290). 'The stage' here refers to the person's capability set. This means that, when all the prerequisites are in place, the individual always has the freedom to choose whether or not to utilise their capability set (i.e. their available resources and conversion factors) in order to reach the goal in question.

2.3.5 *Goals of Value – Personal Goals*

The goals that an individual has reason to value can be defined as 'goals of value'. These goals are unique to each person and should be independent of the person's functional level or health status. However, there is a challenge in that individuals adapt their goals of value to their current life situation, meaning that expectations may affect the choice of goals.

2.3.6 *Justice – A Person's Right to Achieve Goals of Value*

As stated in the background section above, both Nussbaum and Sen argue that the capability approach needs to be combined with a focus on human rights. This is applied in AgeCap through an overarching principle that every person has the right to be able to perform actions in order to achieve their own goals of value. Nussbaum claims that capabilities are the political goal but, as stated earlier in this chapter, every person must then be free to decide whether or not to use the provided tools to achieve a certain goal. People are not to be viewed as passive recipients, and the important inclusion of the keyword 'choice' in the capability approach respects their freedom (Nussbaum, 1997). Justice in the capability approach considers both the right to achieve goals, and also the right to freedom of choice. This freedom to choose is dependent on determinants and different arrangements within a society; for example, facilities within the healthcare system. Furthermore, sociocultural values and traditions that appear in different unique settings can be either 'freedom facilitators' or 'freedom inhibitors', which directly or indirectly affect the person's ability to choose and to achieve their goals of value.

2.4 A Graphical Illustration of the AgeCap Capability Approach

To facilitate the application of the capability approach within our research setting, and to make it more accessible to different target groups within society, the AgeCap Steering Committee decided that a graphic illustration of the AgeCap framework of capability should be created in collaboration with graphic designers and the Sahlgrenska Academy at the University of Gothenburg.

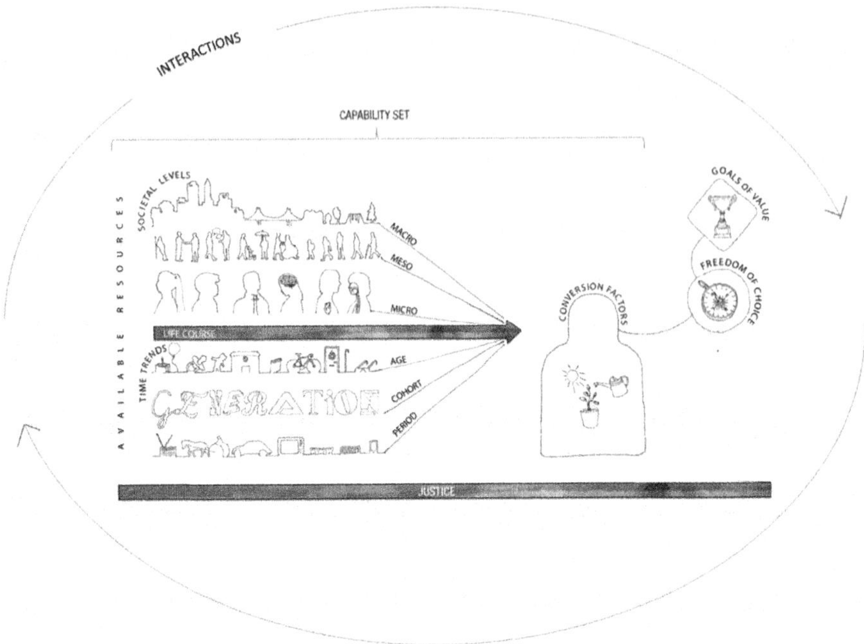

Fig. 2.2 A graphic illustration of the AgeCap capability approach

2.5 Challenges and Reflections

The development of a conceptual framework within a broad, multidisciplinary research centre such as AgeCap entailed several challenges that required reflection. Although it was of great importance to create a common foundation and to share a common view of the key concept of capability, there were also great difficulties involved in making this view applicable to all research fields. The framework has the aim of explaining and simplifying the concept of capability, yet retaining an awareness of the challenges related to our multidisciplinary setting. Thus, the conceptual framework was developed mainly to serve as a platform for researchers to use in whatever way they found most relevant from their own perspective.

2.5.1 How Could the Framework Be Applied?

The framework was developed to guide discussions regarding research on capability in ageing, and to understand the complex associations between the different factors that influence ageing and health. Is it possible or even relevant to apply the AgeCap capability approach in our research? And if so, how could it be done? Must the concept of capability be measured and included as a core factor in our research project from the beginning, or could it merely be applied as an overarching perspective that permeates projects from method to discussion? The most reasonable answer ought to be: 'it depends'. It depends on the research question, the research setting, the field and the interests of the individual researcher.

The main purpose of AgeCap is to investigate capability in ageing as demonstrated and seen in the following chapters of this book. In some research projects, the inclusion of the concept is very straightforward and obvious, while in others the connection between the investigated factors and capability is less clear. Different research programmes, as well as specific collaborations and research questions, focus on various different areas and levels of the theoretical framework of capability. For example, at the micro-level, genetic, cognitive and behavioural factors may be evaluated, while at the macro-level researchers might be investigating factors related to the law, ageism and culture. However, all projects within AgeCap aim to fulfil our common goal – to enable and enhance capability in ageing and thereby to contribute to increased quality of life and societal participation for older people.

The graphic illustration may also be applied outside the research community in order to make the general public feel more included in the research that is planned and performed within AgeCap. It is an endeavour to make our theoretical framework more accessible so as to dismantle the wall between researchers, older people and the general public.

2.5.2 *What Is Freedom of Choice?*

What constitutes a 'free' choice? How can we know if a person has the genuine opportunity and freedom to realise a goal that he or she has reason to value? Is 'freedom of choice' the same for a person with largely preserved cognitive abilities as it is for a person affected by dementia? These questions are important to keep in mind and discuss in relation to the capability approach.

2.5.3 *Goals of Value – Subjective or Objective?*

A person may not think they have the required abilities to achieve a certain goal, and may therefore exclude it as a goal worth striving for. Is this important to consider? Do we all have the same mindset towards reachable goals, or is it more realistic that each person defines their goals in line with their expectations and current life situation? Who decides which goals are valuable or not? Is it up to the researcher, or the individual? This question is a dividing line between Sen and Nussbaum – whether Nussbaum's 'list' (see a simplified version in Box 2.1) should be applied or not. This list was created by Nussbaum with the aim of deciding upon ten morally relevant capabilities and goals of value (Nussbaum, 1997). Sen criticises this list and emphasises that all capabilities and goals of value are morally relevant, and that a

Box 2.1: Nussbaum's List in Brief. The Complete List Can Be Found Elsewhere (Nussbaum, 1997)

Being able to live a life of normal length

Having physical health, reproductive health, food and shelter

Being able to move freely and safely, not being exposed to violence, having sexual freedom

Being able to use the senses, imagination, thought, education, freedom of speech

Being able to have attachments to things and people outside ourselves, to feel devotion, love, grief, desire, gratitude and anger

Being able to form a conception of the good and to engage in critical reflection about the planning of one's life

Affiliation, living with others, being treated with respect and dignity, absence of discrimination due to ethnicity, sexual orientation, religion etc.

Being able to live with concern for and in relation to animals, plants and the world of nature

Being able to laugh, play and enjoy recreational activities

Political and material control over one's environment, political participation, having the right to employment

goal of value can only be expressed and chosen by a person themselves (Sen, 2005). On the other hand, Nussbaum criticises Sen for not having a list, because she thinks that considering justice demands making a distinction between morally relevant and non-relevant capabilities (Nussbaum, 1997). However, it can be very difficult to distinguish a clear line between goals, available resources and conversion factors. Thus, what is the difference between subjective and objective goals of value? Subjective goals of value are retrieved from the person, e.g. by asking an open question, such as: 'what is most important to you?' or 'which aspects of life mean the most to you?' Objective goals of value are predefined, and are not chosen by the person. Two examples of objective goals of value are Nussbaum's list and the ICECAP-O questionnaire, which will be addressed in Chap. 3.

2.6 Summary and Future Directions

The conceptual framework of capability and the graphic illustration introduced in this chapter were developed as an endeavour to meet the pronounced need for a shared platform related to capability in ageing within AgeCap, and to make our theoretical framework more accessible to the general public. The framework is based on the capability approach that was developed by Sen, Nussbaum and Robeyns (Sen, 2009; Nussbaum, 1997; Robeyns, 2005), and adapted for the multidisciplinary ageing context of AgeCap. The research questions within AgeCap typically exist at several levels and within different parts of the framework. Due to the difficulty of considering the entire capability approach in each specific project, some research projects will utilise the theoretical framework more than others. Each piece of enhanced knowledge related to capability that is produced by AgeCap collaborations will thus play an important role in our research context.

The conceptual framework of capability represents an indicative starting point for investigating capability in ageing, and to guide the reasoning and discussions within our multidisciplinary setting. Furthermore, it may facilitate our understanding of the complex associations between ageing and health within our many research fields. AgeCap researchers are encouraged to use the framework in whichever way they find relevant from their own perspective in order to achieve our joint goal of increasing the quality of life and societal participation of older adults.

References

Nussbaum, M. C. (1997). Capabilities and human rights. *Fordham Law Review, 66*(2), 273–300.

Robeyns, I. (2005). The capability approach: A theoretical survey. *Journal of Human Development, 6*(1), 93–114.

Sen, A. (2005). Human rights and capabilities. *Journal of Human Development, 6*(2), 151–166.

Sen, A. (2009). *The idea of justice*. Belknap Press of Harvard University Press.

Chapter 3
The ICECAP-O Measure

Susanne Gustafsson and Helena Hörder

3.1 Analytical Synopsis

The ICECAP-O is a measure of capability in older people. It focuses on wellbeing defined in a broad sense, rather than health states, and is founded on Amartya Sen's conceptualisation of capability. The ICECAP-O contains five attributes: *Attachment*, *Security*, *Role*, *Enjoyment* and *Control*. A measure focusing on the capabilities of older people may be especially valuable for the evaluation of programmes targeting public health, interventions crossing health and social care boundaries, multidisciplinary actions and economic evaluations.

There is a lack of measures such as the ICECAP-O in the context of either research or health and social care interventions in Sweden. Therefore, a Swedish version of the ICECAP-O was established, by following guidelines for translation and cross-cultural adaptation, including forward–backward translation, committee

S. Gustafsson (✉)
Department of Rehabilitation, Jönköping University, School of Health and Welfare, Jönköping, Sweden

Department of Health and Rehabilitation, Institute of Neuroscience and Physiology, The Sahlgrenska Academy at Gothenburg University, Gothenburg, Sweden

Centre for Ageing and Health – AgeCap, University of Gothenburg, Gothenburg, Sweden
e-mail: susanne.gustafsson@ju.se

H. Hörder
Centre for Ageing and Health – AgeCap, University of Gothenburg, Gothenburg, Sweden

Orthopedics, Department of Clinical Sciences, Lund (IKVL), Lund University, Lund, Sweden

Arthro Therapeutics, Malmö, Sweden

Neuropsychiatric Epidemiology Unit, Department of Psychiatry and Neurochemistry, Institute of Neuroscience and Physiology, Sahlgrenska Academy at the University of Gothenburg, Gothenburg, Sweden

H. Falk Erhag et al. (eds.), *A Multidisciplinary Approach to Capability in Age and Ageing*, International Perspectives on Aging 31,
https://doi.org/10.1007/978-3-030-78063-0_3

review and pre-test. Studies evaluating the reliability and validity of the Swedish version of the ICECAP-O showed that it seems to measure what it is supposed to measure, and that acceptability is satisfactory. Even so, the attribute *Control* might be considered in need of a minor overhaul for use in the Swedish context, and a layout adapted for visually impaired people is considered desirable. In addition, a short statement in parentheses after each attribute, with an example clarifying its meaning, is proposed to support a more thorough guidance.

The Swedish version of ICECAP-O also showed high test–retest reliability for the index score, but agreement for individual items was problematic. Further studies on more diverse groups of older people, in different contexts and with different time frames, are needed. As a final point, we recommend the use of the ICECAP-O in health and social care, and in the evaluation of interventions and longitudinal research studies where older people's wellbeing is in focus.

3.2 Introduction

The Investigating Choice Experiments for the Preferences of Older People—CAPability Index (ICECAP-O) (Grewal et al., 2006) is a self-rated measure that focuses on wellbeing defined in a broad sense, rather than just health. In general, wellbeing measures aim to capture when people feel satisfied or content with life. They often contain indicators of the quality of people's relationships, their positive emotions, resilience and the realisation of their potential (Diener & Seligman, 2004). Wellbeing is associated with numerous benefits related to health, work, family and economics (Lyubomirsky et al., 2005).

The ICECAP-O is one of the few measures of wellbeing that taps into the concept of capability, i.e. the opportunities to 'do' and 'be' the things that a person deems important in life. It was originally developed for use in economic evaluations by researchers at the University of Birmingham in the UK. The ICECAP-O is tailored for older people (aged 65 years and older), and is founded on Amartya Sen's conceptualisation of capability (Sen, 1993, 2009). Capability is considered a more appropriate evaluative space than function (health status) because two people may both have a specific function, but only one may have the actual possibility to fulfil this function in action or in being (i.e., capability). This approach advocates assessing capability (what a person *can* do) rather than functioning (what a person *actually* does), in order to avoid imposing a specific idea of what a good life constitutes, and to reflect the importance of freedom to choose (Sen, 1993).

Older people might not have equal opportunities to enjoy good health due to factors at the individual (micro), group (meso) and/or societal (macro) levels. The combination of personal factors, including physical health and cognition, group factors such as family, friends and community, and societal factors, exemplified and executed by laws and healthcare services, may at any given time form the basis for a person's capability set; i.e., what the person actually can or cannot do (Sen, 2009). For instance, two older people may both value being as independent in everyday life as possible. One of these person's legs works well resulting in needing few resources to be mobile, while the other person may have an impairment/disability resulting in an increased need for resources, e.g., technical aids and/or assistance from another person, to achieve the same level of mobility. Hence, capability could be considered as the effective possibilities that a person has to convert their resources into achieving a desired goal (Sen, 1993), such as being independent in everyday life, as illustrated in the example.

A measure that captures the capabilities of older people may be especially valuable for the evaluation of programmes targeting public health, interventions crossing health and social care boundaries, multidisciplinary actions and economic evaluation (Coast et al., 2008a). It may also be useful in longitudinal research studies exploring aspects of older people's health and wellbeing, such as the H70-studies (Rinder et al., 1975; Rydberg Sterner et al., 2019) conducted by the Centre for Ageing and Heath (AGECAP) at the University of Gothenburg, Sweden.

3.3 Development of the Original ICECAP-O

The ICECAP-O measure was first developed based on findings from rigorous qualitative and quantitative research with older people in the UK (Coast et al., 2008a, b; Flynn et al., 2011; Grewal et al., 2006). In addition to the ICECAP-O, which is tailored for older people, there is also a version targeting all adults, the ICECAP-A (Al-Janabi et al., 2012), and a version for use in end-of-life care, the ICECAP-SCM (Coast et al., 2016). The final English-language version of the ICECAP-O contains five attributes that were found to be important for capability: *Attachment* – love and friendship; *Security* – thinking about the future without concern; *Role* – doing things that make you feel valued; *Enjoyment* – enjoyment and pleasure; and *Control* – independence (Coast et al., 2008a). The ICECAP-O has a four-level response option scale that is described as statements representing: 'none', 'a little', 'a lot', and 'full capability'. For example, the response options for the last attribute, *Control* – independence, are: 'I am able to be completely independent' (level 4), 'I am able to be independent in many things' (level 3), 'I am able to be independent in a few things' (level 2), and 'I am unable to be at all independent' (level 1). The response option values (4 to 1), are anchored to a best–worst scaling, ranging from 1.00 (full capability) to 0.00 (no capability). A total index score, based on a tariff computed from population-based values in the UK, is thus obtained (Coast et al., 2008a; Flynn et al., 2007). In a survey study, including 809 individuals aged 65 years and older in the UK, the mean ICECAP-O index score was 0.832. Seven percent of the participants in this study gave answers indicating that they considered themselves to be in the top ICECAP-O state (1.00 = full capability). The same study also found that poor physical and psychological health, living alone and infrequent socialising were associated with lower measured capability according to the ICECAP-O.

That impaired physical health is associated with a lower mean index score was also confirmed for osteoarthritis patients requiring joint replacement (Mitchell et al., 2013). In an Australian study (Couzner et al., 2013), in which 786 people aged 65 years and older participated, men had a slightly lower mean index score (0.821) than women (0.836). In this study, an association with lower levels of the index score were found for people born outside Australia, those having an injury or disability and those with a lower income.

Reliability, validity and feasibility testing for the English-language version of the ICECAP-O, as well as versions translated into other languages, are ongoing. There is evidence, for example, of construct validity (Coast et al., 2008b), face validity (Horwood et al., 2014) and validity for a post-hospitalised older population in the Netherlands (Makai et al., 2013). The ICECAP-O questionnaire is freely available on the University of Birmingham's webpage (University of Birmingham, 2021).

3.4 The Swedish Version of the ICECAP-O

There is a lack of measures such as the ICECAP-O in the context of research or health and social care interventions in Sweden. Implementing a questionnaire developed and tested in a specific context (e.g. the UK) in a dissimilar context (e.g. Sweden) requires cross-cultural adaptation. Therefore, a Swedish version of the ICECAP-O was established by following guidelines for translation and cross-cultural adaptation, including forward–backward translation, committee review and pre-test (Guillemin et al., 1993). Thereafter, two studies nested within an ongoing comprehensive population-based study of health among older people, the Gothenburg Birth Cohort Studies (H70), Sweden (Rinder et al., 1975; Rydberg Sterner et al., 2019), were performed.

3.5 Reliability Testing

The first study (Hörder et al., 2016), examined test–retest reliability and item relevance. It included 39 70-year-olds from the H70 study (Rinder et al., 1975; Rydberg Sterner et al., 2019), who answered the ICECAP-O on two occasions at approximately two-week intervals. The mean ICECAP-O index score was 0.86 on test occasion one and 0.84 on test occasion two. This result indicated that the index has good test–retest reliability, similar to that observed in a Dutch study (Van Leeuwen et al., 2015) that focused on frail older adults. On the other hand, the absolute agreement for each item was only low to moderate in the study. Good reliability for the index, despite the low absolute agreement for individual items, could be explained by the fact that most item changes involved shifts from 'full capability' (level 4) to 'a lot' (level 3), and these levels have very similar weighting in the tariff, in contrast to the much larger difference in weighting between the two lowest levels, 'a little' (level 2) and 'no capability' (level 1) (Coast et al., 2008, b). Furthermore, about

40% included both lower and higher ratings on individual items on the second test occasion, resulting in a relatively consistent index score.

Our study was the first to examine test–retest agreement for individual ICECAP-O items. A partial explanation for the observed item inconsistency might be related to the age of the participants. In a general population-based British study that utilised the ICECAP-A (adult) (Al-Janabi et al., 2015), greater age was associated with more inconsistent item ratings. Another possible explanation for test–retest item inconsistency might be related to differences in available time for completion of the questionnaire. On the first occasion, the ICECAP-O was included in an extensive questionnaire packet that was administered in connection with a comprehensive health examination. In contrast, the retest was completed at home at the participant's leisure. This meant that participants were free to take their time and reflect upon ICECAP-O item response options, which could have had an impact on both interpretation and choice of response. In a think-aloud study, people were shown to vary in interpretations when rating capabilities (Al-Janabi et al., 2013).

Previous studies have shown slightly lower reliability for the ICECAP-A index compared to EuroQoL (Al-Janabi et al., 2013), a well-known Quality of Life measure. As highlighted by others (Al-Janabi et al., 2013), more thorough guidance might be one way to achieve more consistent interpretations of capabilities. In addition, participants' ratings of item relevance showed that attachment was valued most highly, followed by control, role, security and finally enjoyment. This order is similar to that observed in the original British study on older people (Coast et al., 2008a).

Some important limitations of the test–retest study need to be mentioned. The sample was relatively homogeneous and small in size. Therefore, reliability testing is necessary for other age groups. A wider variation in medical conditions and functional abilities is to be anticipated in older age groups, and this would be expected to result in a larger variation in item responses.

3.6 Validity Testing

The second study (Gustafsson et al., 2017) evaluated the face and content validity and acceptability of the ICECAP-O. The applied method was cognitive interviews, which is a research method used to detect any problems respondents are having in understanding survey instructions and items, and in formulating answers (García, 2011). Eighteen 70-year-old community-dwelling individuals from the previously mentioned H70 study participated.

Overall, the results showed that the attributes listed in the ICECAP-O measure were interpreted as anticipated and the extent to which participants 'struggled' to complete the measure was moderate. Three participants (18%) had problems completing the measure, compared with 25% reported for the original British version (Horwood et al., 2014). The participants discussed all the attributes in the ICECAP-O measure during the interviews in terms of both significance/meaning and disincentives for capability, indicating that they were all relevant and essential for the purposes of the measure. The results also showed that most participants perceived the attributes to be understandable, even though the meaning of *Control* carried some uncertainty. One possible explanation is that participants in the study were community-dwelling 70-year-olds who had remained in relatively good health with no or little experience of being dependent in the activities of daily life, attributes that characterise 'the third age' (Baltes & Smith, 2003). Finally, participants made suggestions for an improved questionnaire format with larger text size to meet the needs of visually impaired respondents, as well as the addition of a short statement in parentheses after each attribute giving a description or an example to clarify its meaning. The latter suggestion was intended to support a more thorough guidance when considering the answer options.

This study also had some issues regarding its methodology that need to be highlighted. Firstly, only 18 older people were recruited, which some may consider too few, but the number of participants is in accordance with Lee's (2014) recommended sample size of approximately 15 participants in cognitive interviews within cross-cultural research. However, in addition to being 70 years old and community dwelling, all the participants were in relatively good health, lived in the same city, had a generally high education level and only two lived alone. These factors imply that this study entailed a relatively homogeneous group of participants, which may have affected the results. Further evaluation of face and content validity, and also acceptability, by including more diverse groups of older people in terms of age, health status, and ability to speak Swedish, as well as including those living in senior housing and rural areas, is thus recommended.

3.7 Summary

The Swedish version of the ICECAP-O seems to measure what it is supposed to measure, and acceptability is satisfactory. Even so, the attribute *Control* (i.e., independence) might be considered in need of a minor overhaul for use in the Swedish context, and a layout adapted for visually impaired respondents is desirable. In addition, a short statement in parentheses after each attribute with an example clarifying its meaning is proposed in order to support a more thorough guidance. The Swedish version also showed high test–retest reliability for the index score, but agreement for individual items was problematic. Further studies that include more diverse groups of older people in different contexts and with different time frames, are needed.

3.8 Conclusion

To conclude, the Swedish version of the ICECAP-O provides a promising approach to self-reported capability in the older population. ICECAP-O seems to capture the capability of older people and may therefore be especially valuable for the evaluation of programmes targeting public health, interventions crossing health and social care boundaries, multidisciplinary actions, economic evaluations and longitudinal studies. These assumptions are in line with a review from 2019 (Proud et al., 2019), reporting that publications relating to the ICECAP-O have now shifted from assessments of its psychometric properties to the utilisation of the measure in different contexts. Consequently, we recommend the use of the Swedish version of the ICECAP-O in evaluations of health and social care, and in interventions and longitudinal research studies where older people's capabilities are in focus.

References

Al-Janabi, H., Flynn, T. N., & Coast, J. (2012). Development of a self-report measure of capability wellbeing for adults: The ICECAP-A. *Quality of Life Research, 21*(1), 167–176. https://doi.org/10.1007/s11136-011-9927-2

Al-Janabi, H., Flynn, T. N., Peters, T. J., et al. (2015). Test-retest reliability of capability measurement in the UK general population. *Health Economics (United Kingdom), 24*(5), 625 630. https://doi.org/10.1002/hec.3100

Al-Janabi, H., Keeley, T., Mitchell, P., et al. (2013). Can capabilities be self-reported? A think aloud study. *Social Science and Medicine, 87*, 116–122. https://doi.org/10.1016/j.socscimed.2013.03.035

Baltes, P. B., & Smith, J. (2003). New frontiers in the future of aging: From successful aging of the young old to the dilemmas of the fourth age. *Gerontology, 49*(2), 123–135.

Coast, J., Bailey, C., Canaway, A., et al. (2016). Measuring and valuing outcomes for care at the end of life: The capability approach. In J. Round (Ed.), *Care at the end of life: An economic perspective* (pp. 89–101). Springer/Adis, eBook.

Coast, J., Flynn, T. N., Natarajan, L., et al. (2008a). Valuing the ICECAP capability index for older people. *Social Science and Medicine, 67*(5), 874–882. https://doi.org/10.1016/j.socscimed.2008.05.015

Coast, J., Peters, T. J., Natarajan, L., et al. (2008b). An assessment of the construct validity of the descriptive system for the ICECAP capability measure for older people. *Quality of Life Research, 17*(7), 967–976. https://doi.org/10.1007/s11136-008-9372-z

Couzner, L., Ratcliffe, J., Lester, L., et al. (2013). Measuring and valuing quality of life for public health research: Application of the ICECAP-O capability index in the Australian general population. *International Journal of Public Health, 58*(3), 367–376. https://doi.org/10.1007/s00038-012-0407-4

Diener, E., & Seligman, M. E. P. (2004). Beyond money: Toward an economy of well-being. *Psychological Science in the Public Interest, Supplement, 5*(1), 1–31.

Flynn, T. N., Louviere, J. J., Peters, T. J., et al. (2007). Best-worst scaling: What it can do for health care research and how to do it. *Journal of Health Economics, 26*, 171–189.

Flynn, T. N., Chan, P., Coast, J., & Peters, T. J. (2011). Assessing quality of life among British older people using the ICEPOP CAPability (ICECAP-O) measure. *Applied Health Economics and Health Policy, 9*(5), 317–329. https://doi.org/10.2165/11594150-000000000-00000

García, A. A. (2011). Cognitive interviews to test and refine questionnaires. *Public Health Nursing, 28*(5), 444–450. https://doi.org/10.1111/j.1525-1446.2010.00938.x

Grewal, I., Lewis, J., Flynn, T., et al. (2006). Developing attributes for a generic quality of life measure for older people: Preferences or capabilities? *Social Science and Medicine, 62*(8), 1891–1901. https://doi.org/10.1016/j.socscimed.2005.08.023

Guillemin, F., Bombardier, C., & Beaton, D. (1993). Cross-cultural adaptation of health-related quality of life measures: Literature review and proposed guidelines. *Journal of Clinical Epidemiology, 46*(12), 1417–1432. https://doi.org/10.1016/0895-4356(93)90142-N

Gustafsson, S., Hörder, H., Ottenvall-Hammar, I., et al. (2017). Face and content validity and acceptability of the ICECAP-O capability measure for Sweden: Cognitive interviews with participants from the Gothenburg H70 study. *Health Psychology Research, 6*(1), 6496. https://doi.org/10.4081/hpr.2018.6496

Horwood, J., Sutton, E., & Coast, J. (2014). Evaluating the face validity of the ICECAP-O capabilities measure: A 'think aloud' study with hip and knee arthroplasty patients. *Applied Research in Quality of Life, 9*(3), 667–682. https://doi.org/10.1007/s11482-013-9264-4

Hörder, H., Gustafsson, S., Rydberg, T., Skoog, I., & Waern, M. (2016). A cross-cultural adaptation of the ICECAP-O: Test–retest reliability and item relevance in Swedish 70-year-olds. *Societies, 6*(4), 30.

Lee, J. (2014). Conducting cognitive interviews in cross-national settings. *Assessment, 21*(2), 227–240. https://doi.org/10.1177/1073191112436671

Lyubomirsky, S., King, L., & Diener, E. (2005). The benefits of frequent positive affect: Does happiness lead to success? *Psychological Bulletin, 131*(6), 803–855. https://doi.org/10.1037/0033-2909.131.6.803

Makai, P., Koopmanschap, M. A., Brouwer, W. B. F., et al. (2013). A validation of the ICECAP-O in a population of post-hospitalized older people in the Netherlands. *Health and Quality of Life Outcomes, 11*(1). https://doi.org/10.1186/1477-7525-11-57

Mitchell, P. M., Roberts, T. E., Barton, P. M., et al. (2013). Predicting the ICECAP-O capability index from the WOMAC osteoarthritis index: Is mapping onto capability from condition-specific health status questionnaires feasible? *Medical Decision Making, 33*(4), 547–557. https://doi.org/10.1177/0272989X12475092

Proud, L., McLoughlin, C., & Kinghorn, P. (2019). ICECAP-O, the current state of play: A systematic review of studies reporting the psychometric properties and use of the instrument over the decade since its publication. *Quality of Life Research, 28*(6), 1429–1439. https://doi.org/10.1007/s11136-019-02114-y

Rinder, L., Roupe, S., Steen, B., & Svanborg, A. (1975). Seventy year old people in Gothenburg: A population study in an industrialised Swedish city. I. General presentation of the study. *Acta Medica Scandinavica, 198*(5), 397–407.

Rydberg Sterner, T., Ahlner, F., Blennow, K., et al. (2019). The Gothenburg H70 birth cohort study 2014–16: Design, methods and study population. *European Journal of Epidemiology, 34*(2), 191–209. https://doi.org/10.1007/s10654-018-0459-8

Sen, A. (1993). *Capability and well-being* (A. Sen, Ed.). Clarendon.

Sen, A. (2009). *The idea of justice*. Belknap Press of Harvard University Press.

University of Birmingham. (2021). ICECAP-O. Retrieved from http://www.birmingham.ac.uk/research/activity/mds/projects/HaPS/HE/ICECAP/ICECAP-O/index.aspx

Van Leeuwen, K. M., Jansen, A. P. D., Muntinga, M. E., et al. (2015). Exploration of the content validity and feasibility of the EQ-5D-3L, ICECAP-O and ASCOT in older adults. *BMC Health Services Research, 15*(1). https://doi.org/10.1186/s12913-015-0862-8

Chapter 4
The Capability Approach in Epidemiological Studies

Ingmar Skoog, Hanna Falk Erhag, Silke Kern, Therese Rydberg Sterner, Jessica Samuelsson, and Anna Zettergren

4.1 Introduction

Population epidemiology is the science that deals with disorders and certain conditions at the population level, i.e. at the macro-level. In contrast to experimental studies, the scientist in epidemiology cannot manipulate conditions to make studies of associations as pure as possible. This might be seen as a disadvantage, but is actually an advantage because epidemiology studies conditions at the place where they are occurring, i.e. in real life. The science of epidemiological studies examines the occurrence of diseases, risk and protective factors for diseases and the prognosis of different disorders and conditions in different populations.

Population epidemiologists may also study the entire course of disorders, beginning with very mild symptoms occurring before the individual presents to the healthcare system. This contrasts with clinical studies, which can only study patients who have sought help from the healthcare system. The latter studies are thus

I. Skoog (✉)
Neuropsychiatric Epidemiology Unit, Department of Psychiatry and Neurochemistry, Institute of Neuroscience and Physiology, Sahlgrenska Academy at the University of Gothenburg, Gothenburg, Sweden

Centre for Ageing and Health – AgeCap, University of Gothenburg, Gothenburg, Sweden

Region Västra Götaland, Sahlgrenska University Hospital, Psychiatry, Cognition and Old Age Psychiatry Clinic, Gothenburg, Sweden
e-mail: ingmar.skoog@neuro.gu.se

H. Falk Erhag
Neuropsychiatric Epidemiology Unit, Department of Psychiatry and Neurochemistry, Institute of Neuroscience and Physiology, Sahlgrenska Academy at the University of Gothenburg, Gothenburg, Sweden

Centre for Ageing and Health – AgeCap, University of Gothenburg, Gothenburg, Sweden

Institute of Health and Care Sciences, Sahlgrenska Academy at the University of Gothenburg, Gothenburg, Sweden
e-mail: hanna.falk@gu.se

H. Falk Erhag et al. (eds.), *A Multidisciplinary Approach to Capability in Age and Ageing*, International Perspectives on Aging 31,
https://doi.org/10.1007/978-3-030-78063-0_4

influenced by the fact that individuals who seek help differ from those who do not regarding a number of factors. The occurrence of disorders is measured as prevalence and incidence. Prevalence is the number of individuals affected by a disease divided by the number of people living in the target population during a certain time period, while incidence is the number of new cases that occur during a certain time period. Prevalence is related to the burden of the disease for society, while incidence is related to the risk of developing the disease.

The capability approach is an ideal framework for epidemiological studies because it captures the dynamic and multiple processes involved in these types of studies, in relation to both time and space, as well as socioeconomic, psychological and biological factors. Determinants for common disorders and conditions include complex interactions among a multitude of factors acting between and within macro-, meso- and micro-levels during the life-course of an individual. Each of these may have a small positive or negative impact on the outcome (e.g. dementia, cognitive function, depression, well-being, functional ability), but may together have a large or substantial impact at the micro-, meso- and macro-levels depending on the individual or societal conversion factors. The latter may be related to factors such as cognitive, physical and social reserve at the individual level, or the effect of the welfare state and educational systems at the societal level.

The ultimate goal of population epidemiology is to prevent diseases and functional limitations, and to increase well-being, thus increasing capability at the individual and societal level. However, what may constitute a small risk at the individual micro-level may have a large impact on the burden of disease at the population level, i.e. at the macro-level, in both the short and long term. However, findings from observational studies do not always translate into results in randomised controlled trials (RCT), which are the gold standard for clinical trials. One reason could be time of follow-up. While observational population studies more or less have a

S. Kern
Neuropsychiatric Epidemiology Unit, Department of Psychiatry and Neurochemistry, Institute of Neuroscience and Physiology, Sahlgrenska Academy at the University of Gothenburg, Gothenburg, Sweden

Centre for Ageing and Health – AgeCap, University of Gothenburg, Gothenburg, Sweden

Västra Götaland, Sahlgrenska University Hospital, Psychiatry, Cognition and Old Age Psychiatry Clinic, Gothenburg, Sweden
e-mail: silke.kern@neuro.gu.se

T. Rydberg Sterner · J. Samuelsson · A. Zettergren
Neuropsychiatric Epidemiology Unit, Department of Psychiatry and Neurochemistry, Institute of Neuroscience and Physiology, Sahlgrenska Academy at the University of Gothenburg, Gothenburg, Sweden

Centre for Ageing and Health – AgeCap, University of Gothenburg, Gothenburg, Sweden
e-mail: therese.rydberg.sterner@gu.se; jessica.samuelsson@neuro.gu.se; anna.zettergren@neuro.gu.se

lifetime perspective and act at the macro-level, RCTs could be regarded as acting at a meso- or micro-level, due to selection criteria for the individuals who participate, and they often have short follow-ups, not more than 5–6 years.

Primary prevention refers to interventions at the population level in individuals without symptoms or signs of a particular disorder (Skoog & Gustafson, 2006). This could be vaccination against a virus, or campaigns to increase physical activity, change to healthier diets or cessation of smoking. Primary prevention may have a large impact at the macro-level by decreasing prevalence and incidence, but the effect on capability at the micro- and meso-levels is not easy to measure, and not always appreciated by the individual. Secondary prevention acts on individuals who have a risk factor, but no diagnosis (Skoog, 1999). One example of secondary prevention is the treatment of hypertension to prevent stroke or myocardial infarction. Screening to detect disorders very early, before a diagnosis, is also part of secondary prevention, e.g. screening for breast cancer or prostate cancer. Secondary prevention is also related to macro-level effects, but also has a clearer effect at the micro- and meso-levels. Tertiary prevention refers to treatment when a disorder is already present. At this stage, treatment is mainly conducted at the micro-level, and its impact is mainly felt at the micro- and meso-levels. However, when treatment is introduced for a disorder that was previously lethal or resulted in long-term care, it may also have an impact at the macro-level. For example, if a treatment were introduced that slowed down the course of Alzheimer's disease or treated the disorder completely, it would have a huge effect on the costs of elderly care for society, i.e. for capability at the macro-level.

Population studies could thus be seen as acting at the macro-level, because they are supposed to study representative samples of populations. This is especially true in the study of prevalence, which is related to the burden of a disorder on society, i.e. with capability at the macro-level. Common chronic disorders, such as cardiovascular disorder, depression or dementia, lead to costs at the macro-level for the healthcare sector, for sick leave and for home care. The more severe a common disorder is, and the more widespread it is, the greater the costs for society and the greater the suffering for individuals and their families, i.e. the more it will affect capability at macro-, meso- and micro-levels. A severe rare disorder, on the other hand, leads to costs and suffering at the micro- and meso-levels, but may not have a large impact at the macro-level.

Risk and protective factors thus act at macro-, micro- or meso-levels. Some risk factors act on capability at more than one level. One example is education. A lower level of education is a risk factor for most of the common disorders in old age, e.g. dementia (Wang et al., 2012), depression (Skoog, 2011) and cardiovascular disorders (Chen et al., 2021), which all influence capability. At the macro-level, years of education, the quality of education, cost of education and the number of pupils in a school class are all dependent on political decisions taken at the macro-level. The effect of education is also dependent at the meso-level, for example the quality of teachers, the school, the influence of parents and family and the economic situation at home. At the micro-level, educational attainment is dependent on each individual's intellectual capacity and wishes. The impact of education is also strongly dependent on socioeconomic circumstances, but these two conditions often have independent influences on the risk of dementia. Thus the simple finding of increased risk of dementia, depression and cardiovascular disorders with lower levels of education is dependent on a number of factors that act and interact at the macro-, meso- and micro-levels.

It needs to be emphasised that associations between risk factors and disease may not be stable between populations due to differences at the meso-levels between populations (e.g. differences in socioeconomic factors, educational level, climate, animal populations, political decisions, population density, access to healthcare and medication and a number of other factors). This is one obvious reason why findings from one population may be difficult to replicate in another.

Findings and risk factors may also differ between historical periods. In our H70 studies, which are representative population studies conducted among different birth cohorts of 70-year-olds born between 1901–1902 (first examined in 1971–1972) and 1944 (first examined in 2014) and followed until death (Rydberg Sterner et al., 2019a; Skoog, 2004), we have found a number of significant changes over time. For example, cognitive (Karlsson et al., 2015; Thorvaldsson et al., 2017) and physical function have improved, blood pressure has declined (Zhi et al., 2013; Joas et al., 2017), BMI has increased (Zhi et al., 2013), the prevalence of dementia (Skoog et al., 2017; Skoog, 2016; Wu et al., 2016, 2017), impairment in activities of daily living (Falk et al., 2014; Falk Erhag et al., 2021), depression (Rydberg Sterner et al., 2019b) and sleep problems (Skoog et al., 2019) has decreased, educational level, alcohol consumption (Ahlner et al., 2018) and sexual activity (Beckman et al., 2008) have increased, and even the overall personality of the population has changed considerably (Rydberg Sterner et al., 2019b; Billstedt et al., 2013, 2017). The greatest changes over time were observed in women. An interesting finding was that a restricted social network was a risk factor for depression in the 1970s, but not in the 2000s (Sjöberg et al., 2013). Thus, what is true in one time period may not be true in another. Reasons for the changes are to be found in macro-level changes in education, gender roles, socioeconomic circumstances, living and working conditions, healthcare and advances in medical science, such as the introduction of effective drugs against infections and hypertension (Skoog, 2016).

One of the most important aspects of epidemiology is to evaluate whether certain associations between risk factors and outcomes, or between disorders and consequences, are influenced by confounding factors. This is often achieved using statistical methods, such as regression analyses, where the independent effect of a particular factor is examined by controlling for other, associated factors. Age is one of the most important confounding factors for many associations, but the effect of age might also be confounded by age-related factors. One example is the reported association between age and death in individuals with Covid-19. When age was analysed in isolation, without taking other age-related factors into consideration, it became a very strong predictor for death. However, in Sweden, 75% of all deaths occurred in the small group (3%) receiving old-age care (home care and nursing homes) (www.socialstyrelsen.se/en/). Taking this into consideration, the age-related effect was considerably attenuated.

In the following, we will discuss certain concepts that are related to the epidemiology of capability in ageing, such as specific conditions that are important for capability, including cognitive function, mental health (mostly depression), multimorbidity and functional ability, and factors that may affect these conditions and affect capability in general, such as the non-modifiable factor of genetics (a trait) and the modifiable factor of nutrition (a state).

Cognitive function and mental health are among the most important determinants for capability in old age. Mental and cognitive health in older populations are positioned along a continuum, from complete wellbeing to defined disorders, such as dementia (e.g. Alzheimer's disease) and other mental disorders (e.g. depression). Even mild mental conditions have a profound impact on health, and how a person adapts to ageing and its related disorders, and thus to the individual's capability. Recently, we reported that pathological biomarkers for Alzheimer's disease are present in 45% of completely normal 70-year-olds (Kern et al., 2018), extending the continuum into symptom-free individuals, in whom the disorder has not yet had an impact on capability. The relevance of these subclinical conditions can only be studied in longitudinal, population-based samples.

4.2 Cognitive Function and Capability

Cognitive function in the population is positioned along a continuum from high to normal function, to subclinical stages (defined as having pathological biomarkers but normal cognitive function), to mild cognitive impairment (defined as decline in cognitive function without impairment in activities of daily life) to dementia (defined as cognitive impairment with impairment in social and functional abilities). The prevalence of dementia increases from 3% at ages 70–75 years to 52% in 95-year-olds (Börjesson Hansson et al., 2004). Mild cognitive impairment is even more common.

Dementia is the most important factor affecting capability in older people at the macro-, meso- and micro-levels, affecting the costs of care for society, the family of the person with dementia, and the individual who suffers from the disease, having an impact on all aspects of the individual person. The two most common forms of dementia are Alzheimer's disease (AD) and vascular dementia. Risk factors for AD at the macro-level include low educational level, and low socioeconomic status (Hasselgren et al. 2018; Wu et al., 2018). The prevalence of dementia is also related to time-trends and thus to historical periods at the macro-level. This is reflected in reports that the prevalence and incidence of dementia has declined during recent years, and is lower in later-born birth cohorts (Skoog, 2016; Wu et al., 2017).

The risk of dementia is also related to dietary patterns, which may be due to macro-, meso- and micro-level circumstances. At the meso-level, the risk of dementia is related to social networks and the type of work the individual has had. At the micro-level are genetic factors, such as possession of the *APOE* e4 allele, and risk factors, such as low educational level (Hasselgren et al., 2018), psychological stress

(Johansson et al., 2010), poor sleep, neuroticism (Johansson et al., 2014), poor lung function (Guo et al., 2007) and cardiovascular risk factors, such as hypertension (Skoog et al., 1996; Joas et al., 2012), being overweight (Gustafson et al., 2003), diabetes mellitus (Mehlig et al., 2014) and hypercholesterolemia, as well as protective factors, which could be regarded as conversion factors, such as midlife fitness (Hörder et al., 2018), and physical and cognitive activities (Najar et al., 2019). The importance of risk factors may also differ depending on the age at which they are measured. For example, stroke and Alzheimer encephalopathy are related to dementia, but the relative risk is lower in nonagenarians compared to septuagenarians and octogenarians (Andersson et al., 2012).

The different risk factors also interact in a complicated way. We recently reported that possession of the *APOE* ε4 allele and socioeconomic status interacted in the determination of time to dementia onset (Hasselgren et al., 2018). At the most fine-grained micro-level, the brain changes in Alzheimer's disease, as reflected by neurochemical changes in the cerebrospinal fluid, may influence cognitive change. For example, in a cooperation project with the Mayo Clinic, Rochester USA, higher levels of the protein neurofilament light, an unspecific biomarker for neurodegeneration, in cerebrospinal fluid was associated with higher risk of decline from normal cognition to mild cognitive impairment (Kern et al., 2019). This is important at the macro-, meso- and micro-levels because neurodegeneration leads to cognitive decline, which leads to societal costs for healthcare at the macro-level as patients with MCI and dementia may need more attention from professional caregivers at the meso-level. This, in turn, may lead to changes in political regulations at the macro-level and is related to less capability at the meso- and micro-levels.

4.3 Depression and Capability

Another common condition that negatively affects capability in older adults is depression, which is a syndrome characterised by low mood, loss of interest, loss of appetite, sleep problems, cognitive symptoms, motor retardation, guilt and suicidal feelings. Depression is one of the most common mental disorders in old age (Skoog, 2011), and is one of the leading causes of the global burden of disease among both men and women (Ferrari et al., 2010). During the past decade, depression has been ranked as the third-to-fifth most common cause of years lived with disability (YLD) (James et al., 2018). The prevalence among older populations is approximately 10%, including 1–5% with major depression (Fiske et al., 2009). From a lifetime perspective, approximately 40% of women have had major depression, rising to 70% if minor depression is included (Skoog et al., in manuscript). Depression is related to a number of consequences influencing capability at the macro-, meso- and micro-levels. At the macro-level, depression is related to an increased use of health services, a need for home care and, among younger ages, an increase in sick leave. At the meso-level, it affects the social network, family and workplace. At the micro-level, it is related to decreases in well-being, life satisfaction and cognitive function, an increased risk of suicide and increased risk of somatic conditions, such as stroke and myocardial infarction, and an increased non-suicidal mortality rate (Skoog, 2011). Thus, depression is a major factor affecting capability, not only in old age, but also from a lifetime perspective.

Depression may thus affect, and be affected by, available resources at all societal levels. At the **macro-level**, risk factors for depression include poverty, discrimination, national pension systems, unemployment rates, disasters, other negative historical events and access to healthcare. Depression is related to increased use of healthcare and home-care services (Skoog, 2011), and is thus associated with higher direct and indirect costs for all age groups (König et al., 2019), especially older age groups, healthcare-related costs, lost productivity or premature death by suicide (Greenberg et al., 2015). Late-life depression is associated with early retirement (Zuelke et al., 2020), which may not only affect household finances, but will also generate productivity loss and lower income tax revenue at a societal level. Today, older adults are healthier than those of previous generations. Higher levels of depression in the population will prevent the potential societal benefits stemming from having older adults working beyond retirement age. Besides economic factors, another important macro-level issue related to late-life depression is the lack of access to mental healthcare. Globally, there is an unmet need for mental healthcare (Dakic, 2019). In a focus-group study from the H70 studies (Rydberg Sterner et al., 2020), participants expressed an awareness of the lack of access to specialised mental healthcare in Sweden, both from their own experiences and from media reporting. In addition, they were frustrated by the lack of psychotherapeutic options for the treatment of depression. It has been shown that antidepressants are prescribed to older adults by default, due to lack of time for discussion about other treatment options (Overend et al., 2015). The Swedish National Board of Health and Welfare acknowledges that depressed older adults have less access to specialised care and psychotherapeutic alternatives than their younger counterparts (Socialstyrelsen 2018; Socialstyrelsen 2019). Our participants did not trust that they would be prioritised by healthcare services if depression recurred. The lack of access to mental healthcare may have adverse effects on future help-seeking behaviour.

At the **meso-level**, risk factors for depression include poor social networks, lower socioeconomic status in relation to others, living in a poor environment, negative life events, an unhappy marriage or divorce and a family history of depression (Skoog, 2011). Among the core symptoms of depression are diminished interest in one's surroundings and lack of initiative. This may negatively affect one's ability to socialise with family and friends, which may generate a feeling of loneliness or lack of social support (Hsueh et al., 2019). Feeling lonely or experiencing a lack of social support may, in turn, increase the risk of depression (Bergdahl et al., 2007). Social support provided by a spouse, friends or family members is reported to be protective against late-life depression (Gariepy et al., 2016; Tengku Mohd et al., 2019). The effects may include decreased levels of psychosocial stress due to emotional or economic support (Carr & Springer, 2010). The perception of social support is also suggested to act as a buffer by decreasing the risk of depression when exposed to negative life events (Hashimoto et al., 1999).

Having late-life depression may be accompanied by social stigma, generating a barrier towards reaching out to others (Rydberg Sterner et al., 2020). This barrier may entail the fear of not being understood, or being perceived as burdensome or weak (Rydberg Sterner et al., 2020; Black et al., 2007; Conner et al., 2010). Older adults with decreased capability due to depression may not be able to help others to the same extent as before. This may cause a great deal of frustration among those who are depressed, as they still have a strong need to be needed (Rydberg Sterner et al., 2020). However, having a social network per se is not necessarily beneficial in relation to late-life depression. As an example, social relationships may entail emotional, physical or financial abuse (Poole & Rietschlin, 2012; Roh et al., 2016), or marital dissatisfaction (Woods et al., 2019), which may contribute to an elevated risk of depression.

At the **micro-level**, risk factors for depression include genetic factors, somatic health, personality, smoking, a low level of education, cardiovascular disorders (Skoog, 2011) and several other somatic disorders (Skoog, 2011). Depression may be both a consequence and a cause of somatic disorders, for example in relation to stroke (Liebetrau et al., 2008; Bos et al., 2008). Risk factors for depression may already present during foetal development, perhaps due to early programming as a response to the intrauterine environment, indicating the role of epigenetics (Barker, 2003; Hodes, 2013). In addition, lower birth weight (Gudmundsson et al., 2011) has been related to depression. It has also been reported that old-age depression is related to lower levels of physical activity (Gudmundsson et al., 2015). Depression, including mild subsyndromal symptoms, may affect an older person's available resources at the micro-level in several ways. The consequences of depression include poor quality of life, disability, cognitive decline, suicide, increased mortality rate and increased risk of cardiovascular disease (CaD) (Skoog, 2011).

Mental health may also be considered a personal conversion factor within the framework of capability. Suffering from mental illness, such as depression, may reduce an older person's ability to utilise available resources, in order to reach goals of value. For example, a valued goal for an older person may be to spend every Sunday afternoon playing video games with his/her grandchildren. Even where all the available resources are present, such as access to public transport (macro-level), having positive relationships with the grandchildren (meso-level) and having sufficient economic resources to travel and to buy video games (micro-level), late-life depression may be a barrier to achieving this goal (lacking conversion factor). From a capability perspective, there is also a challenge in that individuals adapt their goals of value to their current life situation, meaning that expectations may affect the choice of goals. Older adults may perceive some goals as being out of reach due to having depression, compared to their life perceptions before having depression. It may also be questioned whether a person with mental illness has the same freedom of choice as those without. Depression may be perceived as a restraining factor because the person may feel as though he/she is no longer in control of his/her own body.

4.4 Multimorbidity and Capability

Multimorbidity can be defined as the co-occurrence of multiple chronic conditions within the same individual (Christensen et al., 2009; Fried et al., 2004). Studies show that multimorbidity increases the likelihood of death, functional disability and institutionalisation, over and above the risk attributable to individual diseases (Formiga et al., 2013). In Sweden, multimorbidity affects more than half of those aged 78 years and older (Marengoni et al., 2008), and in the USA more than two thirds of all older Medicaid beneficiaries have two or more chronic conditions (Fried et al., 2004). Thus, multimorbidity is an important determinant of capability in old age. In light of this, it is surprising that relatively little is known about how diseases are distributed and co-occur in the same individual, and how conversion factors, such as social ties and personal and situational antecedents, might affect functional disability, frailty and dependence in physically vulnerable older people (Marengoni et al., 2011; Fortin et al., 2012). By definition, older people with multimorbidity are heterogeneous in terms of severity of illness, functional status, prognosis and risk of adverse events, even when diagnosed with the same pattern of conditions. Studies show that there are gender differences in terms of clinical characteristics in patients with multimorbidity (Marengoni et al., 2008, 2011), and that there is a strong relationship between social ties and health (Ferlander & Mäkinen, 2009), as well as differences in symptoms experienced by different age groups (Zambroski et al., 2005).

Unlike single chronic conditions, for which strong epidemiological data is available, existing prevalence estimates of multimorbidity in older persons range from 55% to 98%, making it difficult to determine whether differences between studies are real or due to a wide variety of methodological issues (Marengoni et al., 2011). The operational definition of multimorbidity and the methods used for data collection are particularly critical issues that need consideration when studying prevalence estimates. Defining multimorbidity as two or more chronic conditions means that both individuals who may live relatively unaffected by multimorbidity, as well as those who face severe functional loss, are included in the definition (Fortin et al., 2005). Since multiple chronic conditions often represent the norm in older people, multimorbidity needs to be evaluated in relation to illness distress, disease severity and level of impairment at the macro-, meso- and micro-levels.

The lack of conceptual schemes guiding the terminology, measurements and hypotheses in the study of multimorbidity also makes it difficult to meaningfully compare findings from different studies. Relationships between pathology, impairment and illness distress can be as much a function of psychosocial characteristics at the meso- and macro-levels as it can be related to number of diagnoses or disease severity at the micro-level (Femia et al., 2001). Thus, how multimorbidity affects capability is dependent on all levels. At the macro-level, it is related to political decisions on the availability and quality of home care and aid devices, and how pharmacological research is able to find new drugs. At the meso-level, it is dependent on factors such as the condition of the home and access to help from relatives and friends. At the micro-level, it is dependent on factors such as severity of diseases, personality and physical reserves.

4.5 Functional Ability and Capability

As the average expected lifespan increases, an important issue is whether the years added to life are characterised by good health and independence or by health problems and dependence, i.e. by high or low capability. Disability refers to the negative aspects of the interaction between a person and their environment (i.e. deficits), which leads to limitations in their activity and restrictions in their social participation (Üstün et al., 2010). Dependence, which severely affects all aspects of capability, arises when conversion factors, such as adaptation of the environment or the use of technical aids, can no longer compensate for the disability, which results in the need for help from a third person (Verbrugge & Jette, 1994).

At the micro-level, research on disability in old age has identified non-modifiable risk factors, such as age, gender and genetics, and modifiable factors, such as age-related diseases, impairments, functional limitations, poor coping skills, sedentary lifestyles and other unhealthy behaviours, and at the meso- and macro-levels, social and environmental obstacles (Vermeulen et al., 2011; Taş et al., 2007; Heikkinen, 2006; Stuck et al., 1999). It is common to distinguish between disabilities in the performance of the primary or basic activities of daily living (ADLs) on the one hand, and secondary or instrumental activities of daily living (IADLs) on the other. In comparison to disease prevalence, indicators such as ADL and IADL disability, which reflect the cumulative effects of morbidity, are more revealing in terms of describing health and capability in older populations because of the high rates of co-morbidity and the interaction between disease and the ageing process (Parker et al., 2008; Manton et al., 1993). Research shows that dependence in ADL is associated with increased risk of mortality (Millán-Calenti et al., 2010), and that those individuals who are dependent in ADL are also likely to be dependent in IADL (Wang et al., 2019).

At the macro-level, severe disability poses a significant financial burden on healthcare services since it often results in loss of independence, requiring the provision of round-the-clock assistance (Verropoulou & Tsimbos, 2017). Although disability rates increase with age, in particular among the oldest-old (Wang et al., 2019), there is much debate about whether later-born cohorts of older adults will face the same disability rates as earlier-born cohorts. Many studies have suggested a compression of morbidity, implying that the future care needs of older adults will not follow the demographic prognoses. Several recent studies have shown that later-born cohorts of older adults are healthier and more active than earlier-born cohorts, displaying great plasticity and variability between individuals in health status, quality of life and wellbeing in later life. For example, it has been shown that, between 2004 and 2013, there was a declining trend in ADL disability among adults older than 65 years in Europe (Verropoulou & Tsimbos, 2017). However, there is great variability in prevalence between studies. Among older adults in Spain (mean age 75 years), 35% reported problems in at least one ADL activity, and 54% in at least one IADL activity (Millán-Calenti et al., 2009). In Ireland, among persons aged 75 to 79 years, 15% reported problems in at least one ADL activity, and 13% in at least one IADL activity (Connolly et al., 2017). Among Swedish 75-year-olds born in 1930, only 6% reported disability for at least one ADL activity and 13% with IADL, compared to 14% and 33%, respectively, in 75-year-olds born in 1901–1902 (Falk et al., 2014). However, in 90–94-year-olds, 71% reported ADL disability, and this figure rose to 89% in 95–99-year-olds, and 97% in centenarians (Berlau et al., 2009).

Sweden has had a large proportion of older adults in the population for many years and still leads the world regarding the proportion of very old people. Epidemiology has traditionally focused on the prevalence of specific diseases or conditions within a population, which affects society at the macro-level. While disease indicators reflect the need for medical care, indicators of disability and functioning are more helpful for capturing both living conditions and potential care needs. Estimating disability among community-dwelling older adults may help policymakers to plan and prepare for the needs of this population. At a time when society is faced with demographic transformations, an important public health issue at the macro-level is how to prevent or postpone the onset of disability in old age, since this is one of the central components fuelling cost increases at the macro-level (Verropoulou & Tsimbos, 2017; Parker et al., 2008) and low capability at the micro-level. Studying health in the older population of Swedish citizens is particularly relevant because the proportion of this age group is large compared to other western countries (Parker et al., 2008). In the context of increasing numbers of older adults, and conflicting findings among studies on disability trends, the comparison of levels of disability between birth cohorts can be of great significance.

4.6 Genetics and Capability

Genetics has a fundamental impact on older individuals' capability at the micro-level, since variations within the DNA constitute the molecular basis for our level of vulnerability to, or protection against, age-related disease, frailty and biological ageing. Although some disorders/traits are caused by a single genetic factor (i.e. they are monogenetic), the majority of disorders/traits, among both young and old individuals, are polygenic (also known as complex) and caused by variations in numerous genes in combination with environmental and lifestyle factors at the micro-, meso- and macro-levels. Genetic factors act at the micro-level of individuals' available resources, but findings in genetic research can have a great impact at all societal levels due to their importance for understanding disease pathogenesis, for the work with identifying potential drug targets, for identifying individuals who will benefit from preventative efforts, and for the inclusion of individuals in clinical trials. Within dementia research, it has been demonstrated that both the 'high effect' gene *APOE* (i.e. the *APOE ε4* allele) and combinations of genetic variants into genetic risk scores (i.e. PRS = polygenic risk scores) are useful for identifying individuals at risk of disease (Altmann et al., 2020). Within the frame of the H70 studies, an increasing risk of developing dementia with an increasing PRS for Alzheimer's disease was seen among individuals who were *APOE ε4* negatives (Najar et al., 2021). Furthermore, *APOE* was associated with the Alzheimer's disease biomarkers cerebrospinal fluid Aβ42, t-tau, and p-tau, and PRS for Alzheimer's disease was associated with cerebrospinal fluid Aβ42 and NfL, among cognitively healthy 70-year-olds (Kern et al., 2018; Skoog et al., 2021). Moreover, an association between the *APOE ε4* allele and a larger decline in grip strength between the ages of 75 and 79 years (Skoog, 2016) was found. This association was independent of cognitive function, indicating either an association independent of dementia, or an association at a very early stage of the disease.

There is an overlap in genetic factors that is important for age-related disorders (i.e. one genetic factor can be associated with several different phenotypes = pleiotropy). Results from the H70 studies have shown associations between the genes *APOE* and *ACE* (angiotensin-converting enzyme) and both dementia and late-life major depression (Skoog et al., 2015; Zettergren et al., 2017). There are also genetic overlaps between different forms of dementia disorders, and between dementia and cardiovascular and metabolic disorders (Guerreiro et al., 2020). Moreover, genetic factors interact with environmental and lifestyle factors at the macro-, meso- and micro-levels. One example from the H70 studies is the discovery of interactions between genetic and social factors in relation to dementia risk among men, implying that socioeconomic status modifies the effect of *APOE ε4*, whereas, among women, high socioeconomic status does not seem to exhibit the same 'compensatory ability' (Hasselgren et al., 2019). Furthermore, a meso-level factor, such as control over one's work, was suggested to be the most influential work environment factor on the effect of *APOE ε4*, albeit in different ways among men and women (Hasselgren et al. 2018).

Genetics can also influence individuals' ability to cope with disease and ageing at an emotional level, since genetic factors are known to be associated with personality and behavioural traits (Sanchez-Roige et al., 2018). Twin studies of heritability have found that genetic factors account for a substantial part of the variance in individuals' self-rated health (Christensen et al., 1999; Leinonen et al., 2005). Self-rated health is a subjective, general indicator that strongly predicts mortality. Important domains known to influence self-rated health, and subsequent mortality, include individual and cultural beliefs and health behaviours, chronic illness, depression, cognitive function, socioeconomic status, functional impairment and physical activity (Leinonen et al., 2001; Leinonen et al., 2002; Stanojevic Jerkovic et al., 2015; Galenkamp et al., 2013). In a study of well-established longevity genes in relation to self-rated health, an association was found between the gene *FOXO3* and self-rated health in individuals aged 75–85 years from the H70 studies (Zettergren et al., 2018). Interestingly, the association between *FOXO3* and self-rated health was not influenced by cognitive or mental functioning. Thus, an apparently micro-level factor, such as genetics, may influence capability at the macro-, meso- and micro-levels.

4.7 Diet and Capability

Diet may influence capability in a number of ways, such as our health in general or as a risk factor for certain diseases. Diet is affected by factors at the micro-, meso- and macro-levels. At the macro level, what we eat is affected by cultural and historical norms in society, by guidelines from the authorities and by the availability of certain foods. At the meso-level, it is affected by preferences among family and friends, and the socioeconomic situation of the family. At the micro-level it is affected by a number of factors, including personal preferences. Global and national dietary guidelines recommend dietary patterns containing nutrient-dense foods, such as vegetables, pulses, nuts, wholegrain cereals, low-fat dairy products and fish, as well as a limited intake of red and processed meat, refined cereals, high-fat dairy products, high-sugar foods/drinks and alcoholic beverages in order to promote health and reduce the risk of disease (Nordic Council of Ministers, 2012; Herforth et al., 2019). Obesity and chronic age-related non-communicable diseases, such as cardiovascular disease, diabetes and dementia, can in part be prevented or delayed by means of a healthy lifestyle and healthy dietary habits (Global burden of disease 2017 Diet collaborators, 2019, Samadi et al., 2019, Ley et al., 2014, Rodríguez-Monforte et al., 2015). In this case, diet acts as a conversion factor.

In Sweden, dietary habits among healthy older people are generally better than among younger adults (Swedish food agency, 2012). Results from the H70 birth cohort study show that dietary patterns among five birth cohorts of 70-year-olds have changed during the past five decades, with an increase in healthy foods and a higher nutrient density in later-born birth cohorts (Samuelsson et al., 2019). However, the intake of alcohol has increased and about 30% of the participants had an intake above the Swedish Food Agency's recommendation in 2014–2016 (Samuelsson et al., 2019; Nordic Council of Ministers, 2012).

There is an increased risk of malnutrition related to ageing and chronic illness (Cederholm et al., 2019), and malnutrition (both undernutrition and obesity) plays a key role in the pathogenesis of frailty, sarcopenia and cognitive decline (Volkert et al., 2019; Cruz-Jentoft et al., 2017; Cederholm et al., 2019; Ma & Chan, 2020; Gómez-Gómez & Zapico, 2019). Frailty and sarcopenia are associated with dependency, and preventive strategies could improve quality of life and well-being among older adults (Cruz-Jentoft et al., 2017; Govindaraju et al., 2018). In addition to chronic illness, there are several factors at the micro-level that could affect dietary intake among older adults. Sensory impairments (e.g., loss of taste and smell), gastrointestinal motility changes and diminished hunger and satiety control mechanisms are some of many physiological changes related to ageing that may affect appetite and lead to a decrease in food intake (Cox et al., 2019). Psychosocial and environmental changes, such as isolation, loneliness, inadequate finances and depression may have a negative impact on food intake (Landi et al., 2016), and socioeconomic factors such as being unmarried, male sex, lower level of education, functional limitations and smoking have been associated with the risk of a poor-quality diet and malnutrition (Katsas et al., 2020; Nazri et al., 2020). Obesity, with its well-known negative health consequences, is an increasing problem among older people (von Berens et al., 2020; Bischoff et al., 2017). In the H70 birth cohort study (at 75 years), and the Uppsala Longitudinal Study of Adult Men (at 87 years), 4% of the women and 10–11% of the men were obese (von Berens et al., 2020). Globally, these numbers range between 18–30% (>65 years) (Gallus et al., 2015; Porter Starr et al., 2016). Effective dietary education, meal service and dietary interventions at macro to micro societal levels could reduce the risk of disease, improve health and increase quality of life and capability among older adults (Volkert et al., 2019, Global burden of disease 2017 Diet collaborators, 2019, Govindaraju et al., 2018, Zhou et al., 2018).

4.8 Conclusion

In this chapter, we have discussed how the capability approach can be used in epidemiology in general, and in old age in particular, using examples from specific conditions, such as cognitive function and dementia, depression, multimorbidity and functional ability, and non-modifiable and modifiable risk factors, such as genetics and nutrition. It can be seen that the capability approach is a valuable tool in epidemiological studies. In these types of studies, capability is the final outcome of the dynamic interactions between a multitude of factors at the micro-, meso- and macro-levels that lead to disorders and other conditions, which lead to restrictions in the individual's ability to perform actions in order to reach goals that he or she has reason to value.

References

Altmann, A., Scelsi, M. A., Shoai, M., De Silva, E., Aksman, L. M., Cash, D. M., Hardy, J., & Schott, J. M. (2020). A comprehensive analysis of methods for assessing polygenic burden on Alzheimer's disease pathology and risk beyond APOE. *Brain Communication, 2*, fcz047.

Ahlner, F., Sigström, R., Rydberg Sterner, T., Mellqvist Fässberg, M., Kern, S., Östling, S., Waern, M., & Skoog, I. (2018). Increased alcohol consumption among Swedish 70-year-olds 1976-2016: Analysis of data from the Gothenburg H70 birth cohort studies, Sweden. *Alcoholism, Clinical and Experimental Research, 42*, 2403–2412.

Andersson, M., Guo, X., Börjesson-Hanson, A., Liebetrau, M., Östling, S., & Skoog, I. (2012). A population-based study on dementia and stroke in 97-year-olds. *Age and Ageing, 41*(4), 529–533.

Barker, D. J. (2003). The developmental origins of adult disease. *European Journal of Epidemiology, 18*, 733–736.

Beckman, N., Waern, M., Gustafson, D., & Skoog, I. (2008). Secular trends in self reported sexual activity and satisfaction in Swedish 70 year olds: Cross sectional survey of four populations, 1971–2001. *British Medical Journal, 337*, 151–154.

Bergdahl, E., Allard, P., Alex, L., Lundman, B., & Gustafson, Y. (2007). Gender differences in depression among the very old. *International Psychogeriatrics, 19*(6), 1125–1140.

Berlau, D. J., Corrada, M. M., & Kawas, C. (2009). The prevalence of disability in the oldest-old is high and continues to increase with age: Findings from the 90+ study. *International Journal of Geriatric Psychiatry, 24*(11), 1217–1225.

Bischoff, S. C., Boirie, Y., Cederholm, T., Chourdakis, M., Cuerda, C., Delzenne, N. M., Deutz, N. E., Fouque, D., Genton, L., Gil, C., Koletzko, B., Leon-Sanz, M., Shamir, R., Singer, J., Singer, P., Stroebele-Benschop, N., Thorell, A., Weimann, A., & Barazzoni, R. (2017). Towards a multidisciplinary approach to understand and manage obesity and related diseases. *Clinical Nutrition, 36*, 917–938.

Billstedt, E., Waern, M., Duberstein, P., Marlow, T., Hellström, T., Ostling, S., & Skoog, I. (2013). Secular changes in personality: Study on 75-year-olds examined in 1976-77 and 2005-2006. *International Journal of Geriatric Psychiatry, 28*, 298–304.

Billstedt, E., Falk, H., Duberstein, P., Waern, M., Östling, S., Hällström, T., & Skoog, I. (2017). Time trends in Murray[1]s psychological needs over three decades in Swedish 75-year olds. *Gerontology, 63*(1), 45–54.

Black, H. K., White, T., & Hannum, S. M. (2007). The lived experience of depression in elderly African American women. *The Journals of Gerontology. Series B, Psychological Sciences and Social Sciences, 62*(6), S392–S398.

Bos, M. J., Lindén, T., Koudstaal, P. J., Hofman, A., Skoog, I., Breteler, M. M., & Tiemeier, H. (2008). Depressive symptoms and risk of stroke: The Rotterdam study. *Journal of Neurology, Neurosurgery, and Psychiatry, 79*, 997–1001.

Börjesson Hansson, A., Edin, E., Gislason, T., & Skoog, I. (2004). The prevalence of dementia in 95-year-olds. *Neurology, 63*, 2436–2438.

Carr, D., & Springer, K. W. (2010). Advances in families and Health Research in the 21st century. *Journal of Marriage and the Family, 72*(3), 743–761.

Cederholm, T., Jensen, G. L., Correia, M., Gonzalez, M. C., Fukushima, R., Higashiguchi, T., Baptista, G., Barazzoni, R., Blaauw, R., Coats, A., Crivelli, A., Evans, D. C., Gramlich, L., Fuchs-Tarlovsky, V., Keller, H., Llido, L., Malone, A., Mogensen, K. M., Morley, J. E., Muscaritoli, M., Nyulasi, I., Pirlich, M., Pisprasert, V., De Van Der Schueren, M. A. E., Siltharm, S., Singer, P., Tappenden, K., Velasco, N., Waitzberg, D., Yamwong, P., Yu, J., Van Gossum, A., & Compher, C. (2019). GLIM criteria for the diagnosis of malnutrition - A consensus report from the global clinical nutrition community. *Clinical Nutrition, 38*, 1–9.

Chen, L., Tan, Y., Yu, C., Guo, Y., Pei, P., Yang, L., Chen, Y., Du, H., Wang, X., Chen, J., Chen, Z., Lv, J., Li, L., & China Kadoorie Biobank Collaborative Group. (2021). Educational disparities in ischaemic heart disease among 0.5 million Chinese adults: A cohort study. *Journal of Epidemiology and Community Health*,jech-2020-216314. https://doi.org/10.1136/jech-2020-216314. Online ahead of print.

Christensen, K., Holm, N. V., Mcgue, M., Corder, L., & Vaupel, J. W. (1999). A Danish population-based twin study on general health in the elderly. *Journal of Aging and Health, 11*, 49–64.

Christensen, K., Doblhammer, G., Rau, R., & Vaupel, J. W. (2009). Ageing populations: The challenges ahead. *The Lancet, 374*(9696), 1196–1208.

Conner, K. O., Lee, B., Mayers, V., Robinson, D., Reynolds, C. F., Albert, S., et al. (2010). Attitudes and beliefs about mental health among African American older adults suffering from depression. *Journal of Aging Studies, 24*(4), 266–277.

Connolly, D., Garvey, J., & McKee, G. (2017). Factors associated with ADL/IADL disability in community dwelling older adults in the Irish longitudinal study on ageing (TILDA). *Disability and Rehabilitation, 39*(8), 809–816.

Cox, N. J., Ibrahim, K., Sayer, A. A., Robinson, S. M., & Roberts, H. C. (2019). Assessment and treatment of the anorexia of aging: A systematic review. *Nutrients, 11*.

Cruz-Jentoft, A. J., Kiesswetter, E., Drey, M., & Sieber, C. C. (2017). Nutrition, frailty, and sarcopenia. *Aging Clinical and Experimental Research, 29*, 43–48.

Dakic T. (2019). Mental health burden and unmet needs for treatment: a call for justice. *Br J Psychiatry, 216*(5), 241–242. https://doi.org/10.1192/bjp.2019.254

Falk, H., Johansson, L., Östling, S., Thøgersen Agerholm, K., Staun, M., Høst Dørfinger, L., & Skoog, I. (2014). Functional disability and ability 75-year-olds: A comparison of two Swedish cohorts born 30 years apart. *Age and Ageing, 43*(5), 636–641. https://doi.org/10.1093/ageing/afu018. Epub 2014 Mar 3.

Falk Erhag, H., Wetterberg, H., Johansson, L., Rydén, L., & Skoog, I. (2021). ADL and IADL disability in Swedish 85-year-olds born three decades apart – Findings from the H70 study. *Age and Ageing*. In Press.

Ferlander, S., & Mäkinen, I. H. (2009). Social capital, gender and self-rated health. Evidence from the Moscow health survey 2004. *Social Science & Medicine, 69*(9), 1323–1332.

Ferrari, A. J., Charlson, F. J., Norman, R. E., Patten, S. B., Freedman, G., Murray, C. J., et al. (2010). Burden of depressive disorders by country, sex, age, and year: Findings from the global burden of disease study. *PLoS Medicine, 10*(11), e1001547.

Femia, E. E., Zarit, S. H., & Johansson, B. (2001). The disablement process in very late life: A study of the oldest-old in Sweden. *The Journals of Gerontology Series B: Psychological Sciences and Social Sciences, 56*(1), P12–P23.

Fiske, A., Wetherell, J. L., & Gatz, M. (2009). Depression in older adults. *Annual Review of Clinical Psychology, 5*, 363–389.

Fried, L. P., Ferrucci, L., Darer, J., Williamson, J. D., & Anderson, G. (2004). Untangling the concepts of disability, frailty, and comorbidity: Implications for improved targeting and care. *The Journals of Gerontology Series A: Biological Sciences and Medical Sciences, 59*(3), M255–M263.

Formiga, F., Ferrer, A., Sanz, H., Marengoni, A., Alburquerque, J., Pujol, R., & Octabaix Study Members. (2013). Patterns of comorbidity and multimorbidity in the oldest old: The Octabaix study. *European Journal of Internal Medicine, 24*(1), 40–44.

Fortin, M., Bravo, G., Hudon, C., Vanasse, A., & Lapointe, L. (2005). Prevalence of multimorbidity among adults seen in family practice. *The Annals of Family Medicine, 3*(3), 223–228.

Fortin, M., Stewart, M., Poitras, M. E., Almirall, J., & Maddocks, H. (2012). A systematic review of prevalence studies on multimorbidity: Toward a more uniform methodology. *The Annals of Family Medicine, 10*(2), 142–151.

Gallus, S., Lugo, A., Murisic, B., Bosetti, C., Boffetta, P., & La Vecchia, C. (2015). Overweight and obesity in 16 European countries. *European Journal of Nutrition, 54*, 679–689.

Gómez-Gómez, M. E., & Zapico, S. C. (2019). Frailty, cognitive decline, neurodegenerative diseases and nutrition interventions. *International Journal of Molecular Science, 20*.

Govindaraju, T., Sahle, B. W., Mccaffrey, T. A., Mcneil, J. J., & Owen, A. J. (2018). Dietary patterns and quality of life in older adults: A systematic review. *Nutrients, 10*.

Galenkamp, H., Braam, A. W., Huisman, M., & Deeg, D. J. (2013). Seventeen-year time trend in poor self-rated health in older adults: Changing contributions of chronic diseases and disability. *European Journal of Public Health, 23*, 511–517.

Guerreiro, R., Gibbons, E., Tabuas-Pereira, M., Kun-Rodrigues, C., Santo, G. C., & Bras, J. (2020). Genetic architecture of common non-Alzheimer's disease dementias. *Neurobiology of Disease, 142*, 104946.

Gariepy, G., Honkaniemi, H., & Quesnel-Vallee, A. (2016). Social support and protection from depression: Systematic review of current findings in Western countries. *The British Journal of Psychiatry, 209*(4), 284–293.

Global burden of disease 2017 Diet collaborators. (2019). Health effects of dietary risks in 195 countries, 1990–2017: A systematic analysis for the Global Burden of Disease Study 2017. *Lancet, 393*, 1958–1972.

Greenberg, P. E., Fournier, A. A., Sisitsky, T., Pike, C. T., & Kessler, R. C. (2015). The economic burden of adults with major depressive disorder in the United States (2005 and 2010). *The Journal of Clinical Psychiatry, 76*(2), 155–162.

Gudmundsson, P., Andersson, S., Gustafson, D., Waern, M., Ostling, S., Hällström, T., Palsson, S., Skoog, I., & Hulthen, L. (2011). Depression in Swedish women: Relationship to factors at birth. *European Journal of Epidemiology, 26*(1), 55–60.

Gudmundsson, P., Lindwall, M., Gustafson, D. R., Ostling, S., Hallstrom, T., Waern, M., et al. (2015). Longitudinal associations between physical activity and depression scores in Swedish women followed 32 years. *Acta Psychiatrica Scandinavica, 132*(6), 451–458.

Guo, X., Waern, M., Sjögren, K., Lissner, L., Bengtsson, C., Björkelund, C., Östling, S., Gustafson, D., & Skoog, I. (2007). Midlife lung function and incidence of Alzheimer's disease: a 29-year longitudinal study in women. *Neurobiology of Aging, 28*, 343–350.

Gustafson, D., Rothenberg, E., Blennow, K., Steen, B., & Skoog, I. (2003). An 18-year follow-up of overweight and risk of Alzheimer disease. *Archives of Internal Medicine, 163*, 1524–1528.

Hashimoto, K., Kurita, H., Haratani, T., Fujii, K., & Ishibashi, T. (1999). Direct and buffering effects of social support on depressive symptoms of the elderly with home help. *Psychiatry and Clinical Neurosciences, 53*(1), 95–100.

Hasselgren, C., Dellve, L., Ekbrand, H., Zettergren, A., Zetterberg, H., Blennow, K., Skoog, I., & Halleröd, B. (2018). Socioeconomic status, gender, and dementia: The influence of work environment exposures and their interactions with APOE varepsilon4. *SSM Population Health, 5*, 171–179.

Hasselgren, C., Ekbrand, H., Fössberg, M. M., Zettergren, A., Zetterberg, H., Blennow, K., Skoog, I. & Hallerod, B. (2019). APOE ε4 and the long arm of social inequality: Estimated effects of socioeconomic status and sex on the timing of dementia onset. *Ageing & Society, 39*, 1951–1975.

Heikkinen, E. (2006). Disability and physical activity in late life—research models and approaches. *European Review of Aging and Physical Activity, 3*(1), 3–9.

Herforth, A., Arimond, M., Álvarez-Sánchez, C., Coates, J., Christianson, K., & Muehlhoff, E. (2019). A global review of food-based dietary guidelines. *Advances in Nutrition, 10*, 590–605.

Hodes, G. (2013). Sex, stress, and epigenetics: Regulation of behavior in animal models of mood disorders. *Biology of Sex Differences, 4*(1). https://doi.org/10.1186/2042-6410-4-1

Hsueh, Y. C., Chen, C. Y., Hsiao, Y. C., & Lin, C. C. (2019). A longitudinal, cross-lagged panel analysis of loneliness and depression among community-based older adults. *Journal of Elder Abuse & Neglect, 31*(4–5), 281–293.

Hörder, H., Johansson, L., Guo, X., Grimby, G., Kern, S., Östling, S., & Skoog, I. (2018). Midlife cardiovascular fitness and dementia: A 44-year longitudinal population study in women. *Neurology, 90*(15), e1298–e1305.

James, S. L., Abate, D., Abate, K. H., Abay, S. M., Abbafati, C., Abbasi, N., et al. (2018). Global, regional, and national incidence, prevalence, and years lived with disability for 354 diseases and injuries for 195 countries and territories, 1990-2017: a systematic analysis for the global burden of disease study 2017. *Lancet, 392*(10159), 1789–1858.

Joas, E., Bäckman, K., Gustafson, D., Ostling, S., Waern, M., Guo, X., & Skoog, I. (2012). Blood pressure trajectories from midlife to late life in relation to dementia in women followed for 37 years. *Hypertension, 59*(4), 796–801.

Joas, E., Guo, X., Kern, S., Östling, S., & Skoog, I. (2017). Sex differences in time trends of blood pressure among Swedish septuagenarians examined three decades apart: a longitudinal population study. *Journal of Hypertension, 35*(7), 1424–1431.

Johansson, L., Guo, X., Waern, M., Östling, S., Gustafson, D., Bengtsson, C., & Skoog, I. (2010). Mid-life psychological stress and risk of dementia: A 35-year longitudinal population study. *Brain, 133*(Pt 8), 2217–2224.

Johansson, L., Guo, X., Duberstein, P. R., Hällström, T., Waern, M., Östling, S., & Skoog, I. (2014). Midlife personality and risk of Alzheimer's disease and distress: a 38 year follow-up. *Neurology, 83*(17), 1538–1544.

Karlsson, P., Thorvaldsson, V., Skoog, I., Gudmundsson, P., & Johansson, B. (2015). Birth cohort differences in fluid cognition in old age: Comparisons of trends in levels and change trajectories over 30 years in three population-based samples. *Psychology and Aging, 30*(1), 83–94.

Katsas, K., Mamalaki, E., Kontogianni, M. D., Anastasiou, C. A., Kosmidis, M. H., Varlamis, I., Hadjigeorgiou, G. M., Dardiotis, E., Sakka, P., Scarmeas, N., & Yannakoulia, M. (2020). Malnutrition in older adults: Correlations with social, diet-related, and neuropsychological factors. *Nutrition, 71*, 110640.

Kern, S., Zetterberg, H., Kern, J., Zettergren, A., Waern, M., Höglund, K., Andreasson, U., Wetterberg, H., Börjesson-Hanson, A., Blennow, K., & Skoog, I. (2018). Prevalence of preclinical Alzheimer disease: Comparison of current classification systems. *Neurology, 90*(19), e1682–e1691.

Kern, S., Syrjanen, J. A., Blennow, K., Zetterberg, H., Skoog, I., Waern, M., Hagen, C. E., van Harten, A. C., Knopman, D. S., & Jack Jr CRPetersen RP, Mielke MM. (2019). Cerebrospinal fluid Neurofilament light protein and risk of mild cognitive impairment among cognitively unimpaired individuals. *JAMA Neurology, 76*(2), 187–193.

König, H., König, H. H., & Konnopka, A. (2019). The excess costs of depression: a systematic review and meta-analysis. *Epidemiology and Psychiatric Sciences, 29*, e30. https://doi.org/10.1017/S2045796019000180

Landi, F., Calvani, R., Tosato, M., Martone, A. M., Ortolani, E., Savera, G., Sisto, A., & Marzetti, E. (2016). Anorexia of aging: Risk factors, consequences, and potential treatments. *Nutrients, 8*, 69–69.

Ley, S. H., Hamdy, O., Mohan, V., & Hu, F. B. (2014). Prevention and management of type 2 diabetes: Dietary components and nutritional strategies. *Lancet, 383*, 1999–2007.

Liebetrau, M., Steen, B., & Skoog, I. (2008). Depression as a risk factor for the incidence of first-ever stroke in 85-year-olds. *Stroke, 39*, 1960–1965.

Leinonen, R., Heikkinen, E., & Jylha, M. (2001). Predictors of decline in self-assessments of health among older people--a 5-year longitudinal study. *Social Science & Medicine, 52*, 1329–1341.

Leinonen, R., Heikkinen, E., & Jylha, M. (2002). Changes in health, functional performance and activity predict changes in self-rated health: a 10-year follow-up study in older people. *Archives of Gerontology and Geriatrics, 35*, 79–92.

Leinonen, R., Kaprio, J., Jylha, M., Tolvanen, A., Koskenvuo, M., Heikkinen, E., & Rantanen, T. (2005). Genetic influences underlying self-rated health in older female twins. *Journal of the American Geriatrics Society, 53*, 1002–1007.

Ma, L., & Chan, P. (2020). Understanding the physiological links between physical frailty and cognitive decline. *Aging and Disease, 11*, 405–418.

Manton, K. G., Corder, L. S., & Stallard, E. (1993). Estimates of change in chronic disability and institutional incidence and prevalence rates in the US elderly population from the 1982, 1984, and 1989 National Long Term Care Survey. *Journal of Gerontology, 48*(4), S153–S166.

Marengoni, A., Winblad, B., Karp, A., & Fratiglioni, L. (2008). Prevalence of chronic diseases and multimorbidity among the elderly population in Sweden. *American Journal of Public Health, 98*(7), 1198–1200.

Marengoni, A., Angleman, S., Melis, R., Mangialasche, F., Karp, A., Garmen, A., et al. (2011). Aging with multimorbidity: a systematic review of the literature. *Ageing Research Reviews, 10*(4), 430–439.

Mehlig, K., Skoog, I., Waern, M., Miao Jonasson, J., Lapidus, L., Björkelund, C., Ostling, S., & Lissner, L. (2014). Physical activity, weight status, diabetes and dementia: A 34-year follow-up of the population study of women in Gothenburg. *Neuroepidemiology, 42*(4), 252–259.

Millán-Calenti, J. C., Tubío, J., Pita-Fernández, S., González-Abraldes, I., Lorenzo, T., Fernández-Arruty, T., & Maseda, A. (2010). Prevalence of functional disability in activities of daily living (ADL), instrumental activities of daily living (IADL) and associated factors, as predictors of morbidity and mortality. *Archives of Gerontology and Geriatrics, 50*(3), 306–310.

Millán-Calenti, J. C., Tubío, J., Pita-Fernández, S., González-Abraldes, I., Lorenzo, T., & Maseda, A. (2009). Prevalence of cognitive impairment: Effects of level of education, age, sex and associated factors. *Dementia and Geriatric Cognitive Disorders, 28*(5), 440–445.

Najar, J., Östling, S., Gudmundsson, P., Sundh, V., Johansson, L., Kern, S., Guo, X., Hällström, T., & Skoog, I. (2019). Cognitive and physical activity and dementia. A 44-year longitudinal population study of women. *Neurology, 92*(12), e1322–e1330.

Najar, J., Van Der Lee, S. J., Joas, E., Wetterberg, H., Hardy, J., Guerreiro, R., Bras, J., Waern, M., Kern, S., Zetterberg, H., Blennow, K., Skoog, I., & Zettergren, A. (2021). Polygenic risk scores for Alzheimer's disease are related to dementia risk in APOE varepsilon4 negatives. *Alzheimers Dement (Amst), 13*, e12142.

Nazri, N. S., Vanoh, D., & Leng, S. K. (2020). Malnutrition, low diet quality and its risk factors among older adults with low socio-economic status: a scoping review. *Nutrition Research Reviews*, 1–10.

Nordic Council of Ministers. (2012). *Nordic Nutrition Recommendations 2012: Integrating nutrition and physical activity*.

Overend, K., Bosanquet, K., Bailey, D., Foster, D., Gascoyne, S., Lewis, H., et al. (2015). Revealing hidden depression in older people: a qualitative study within a randomised controlled trial. *BMC Family Practice, 16*, 142.

Parker, M. G., Schön, P., Lagergren, M., & Thorslund, M. (2008). Functional ability in the elderly Swedish population from 1980 to 2005. *European Journal of Ageing, 5*(4), 299–309.

Poole, C., & Rietschlin, J. (2012). Intimate partner victimization among adults aged 60 and older: An analysis of the 1999 and 2004 general social survey. *Journal of Elder Abuse & Neglect, 24*(2), 120–137.

Porter Starr, K. N., Mcdonald, S. R., Weidner, J. A., & Bales, C. W. (2016). Challenges in the Management of Geriatric Obesity in high risk populations. *Nutrients, 8*.

Roh, S., Burnette, C. E., Lee, K. H., Lee, Y. S., & Easton, S. D. (2016). Risk and protective factors for depressive symptoms among indigenous older adults: Intimate partner violence (IPV) and social support. *Journal of Gerontological Social Work*, 1–16. https://doi.org/10.1080/01634372.2016.1214659

Rodríguez-Monforte, M., Flores-Mateo, G., & Sánchez, E. (2015). Dietary patterns and CVD: a systematic review and meta-analysis of observational studies. *The British Journal of Nutrition, 114*, 1341–1359.

Rydberg Sterner, T., Ahlner, F., Blennow, K., Dahlin-Ivanoff, S., Falk, H., Havstam Johansson, L., Hoff, M., Holm, M., Hörder, H., Jacobsson, T., Johansson, B., Johansson, L., Kern, J., Kern, S., Machado, A., Mellqvist Fässberg, M., Nilsson, J., Ribbe, M., Rothenberg, E., Rydén, L., Sadeghi, A., Sacuiu, S., Samuelsson, J., Sigström, R., Skoog, J., Thorvaldsson, V., Waern, M., Westman, E., Wetterberg, H., Zetterberg, H., Zetterberg, M., Zettergren, A., Östling, S., & Skoog, I. (2019a). The Gothenburg H70 birth cohort study 2014-16: Design, methods and study population. *European Journal of Epidemiology, 34*(2), 191–209.

Rydberg Sterner, T., Gudmundsson, P., Sigström, R., Ahlner, F., Seidu, N., Zettergren, A., Kern, S., Östling, S., Waern, M., & Skoog, I. (2019b). Depression and neuroticism decrease among women but not among men between 1976-2016 in Swedish septuagenarians. *Acta Psychiatrica Scandinavica, 139*(4), 381–394.

Rydberg Sterner, T., Dahlin-Ivanoff, S., Gudmundsson, P., Wiktorsson, S., Hed, S., Falk, H., Skoog, I., & Waern, M. (2020). 'I wanted to talk about it, but I couldn't', an H70 focus group study about experiencing depression in early late life. *BMC Geriatrics, 20*(1), 528. https://doi.org/10.1186/s12877-020-01908-x. PMID: 33287708.

Samadi, M., Moradi, S., Moradinazar, M., Mostafai, R., & Pasdar, Y. (2019). Dietary pattern in relation to the risk of Alzheimer's disease: a systematic review. *Neurological Sciences, 40*, 2031–2043.

Samuelsson, J., Rothenberg, E., Lissner, L., Eiben, G., Zettergren, A., & Skoog, I. (2019). Time trends in nutrient intake and dietary patterns among five birth cohorts of 70-year-olds examined 1971–2016: Results from the Gothenburg H70 birth cohort studies, Sweden. *Nutrition Journal, 18*, 66.

Sanchez-Roige, S., Gray, J. C., Mackillop, J., Chen, C. H., & Palmer, A. A. (2018). The genetics of human personality. *Genes, Brain, and Behavior, 17*, e12439.

Sjöberg, L., Östling, S., Waern, M., Falk, H., & Skoog, I. (2013). Secular changes in the relation between depression and social factors. A study of two birth cohorts of Swedish septuagenarians followed for 5 years. *Journal of Affective Disorders, 150*(2), 245–252.

Skoog, I. (1999). Possibilities for secondary prevention of alzheimer's disease. In R. Mayeux & Y. Christen (Eds.), *The epidemiology of alzheimer's disease: From gene to prevention*. Springer.

Skoog, I. (2004). Psychiatric epidemiology of old age: The H70 study - the NAPE lecture 2003. *Acta Psychiatrica Scandinavica, 109*, 4–18.

Skoog, I. (2011). Psychiatric disorders in the elderly. *Canadian Journal of Psychiatry, 56*(7), 387–397.

Skoog, I. (2016). Dementia: Dementia incidence - the times, they are a-changing.Nat. *Revista de Neurologia, 12*(6), 316–318.

Skoog, I., & Gustafson, D. (2006). Lessons learned from primary prevention trials in dementia. In K. Rockwood & S. Gauthier (Eds.), *Trial designs and outcomes in dementia therapeutic research* (pp. 189–211). Taylor & Francis.

Skoog, I., Lernfelt, B., Landahl, S., Palmertz, B., Andreasson, L.-A., Nilsson, L., Persson, G., Odén, A., & Svanborg, A. (1996). A 15-year longitudinal study on blood pressure and dementia. *Lancet, 347*, 1141–1145.

Skoog, I., Waern, M., Duberstein, P., Blennow, K., Zetterberg, H., Borjesson-Hanson, A., Ostling, S., Guo, X., Kern, J., Gustafson, D., Gudmundsson, P., Marlow, T., & Kern, S. (2015). A 9-year prospective population-based study on the association between the APOE*E4 allele and late-life depression in Sweden. *Biological Psychiatry, 78*, 730–736.

Skoog, I., Börjesson-Hanson, A., Kern, S., Johansson, L., Falk, H., Sigström, R., & Östling, S. (2017). Decreasing prevalence of dementia in 85-year olds examined 22 years apart: The influence of education and stroke. *Scientific Reports, 7*(1), 6136.

Skoog, J., Jönsson, H., Sigström, R., Östling, S., Falk, H., Waern, M., Thorvaldsson, V., Skoog, I., & Johansson, B. (2019). Do later-born birth cohorts of septuagenarians sleep better? A prospective population-based study of two birth cohorts of 70-year-olds. *Sleep, 42*(1).

Skoog, I., Kern, S., Najar, J., Guerreiro, R., Bras, J., Waern, M., Zetterberg, H., Blennow, K., & Zettergren, A. (2021). A non-APOE polygenic risk score for Alzheimer's disease is associated with CSF neurofilament light in a representative sample of cognitively unimpaired 70-year-olds. *The Journals of Gerontology. Series A, Biological Sciences and Medical Sciences*.

Socialstyrelsen. Psykisk ohälsa hos personer 65 år och äldre [Mental illness among persons older than 65 years]. (2018). https://www.socialstyrelsen.se/globalassets/sharepoint-dokument/artikelkatalog/oppna-jamforelser/2018-9-12.pdf. Accessed 11 Jan 2020.

Socialstyrelsen. Vård och omsorg om äldre - Lägesrapport 2019 [Health and social care for older adults]. (2019). https://www.socialstyrelsen.se/globalassets/sharepoint-dokument/artikelkatalog/ovrigt/2019-3-18.pdf. Accessed 6 Feb 2020.

Stanojevic Jerkovic, O., Sauliune, S., Sumskas, L., Birt, C., & Kersnik, J. (2015). Determinants of self-rated health in elderly populations in urban areas in Slovenia, Lithuania and UK: Findings of the EURO-URHIS 2 survey. *European Journal of Public Health*.

Stuck, A. E., Walthert, J. M., Nikolaus, T., Büla, C. J., Hohmann, C., & Beck, J. C. (1999). Risk factors for functional status decline in community-living elderly people: a systematic literature review. *Social Science & Medicine, 48*(4), 445–469.

Swedish Food Agency. (2012). *Riksmaten – vuxna 2010–11*. Livsmedels- och näringsintag bland vuxna i Sverige.

Taş, Ü., Verhagen, A. P., Bierma-Zeinstra, S. M., Hofman, A., Odding, E., Pols, H. A., & Koes, B. W. (2007). Incidence and risk factors of disability in the elderly: The Rotterdam study. *Preventive Medicine, 44*(3), 272–278.

Tengku Mohd, T. A. M., Yunus, R. M., Hairi, F., Hairi, N. N., & Choo, W. Y. (2019). Social support and depression among community dwelling older adults in Asia: a systematic review. *BMJ Open, 9*(7), e026667. https://doi.org/10.1136/bmjopen-2018-026667

Thorvaldsson, V., Karlsson, P., Skoog, J., Skoog, I., & Johansson, B. (2017). Better cognition in new birth cohorts of 70 year olds, but greater decline thereafter. *The Journals of Gerontology. Series B, Psychological Sciences and Social Sciences, 72*(1), 16–24.

Üstün, T. B., Kostanjsek, N., Chatterji, S., & Rehm, J. (Eds.). (2010). *Measuring health and disability: Manual for WHO disability assessment schedule WHODAS 2.0*. World Health Organization.

Wang, H.-X., Gustafson, D. R., Kivipelto, M., Pedersen, N. L., Skoog, I., Windblad, B., & Fratiglioni, L. (2012). Education halves the risk of dementia due to apolipoprotein epsilon 4 allele: A collaborative study from the Swedish brain power initiative. *Neurobiology of Aging, 33*(5), 1007.e1–1007.e7.

Wang, Y., Xu, L., Qin, W., Zhang, J., Xia, Y., Jing, X., … Li, Y. (2019). Gender difference in general self-efficacy among young-old elderly aged 60–74 in rural Shandong China: A cross-sectional survey. *International Journal of Environmental Research and Public Health, 16*(24), 5070.

Verbrugge, L. M., & Jette, A. M. (1994). The disablement process. *Social Science & Medicine, 38*(1), 1–14.

Vermeulen, J., Neyens, J. C., van Rossum, E., Spreeuwenberg, M. D., & de Witte, L. P. (2011). Predicting ADL disability in community-dwelling elderly people using physical frailty indicators: A systematic review. *BMC Geriatrics, 11*(1), 1–11.

Verropoulou, G., & Tsimbos, C. (2017). Disability trends among older adults in ten European countries over 2004-2013, using various indicators and survey of health, ageing and retirement in Europe (SHARE) data. *Ageing and Society, 37*(10), 2152.

Woods, S. B., Priest, J. B., Signs, T. L., & Maier, C. A. (2019). In sickness and in health: The longitudinal associations between marital dissatisfaction, depression and spousal health. *Journal of Family Therapy, 41*, 102–125.

Volkert, D., Beck, A. M., Cederholm, T., Cruz-Jentoft, A., Goisser, S., Hooper, L., Kiesswetter, E., Maggio, M., Raynaud-Simon, A., Sieber, C. C., Sobotka, L., Van Asselt, D., Wirth, R., & Bischoff, S. C. (2019). ESPEN guideline on clinical nutrition and hydration in geriatrics. *Clinical Nutrition, 38*, 10–47.

Von Berens, Å., Obling, S. R., Nydahl, M., Koochek, A., Lissner, L., Skoog, I., Frändin, K., Skoglund, E., Rothenberg, E., & Cederholm, T. (2020). Sarcopenic obesity and associations with mortality in older women and men - a prospective observational study. *BMC Geriatrics, 20*, 199.

Wu, Y.-T., Fratiglioni, L., Matthews, F. E., Lobo, A., Breteler, M. M. B., Skoog, I., & Brayne, C. (2016). Dementia occurrence in Europe: Epidemiological evidence and implications for current policy making. *Lancet Neurology, 15*(1), 116–124.

Wu, Y. T., Beiser, A. S., Breteler, M. M. B., Fratiglioni, L., Helmer, C., Hendrie, H. C., Honda, H., Ikram, M. A., Langa, K. M., Lobo, A., Matthews, F. E., Ohara, T., Pérès, K., Qiu, C., Seshadri, S., Sjölund, B. M., Skoog, I., & Brayne, C. (2017). The changing prevalence and incidence of dementia over time - current evidence. *Nature Reviews. Neurology, 13*(6), 327–339.

Wu, J., Hasselgren, C., Zettergren, A., Zetterberg, H., Blennow, K., Skoog, I., & Halleröd, B. (2018). The impact of social networks and APOE e4 on dementia among older adults: Tests of possible interactions. *Aging & Mental Health, 27*, 1–10. [Epub ahead of print].

Zambroski, C. H., Moser, D. K., Bhat, G., & Ziegler, C. (2005). Impact of symptom prevalence and symptom burden on quality of life in patients with heart failure. *European Journal of Cardiovascular Nursing, 4*(3), 198–206.

Zhi, X., Joas, E., Waern, M., Östling, S., Börjesson-Hanson, A., & Skoog, I. (2013). Prevalence of cardiovascular disorders and risk factors in two 75-year-olds birth cohorts examined in 1976-77 and 2005-06. *Aging Clinical and Experimental Research, 25*, 377–383.

Zhou, X., Perez-Cueto, F. J. A., Santos, Q. D., Monteleone, E., Giboreau, A., Appleton, K. M., Bjørner, T., Bredie, W. L. P., & Hartwell, H. (2018). A systematic review of behavioural interventions promoting healthy eating among older people. *Nutrients, 10*.

Zuelke, A. E., Roehr, S., Schroeter, M. L., Witte, A. V., Hinz, A., Glaesmer, H., Engel, C., Enzenbach, C., Zachariae, S., Zeynalova, S., Loeffler, M., Villringer, A., & Riedel-Heller, S. G. (2020). Depressive symptomatology in early retirees associated with reason for retirement—Results from the population-based LIFE-adult-study. *Frontiers in Psychiatry, 11*, 565442. https://doi.org/10.3389/fpsyt.2020.565442

Zettergren, A., Kern, S., Gustafson, D., Gudmundsson, P., Sigstrom, R., Ostling, S., Eriksson, E., Zetterberg, H., Blennow, K., & Skoog, I. (2017). The ACE gene is associated with late-life major depression and age at dementia onset in a population-based cohort. *The American Journal of Geriatric Psychiatry, 25*, 170–177.

Zettergren, A., Kern, S., Ryden, L., Ostling, S., Blennow, K., Zetterberg, H., Falk, H., & Skoog, I. (2018). Genetic variation in FOXO3 is associated with self-rated health in a population-based sample of older individuals. *The Journals of Gerontology. Series A, Biological Sciences and Medical Sciences, 73*, 1453–1458.

Chapter 5
Good Self-Rated Health as an Indicator of Personal Capability in Old Age

Hanna Falk Erhag

5.1 Introduction

The goal of nursing research is to develop a body of knowledge that will support and advance nursing practice (Risjord, 2010). The distinctiveness of the discipline lies in its holistic and life-world perspective, focusing on subjective experiences of illness and health, as well as personal interpretations and understandings of human existence. Many nurse researchers tend to use qualitative methodology that aims to generate in-depth understandings of human existence in close proximity to those being studied.

The questions that nurse researchers ask, as well as the methods they use to answer these questions, depend on their general perspective on how the world works – a paradigm, or multiple paradigms, that help researchers to sharpen their focus on the phenomena under study (Polit & Beck, 2018; Risjord, 2010). For example, according to the constructivist paradigm, reality is not permanent but rather a construction that exists within a certain context that is interpreted differently in people's minds, and can therefore never be either verified or falsified (Polit & Beck, 2018). In order to study the multiple interpretations of reality that exist in people's minds, knowledge is said to be maximised when the distance between

H. Falk Erhag (✉)
Neuropsychiatric Epidemiology Unit, Department of Psychiatry and Neurochemistry, Institute of Neuroscience and Physiology, Sahlgrenska Academy at the University of Gothenburg, Gothenburg, Sweden

Centre for Ageing and Health – AgeCap, University of Gothenburg, Gothenburg, Sweden

Institute of Health and Care Sciences, Sahlgrenska Academy at the University of Gothenburg, Gothenburg, Sweden
e-mail: hanna.falk@gu.se

H. Falk Erhag et al. (eds.), *A Multidisciplinary Approach to Capability in Age and Ageing*, International Perspectives on Aging 31,
https://doi.org/10.1007/978-3-030-78063-0_5

researcher and study participants is minimised. In contrast, according to the postpositivist paradigm, reality exists independently of human observation, nature is ordered although strict objectivity is impossible, and determinism refers to the assumption that all phenomena have antecedent causes. Within this paradigm, the nurse researcher sees objectivity as a goal and unbiased materials are gathered in order to describe and understand what reality probably is (Denzin & Lincoln, 2017).

Although there seem to be distinctive differences between these two paradigms, they have features in common. For example, that the goal of research is to seek truth regarding the phenomena under study, provide answers and solve problems. These commonalities make it possible to combine paradigms and scientific methods. For example, in nursing research, subjective experiences of health and illness have traditionally been studied using qualitative methodology within a constructivist research paradigm. However, subjective experiences can also be operationalised into quantifiable measures that can lend themselves to being studied at a collective level in large and representative samples of older adults over time. While epidemiology could benefit nursing, both as a research discipline and a clinical practice, it still seems to be significantly underused and poorly understood (Whitehead, 2003; 2000).

Epidemiology, or the study of the frequency, distribution and determinants of disease, has its roots in the scientific study of epidemics (McMahon & Pugh, 1970), and is primarily a quantitative discipline that investigates reports of multiple occurrences of a disease in close proximity to each other. Firmly embedded within medicine, and primarily adopting the postpositivist paradigm of the natural sciences, traditional epidemiology could be viewed as ill-equipped to contribute to a model of nursing. However, since its beginnings, the scope of epidemiology, its range of designs and impact on healthcare and policy have developed to also include studies of subjective experiences of health and illness in relation to a variety of factors (Jacobsen, 2021), and several healthcare-related policies influencing the practice of nurses are a consequence of epidemiological studies of health and illness (Whitehead, 2000).

Traditionally, nursing has had little time for epidemiology, perceiving it as both a discipline and a practice that is firmly embedded in positivistic science. Nursing, however, is an eclectic discipline which has drawn upon many epistemologies and methodologies in its quest for a holistic and life-world perspective (Jacobsen, 2021; Ahrens & Pigeot, 2014). Epidemiological studies can be either descriptive or explanatory. In the former, the aim is to describe the natural history of disease, the frequency or incidence of health outcomes or health determinants and their temporal or geographical variation. In the latter, the aim is to contribute to the search for the causes of health-related events, in particular by isolating the effects of specific factors (Whitehead, 2000; Ahrens & Pigeot, 2014). Both perspectives are needed in studies of self-rated health during the fourth age in order to determine whether it can be used as an indicator of personal capability to master the gains and losses of late life, given changing reference points, cultural norms and multiple comparisons. Although we have seen extensive research on self-rated health during the last 70 years, there is still limited understanding of the dimensions to which older adults refer when evaluating their own health and how those dimensions act and interact in the evaluation process, or how these assessments reflect their resilience and capacity to maintain and regain normal levels of functioning in the face of risks and losses in late life, especially during the fourth age.

5.2 Views on Ageing and Old Age

At the biological level, ageing is a result of the impact of an accumulation of a wide variety of molecular and cellular damage over time (World Health Organisation, 2015a, 2020). Ageing can also be regarded as the process of a person living a long life extending beyond the period of reproductive fitness. However, age-related changes are neither linear nor consistent, and only loosely associated with a person's chronological age in years. Globally, people are living longer, and population ageing is one of the most significant social transformations of the twenty-first century, constituting both a great success for humanity and a global challenge (World Health Organisation, 2020; Sanderson & Scherbov, 2007). Around the world, older adults make up the fastest growing segment of the population and, by 2050, the proportion of those older than 85 years will have nearly doubled compared with today (United Nations World Population Prospects, 2019). The uncertainty over the rate and nature of ageing has been the subject of a number of debates over the years (Higgs & Gilleard, 2015). Research findings that show considerable variation between populations, trends in the delayed onset of morbidity, less steep decline, and a greater compression of morbidity, points towards the fact that we are facing a real change in the process of ageing, and that those growing old today differ greatly from those growing old at the beginning of the twentieth century. It becomes more and more evident that chronological age has lost quite a lot of its credibility as a marker of old age. While some 85-year-olds enjoy extremely good health and functioning, other 85-year-olds are frail and require significant help from others in order to manage (World Health Organisation, 2020). The variability between individuals seems to be increasing and the older population is becoming more heterogeneous.

The term 'the fourth age' was coined by gerontologists in the late 1980s (Laslett, 1987, 1991). Following a then well-established tradition of ordering the life course into different distinct stages based on chronological age-spans, Laslett coupled the term 'third age' with a 'fourth age', and in doing so drew attention to one of the most important oppositions in later life – the distinction between fit, healthy and productive late life and ill, frail, impaired and dependent late life (Higgs & Gilleard, 2015). The idea that people can be assigned to one of these two positions had previously been proposed by other researchers, for example Neugarten's distinction between the 'young old' versus the 'old-old', introduced in the mid-1970s (Neugarten, 1974). An appealing aspect of Laslett's view on ageing is that it takes little notice of chronological age. Rather, it is the functional status of the individual that determines whether a person is assigned to one or the other of these statuses (Higgs & Gilleard, 2015). Functional disability is defined by most laypersons as 'the inability to do something' (Mitra, 2006; Albrecht et al., 2001). It can be defined and operationalised by the presence of limitations in performing the necessary activities of daily living such as eating, dressing, using the toilet, getting out of bed, walking or activities related to household maintenance such as cooking, shopping and managing bills or one's medication. Any difficulty in performing these tasks compromises a person's ability to live an independent life, their health and wellbeing and their status as an autonomous individual (Staudinger et al., 1995). According to the World Health Organisation (2015b), functional disability in old age has its origins in a health condition that gives rise to problems with body function or structure causing loss or deviation, problems in the execution of tasks, and participation restrictions within contextual factors. In relation to self-rated health as an indicator of personal capability during the fourth age, this view of disability is useful in that it incorporates both objective and subjective aspects. For example, physical losses and functional disability may be coped with by shifting from a temporal comparison of the present health status with previous health, to a social comparison with people of the same age (Spuling et al., 2015). Ultimately, comparing oneself favourably to others affects personal capability and self-rated health in that it influences cognitive coping efforts to manage stress. In addition, conceptions of health might change over historical time. What was considered good health in old age some fifty years ago might not be relevant to those growing old in 2020.

How we choose to view ageing and define old age has major implications for our research practice. In addition to Laslett's third and fourth ages, which focus on distinctions between fit, healthy and productive late life and ill, frail, impaired and dependent late life (Higgs & Gilleard, 2015), concepts such as resilience and reserve capacity play an important role because they can provide insights into why some older adults, despite chronic illness and functional disability, rate their health as good. Resilience refers to the ability to bounce back from adversity and to regain levels of functioning after setbacks such as illness, trauma or loss (Staudinger et al., 1995). It also has to do with the ability to adapt to changes, to develop and to create a 'new normal'. It could be postulated that high levels of resilience in late life can be viewed as a conversion factor that enables the individual to use his or her full potential, thus improving personal capability as well as self-rated health.

5.3 What Is Health and How Can It Be Defined?

From a nursing perspective, health is more than just the absence of illness – it is an active process in which the person moves towards his or her maximum potential, and the experience of health and illness is influenced by the psychological and social fabric of the environment as well as biological factors (Leininger, 1988). Because health is individually defined by each person, and affected by numerous factors, a standard definition is difficult. According to the World Health Organisation, health includes not only physical and mental health, but also social wellbeing (World Health Organisation, 2020). Lay definitions of health are influenced by historical and local contexts, whether respondents are referring to health in general or to their own health and personal experiences and observations (Milte et al., 2014).

Symptoms, or the subjective experience of illness, emerge when the habitual equilibrium of the person has been disturbed and interpreted as a bodily message (Malterud et al., 2015). How this 'bodily message' is perceived is based on the reality of the person, including physiological, psychological, social, cultural and behavioural components (Wallström & Ekman, 2018). The relationship between subjective experiences of health and illness on the one hand, and objective indicators of disease and functioning on the other, is extremely complex and multidimensional. In contrast to illness, disease can be defined as an organic phenomenon that is detected through signs of malfunction and/or abnormality, independent of subjective experience (Dodd et al., 2001). However, disease and illness are interdependent concepts that influence each other in the sense that medical knowledge and medical terminology affect the subjective experience of illness. In many ways, the epistemic and normative differences between disease and illness provide a perspective on human ailments that distinguishes nursing from other disciplines investigating similar research problems.

When it comes to health in late life, there is a gradual decrease in physical and mental capacity and a growing risk of health problems. However, these changes are neither linear nor consistent, and they are only loosely associated with a person's chronological age in years. In 1987, Rowe and Kahn defined successful ageing as "low probability of disease and disease-related disability and risk factors, with high cognitive and physical functional capacity, and active engagement with life" (Rowe & Kahn, 1997). Their goal was to contribute a more nuanced perspective on health in old age at a time when most researchers were only emphasising the role of chronological age in determining an individual's health, concentrating on average age-related losses across different age-groups, and neglecting the substantial variability between individuals and heterogeneity within age-groups (Lu et al., 2019). In addition, Rowe and Kahn distinguished between 'usual' and 'successful' ageing, where 'usual' referred to those declines in function and fitness normally associated with advancing age. Over the years, the concept of successful ageing has paved the way for other concepts, such as 'optimal ageing' and 'healthy ageing', which are more inclusive and focused on the optimisation of opportunities for health, participation, security and quality of life, rather than emphasising the selective survivorship of successful agers (Fuchs et al., 2013).

5.4 What Is Self-Rated Health and How Can It Be Measured?

Hardly any other measure of health is more widely used or more poorly understood than self-rated health (Jylhä, 2009). It is based on the all-inclusive, sensitive, yet non-specific question: 'In general, how would you rate your health?' with response options ranging from 'very good' to 'very poor' on a four- or five-point scale. Alternative wording often use reference points to anchor the assessment, such as comparing the present health status with previous health (self-comparative) or same-aged peers (age-comparative). Regardless of the exact wording, the question delegates to the individual the task of synthesising, in a single evaluation, the many dimensions (physical, mental, functional and emotional) that make up the complex concept of health. This seemingly simple question has been one of the most frequently used health indicators in research since the 1960s (Maddox, 1962; Garrity et al., 1978). However, despite its extensive use, our understanding of the processes that direct a person to rate his or her health is still limited (Lisko et al., 2020), and the measure's most important benefit, as well as its main drawback, is the limited control over what respondents consider when rating their health. In other words, what people integrate and summarise across the health domains, as well as the psychological filters that play a vital role in any self-rating, are themselves part of the assessment rather than factors that need to be controlled for (Jylhä, 2009, 2010).

Several studies have confirmed that self-rated health is influenced by many factors, deriving from various dimensions, mainly, but not exclusively, related to health (Golini & Egidi, 2016). Chronic illness, multimorbidity, functional impairment and psychological wellbeing, as well as demographic factors such as sex, educational attainment, social networks and social class have been pointed out as major determinants of self-rated health in older adults (DeSalvo et al. 2006; Nummela et al., 2011; Verroupoulou, 2009; Jylhä et al., 2006; Jylhä, 2009). There are also studies emphasising early life factors, personality traits and mood as potential determinants in self-assessments of health (Segerstrom, 2014; Kasai et al., 2013), as well as physical and cognitive functioning (Golini & Egidi, 2016). The number of factors potentially influencing the self-rated health of older adults seems endless and, in most cases, depends on the available dataset. For example, Mantzavinis and colleagues (2005) showed that, in 57 studies on self-rated health published in 2002, 133 different determinants were considered. In addition, the relationship between self-rated health and mortality is well established in the literature (Idler & Benyamini, 1997). Several explanations for this relationship have been suggested, including the 'trajectory hypothesis' (Wolinsky & Tierney, 1998), which posits that self-rated health reflects changes in health and life circumstances, past experiences and expectations. These changes might be especially relevant to those in the fourth age, a population with high rates of mortality and morbidity, who thus are likely to employ evaluative processes that differ from other age groups when reporting self-rated health. Several studies have shown that the link between symptoms of illness, diagnosed conditions and functional status on the one hand, and self-rated health on the other, weakens with age (Cheng et al., 2007; Schnittker, 2005), and that, given a comparable level of disease and functioning, older olds tend to rate their health more positively than younger olds (Ferraro, 1980). It has also been proposed that older olds are less likely to change their self-evaluation of their health in response to changing disease status than younger olds (Heller et al., 2009). As a primary explanation, most studies put forward mechanisms of successful adaptation to declining health, revised expectations or comparison mechanisms.

Undoubtedly, social comparison with others (Festinger, 1954) and temporal comparison with previous health states (Albert, 1977) play an important role in the self-rating process, and comparison theories can guide studies investigating the effects of reference points on self-rated health in later life. Comparison theories propose that individuals use reference points to evaluate current personal attributes such as self-rated health. For example, according to the theory of enhanced social downgrading (i.e. comparing oneself favourably to others), older adults have been found to compare themselves favourably against negative stereotypical attributes by creating a positive distance between themselves and the comparison group (Heckhausen & Brim, 1997). There are also studies in which older adults have been asked to temporally compare their current health status with past health status, which in many cases have highlighted functional loss and impairment and therefore yielded more negative health evaluations (Heller et al., 2009).

The complex cognitive process of individual health evaluation is infused with the demographic and socio-economic characteristics of the individual, and the evaluation consists of three phases (Jylhä, 2009). In the first phase, the individual identifies the components and relevant information that need to be taken into consideration in the self-evaluation; for example, symptoms of illness, medical treatments, problems in body function or structure causing a loss or deviation, problems in the execution of tasks or maintaining control over the environment. In the second phase, the individual has to decide how these components are ordered in terms of priority, based on social and temporal comparisons as well as their interrelationships. In the third step, the person has to choose which response alternative on the four- or five-point scale corresponds best. Studies show that the health aspects that older people take into account during the first phase of the evaluation process differ to some extent from those that younger people consider when rating their health (Peersman et al., 2012). In addition, older people may downgrade their aspirations and expectations about their health, which can be regarded as highly desirable adaptive responses to health decline (Tornstam, 1975).

In addition to the cognitive processes and theories of social and temporal comparison, conceptions of health might change over historical time, and the societal value ascribed to certain aspects of life also influence how we rate our health. Different birth cohorts grow old in different societal contexts, which might be associated with varying interpretations and understandings of health. If, for example, the societal value of autonomy and independence in old age had increased during the previous century, then it would follow that functional disability may have gained importance as a marker of poor self-rated health in later-born birth cohorts compared to earlier-born cohorts. As such, the associative strength between predictors and self-rated health might depend not only on age but also on birth cohort. According to Spuling et al. (2015), predictors of self-rated health can be either invariant (i.e. having a constant influence on self-rated health across age-groups and cohorts), age contextual (i.e. having a changing influence with advancing age), or cohort contextual (i.e. having a changing influence across different birth cohorts). The complexity surrounding self-rated health as a measure can be overwhelming, and the potentially changing reference points and different predictors across cohorts (i.e. historical time) make it challenging to study empirically. However, these challenges are also what makes self-rated health so fascinating and potentially useful as an indicator of more latent variables, such as personal capability.

5.5 Good Self-Rated Health as an Indicator of Personal Capability

The capability approach is a broad normative framework for the evaluation of individual wellbeing and social arrangements, the design of policies and plans about social change in society (Robeyns, 2005). At the individual level, this approach can be used to evaluate a wide range of aspects of health and functioning. The core characteristic of the capability approach is its focus on what people are effectively able to do and to be – their capabilities. Although a person's capabilities are dependent on a wide variety of factors, at the individual level it is the experience of symptoms, chronic illnesses and functional disability that are paramount for people's ability to function and to engage in the actions and activities they want to undertake. In addition to factors or resources at the individual micro-level, a person's capability is also conditioned by factors at several societal levels. The macro-level refers, among other things, to laws that regulate social security and healthcare systems, and affect the social imaginary of the third and fourth ages, as well as ageist attitudes and prejudice that diminish older adults. The meso-level refers, for example, to the arrangements in which everyday life is embedded. In relation to self-rated health, lack of social capital (i.e. the actual and potential social resources available to individuals, groups or communities) has been associated with poor self-rated health and adverse health outcomes in several studies (DeSalvo et al., 2006; Kawachi et al., 2008). For example, lack of social integration (i.e. actual or perceived connectedness with others within social groups, communities and networks) have been shown to be a risk factor for poor self-rated health (Engström et al., 2008), and bridging social capital have been shown to be closely related to both psychological wellbeing and quality of life (Courtin & Knapp, 2017).

According to the capability approach, conversion factors refer to a person's ability to actually convert available resources into the goals that he or she has reason to value. At the personal level, an important conversion factor is resilience. This means having the ability to adapt to changes, to develop, to bounce back from adversity and to regain levels of functioning after setbacks such as illness, trauma or loss (Staudinger et al., 1995). In relation to good self-rated health as an indicator of personal capability, an individual showing high levels of resilience is better equipped to master the gains and losses of late life compared to an individual without resilience, given the same conditions and available resources.

5.6 Epidemiological Studies of Self-Rated Health as an Indicator of Personal Capability in the Fourth Age

The Gothenburg H70 Birth Cohort Studies (H70 studies) are multidisciplinary epidemiological studies examining representative birth cohorts of older populations in Gothenburg, Sweden. The first study started in 1971. So far, six birth cohorts with baseline examination at age 70 have been followed longitudinally, and more than 700 scientific papers have been published based on these data since 1971. Examinations have been virtually identical between studies in order to enhance the possibilities of comparisons between birth cohorts and examination years. This generates an opportunity to study time trends in age-related risk and protective factors, subjective experiences such as self-rated health, preclinical markers and the prevalence and incidence of disease. In addition, new and modern types of assessment have been added over the years in order to keep the H70 studies innovative and up-to-date with modern techniques. The overarching aim of the H70 studies is to examine the impact of mental, somatic and social health on the functional ability and wellbeing of individuals aged 70 years and older, taking into account their complex interactions with age, sex, gender, socioeconomic gradients, environmental exposures, psychosocial, neurobiological and genetic factors. The self-rated health question has been included since the first examination in 1971, using either a neutral or global reference (i.e., how would you rate your health in general?), or stipulating a reference point to anchor the assessment, such as comparing current health with previous health (self-comparative) or same-aged peers (age-comparative). These reference points can have a significant effect on the health assessment process and should not be used interchangeably. So far, we have identified self-rated health questions with identical wording and response options in five birth cohorts examined at 70, 74, 79, 85, 88, 90 and 95 years of age, which enables us to combine cross-sectional and longitudinal data that allows comparison of age-group differences in cross-section with individual changes over time in the longitudinal section. The H70 study provides important insights into how predictors of self-rated health can either show a constant influence across age-groups and birth cohorts (i.e. invariant predictors), show a changing influence across different birth cohorts (i.e. cohort-contextual predictors), or show a changing influence with advancing age (age-contextual predictors). Our research programme investigating self-rated health has two main themes, one focusing on the structure of self-rated health and the other on the reweighting process, the shifting meanings of self-evaluation of health and changing reference points. In the first theme, we are identifying the direct and indirect influences of various factors that have been shown to predict self-rated health in previous studies. For example demographic factors (sex, education, social class etc.), health-related factors (i.e. number of chronic conditions, functional disability, physical activity etc.), factors related to psychological wellbeing (i.e. life satisfaction, depressive symptoms, positive affect etc.), and factors related to social capital and social integration.

Previous studies have demonstrated, for example, that individuals show stability in their self-evaluations and often maintain good self-rated health into old age despite a worsening in physical health status, suggesting that health-related factors become less important self-rated health predictors with advancing age, and that factors related to psychological wellbeing, for example positive affect or depressive symptoms, become more important (Benyamini et al., 2000). In addition, due to historically changing conceptions of health, factors related to psychological wellbeing could also be subject to cohort effects. We therefore hypothesise that health-related factors will show a decreasing association with self-rated health with advancing age (i.e. age-contextual predictors of decreasing strength), that factors related to psychological wellbeing will show an increasing association with self-rated health with advancing age (i.e. age-contextual predictors of increasing strength), and that factors related to psychological wellbeing are not only age-contextual predictors but additionally are subject to cohort effects (i.e. cohort-contextual predictors of increasing strength).

In order to examine the reweighting process, the shifting meanings of the self-evaluation of health and changing reference points, we compare whether questions using either a neutral or global reference (i.e., how would you rate your health in general?), or stipulating a reference point to anchor the assessment, such as comparing current health with previous health (self-comparative) or same-aged peers (age-comparative) are equivalent measures of health perception in older adults. We also explore how subjective age (i.e. if individuals experience themselves as younger as or older than their actual age) affects self-rated health and how this association can be mediated by life satisfaction and psychological wellbeing.

References

Ahrens, W., & Pigeot, I. (Eds.). (2014). *Handbook of epidemiology*. Springer.

Albert, S. (1977). Temporal comparison theory. *Psychological Review, 84*, 485–503.

Albrecht, G. L., Seelman, K. D., & Bury, M. (Eds.). (2001). *Handbook of disability studies*. Sage.

Benyamini, Y., Idler, E. L., Leventhal, H., & Leventhal, E. A. (2000). Positive affect and function as influences on self-assessments of health: Expanding our view beyond illness and disability. *The Journals of Gerontology: Series B: Psychological Sciences and Social Sciences, 55*, 107–116.

Cheng, S. T., Fung, H., & Chan, A. (2007). Maintaining self-rated health through social comparison in old age. *The Journals of Gerontology. Series B, Psychological Sciences and Social Sciences, 62*, 277–285.

Courtin, E., & Knapp, M. (2017). Social isolation, loneliness and health in old age: a scoping review. *Health & Social Care in the Community, 25*(3), 799–812.

Denzin, N. K., & Lincoln, Y. S. (Eds.). (2017). *The Sage handbook of qualitative research*. Sage.

DeSalvo, K. B., Bloser, N., Reynolds, K., He, J., & Muntner, P. (2006). Mortality prediction with a single general self-rated health question. *Journal of General Internal Medicine, 21*(3), 267.

Dodd, M., Janson, S., Facione, N., Faucett, J., Froelicher, E. S., Humphreys, J., … Taylor, D. (2001). Advancing the science of symptom management. *Journal of Advanced Nursing, 33*(5), 668–676.

Engström, K., Mattsson, F., Järleborg, A., & Hallqvist, J. (2008). Contextual social capital as a risk factor for poor self-rated health: A multilevel analysis. *Social Science & Medicine, 66*(11), 2268–2280.

Ferraro, K. F. (1980). Self-ratings of health among the old and the old-old. *Journal of Health and Social Behavior, 21*, 377–383.

Festinger, L. (1954). A theory of social comparison processes. *Human Relations, 7*(2), 117–140.

Fuchs, J., Scheidt-Nave, C., Hinrichs, T., Mergenthaler, A., Stein, J., Riedel-Heller, S. G., & Grill, E. (2013). Indicators for healthy ageing – A debate. *International Journal of Environmental Research and Public Health, 10*(12), 6630–6644.

Garrity, T. F., Somes, G. W., & Marx, M. B. (1978). Factors influencing self-assessment of health. *Social Science & Medicine. Part A: Medical Psychology & Medical Sociology, 12*, 77–81.

Golini, N., & Egidi, V. (2016). The latent dimensions of poor self-rated health: How chronic diseases, functional and emotional dimensions interact influencing self-rated health in Italian elderly. *Social Indicators Research, 128*(1), 321–339.

Heckhausen, J., & Brim, O. G. (1997). Perceived problems for self and others: Self-protection by social downgrading throughout adulthood. *Psychology & Aging, 12*, 610–619.

Heller, D. A., Ahern, F. M., Pringle, K. E., & Brown, T. V. (2009). Among older adults, the responsiveness of self-rated health to changes in Charlson comorbidity was moderated by age and baseline comorbidity. *Journal of Clinical Epidemiology, 62*, 177–187.

Higgs, P., & Gilleard, C. (2015). *Rethinking old age: Theorising the fourth age*. Macmillan International Higher Education.

Idler, E. L., & Benyamini, Y. (1997). Self-rated health and mortality: A review of twenty-seven community studies. *Journal of Health and Social Behavior, 38*, 21–37.

Jacobsen, K. H. (2021). *Introduction to health research methods: A practical guide* (3rd ed.). Jones & Bartlett Learning.

Jylhä, M. (2009). What is self-rated health and why does it predict mortality? Towards a unified conceptual model. *Social Science & Medicine, 69*(3), 307–316.

Jylhä, M. (2010). Self-rated health between psychology and biology. A response to Huisman and Deeg. *Social Science & Medicine, 70*(5), 655–657.

Jylhä, M., Volpato, S., & Guralnik, J. A. (2006). Self-rated health showed a graded association with frequently used biomarkers in a large population sample. *Journal of Clinical Epidemiology, 59*(5), 465–471.

Kasai, Y., Suzuki, E., Iwase, T., Doi, H., & Takao, S. (2013). Type D personality is associated with psychological distress and poor self-rated health among the elderly: A population-based study in Japan. *PLoS One, 8*(10), e77918.

Kawachi, I., Subramanian, S., & Kim, D. (2008). Social capital and health. In I. Kawachi, S. Subramanian, & D. Kim (Eds.), *Social Capital and Health*. Springer.

Laslett, P. (1987). The emergence of the Third Age. *Ageing and Society, 7*, 133–160.

Laslett, P. (1991). *A fresh map of life: The emergence of the Third Age*. Wiedenfield and Nicholson.

Leininger, M. M. (Ed.). (1988). *Care: The essence of nursing and health*. Wayne State University Press.

Lisko, I., Törmäkangas, T., & Jylhä, M. (2020). Structure of self-rated health among the oldest old: Analyses in the total population and those living with dementia. *SSM Population Health, 18*(11), 100567.

Lu, W., Pikhart, H., & Sacker, A. (2019). Domains and measurements of healthy aging in epidemiological studies: A review. *The Gerontologist, 59*(4), 294–310.

Maddox, G. L. (1962). Some correlates of differences in self-assessment of health status among the elderly. *Journal of Gerontology, 17*, 180–185.

Malterud, K., Guassora, A. D., Graungaard, A. H., & Reventlow, S. (2015). Understanding medical symptoms: A conceptual review and analysis. *Theoretical Medicine and Bioethics, 36*(6), 411–424.

Mantzavinis, G. D., Pappas, N., Dimoliatis, I. D., & Ioannidis, J. P. (2005). Multivariate models of self-reported health often neglected essential candidate determinants and methodological issues. *Journal of Clinical Epidemiology, 58*(5), 436–443.
McMahon, B., & Pugh, T. F. (1970). *Epidemiological principles and methods*. Little Brown.
Milte, C. M., Walker, R., Luszcz, M. A., Lancsar, E., Kaambwa, B., & Ratcliffe, J. (2014). How important is health status in defining quality of life for older people? An exploratory study of the views of older South Australians. *Applied Health Economics and Health Policy, 12*(1), 73–84.
Mitra, S. (2006). The capability approach and disability. *Journal of Disability and Policy Studies, 16*(4), 236–247.
Neugarten, B. L. (1974). Age groups in American society and the rise of the young-old. *The Annals of the American Academy of Political and Social Science, 415*(1), 187–198.
Nummela, O., Seppänen, M., & Uutela, A. (2011). The effect of loneliness and change in loneliness on self-rated health (SRH): A longitudinal study among aging people. *Archives of Gerontology and Geriatrics, 53*(2), 163–167.
Peersman, W., Cambier, D., De Maeseneer, J., & Willems, S. (2012). Gender, educational and age differences in meanings that underlie global self-rated health. *International Journal of Public Health, 57*, 513–523.
Polit, D. F., & Beck, C. T. (2018). *Essentials of nursing research: Appraising evidence for nursing practice*. Wolters Kluwer.
Risjord, M. (2010). *Nursing knowledge: Science, practice, and philosophy*. Wiley.
Robeyns, I. (2005). The capability approach: A theoretical survey. *Journal of Human Development, 6*(1), 93–117.
Rowe, J. W., & Kahn, R. L. (1997). Successful aging. *The Gerontologist, 37*(4), 433–440.
Sanderson, W. C., & Scherbov, S. (2007). A new perspective on population ageing. *Demographic Research, 16*, 27–58.
Schnittker, J. (2005). When mental health becomes health: Age and the shifting meaning of self-evaluations of general health. *The Milban Quarterly, 83*, 397–423.
Segerstrom, S. C. (2014). Affect and self-rated health: A dynamic approach with older adults. *Health Psychology, 33*(7), 720.
Spuling, S. M., Wurm, S., Tesch-Römer, C., & Huxhold, O. (2015). Changing predictors of self-rated health: Disentangling age and cohort effects. *Psychology and Aging, 30*(2), 462.
Staudinger, U. M., Marsiske, M., & Baltes, P. B. (1995). Resilience and reserve capacity in later adulthood: Potentials and limits of development across the life span. *Developmental Psychopathology, 2*, 801–847.
Tornstam, L. (1975). Health and self-perception: A systems theoretical approach. *The Gerontologist, 15*, 264–270.
United Nations World Population Prospects. (2019). https://unstats.un.org/unsd/publications/. Accessed 2 Nov 2020 .
Verroupoulou, G. (2009). Key elements composing self-rated health in older adults: a comparative study of 11. European Countries. *European Journal of Ageing, 6*, 213–226.
Wallström, S., & Ekman, I. (2018). Person-centred care in clinical assessment. *European Journal of Cardiovascular Nursing, 17*(7), 576–579.
Whitehead, D. (2000). Is there a place for epidemiology in nursing? *Nursing Standard, 14*(42), 35.
Whitehead, D. (2003). Evaluating health promotion: a model for nursing practice. *Journal of Advanced Nursing, 41*(5), 490–498.
Wolinsky, F. D., & Tierney, W. M. (1998). Self-rated health and adverse health outcomes: An exploration and refinement of the trajectory hypothesis. *The Journals of Gerontology Series B: Psychological Sciences and Social Sciences, 53*(6), S336–S340.
World Health Organization. (2015a). *World report on ageing and health*. WHO.
World Health Organization. (2015b). *WHO global disability action plan 2014–2021. Better health for all people with disability*. WHO.
World Health Organization. (2020). *Decade of healthy ageing: Baseline report*. WHO.

Chapter 6
Capability in Research on Cognition and Well-being in Ageing and Retirement

Boo Johansson, Anne Ingeborg Berg, Pär Bjälkebring, Marcus Praetorius Björk, Yvonne Brehmer, Sandra Buratti, Isabelle Hansson, Linda Hassing, Georg Henning, Marie Kivi, Stefanie König, Magnus Lindwall, Sindre Rolstad, Johan Skoog, Valgeir Thorvaldsson, and Linn Elena Zulka

Capability is broadly defined as an individual's ability to perform actions in order to reach their own valued goals (Sen, 1985). The actual and observed capabilities are, however, more or less complex products, conditioned and influenced by numerous factors at the macro, meso and micro levels. The macro-level includes societal factors such as laws and regulations, pension systems, healthcare and social support systems. The meso-level includes dimensions of community involvement, social integration and networks, and the workplace and related retirement conditions. The micro-level is represented by individual factors, such as cognitive, mental and physical health. The main research focus within the ADA-Gero research group is on change and continuity at the individual or micro-level, although based on an understanding of the roles and influences of many macro- and meso-related circumstances.

Psychology is the science of brain and behaviour in which we as researchers explore the fundamental mechanisms involved in various mental processes, as well as personality dimensions that enable us to master challenges and the environment differently. The specific research questions addressed in the psychology of ageing are: how and why do developmental trajectories unfold in a certain manner with

---

B. Johansson (✉) · A. I. Berg · P. Bjälkebring · M. Praetorius Björk · Y. Brehmer · S. Buratti
I. Hansson · L. Hassing · G. Henning · M. Kivi · S. König · M. Lindwall · S. Rolstad
J. Skoog · V. Thorvaldsson · L. Elena Zulka
Department of Psychology, University of Gothenburg, Gothenburg, Sweden

Centre for Ageing and Health – AgeCap, University of Gothenburg, Gothenburg, Sweden
e-mail: boo.johansson@psy.gu.se; anne.berg@psy.gu.se; pop-par.bjalkebring@psy.gu.se; marcus.praetorius.bjork@vgregion.se; y.brehmer@tilburguniversity.edu; sandra.buratti@psy.gu.se; isabelle.hansson@psy.gu.se; linda.hassing@psy.gu.se; georg.henning@psy.gu.se; marie.kivi@psy.gu.se; stefanie.konig@psy.gu.se; magnus.lindwall@gu.se; sindre.rolstad@neuro.gu.se; johan.skoog@psy.gu.se; valgeir.thorvaldsson@psy.gu.se; linn.zulka@psy.gu.se

H. Falk Erhag et al. (eds.), *A Multidisciplinary Approach to Capability in Age and Ageing*, International Perspectives on Aging 31,
https://doi.org/10.1007/978-3-030-78063-0_6

increasing age, and especially in older age? Based on a life-span perspective, we examine whether observed outcomes represent behavioural continuity, fundamental neurobiological ageing or disease-related changes. In this respect, the outcomes are seen as the products of a lifelong interplay between genetic and environmental influences. This makes it necessary to consider how the societal and historical contexts tend to influence individual ageing and outcomes in cohorts exposed to similar or non-shared environments.

6.1 Capability and Cognition

At the micro-level, the orchestration of several specialised cognitive abilities contributes to the overall cognitive capacity required for efficient environmental interaction, adaption and well-being. These cognitive abilities include, among others: perception, attention, processing speed, spatial orientation, language, memory processes, logical reasoning, decision-making and cognitive flexibility.

Cognitive ageing may not only alter older adults' ability to respond to and perform cognitively demanding tasks and operations, but may also change the ways in which individuals perceive and master cognitive tasks and demands. Fluid abilities refer to those cognitive processes that are typically used to solve novel challenges that are relatively independent of previous knowledge and acquired facts, and these generally show a decline after age 60–70 (Rönnlund et al., 2005). Our abilities to engage in solving tasks that require acquired knowledge and skills, also known as crystallised intelligence, are less affected and remain better preserved in later life (Thorvaldsson et al., 2006).

The probability of decline and compromised cognition unfortunately increases in later life, which may jeopardise older adults' ability to function in everyday life, and not only in a laboratory setting. Apart from normative age-related changes, a more compromised cognition is mainly produced by dementia disorders (Thorvaldsson et al., 2011) and other age-related diseases affecting the brain's integrity. Our own, as well as societal, expectations of cognitive ageing are also important (Robertson et al., 2016). Efforts to prevent cognitive decline and the identification of factors that can protect and promote preserved cognitive functioning are therefore important research targets in cognitive ageing research. In this context, the importance of lifestyle (e.g., physical activity, a healthy diet, no tobacco or alcohol use) and a stimulating environment (enrichment) is often stressed (e.g., Hassing, 2018; Hertzog et al., 2009; Lindwall et al., 2012). Intact cognition represents a core component for reaching personally valued goals, but also for generating and prioritising such goals. In this respect, cognitive abilities are also crucial for mastering many environmental demands at the meso- and macro-levels, as well as for coping with one's own decremental changes in body and brain, whether produced by disease processes or normative age-related changes.

A core idea in current cognitive ageing research is that ageing and cognitive capabilities need to be studied using research designs that allow analyses of between-person differences in within-person changes. Longitudinal designs are required to distinguish between-person (i.e., how an individual differs from others) and within-person variability (i.e., how an individual changes over time relative to his/her previous values and performance). In multidisciplinary longitudinal studies based on representative samples, like the H70 research programme, we have opportunities to study cognitive functioning at the population level, manifested as aggregated change or preserved functioning at the individual level. In addition, such a research programme allows us to study how observed outcomes are associated with previous lifespan influences, as well as with current health and socio-cultural conditions.

Our lives, and consequently our ageing, are always embedded in a historical context. Lifespan influences and exposures can differ substantially across generations. Comparisons of cognitive trajectories for various birth cohorts generally show superior performance levels in later-born cohorts (Rönnlund et al., 2013; Schaie & Strother, 1968). The reasons for this improvement have been ascribed to multiple factors, including better nutrition (Lynn, 1998) and a more extended education (Rönnlund & Nilsson, 2009). Our own and other studies, however, indicate a more marked decline, although from a higher level, in later birth cohorts, even for relatively simple tasks, requiring people to perceive, identify and then react and respond as quickly as possible (see Fig. 6.1; Gerstorf et al., 2011; Karlsson et al., 2015; Thorvaldsson et al., 2017).

An increasingly important focus in cognitive ageing research is on strategies to promote active and successful cognitive ageing and on the use of potentially compensatory strategies to master and cope with compromised abilities. These efforts are directly in line with the aim of improving the capabilities of older adults. Studies on brain plasticity during ageing provide support for old ideas concerning the 'use it or lose it hypothesis' (Bielak, 2010; Salthouse, 2006), with various mental exercises and activity engagements seeming to partly counteract age-related cognitive decline and the risk of later dementia.

The cognitive reserve hypothesis (Stern, 2002) represents another important conceptual framework for research on cognitive ageing in its attempt to account for the incongruence between brain pathology/damage and its functional and clinical manifestations. Findings of weak relationships between neuronal brain damage and functional outcomes are attributed to differences in brain resilience and the abilities to use compensatory strategies and pre-existing cognitive networks to cope with cognitive challenges (Rolstad et al., 2009). Experiences across the lifespan, such as educational, occupational and recreational attainment (Hassing, 2017), seem to enhance cognitive reserves and improve our ability to better withstand age-related cognitive decline due to compromised brain functioning.

According to the cognitive reserve hypothesis, there is a potential to counteract age-related cognitive decline. An enriched environment with cognitive demands that match personal preferences, including extended work-related cognitive stimulation (i.e., working to a greater age or by promoting participation in bridge employment; and/or voluntary work) may mitigate decline (Mitchell et al., 2012). With between-person differences in mind, it should be noted that certain types of

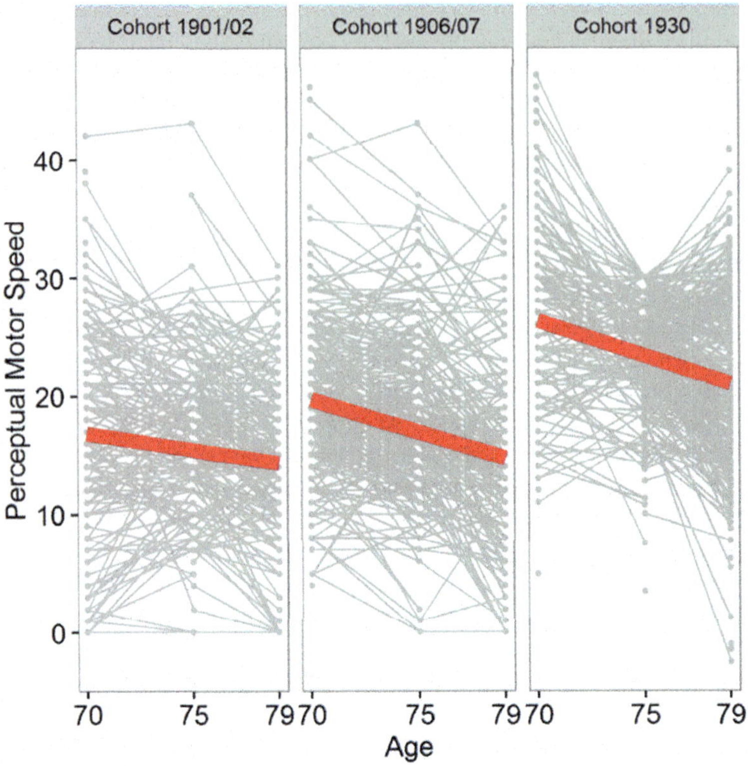

Fig. 6.1 Examples of raw score trajectories for a perceptual motor speed performance in cohorts born 1901/02, 1906/07 and 1930 and examined at ages 70, 75 and 79 in the H70 study. The red lines refer to the estimated average change trajectories (Thorvaldsson et al., 2017)

cognitive stimulation might not be feasible or even possible for everyone. For example, the possibility of bridge employment would not only depend on external circumstances (e.g., company employer), but also on the individual possessing sufficient cognitive abilities to take part in the planning and learning requirements associated with the position (Stafford et al., 2017). In cases like these, the individual's actual freedom of choice becomes important. Freedom of choice is a central aspect of Sen's capability model, along with available resources and conversion factors (Sen, 1992). More specifically, freedom of choice entails the possibility to realise goals that a person has reason to value. However, compromised cognitive abilities are likely to delimit the number of potential choices. For example, continuing employment beyond retirement age is unlikely to be offered to individuals lacking the cognitive ability to adapt to changing needs. In this context, education and lifelong learning have important roles to play in enhancing cognitive reserves and flexibility, which in turn can promote the capacity to counteract detrimental age-related brain changes. Although education does not have a direct influence on cognitive ageing, recent studies suggest that it affects overall health behaviour and the socioeconomic conditions related to a more active and successful cognitive ageing (Clouston et al., 2015). In this respect, preserved or at least 'good enough' cognitive health becomes important for realising capability in old age.

6.2 Capability and Subjective Well-being

At the heart of the capability approach is the idea of individual agency and that each individual should have the right to live the life that she or he desires (Robeyns, 2005). Thus, the capability approach emphasises the individual's right to define personal goals and how these can best be reached. Capability can never be appropriately studied if the individual's own perspective is neglected because how capability is experienced serves as an indicator of the extent to which individuals feel that they actually have the life they desire. In this respect, capability is closely related to subjective well-being, and more specifically to life satisfaction, defined as the individual's evaluation of satisfaction with their life as a whole (Diener, 1984).

Subjective well-being is a central indicator of psychological health and vitality in late life (Smith & Ryan, 2015), and it serves as an important predictor of future health status and longevity (Diener & Chan, 2011). Subjective evaluations of life are relevant within the capability approach because they include judgements about the current life situation relative to the ideal (Schimmack et al., 2002), and therefore capture the discrepancy between perceived and anticipated conditions (Diener et al., 1998). Research has demonstrated that numerous individual and situational factors contribute to individual differences in subjective well-being (e.g., Berg et al., 2006) but also that life satisfaction tends to vary systematically with increasing age (Diener, 2013). From an adult developmental and ageing perspective, people generally seem to become more satisfied with their lives during the period from their 40s until their early 70s, when life satisfaction peaks and thereafter declines (Baird et al., 2010).

The fact that happiness increases over the lifespan at the same time as the individual is more likely to be facing age-related declines in functional capacities is generally referred to as the paradox of well-being (e.g., Mroczek & Kolarz, 1998). The explanations for these findings include an increase in adaptive capacity over the lifespan (i.e., the selection, optimisation and compensation (SOC) model; Baltes, 1997) and aspects of age-related maturation and improved emotional regulation (i.e., the socioemotional selectivity theory (SST); Carstensen et al., 2003). Alternative explanations include age-related differences in the preference for emotional arousal, suggesting that older adults are more likely to prefer satisfaction over intense sensation (Bjälkebring et al., 2015). The somewhat contradictory finding that well-being seems to increase over the life-course implies that psychological factors such as adaptive abilities and emotional regulation are key mechanisms for successful ageing. Lifespan developmental processes relating to psychological health and well-being may in this sense contribute to counterbalancing ageing-related experiences of decline in functional capacities.

The capability approach suggests that available resources represent necessary preconditions for the potential to perform actions and reach valued goals, but that many other circumstances can influence the ability to convert these resources into the functions needed to reach a specific goal (Robeyns, 2006). Research on subjective well-being demonstrates that the availability of resources, as well as the individual's own perception of these resources, is considered when people assess their own well-being (Diener, 2009; Heller et al., 2004). This means that objective circumstances, as well as individual factors and attributes are all of relevance for understanding individual differences in subjective well-being in late adulthood. Our own findings show that individual characteristics such as personality and perceptions of control are generally better predictors of life satisfaction among older adults, compared with objective circumstances such as income, health status or quantity of social relations (Berg et al., 2006; Berg et al., 2011; Berg et al., 2009; Hansson et al., 2018a, b; Henning et al., 2017).

In a recent study on subjective memory, an important marker of one's own perceived cognition related to well-being, in which a sample of men responded to the same questionnaire at age 40, and then 30 years later at age 70, we found that those who reported better overall health and less anxiety also experienced less memory decline up to age 70. Higher stress and depression at age 70, however, were associated with worse subjective memory appearing as early as age 40. The correlation between an overall memory factor at ages 40 and 70 was 0.58, while the correlation between the memory factor at age 70 and retrospective ratings at age 40 was as high as 0.87. These findings suggest that subjective memory is quite consistent, and that we are inclined to preserve a continuity of our own memory functioning over the adult lifespan (Johansson et al., 2020).

Personality, conventionally defined as consistent patterns of individual differences in thoughts, feelings and behaviours, is assumed to influence subjective well-being through its relevance for how people view and evaluate their lives and opportunities (Lucas & Diener, 2009). Among the Big Five personality characteristics: extraversion, agreeableness, conscientiousness, neuroticism and openness (Goldberg, 1993), extraversion and neuroticism constitute the strongest and most reliable predictors of subjective well-being. Relatively higher levels of extraversion and lower levels of neuroticism are associated with higher satisfaction with life (Lucas & Diener, 2009). High scores on extraversion are characterised by sociability, talkativeness and excitability, and a tendency to view life in optimistic terms and experience frequent positive emotions (Costa & McCrae, 1980). High scores on neuroticism, on the other hand, are associated with a tendency to experience negative emotions, such as anger, anxiety and depression. Individuals who score highly on neuroticism are also more emotionally unstable in terms of having frequent mood swings, high irritability and stronger reactions to stress, which are assumed to negatively influence life evaluations (Costa & McCrae, 1980). Research suggests that personality can have a direct impact on life evaluations, but also an indirect effect through its relevance for how a person reacts to and copes with various life challenges (Heller et al., 2004). Our own research shows that individuals with higher levels of extraversion are more likely to report higher satisfaction with life, partially because of a higher perceived resource capability, but also due to an increased probability of building and maintaining resources (Hansson et al., 2019). Individuals with higher scores on neuroticism, on the other hand, are more likely to report lower life satisfaction due to lower perceived resource capability, but also due to an increased vulnerability to resource loss during times of major life events, such as retirement (Hansson et al., 2019).

The capability approach represents a broad theoretical framework that helps us gain a better understanding of the many mechanisms that are involved in determining an individual's capability. The capability framework acknowledges that multiple individual and contextual factors influence the availability of important resources, but also the extent to which an individual can benefit from and convert these resources into the actions needed to achieve a specific goal. In this sense, the capability approach corresponds well with present knowledge about which factors are of relevance for how we view and evaluate our current life situation and overall functioning. We argue, however, that resources and conversion factors are not easily separable, but instead represent parallel processes that simultaneously influence each other. Personality, for instance, can serve as a resource (e.g., extraversion is a key resource in social activities) at the same time as it may influence the ability to use and benefit from other resources (e.g., social participation contributes to stimulating cognitive functions). It is therefore necessary to recognise that psychological resources, such as certain personality characteristics, are likely to influence an individual's capability through its relevance to the availability of resources, as well as the ability to convert these resources into desired functions.

Sleep constitutes a major prerequisite for preserved capability in cognition and well-being throughout life. During ageing, however, we can often observe changes in sleep quantity and quality. People tend to report more early awakenings, increased sleep onset latency, more day-time naps and shorter sleep duration and may therefore show a reduced sleep efficiency, which is defined as the ratio of time spent asleep compared to the amount of time spent in bed (Skoog et al. 2019; Ancoli-Israel, 2009; Cajochen et al., 2006; Roepke & Ancoli-Israel, 2010). In a meta-analysis, Ohayon and colleagues (2004) conclude that total sleep time, sleep efficiency, and the proportion of slow-wave and rapid eye movement sleep decrease with age, while the number of awakenings after sleep onset, as well as sleep latency and proportions of stage 1 and stage 2 sleep tend to increase. Given that sleep affects memory consolidation and emotional well-being, it also represents a significant marker of health and overall functioning. For example, Liu and collaborators (2020) found that periodic sleep disruption for only one night led to impaired functioning of older adults' sleep-related memory consolidation. Sleep patterns may also change over time, not only with age. In a longitudinal study of the prevalence of insomnia, in which we compared and followed two birth cohorts of 70-year-olds born 30 years apart, we found that the prevalence of insomnia was lower in the later birth cohort (about 32% in the birth cohort born in 1901–07, compared with 16% in those born in 1930). Interestingly, the prevalence of insomnia increased from age 70 to 79 only in the later cohort, but at age 79 the prevalence was similar in both cohorts (32%). Insomnia was more common in women, although the sex difference was less pronounced in the later-born birth cohort. Poor sleep has also been associated with a higher incidence of dementia. In another study, we found that early-morning awakenings with an inability to return to sleep, i.e. terminal insomnia, and long sleep duration at age 70 was related to an increased risk of developing dementia (Sindi et al., 2018). A better understanding of the associations between sleep, cognitive decline and well-being is essential in order to design public health and person-oriented interventions that can improve health and wellbeing, and thereby capability, in older adults.

6.3 Cognition and Well-being in the Social Context of Retirement

Retirement marks a significant life event that is often considered the societally defined entrance into 'old age'. Our research team is currently involved in a research programme focusing on older adults' transition to retirement, the HEARTs study (HEalth, Ageing, and Retirement Transition in Sweden; see Lindwall et al., 2017). In this programme, we longitudinally investigate outcomes of the transition to retirement, with a focus on conditions before and after the retirement event. This allows us to investigate whether retirement expectations and life-course experiences affect overall health, cognition and/or well-being. Although our focus is on individual trajectories, these micro-level analyses are conducted in the context of meso- and macro-level conditions. Thus, cognitive health and well-being are considered within the social context in which societal norms and legislation on labour-market participation are confronted with work/life requirements, job demands and individual retirement preferences.

The rationale for implementing the overarching capability framework in research on retirement transitions is that it broadens the perspective beyond that of previously limited accounts focusing mainly on 'work ability' or 'employability'. What an individual can or cannot do at any given time is a reflection of resources or capacities, and whether available resources can be converted into a desired function; for example, preferences to continue working or to retire. Choice is crucial in the capability approach. In particular, the perception of choice and whether an individual feels that he or she has autonomy and 'ownership' of their life, no matter what the actual situation of choice might be.

Being able to work in terms of overall good physical and cognitive health does not necessarily lead to a prolonged working life if the individual is unable to find employment or keep their job (e.g., low employability). Conversely, individuals who in fact have low physical and cognitive capabilities to continue at work may experience that they are unable to exit working life due to the financial consequences (e.g., low pension benefits) or pension-system regulations (e.g., a guaranteed pension at age 65). The individual's motivation to continue working or to retire is crucial and constitutes the key link to capability because it directly relates to the meaning of choice and individual preferences for desired outcomes. Research on multidimensional work motivation (e.g., Gagné, 2014) highlights the difference between autonomous motivation (i.e., actions being performed with a 'full sense of willingness, volition, and choice'; Deci et al., 2017: 20), controlled motivation (i.e. motivation driven by external factors) and amotivation (i.e. lack of any motivation). Our results from the HEARTS study show that people who are more autonomously motivated to work also seem to be more likely to continue working in retirement. Those with low autonomous motivation experience more autonomy after they fully retire. These results support the idea that being able to pursue the activities one values leads to greater well-being (Henning et al., 2019).

The effects of retirement on capability differ most clearly among individuals, given multiple background characteristics and current overall situation. In the HEARTS study, we argue that the retirement transition can serve as a 'lens' (see Fig. 6.2). It can either amplify or mitigate social differences in cognition and well-being, based on factors such as education, occupation and income. In this respect, retirement may have different effects across social groups (König et al., 2018). For example, at the time of retirement we could expect different levels of cognitive functioning between people retiring from jobs characterised by lower versus higher cognitive stimulation, in addition to differences in education and socioeconomic status. Retirement may also trigger adaptations in cognitive functioning. In a recent literature review of longitudinal studies, we revealed mixed evidence for an association between cognition and retirement (Zulka et al., 2019). Among the 20 reviewed studies, nine included prior work demands (e.g. cognitive stimulation at the workplace) as a potential moderator of the relationship between cognitive performance and retirement. A synthesis of these findings provides support for the idea that prior work demands can indeed affect the association. Thus, while retirement seems to be beneficial for blue-collar workers (or retirees from physically demanding jobs), the evidence for white-collar workers (or retirees from cognitively demanding jobs) was less conclusive, with both cognitive improvements and decline being reported

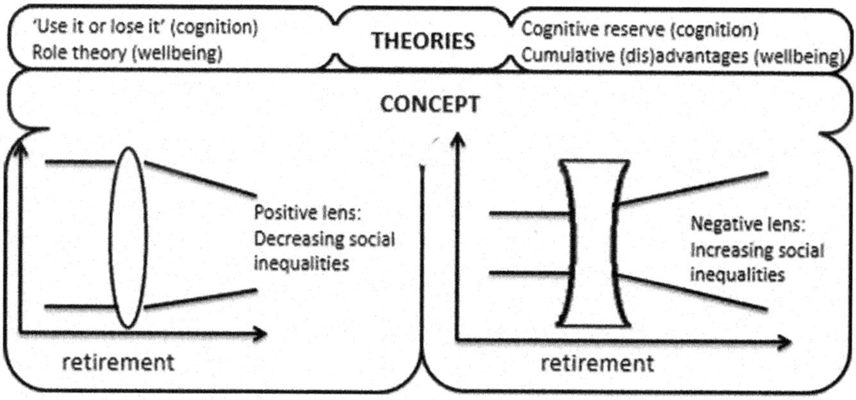

Fig. 6.2 The retirement transitions as a lens for social inequalities (König et al., 2018)

(Zulka et al., 2019). In the HEARTS study, we recently examined the potential impact of prior cognitive work demands as a moderator in the retirement transition. The analyses did not provide support for a significant effect over a more restricted period after the retirement event (Zulka et al., submitted).

Although the above model focuses on outcomes in terms of cognition and well-being, it also highlights other, heterogeneous effects of retirement on capability. The lens perspective is closely linked to the life-course perspective in which multiple factors unfold over the entire lifespan, which contributes to differential lens effects. For example, in HEARTS we found that differences in cognitive functioning due to level of education was smaller in the group of people who had retired compared with those still in the workforce. This result supports the notion of a positive lens (mitigating) effect of retirement on cognitive functioning. However, the opposite result was found for well-being; educational differences in well-being were larger in retirees compared to people who were still working, supporting the notion of a negative lens (amplifying) effect for well-being (König et al., 2018).

Further studies will be conducted to specifically examine the proposed risk of 'a mental and cognitive retirement', ideas largely based on the 'use it or lose it' hypothesis in which retirement is also seen as a major risk of imposing lifestyle changes, with a reduction in cognitive engagement and stimulation. However, cognition and psychological well-being are crucial, as both predictors and outcomes when investigating adaptive processes in the retirement transition. Well-being reflects the achievement of individual preferences, which makes it a core component of defining 'successful retirement' at the individual level. 'Good enough cognition' is, however, required when coping with the challenges associated with this major transition and forming a good life as a retiree.

6.4 Capability in the Context of the COVID-19 Pandemic

The current worldwide COVID-19 pandemic represents a significant threat to overall public health, particularly among vulnerable risk groups. Many countries have enacted a general lockdown, whereas the Swedish policy largely relies on voluntary preventative behaviour and fewer mandatory restrictions, apart from a specific recommendation for social distancing and 'shelter in place' for those aged 70 and older. The overarching goal was to protect older adults, who are considered more vulnerable to a viral infection.

The HEARTS study, with its longitudinal design and annual measurements during the years 2015–2020, provides unique opportunities to investigate the impact of COVID-19 on various aspects of health and well-being. In the 2020 wave, we included a new set of questions to capture levels of worry, risk perception and social distancing in response to the COVID-19 pandemic. Findings based on data collected during one week in the early days of the pandemic (26 March to 2 April 2020 for those aged 65–71) showed that 45% reported high levels of worry about their own, or loved ones', health, and 42% perceived a high risk of being infected by the novel coronavirus (Kivi et al., 2020). A substantial proportion (70%) also worried about adverse effects on social structures and the world economy and 86% perceived a high risk of negative consequences for public health and welfare. Individuals aged 70 and above (defined as a risk group by The Public Health Agency of Sweden) reported avoiding close physical contact with others to a larger extent (79%) than those in the age range 65–69 (69%), and they also perceived the risk of infection as lower (35% and 46%, respectively). Individuals in the age group 70–71 additionally reported less worry about the impact of COVID-19 on their personal finances (20%) compared to those aged 65–69 (28%). Preliminary analyses based on the full wave of data collection in 2020 (N = 3914) showed an average increase in worry about personal (or loved ones') health and an increase in the degree of social distancing between March and May 2020. The previously observed differences in levels of worry about personal finances, the degree of social distancing and the perceived risk of infection between individuals above and below the age of 70 were also mirrored in these analyses.

We further examined changes in four domains of well-being (life satisfaction, financial satisfaction, self-rated health and loneliness) compared to previous years (2015–2020). The findings showed an average decline in self-rated health from 2015 (age 60–66) to 2019 (age 64–70), but an increase in 2020 (age 65–71; Kivi et al., 2020). Financial satisfaction remained stable between 2015 and 2020 but increased in 2020, and life satisfaction showed an average increase between 2015 and 2019, with no deviation in this trend in 2020. Loneliness remained relatively stable between the years 2015 and 2020.

Preliminary analyses based on data from the period March to May (weeks 13–20) 2020 mirrored the effects for life satisfaction, financial satisfaction and self-rated health but, in contrast to the findings in the early days of the COVID-19 pandemic, we found an increase in loneliness compared to previous years. The increase in loneliness was also greater for individuals who responded to the survey later in the spring of 2020. Analyses of differences between individuals above and below the age of 70 further suggest that the positive changes in well-being are more pronounced in the age group 65–69, while individuals above the age of 70 who responded to the survey later in the spring of 2020 reported slightly lower levels of well-being compared to 2019.

The somewhat unexpected finding that older adults rated their well-being during the early phase of the COVID-19 pandemic as highly as, or even higher than, they did in previous years may reflect the fact that older adults refuse to identify themselves as a risk group. They rather tend to view themselves as individuals who are just as capable as others to assess risks and make informed decisions. The fact that Sweden, in contrast to many other countries, did not impose a national lockdown may also contribute to explaining why we found relatively few negative effects on well-being. Another possible explanation is the notion of contrasts, i.e., that the reference point against which the assessment is made has changed. In the context of COVID-19, assessments of personal well-being are likely to be formed in relation to many other possible risks and effects of the pandemic. Circumstances that seemed less satisfying before the pandemic may therefore be given less weight when possible consequences related to COVID-19 are taken into account.

In conclusion, and in contrast to many ageist assumptions about frailty and inability in old age, our findings suggest that the agency and capability of older adults to perform actions and reach valued goals persist, even during a pandemic. It is important to note, however, that the restrictions imposed on older adults are likely to have contributed to the observed increase in loneliness. The specific restrictions imposed on individuals aged 70 and above may also explain why the positive effects were more pronounced in the age group 65–69. The authorities should therefore consider the risk of compromised capability among older adults due to age-specific restrictions during times of pandemic.

6.4.1 In Sum

The core ideas of the capability approach are influencing ongoing and planned research on cognition, subjective well-being and retirement conducted by members of the ADA-Gero research team. From our psychological perspective, the approach emphasises the need to contextualise the micro-level perspective on ageing individuals' cognition and well-being within the meso- and macro-level influences that affect the realisation of personal goals. This means that we certainly realise that ageing trajectories are always embedded in a specific historical and sociocultural context in which societal systems regulate brain–behaviour relationships according to the age of their members. The capability approach constitutes a theoretical framework that is well suited to a broader understanding of the factors and mechanisms involved in shaping age-related developmental and psychological processes across the life course, and especially in late life.

References

Ancoli-Israel, S. (2009). Sleep and its disorders in aging populations. *Sleep Medicine,, 10*(Suppl 1), S7–S11. https://doi.org/10.1016/j.sleep.2009.07.004.

Baird, B. M., Lucas, R. E., & Donnellan, M. B. (2010). Life satisfaction across the lifespan: Findings from two nationally representative panel studies. *Social Indicators Research, 99*, 183–203. https://doi.org/10.1007/s11205-010-9584-9

Baltes, P. (1997). On the incomplete architecture of human ontogeny: Selection, optimization, and compensation as foundation of developmental theory. *American Psychologist, 52*, 366–380. https://doi.org/10.1037/0003-066X.52.4.366

Berg, A. I., Hassing, L. B., McClearn, G. E., & Johansson, B. (2006). What matters for life satisfaction in the oldest-old? *Ageing and Mental Health, 10*, 257–264. https://doi.org/10.1080/13607860500409435

Berg, A. I., Hoffman, L., Hassing, L. B., McClearn, G. E., & Johansson, B. (2009). What matters, and what matters most, for change in life satisfaction in the oldest-old? A study over

6 years among individuals 80+. *Ageing and Mental Health, 13*, 191–201. https://doi.org/10.1080/13607860802342227

Berg, A. I., Hassing, L. B., Thorvaldsson, V., & Johansson, B. (2011). Personality and personal control make a difference for life satisfaction in the oldest-old: Findings in a longitudinal population-based study of individuals 80 and older. *European Journal of Ageing, 8*, 13–20. https://doi.org/10.1007/s10433-011-0181-9

Bielak, A. A. M. (2010). How can we not 'lose it' if we still don't understand how to 'use it'? Unanswered questions about the influence of activity participation on cognitive performance in older age: A mini-review. *Gerontology, 56*, 507–519. https://doi.org/10.1159/000264918

Bjälkebring, P., Västfjäll, D., & Johansson, B. (2015). Happiness and arousal: Framing happiness as arousing results in lower happiness ratings for older adults. *Frontiers in Psychology, 6*, 706. https://doi.org/10.3389/fpsyg.2015.00706

Cajochen, C., Munch, M., Knoblauch, V., Blatter, K., & Wirz-Justice, A. (2006). Age-related changes in the circadian and homeostatic regulation of human sleep. *Chronobiology International, 23*(1–2), 461–474. https://doi.org/10.1080/07420520500545813

Carstensen, L. L., Fung, H. H., & Charles, S. T. (2003). Socioemotional selectivity theory and the regulation of emotion in the second half of life. *Motivation and Emotion, 27*, 103–123. https://doi.org/10.1023/A:1024569803230

Clouston, S. A., Glymour, M., & Terrera, G. M. (2015). Educational inequalities in ageing-related declines in fluid cognition and the onset of cognitive pathology. *Alzheimers Dement (Amst), 1*, 303–310. https://doi.org/10.1016/j.dadm.2015.06.001

Costa, P. T., & McCrae, R. R. (1980). Influence of extraversion and neuroticism on subjective well-being: Happy and unhappy people. *Journal of Personality and Social Psychology, 38*, 668–678. https://doi.org/10.1037/0022-3514.38.4.668

Deci, E. L., Olafsen, A. H., & Ryan, R. M. (2017). Self-determination theory in work organizations: The state of a science. *Annual Review of Organizational Psychology and Organizational Behavior, 4*, 19–43. https://doi.org/10.1146/annurev-orgpsych-032516-113108

Diener, E. (1984). Subjective Well-being. *Psychological Bulletin, 95*, 542–575. https://doi.org/10.1037/0033-2909.95.3.542

Diener, E. (2009). *The science of Well-being: The collected works of Ed Diener*. Springer.

Diener, E. (2013). The remarkable changes in the science of subjective well-being. *Perspectives on Psychological Science, 8*, 663–666. https://doi.org/10.1177/1745691613507583

Diener, E., & Chan, M. Y. (2011). Happy people live longer: Subjective well-being contributes to health and longevity. *Applied Psychology: Health and Well-Being, 3*, 1–43. https://doi.org/10.1037/e675972011-001

Diener, E., Sapyta, J., & Suh, E. (1998). Subjective well-being is essential to well-being. *Psychological Inquiry, 9*, 33–37. https://doi.org/10.1207/s15327965pli0901_3

Gagné, M. (2014). *The Oxford handbook of work engagement, motivation, and self-determination theory*. Oxford Library of Psychology.

Gerstorf, D., Ram, N., Hoppman, C., Willis, S. L., & Schaie, K. W. (2011). Cohort differences in cognitive ageing and terminal decline in the Seattle Longitudinal Study. *Developmental Psychology, 47*, 1026–1041. https://doi.org/10.1037/a0023426

Goldberg, L. R. (1993). The structure of phenotypic personality traits. *The American Psychologist, 48*, 26–34. https://doi.org/10.1037/0003-066x.48.1.26

Hansson, I., Buratti, S., Johansson, B., & Berg, A. I. (2018a). Beyond health and economy: Resource interactions in retirement adjustment. *Ageing and Mental Health, 23*, 1546–1554. https://doi.org/10.1080/13607863.2018.1506745

Hansson, I., Buratti, S., Thorvaldsson, V., Johansson, B., & Berg, A. I. (2018b). Changes in life satisfaction in the retirement transition: Interaction effects of transition type and individual resources. *Work, Ageing and Retirement, 4*, 352–366. https://doi.org/10.1093/worker/wax025

Hansson, I., Henning, G., Buratti, S., Lindwall, M., Kivi, M., Johansson, B., & Berg, A. I. (2019). The role of personality in retirement adjustment: Longitudinal evidence for the effects on life satisfaction. *Journal of Personality*. https://doi.org/10.1111/jopy.12516

Hassing, L. B. (2017). Gender differences in the association between leisure activity in adulthood and cognitive function in old age: A prospective longitudinal population-based study. *The Journals of Gerontology: Series B*, gbx170. https://doi.org/10.1093/geronb/gbx170.

Hassing, L. B. (2018). Light alcohol consumption does not protect cognitive function: A longitudinal prospective study. *Frontiers in Ageing Neuroscience*. https://doi.org/10.3389/fnagi.2018.00081

Heller, D., Watson, D., & Ilies, R. (2004). The role of person versus situation in life satisfaction: A critical examination. *Psychological Bulletin, 130*, 574–600. https://doi.org/10.1037/0033-2909.130.4.574

Henning, G., Hansson, I., Berg, A. I., Lindwall, M., & Johansson, B. (2017). The role of personality for subjective well-being in the retirement transition: Comparing variable-and person-oriented models. *Personality and Individual Differences, 116*, 385–392. https://doi.org/10.1016/j.paid.2017.05.017

Henning, G., Stenling, A., Tafvelin, S., Hansson, I., Kivi, M., Johansson, B., & Lindwall, M. (2019). Preretirement work motivation and subsequent retirement adjustment: A self-determination theory perspective. *Work, Ageing and Retirement, 5*, 189–203. https://doi.org/10.1016/j.paid.2017.05.017

Hertzog, C., Kramer, A. F., Wilson, R. S., & Lindenberger, U. (2009). Enrichment effects on adult cognitive development: Can the functional capacity of older adults be preserved and enhanced? *Psychological Science in the Public Interest, 9*, 1–65. https://doi.org/10.1093/workar/way017

Johansson, B., Praetorius Björk, M., & Thorvaldsson, V. (2020). I rate my memory quite similar at age 40 and at age 70: Findings in a Swedish longitudinal study on subjective memory over a 30-year period. *GeroPsych: The Journal of Gerontopsychology and Geriatric Psychiatry*. Advance online publication. https://doi.org/10.1024/1662-9647/a000239

Karlsson, P., Thorvaldsson, V., Skoog, I., Gudmundsson, P., & Johansson, B. (2015). Birth cohort differences in fluid cognition in old age: Comparisons of trends in levels and change trajectories over 30 years in three population-based samples. *Psychology and Ageing, 30*, 83–94. https://doi.org/10.1037/a0038643

Kivi, M., Hansson, I., & Bjälkebring, P. (2020). Up and about: Older adults' well-being during the COVID-19 pandemic in a Swedish longitudinal study. *The Journals of Gerontology. Series B, Psychological Sciences and Social Sciences*. https://doi.org/10.1093/geronb/gbaa084

König, S., Lindwall, M., Henning, G., & Johansson, B. (2018). Retirement as a lens for socioeconomic differences in cognition and well-being. *Nordic Journal of Working Life Studies, 8*, 63–80. https://doi.org/10.18291/njwls.v8i2.106155

Lindwall, M., Cimino, C. R., Gibbons, L. E., Mitchell, M. B., Benitez, A., Brown, C. L., et al. (2012). Dynamic associations of change in physical activity and change in cognitive function: Coordinated analyses of four longitudinal studies. *Journal of Ageing Research*. https://doi.org/10.1155/2012/493598

Lindwall, M., Berg, A. I., Bjälkebring, P., Buratti, S., Hansson, I., Hassing, L., … Johansson, B. (2017). Psychological health in the retirement transition: Rationale and first findings in the health, ageing and retirement transitions in Sweden (HEARTS) study. *Frontiers in Psychology, 8*, 1634. https://doi.org/10.3389/fpsyg.2017.01634

Liu, X., Peng, X., Peng, P., Li, L., Lei, X., & Yu, J. (2020). The age differences of sleep disruption on mood states and memory performance. *Aging & Mental Health, 24*(9), 1444–1451. https://doi.org/10.1080/13607863.2019.1603286

Lucas, R. E., & Diener, E. (2009). Personality and subjective wellbeing. In E. Diener (Ed.), *The science of well-being: The collected works of Ed Diener* (pp. 75–102). Springer.

Lynn, R. (1998). In support of the nutrition theory. In U. Neisser (Ed.), *The rising curve: Long-term gains in IQ and related measures* (pp. 207–218). American Psychological Association.

Mitchell, M. B., Cimino, C. R., Benitez, A., Brown, C. L., Gibbons, L. E., Kennison, R. F., et al. (2012). Cognitively stimulating activities: Effects on cognition across four studies with up to 21 years of longitudinal data. *Journal of Ageing Research*. https://doi.org/10.1155/2012/461592

Mroczek, D. K., & Kolarz, C. M. (1998). The effect of age on positive and negative affect: A developmental perspective on happiness. *Journal of Personality and Social Psychology, 75*, 1333–1349. https://doi.org/10.1037/0022-3514.75.5.1333

Robertson, D. A., King-Kallimanis, B. L., & Kenny, R. A. (2016). Negative perceptions of ageing predict longitudinal decline in cognitive function. *Psychology and Ageing, 31*, 71–81. https://doi.org/10.1037/pag0000061

Robeyns, I. (2005). The capability approach: A theoretical survey. *Journal of Human Development, 6*, 93–117. https://doi.org/10.1080/146498805200034266

Robeyns, I. (2006). The capability approach in practice. *Journal of Political Philosophy, 14*, 351–376. https://doi.org/10.1111/j.1467-9760.2006.00263.x

Roepke, S. K., & Ancoli-Israel, S. (2010). Sleep disorders in the elderly. *The Indian Journal of Medical Research, 131*, 302–310.

Rolstad, S., Nordlund, A., Eckerström, C., Gustavsson, M. H., & Zetterberg, H. (2009). Biomarkers in relation to cognitive reserve in patients with mild cognitive impairment: Proof of concept. *Dementia and Geriatric Cognitive Disorders, 27*, 194–200. https://doi.org/10.1159/000203130

Rönnlund, M., & Nilsson, L.-G. (2009). Flynn effects on sub-factors of episodic and semantic memory: Parallel gains over time and the same set of determining factors. *Neuropsychologia, 47*, 2174–2180. https://doi.org/10.1016/j.neuropsychologia.2008.11.007

Rönnlund, M., Nyberg, L., Bäckman, L., & Nilsson, L.-G. (2005). Stability, growth, and decline in adult life span development of declarative memory: Cross-sectional and longitudinal data from a population-based study. *Psychology and Ageing, 20*, 3–18. https://doi.org/10.1037/0882-7974.20.1.3

Rönnlund, M., Carlstedt, B., Blomstedt, Y., Nilsson, L.-G., & Weinehall, L. (2013). Secular trends in cognitive test performance: Swedish conscript data 1970:1993. *Intelligence, 41*, 19–24. https://doi.org/10.1016/j.intell.2012.10.001

Salthouse, T. A. (2006). Mental exercise and mental ageing: Evaluating the validity of the 'use it or lose it' hypothesis. *Perspectives on Psychological Science, 1*, 68–87. https://doi.org/10.1111/j.1745-6916.2006.00005.x

Schaie, K. W., & Strother, C. R. (1968). The effect of time and cohort differences on the interpretation of age changes in cognitive behavior. *Multivariate Behavioral Research, 3*, 259–293. https://doi.org/10.1207/s15327906mbr0303_1

Schimmack, U., Diener, E., & Oishi, S. (2002). Life-satisfaction is a momentary judgment and a stable personality characteristic: The use of chronically accessible and stable sources. *Journal of Personality, 70*, 345–384. https://doi.org/10.1111/1467-6494.05008

Sen, A. (1985). *Commodities and capabilities*. Elsevier Science Publishers B.V.

Sen, A. (1992). *Inequality re-examined*. Clarendon Press.

Sindi, S., Kåreholt, I., Johansson, L., Skoog, J., Sjöberg, L., Wang, H. X., … Solomon, A. (2018). Sleep disturbances and dementia risk: A multicenter study. *Alzheimer's & Dementia, 14*(10), 1235–1242. https://doi.org/10.1016/j.jalz.2018.05.012

Skoog, J., Jonsson, H., Sigstrom, R., Ostling, S., Falk, H., Waern, M., … Johansson, B. (2019). Do later-born birth cohorts of septuagenarians sleep better? A prospective population-based study of two birth cohorts of 70-year-olds. *Sleep, 42*(1). https://doi.org/10.1093/sleep/zsy204

Smith, J. H., & Ryan, L. (2015). Psychological vitality in the oldest old. In K. W. Schaie & S. L. Willis (Eds.), *Handbook of the psychology of ageing* (8th ed., pp. 303–319). Elsevier.

Stafford, M., Cooper, R., Cadar, D., Carr, E., Murray, E., Richards, M., … Kuh, D. (2017). Physical and cognitive capability in mid-adulthood as determinants of retirement and extended working life in a British cohort study. *Scandinavian Journal of Work, Environment & Health, 43*, 15–23. https://doi.org/10.5271/sjweh.3589

Stern, Y. (2002). What is cognitive reserve? Theory and research application of the reserve concept. *Journal of the International Neuropsychological Society, 8*, 448–460. https://doi.org/10.1017/S1355617702813248

Thorvaldsson, V., Hofer, S. M., Berg, S., & Johansson, B. (2006). Effects of repeated testing in a longitudinal age-homogenous study of cognitive ageing. *Journal of Gerontology: Psychological Sciences, 61*, 348–354. https://doi.org/10.1093/geronb/61.6.P348

Thorvaldsson, V., MacDonald, S. W. S., Fratiglioni, L., Winblad, B., Kivipelto, M., Laukka, E. J., … Bäckman, L. (2011). Onset and rate of cognitive change before dementia diagnosis: Findings from two Swedish population-based longitudinal studies. *Journal of the International Neuropsychological Society, 17*, 154–162. https://doi.org/10.1017/S1355617710001372

Thorvaldsson, V., Karlsson, P., Skoog, J., Skoog, I., & Johansson, B. (2017). Better cognition in new birth cohorts of 70-year-olds, but greater decline thereafter. *Journal of Gerontology: Psychological Sciences, 72*, 16–24. https://doi.org/10.1093/geronb/gbw125

Zulka, L. E., Hansson, I., & Hassing, L. (2019). Impact of retirement on cognitive function: A literature review. *GeroPsych – The Journal of Gerontopsychology and Geriatric Psychiatry.* https://doi.org/10.1024/1662-9647/a000215

Zulka, L. E., Hansson, I., Thorvaldsson, V., & Hassing, L. (submitted). *Cognitive functioning when retiring: Findings from a Swedish population-based longitudinal study.*

Chapter 7
The Neurochemistry of Alzheimer's Disease: One of the Most Common Causes of Reduced Capability in the Adult Population

Kaj Blennow and Henrik Zetterberg

7.1 Introduction

Alzheimer's disease (AD) is the most common neurodegenerative disease and a major cause of capability impairment in the elderly. The first detectable pathology, which occurs decades before clinical symptom onset, is the accumulation of extracellular amyloid plaques in the brain, which have as their core the 42-amino-acid-long amyloid β (Aβ) protein. Biomarker studies suggest that Aβ accumulation is followed by increased phosphorylation and secretion of tau, a microtubule-associated axonal protein that is highly expressed in cortical neurons. Dysfunctional tau metabolism leads to AD-type neurodegeneration, with the development of dystrophic neurites and intraneuronal neurofibrillary tangles that are composed of

K. Blennow (✉)
Department of Psychiatry and Neurochemistry, Institute of Neuroscience & Physiology, The Sahlgrenska Academy at the University of Gothenburg, Gothenburg, Sweden

Clinical Neurochemistry Laboratory, Sahlgrenska University Hospital, Mölndal, Sweden

Centre for Ageing and Health – AgeCap, University of Gothenburg, Gothenburg, Sweden
e-mail: kaj.blennow@neuro.gu.se

H. Zetterberg
Department of Psychiatry and Neurochemistry, Institute of Neuroscience & Physiology, The Sahlgrenska Academy at the University of Gothenburg, Gothenburg, Sweden

Clinical Neurochemistry Laboratory, Sahlgrenska University Hospital, Mölndal, Sweden

Centre for Ageing and Health – AgeCap, University of Gothenburg, Gothenburg, Sweden

Department of Neurodegenerative Disease, UCL Institute of Neurology, London, UK

UK Dementia Research Institute at UCL, London, UK
e-mail: henrik.zetterberg@clinchem.gu.se

H. Falk Erhag et al. (eds.), *A Multidisciplinary Approach to Capability in Age and Ageing*, International Perspectives on Aging 31,
https://doi.org/10.1007/978-3-030-78063-0_7

hyperphosphorylated and truncated tau proteins. Neurodegeneration translates into the AD clinical syndrome, with neurodegeneration being spatially and temporally associated with the pattern of cognitive deficits that worsen as the disease progresses. Exactly what initiates the amyloidogenic cascade is not known and may well be multifactorial, but the major risk factors are increasing age and the ε4 allele of the apolipoprotein E (*APOE*) gene, which is associated with a major increase in AD risk.

7.1.1 The Molecular Neuropathology of AD

The key microscopic neuropathological features of AD include neuronal and synaptic degeneration, accompanied by different forms of protein aggregates called plaques, neurofibrillary tangles and neuropil threads, Hirano bodies, and granulovacuolar degeneration (Perry, 1986; Terry & Davies, 1980; Tomlinson et al., 1968, 1970). Plaques and tangles are found in the hippocampus and cortex, as well as in subcortical grey matter nuclei, such as the nucleus basalis of Meynert and locus coeruleus (Mann et al., 1985; Tomlinson, 1989), while Hirano bodies and granulovacuolar degeneration are largely restricted to the hippocampus. Plaques and tangles are found with increasing frequency with ageing, including in cognitively unimpaired individuals, and become very common at higher ages (Mann et al., 1984, 1985; Tomlinson, 1989; Dayan, 1970; Mann et al., 1984; Price et al., 2009).

Plaques are primarily composed of aggregated β-amyloid (Aβ), and are rounded extracellular lesions (Masters et al., 1985; Glenner & Wong, 1984) (Fig. 7.1). The majority of Aβ found in plaques ends at position 42 (Aβ42), which is a form of Aβ that is most prone to aggregation, in contrast to Aβ40, which is the most abundant variant. Plaques exist as diffuse plaques that are regarded as being the earliest form, and neuritic plaques, which consist of a central core of amyloid fibres surrounded

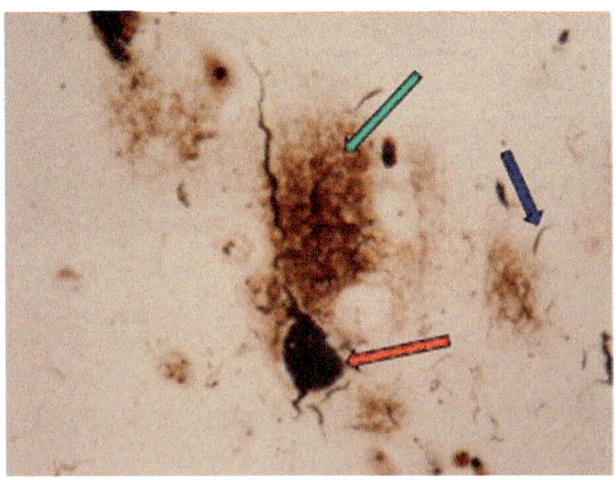

Fig. 7.1 Histology of amyloid plaques and tau pathology in Alzheimer's disease. Plaques (green arrow) are extracellular deposits of β-amyloid (Aβ) surrounded by dystrophic neuritis, while tangles (red arrow) and neuropil threads (blue arrow) are composed abnormally phosphorylated tau protein

by dystrophic neurites filled with fibrillary tau protein, and reactive astrocytes and microglia (Thal et al., 2002). Tangles are located in the neuronal cytoplasm, while neuropil threads are extended structures in the neuropil (Fig. 7.1); both are primarily formed of hyperphosphorylated tau protein (Grundke-Iqbal et al., 1986).

In elderly patients with AD, the number of plaques and tangles varies considerably and overlaps with the number found in cognitively unimpaired elderly people (Mann et al., 1984, 1985; Hansen et al., 1988). A common explanation for this overlap is that elderly patients with AD-type dementia have other pathologies in addition to plaques and tangles, including α-synuclein and TDP-43 deposits, as well as cerebrovascular disease and other pathologies (James et al., 2016; Kovacs et al., 2013). Other frequent points of discussion are whether certain individuals may be more or less susceptible to AD-type pathological changes, whether lifestyle affects the risk or phenotypic expression of the pathologies and whether lifestyle changes could influence the risk of developing dementia from AD. Positive results for multimodal lifestyle interventions have been reported (Ngandu et al., 2015), but an outstanding question is whether such interventions have a direct impact on the neuropathology of AD (a recent biomarker-based study suggests that they do not (Steen Jensen et al., 2016)), or whether they confer protection via ancillary mechanisms such as improved cerebral blood flow, myelination, increased synaptic density or improved immune function. In any case, studies with long-term clinical follow-up suggest that >90% of plaque-positive individuals eventually develop dementia (Buchhave et al., 2012; Rowe et al., 2013), indicating that biomarkers for plaque pathology can be used to identify AD in the preclinical stage of the disease, and thus may have value as tools to enrich the search for asymptomatic AD in intervention studies.

7.2 Clinical Neurochemistry and Fluid Biomarkers

The development of cerebrospinal fluid (CSF) and blood (plasma and serum) biomarkers is a lead project for the Clinical Neurochemistry Laboratory. Such biomarkers for the different types of pathophysiology found in the brains of elderly people have several applications, both in research and in the clinic. Firstly, biomarkers have value in the clinical diagnosis, especially in the early stages of the disease, when symptoms are vague and uncharacteristic. Secondly, biomarkers are key in clinical research to deepen our understanding of the pathogenesis of the disease, for example the time course of different pathologies, how they contribute to the symptoms, how lifestyle and other risk factors may influence the risk of pathological changes, how pathologies may cause subtle changes in behaviour that are not classifiable by traditional clinical criteria and time trends in pathology prevalence, incidence and phenotypic expression (Blennow et al., 2010).

For research on AD and age-related cognitive decline, several highly validated and specific biomarkers are available. Imaging biomarkers include both amyloid and tau positron emission tomography (PET), which give a measure of the density of aggregated amyloid and tau deposits in the brain, and magnetic resonance imaging (MRI), which gives a measure of total and regional brain volume, and thereby degree of neuronal loss. The CSF biomarkers total tau (T-tau), phosphorylated tau (P-tau) and the 42-amino-acid isoform of β-amyloid (Aβ42) reflect the intensity of neuronal and axonal degeneration, the phosphorylation state of tau and tangle formation, and the aggregation and deposition of the Aβ42 peptide into plaques (Blennow & Hampel, 2003). These core AD CSF biomarkers are reviewed below.

7.2.1 The Core CSF Biomarkers for AD

Using enzyme-linked immunosorbent assay (ELISA) methods for T-tau that measure all tau isoforms irrespective of phosphorylation state (Blennow et al., 1995), tau phosphorylated at threonine 181 (P-tau181) (Vanmechelen et al., 2000), and β-amyloid 1-42 (Aβ42) (Andreasen et al. 1999a, b), a very large number of publications have consistently shown that most patients with a clinical diagnosis of AD show the typical 'AD biomarker profile', consisting of increased T-tau and P-tau, together with decreased Aβ42 (Olsson et al., 2016). In line with this, studies in which the diagnosis has been confirmed at autopsy have shown even better diagnostic performance in identifying AD dementia (Koopman et al., 2009; Shaw et al., 2009).

Given that clinical diagnosis is most difficult in the earlier stages of the disease, it is important that AD biomarkers also have high diagnostic accuracy in the mild cognitive impairment (MCI) stage of the disease. MCI is a heterogeneous syndrome that can have many causes; only around 50% of MCI patients will progress to AD dementia. A first study evaluating whether the combination of high tau and low Aβ42 in CSF can predict which MCI patients will progress to AD dementia showed that these core AD CSF biomarkers are already positive at this early clinical stage (Andreasen et al., 1999a, b). Furthermore, the CSF biomarkers had similar concentrations in a new CSF sample taken when patients had reached the dementia stage (Andreasen et al., 1999a, b), suggesting that these CSF biomarkers have already plateaued during the MCI stage, and will not change further during the transition stage.

In 2006, the first study with an extended clinical follow-up, which is needed to ascertain which MCI will not progress to AD dementia, showed that, while cognitively stable MCI cases had normal biomarkers, 95% of MCI patients who progressed to AD dementia had the typical AD CSF biomarker (Hansson et al., 2006). This very high capacity of the core AD CSF biomarkers to identify progressive MCI patients (whom we today call prodromal AD) has been verified by a number of large multicentre studies in Europe (Visser et al., 2009) and the USA (Shaw et al., 2009), and in the Swedish Brain Power study (Mattsson et al., 2009).

7.2.2 CSF Biomarkers in Preclinical AD

An important question for the application of CSF biomarkers in population-based studies is whether they can detect AD pathophysiology in the subset of cognitively unimpaired elderly who have clinically silent pathology. Indeed, in 2003 a first study showed that cognitively unimpaired 85-year-olds who at clinical follow-up had developed AD dementia already had decreased CSF Aβ42 levels in this pre-clinical stage, while both CSF T-tau and P-tau were normal (Skoog et al., 2003). This finding suggests that a CSF test can identify brain amyloid deposition, the central type of AD pathology, preclinically, a finding that was also confirmed in subsequent population-based cohorts of cognitively unimpaired elderly of less advanced age (70–78 years), and even earlier; in a sample taken up to eight years before the appearance of symptoms (Gustafson et al., 2007). Furthermore, these findings support the hypothesis that amyloid deposition (low CSF Aβ42) is present before either neurodegeneration (high T-tau) or tau pathology (high P-tau) is evident. This will facilitate projects examining risk factors for Aβ and tau pathology (and not just their clinical expression) using a molecular epidemiology approach, as discussed in detail below.

7.2.3 New Biomarkers to Monitor Synaptic Dysfunction

Synaptic dysfunction or degeneration is another key feature of AD pathophysiology (Davidsson & Blennow, 1990). Synaptic degeneration correlates more closely with the severity of cognitive disturbances than amyloid plaque load (Terry et al., 1991; DeKosky & Scheff, 1990). Recent studies suggest that early amyloid aggregates, including soluble Aβ oligomers (Shankar et al., 2007) and intracellular Aβ accumulations (Zou et al., 2015), may be the driver behind the synaptic dysfunction with dendritic spine loss in AD.

Combining the core CSF biomarkers for AD with reliable biomarkers to monitor synaptic and dendritic function in longitudinal clinical and epidemiological studies may give clues about AD pathogenesis, specifically the temporal evolution of the different forms of AD pathophysiology, as well as their interrelations, risk factors and relative contributions to cognitive symptoms.

One candidate biomarker for synaptic dysfunction is neurogranin, a dendritic protein expressed in the cortex and hippocampus, which is specifically located in dendritic spines (Represa et al., 1990; Guadano-Ferraz et al., 2005). Neurogranin is involved in synaptic plasticity and the induction of long-term potentiation (LTP) in the hippocampus (Fedorov et al., 1995; Chen et al., 1997), and thus of interest in disorders involving memory dysfunction. In the normal brain, neurogranin expression is highest in the association cortex, while lower neurogranin levels are seen in the cortex and hippocampus of the AD brain (Davidsson & Blennow 1990; Reddy et al., 2005), probably as a consequence of synaptic loss.

A first pilot study on CSF neurogranin as a biomarker for synaptic degeneration in AD found a noticeable increase as compared with cognitively unimpaired individuals of similar age (Thorsell et al., 2010), a finding that could be confirmed in the first study measuring CSF neurogranin by ELISA (Kvartsberg et al., 2015a). High CSF neurogranin in both AD dementia and prodromal AD has subsequently been confirmed in many large studies (Hellwig et al., 2015; Kvartsberg et al., 2015b), including the Alzheimer's Disease Neuroimaging Initiative (ADNI) multicentre study (Portelius et al., 2015). Interestingly, high CSF neurogranin correlates with future rate of neuronal loss and reductions in cortical metabolism (Portelius et al., 2015). Furthermore, increased CSF neurogranin appears to be specific to AD, since normal levels are found in many other neurodegenerative disorders, e.g., frontotemporal dementia, Lewy body dementia and progressive supranuclear palsy (Wellington et al., 2016).

7.3 The Need for Molecular Epidemiology Studies

The vast majority of population-based studies on AD risk profiling have not classified patients or controls using biomarkers reflecting specific AD pathophysiologies, i.e., amyloid and tau pathology (Yu et al., 2020), but instead have examined risk factors for age-related dementia or clinically diagnosed 'probable AD'. Such studies are also hampered by the complex pathophysiology of late-onset AD and the difficulties in making a correct clinical diagnosis. This introduces the risk that a proportion of cognitively unimpaired individuals (classified as control subjects) have preclinical AD pathology and thus limits the ability to correctly identify the underlying type of pathology (AD or other age-related dementias). Indeed, type II diabetes has been found to be a risk factor for 'probable AD' (defined as an 'amnestic dementia') in studies without biomarkers (Lu et al., 2009), while clinical studies validating clinical associations with pathology at autopsy show that the basis for the association between diabetes and cognitive disturbances is through cerebrovascular lesions, and not amyloid plaques or tau pathology (Abner et al., 2016; Nelson et al., 2011). In agreement, population-based studies using biomarkers have found that mid-life risk factors previously claimed to be associated with dementia (or 'probable AD'), such as obesity, smoking, diabetes, hypertension and cardiac disease were not associated with amyloid pathology, but with neurodegeneration (Vemuri et al., 2012). Similarly, GWAS studies have found an association between gene loci and clinically diagnosed 'probable AD', but when these loci are examined in cohorts with autopsy-verified diagnoses, many loci show no association with either amyloid plaques or tau pathology, but with cerebrovascular lesions (Beecham et al., 2014). Conversely, genetic studies using biomarkers for Aβ and tau pathologies as endophenotypes identify slightly different sets of susceptibility genes (Deming et al., 2017), and the association of AD with *APOE* ε4 grows stronger (Andreasson et al., 2014).

In addition, it may be of interest to link modifiable risk factors to specific pathophysiologies following the amyloid (A), tau (T) and neurodegeneration (N) classification system (Jack Jr et al., 2016), in order to understand which risk factors are directly associated with AD, and which are associated with old-age dementia in general.

7.4 Blood Tests will Facilitate the Implementation of Biomarkers in Population-Based Studies

While PET imaging and CSF biomarkers are well-validated tools to measure AD pathophysiology, they have some drawbacks that may make them more difficult to implement in epidemiological studies. PET imaging is expensive and has limited accessibility, and CSF collection by lumbar puncture may be frightening for study participants and regarded as complicated and time-consuming by many clinicians. Thus, the ability to measure proteins linked to AD pathophysiology in blood samples may facilitate the implementation of biomarkers.

Recent technical developments have provided ultrasensitive techniques, such as immuno- magnetic reduction (IMR) and single-molecule array (Simoa), that enable the measurement of brain-derived proteins in blood samples (Andreasson et al., 2016).

7.4.1 Brain Amyloidosis – Plasma Aβ42/40 Ratio

Plasma levels of amyloid β, specifically the Aβ42/40 ratio, are reduced in Alzheimer's disease (AD) and show high concordance with brain amyloidosis as assessed by PET. The explanation is likely to be that the 42-amino-acid-long variant of amyloid β (Aβ42), which is hydrophobic and prone to aggregate (Jarrett et al., 1993), is deposited in amyloid plaques, with a smaller amount being secreted to the CSF (Olsson et al., 2016) and blood. Using the ultrasensitive Simoa technology to measure Aβ42 in plasma (Zetterberg et al., 2011), a statistically significant correlation was found between Aβ42 (and the Aβ42/40 ratio) in plasma and CSF, as well as with amyloid load measured by PET technology (Janelidze et al., 2016). Plasma Aβ42 and Aβ40 can also be measured using fully automated instruments (Palmqvist et al., 2019), and mass spectrometry techniques (Schindler et al., 2019), showing high concordance with amyloid PET measures.

7.4.2 Tau Pathology – Phosphorylated Tau

Tau phosphorylated at position 181 (P-tau181) can be measured in plasma using MSD technology; a first paper showed a marked increase in AD and a clear association with tau PET (Mielke et al., 2018), a finding that was validated in two large clinical cohorts (Janelidze et al., 2020; Thijssen et al., 2020). Importantly, plasma P-tau181 was normal in other tau-pathologies, including frontotemporal dementia, progressive supranuclear palsy and corticobasal degeneration (Thijssen et al., 2020). Another paper presented a method for measuring plasma P-tau181 using the Simoa technique, and showed a marked increase in AD, a clear association with tau pathology measured by PET, but also that plasma P-tau was already increased in individuals with brain amyloidosis, but still a negative tau PET scan (Karikari et al., 2020). Other tau variants, specifically P-tau217, are also measurable in blood samples, with very promising results (Palmqvist et al., 2020). Taken together, these studies indicate that plasma P-tau is a reliable biomarker for tau pathology, which is easily accessible.

7.4.3 Neurodegeneration – Neurofilament Light Protein

Total tau (T-tau) and neurofilament light (NFL) reflect neuronal injury and are measurable in blood. Both these biomarkers show promise as a biomarker for acute neuronal injury (e.g., acute traumatic or hypoxic brain injury), with rapid and dramatic increases that also predict clinical outcome (Moseby-Knappe et al., 2019). However, T-tau in blood only shows a marginal increase in AD, but still correlates with atrophy measured by MRI and reduced cortical metabolism assessed by FDG-PET (Mattsson et al., 2016).

Another neuronal protein, neurofilament light (NFL), can also be measured in blood samples using the Simoa technique (Kuhle et al., 2016). Similar to tau protein, plasma NFL concentrations are increased in both AD dementia and MCI cases (Mattsson et al., 2017). Interestingly, higher plasma NFL concentrations were associated with amyloid deposition (as evaluated by amyloid PET), and predicted progression of cognitive decline and brain atrophy (Mattsson et al., 2017). However, a robust increase in blood NFL levels is found in several neurodegenerative disorders, not only in AD, indicating that it is a non-disease-specific biomarker for axonal degeneration (Lewczuk et al., 2018). Importantly, plasma NFL is already increasing in the preclinical phase of AD (Weston et al., 2017; Preische et al., 2019). These findings support the idea that plasma NFL can be used in the epidemiology setting as a neurodegeneration marker.

In summary, we have witnessed a rapid and successful development of blood biomarkers for specific pathologies in AD, including brain amyloidosis (Aβ42/40 ratio), tau pathology (P-tau), and neurodegeneration (NFL). The implementation of blood biomarkers in epidemiological studies may foster the understanding of lifestyle risk factors for AD, and repeated blood sampling may prove useful to assess the benefits of lifestyle interventions.

References

Abner, E. L., Nelson, P. T., Kryscio, R. J., Schmitt, F. A., Fardo, D. W., Woltjer, R. L., et al. (2016). Diabetes is associated with cerebrovascular but not Alzheimer's disease neuropathology. *Alzheimer's & Dementia: The Journal of the Alzheimer's Association, 12*(8), 882–889.

Andreasen, N., Minthon, L., Clarberg, A., Davidsson, P., Gottfries, J., Vanmechelen, E., et al. (1999a). Sensitivity, specificity, and stability of CSF-tau in AD in a community-based patient sample. *Neurology, 53*(7), 1488–1494.

Andreasen, N., Minthon, L., Vanmechelen, E., Vanderstichele, H., Davidsson, P., Winblad, B., et al. (1999b). Cerebrospinal fluid tau and Abeta42 as predictors of development of Alzheimer's disease in patients with mild cognitive impairment. *Neuroscience Letters, 273*(1), 5–8.

Andreasson, U., Lautner, R., Schott, J. M., Mattsson, N., Hansson, O., Herukka, S. K., et al. (2014). CSF biomarkers for Alzheimer's pathology and the effect size of APOE varepsilon4. *Molecular Psychiatry, 19*(2), 148–149.

Andreasson, U., Blennow, K., & Zetterberg, H. (2016). Update on ultrasensitive technologies to facilitate research on blood biomarkers for central nervous system disorders. *Alzheimers Dement (Amst), 3*, 98–102.

Beecham, G. W., Hamilton, K., Naj, A. C., Martin, E. R., Huentelman, M., Myers, A. J., et al. (2014). Genome-wide association meta-analysis of neuropathologic features of Alzheimer's disease and related dementias. *PLoS Genetics, 10*(9), e1004606.

Blennow, K., & Hampel, H. (2003). CSF markers for incipient Alzheimer's disease. *Lancet Neurology, 2*(10), 605–613.

Blennow, K., Wallin, A., Agren, H., Spenger, C., Siegfried, J., & Vanmechelen, E. (1995). Tau protein in cerebrospinal fluid: a biochemical marker for axonal degeneration in Alzheimer disease? *Molecular and Chemical Neuropathology, 26*(3), 231–245.

Blennow, K., Hampel, H., Weiner, M., & Zetterberg, H. (2010). Cerebrospinal fluid and plasma biomarkers in Alzheimer disease. *Nature Reviews Neurology, 6*(3), 131–144.

Buchhave, P., Minthon, L., Zetterberg, H., Wallin, A. K., Blennow, K., & Hansson, O. (2012). Cerebrospinal fluid levels of beta-amyloid 1-42, but not of tau, are fully changed already 5 to 10 years before the onset of Alzheimer dementia. *Archives of General Psychiatry, 69*(1), 98–106.

Chen, S. J., Sweatt, J. D., & Klann, E. (1997). Enhanced phosphorylation of the postsynaptic protein kinase C substrate RC3/neurogranin during long-term potentiation. *Brain Research, 749*(2), 181–187.

Davidsson, P., & Blennow, K. (1990). Neurochemical dissection of synaptic pathology in Alzheimer's disease. *International Psychogeriatrics / IPA, 10*(1), 11–23.

Dayan, A. D. (1970). Quantitative histological studies on the aged human brain. I. Senile plaques and neurofibrillary tangles in 'normal' patients. *Acta Neuropathologica, 16*(2), 85–94.

DeKosky, S. T., & Scheff, S. W. (1990). Synapse loss in frontal cortex biopsies in Alzheimer's disease: correlation with cognitive severity. *Annals of Neurology, 27*(5), 457–464.

Deming, Y., Li, Z., Kapoor, M., Harari, O., Del-Aguila, J. L., Black, K., et al. (2017). Genome-wide association study identifies four novel loci associated with Alzheimer's endophenotypes and disease modifiers. *Acta Neuropathologica, 133*(5), 839–856.

Fedorov, N. B., Pasinelli, P., Oestreicher, A. B., DeGraan, P. N., & Reymann, K. G. (1995). Antibodies to postsynaptic PKC substrate neurogranin prevent long-term potentiation in hippocampal CA1 neurons. *The European Journal of Neuroscience, 7*(4), 819–822.

Glenner, G. G., & Wong, C. W. (1984). Alzheimer's disease: initial report of the purification and characterization of a novel cerebrovascular amyloid protein. *Biochemical and Biophysical Research Communications, 120*(3), 885–890.

Grundke-Iqbal, I., Iqbal, K., Tung, Y. C., Quinlan, M., Wisniewski, H. M., & Binder, L. I. (1986). Abnormal phosphorylation of the microtubule-associated protein tau (tau) in Alzheimer cytoskeletal pathology. *Proceedings of the National Academy of Sciences of the United States of America, 83*(13), 4913–4917.

Guadano-Ferraz, A., Vinuela, A., Oeding, G., Bernal, J., & Rausell, E. (2005). RC3/neurogranin is expressed in pyramidal neurons of motor and somatosensory cortex in normal and denervated monkeys. *Journal of Comparative Neurology, 493*(4), 554–570.

Gustafson, D. R., Skoog, I., Rosengren, L., Zetterberg, H., & Blennow, K. (2007). Cerebrospinal fluid beta-amyloid 1-42 concentration may predict cognitive decline in older women. *Journal of Neurology, Neurosurgery, and Psychiatry, 78*(5), 461–464.

Hansen, L. A., Deteresa, R., Tobias, H., Alford, M., & Terry, R. D. (1988). Neocortical morphometry and cholinergic neurochemistry in Pick's disease. *The American Journal of Pathology, 131*(3), 507–518.

Hansson, O., Zetterberg, H., Buchhave, P., Londos, E., Blennow, K., & Minthon, L. (2006). Association between CSF biomarkers and incipient Alzheimer's disease in patients with mild cognitive impairment: a follow-up study. *Lancet Neurology, 5*(3), 228–234.

Hellwig, K., Kvartsberg, H., Portelius, E., Andreasson, U., Oberstein, T. J., Lewczuk, P., et al. (2015). Neurogranin and YKL-40: independent markers of synaptic degeneration and neuroinflammation in Alzheimer's disease. *Alzheimer's Research & Therapy, 7*, 74.

Jack, C. R., Jr., Bennett, D. A., Blennow, K., Carrillo, M. C., Feldman, H. H., Frisoni, G. B., et al. (2016). A/T/N: An unbiased descriptive classification scheme for Alzheimer disease biomarkers. *Neurology, 87*(5), 539–547.

James, B. D., Wilson, R. S., Boyle, P. A., Trojanowski, J. Q., Bennett, D. A., & Schneider, J. A. (2016). TDP-43 stage, mixed pathologies, and clinical Alzheimer's-type dementia. *Brain, 139*(11), 2983–2993.

Janelidze, S., Stomrud, E., Palmqvist, S., Zetterberg, H., van Westen, D., Jeromin, A., et al. (2016). Plasma beta-amyloid in Alzheimer's disease and vascular disease. *Scientific Reports, 6*, 26801.

Janelidze, S., Mattsson, N., Palmqvist, S., Smith, R., Beach, T. G., Serrano, G. E., et al. (2020). Plasma P-tau181 in Alzheimer's disease: relationship to other biomarkers, differential diagnosis, neuropathology and longitudinal progression to Alzheimer's dementia. *Nature Medicine, 26*(3), 379–386.

Jarrett, J. T., Berger, E. P., & Lansbury, P. T., Jr. (1993). The carboxy terminus of the beta amyloid protein is critical for the seeding of amyloid formation: implications for the pathogenesis of Alzheimer's disease. *Biochemistry, 32*(18), 4693–4697.

Karikari, T. K., Pascoal, T. A., Ashton, N. J., Janelidze, S., Benedet, A. L., Rodriguez, J. L., et al. (2020). Blood phosphorylated tau 181 as a biomarker for Alzheimer's disease: a diagnostic performance and prediction modelling study using data from four prospective cohorts. *Lancet Neurology, 19*(5), 422–433.

Koopman, K., Le Bastard, N., Martin, J. J., Nagels, G., De Deyn, P. P., & Engelborghs, S. (2009). Improved discrimination of autopsy-confirmed Alzheimer's disease (AD) from non-AD dementias using CSF P-tau(181P). *Neurochemistry International, 55*(4), 214–218.

Kovacs, G. G., Milenkovic, I., Wohrer, A., Hoftberger, R., Gelpi, E., Haberler, C., et al. (2013). Non-Alzheimer neurodegenerative pathologies and their combinations are more frequent than commonly believed in the elderly brain: a community-based autopsy series. *Acta Neuropathologica, 126*(3), 365–384.

Kuhle, J., Barro, C., Andreasson, U., Derfuss, T., Lindberg, R., Sandelius, A., et al. (2016). Comparison of three analytical platforms for quantification of the neurofilament light chain in blood samples: ELISA, electrochemiluminescence immunoassay and Simoa. *Clinical Chemistry and Laboratory Medicine, 54*(10), 1655–1661.

Kvartsberg, H., Duits, F. H., Ingelsson, M., Andreasen, N., Ohrfelt, A., Andersson, K., et al. (2015a). Cerebrospinal fluid levels of the synaptic protein neurogranin correlates with cognitive decline in prodromal Alzheimer's disease. *Alzheimers Dement, 11*(10), 1180–1190.

Kvartsberg, H., Portelius, E., Andreasson, U., Brinkmalm, G., Hellwig, K., Lelental, N., et al. (2015b). Characterization of the postsynaptic protein neurogranin in paired cerebrospinal fluid and plasma samples from Alzheimer's disease patients and healthy controls. *Alzheimer's Research & Therapy, 7*(1), 40.

Lewczuk, P., Riederer, P., O'Bryant, S. E., Verbeek, M. M., Dubois, B., Visser, P. J., et al. (2018). Cerebrospinal fluid and blood biomarkers for neurodegenerative dementias: an update of the consensus of the Task Force on Biological Markers in Psychiatry of the World Federation of Societies of Biological Psychiatry. *The World Journal of Biological Psychiatry, 19*(4), 244–328.

Lu, F. P., Lin, K. P., & Kuo, H. K. (2009). Diabetes and the risk of multi-system aging phenotypes: a systematic review and meta-analysis. *PLoS One, 4*(1), e4144.

Mann, D. M., Yates, P. O., & Marcyniuk, B. (1984). Alzheimer's presenile dementia, senile dementia of Alzheimer type and Down's syndrome in middle age form an age-related continuum of pathological changes. *Neuropathology and Applied Neurobiology, 10*(3), 185–207.

Mann, D. M., Yates, P. O., & Marcyniuk, B. (1985). Some morphometric observations on the cerebral cortex and hippocampus in presenile Alzheimer's disease, senile dementia of Alzheimer type and Down's syndrome in middle age. *Journal of the Neurological Sciences, 69*(3), 139–159.

Masters, C. L., Simms, G., Weinman, N. A., Multhaup, G., McDonald, B. L., & Beyreuther, K. (1985). Amyloid plaque core protein in Alzheimer disease and Down syndrome. *Proceedings of the National Academy of Sciences of the United States of America, 82*(12), 4245–4249.

Mattsson, N., Zetterberg, H., Hansson, O., Andreasen, N., Parnetti, L., Jonsson, M., et al. (2009). CSF biomarkers and incipient Alzheimer disease in patients with mild cognitive impairment. *JAMA: The Journal of the American Medical Association, 302*(4), 385–393.

Mattsson, N., Zetterberg, H., Janelidze, S., Insel, P. S., Andreasson, U., Stomrud, E., et al. (2016). Plasma tau in Alzheimer disease. *Neurology, 87*(17), 1827–1835.

Mattsson, N., Andreasson, U., Zetterberg, H., & Blennow, K. (2017). Alzheimer's disease neuroimaging I. Association of plasma neurofilament light with neurodegeneration in patients with Alzheimer disease. *JAMA Neurology, 74*(5), 557–566.

Mielke, M. M., Hagen, C. E., Xu, J., Chai, X., Vemuri, P., Lowe, V. J., et al. (2018). Plasma phospho-tau181 increases with Alzheimer's disease clinical severity and is associated with tau- and amyloid-positron emission tomography. *Alzheimers Dement, 14*(8), 989–997.

Moseby-Knappe, M., Mattsson, N., Nielsen, N., Zetterberg, H., Blennow, K., Dankiewicz, J., et al. (2019). Serum neurofilament light chain for prognosis of outcome after cardiac arrest. *JAMA Neurology, 76*(1), 64–71.

Nelson, P. T., Head, E., Schmitt, F. A., Davis, P. R., Neltner, J. H., Jicha, G. A., et al. (2011). Alzheimer's disease is not 'brain aging': neuropathological, genetic, and epidemiological human studies. *Acta Neuropathologica, 121*(5), 571–587.

Ngandu, T., Lehtisalo, J., Solomon, A., Levalahti, E., Ahtiluoto, S., Antikainen, R., et al. (2015). A 2-year multidomain intervention of diet, exercise, cognitive training, and vascular risk monitoring versus control to prevent cognitive decline in at-risk elderly people (FINGER): a randomised controlled trial. *Lancet, 385*(9984), 2255–2263.

Olsson, B., Lautner, R., Andreasson, U., Ohrfelt, A., Portelius, E., Bjerke, M., et al. (2016). CSF and blood biomarkers for the diagnosis of Alzheimer's disease: a systematic review and meta-analysis. *Lancet Neurology, 15*(7), 673–684.

Palmqvist, S., Janelidze, S., Stomrud, E., Zetterberg, H., Karl, J., Zink, K., et al. (2019). Performance of fully automated plasma assays as screening tests for Alzheimer disease-related beta-amyloid status. *JAMA Neurology, 76*(9), 1060–1069.

Palmqvist, S., Janelidze, S., Quiroz, Y. T., Zetterberg, H., Lopera, F., Stomrud, E., et al. (2020). Discriminative accuracy of plasma phospho-tau217 for Alzheimer disease vs other neurodegenerative disorders. *JAMA: The Journal of the American Medical Association, 324*(8), 772–781.

Perry, R. H. (1986). Recent advances in neuropathology. *British Medical Bulletin, 42*(1), 34–41.

Portelius, E., Zetterberg, H., Skillback, T., Tornqvist, U., Andreasson, U., Trojanowski, J. Q., et al. (2015). Cerebrospinal fluid neurogranin: relation to cognition and neurodegeneration in Alzheimer's disease. *Brain: A Journal of Neurology, 138*(Pt 11), 3373–3385.

Preische, O., Schultz, S. A., Apel, A., Kuhle, J., Kaeser, S. A., Barro, C., et al. (2019). Serum neurofilament dynamics predicts neurodegeneration and clinical progression in presymptomatic Alzheimer's disease. *Nature Medicine, 25*(2), 277–283.

Price, J. L., McKeel, D. W., Jr., Buckles, V. D., Roe, C. M., Xiong, C., Grundman, M., et al. (2009). Neuropathology of nondemented aging: presumptive evidence for preclinical Alzheimer disease. *Neurobiology of Aging, 30*(7), 1026–1036.

Reddy, P. H., Mani, G., Park, B. S., Jacques, J., Murdoch, G., Whetsell, W., Jr., et al. (2005). Differential loss of synaptic proteins in Alzheimer's disease: implications for synaptic dysfunction. *Journal of Alzheimer's Disease: JAD, 7*(2), 103–117. discussion 73–80.

Represa, A., Deloulme, J. C., Sensenbrenner, M., Ben-Ari, Y., & Baudier, J. (1990). Neurogranin: immunocytochemical localization of a brain-specific protein kinase C substrate. *The Journal of Neuroscience, 10*(12), 3782–3792.

Rowe, C. C., Bourgeat, P., Ellis, K. A., Brown, B., Lim, Y. Y., Mulligan, R., et al. (2013). Predicting Alzheimer disease with beta-amyloid imaging: results from the Australian imaging, biomarkers, and lifestyle study of ageing. *Annals of Neurology, 74*(6), 905–913.

Schindler, S. E., Bollinger, J. G., Ovod, V., Mawuenyega, K. G., Li, Y., Gordon, B. A., et al. (2019). High-precision plasma beta-amyloid 42/40 predicts current and future brain amyloidosis. *Neurology, 93*(17), e1647–e1e59.

Shankar, G. M., Bloodgood, B. L., Townsend, M., Walsh, D. M., Selkoe, D. J., & Sabatini, B. L. (2007). Natural oligomers of the Alzheimer amyloid-beta protein induce reversible synapse loss by modulating an NMDA-type glutamate receptor-dependent signaling pathway. *The Journal of Neuroscience, 27*(11), 2866–2875.

Shaw, L. M., Vanderstichele, H., Knapik-Czajka, M., Clark, C. M., Aisen, P. S., Petersen, R. C., et al. (2009). Cerebrospinal fluid biomarker signature in Alzheimer's disease neuroimaging initiative subjects. *Annals of Neurology, 65*(4), 403–413.

Skoog, I., Davidsson, P., Aevarsson, O., Vanderstichele, H., Vanmechelen, E., & Blennow, K. (2003). Cerebrospinal fluid beta-amyloid 42 is reduced before the onset of sporadic dementia: a population-based study in 85-year-olds. *Dementia and Geriatric Cognitive Disorders, 15*(3), 169–176.

Steen Jensen, C., Portelius, E., Siersma, V., Hogh, P., Wermuth, L., Blennow, K., et al. (2016). Cerebrospinal fluid amyloid beta and tau concentrations are not modulated by 16 weeks of moderate- to high-intensity physical exercise in patients with Alzheimer disease. *Dementia and Geriatric Cognitive Disorders, 42*(3–4), 146–158.

Terry, R. D., & Davies, P. (1980). Dementia of the Alzheimer type. *Annual Review of Neuroscience, 3*, 77–95.

Terry, R. D., Masliah, E., Salmon, D. P., Butters, N., DeTeresa, R., Hill, R., et al. (1991). Physical basis of cognitive alterations in Alzheimer's disease: synapse loss is the major correlate of cognitive impairment. *Annals of Neurology, 30*(4), 572–580.

Thal, D. R., Rub, U., Orantes, M., & Braak, H. (2002). Phases of A beta-deposition in the human brain and its relevance for the development of AD. *Neurology, 58*(12), 1791–1800.

Thijssen, E. H., La Joie, R., Wolf, A., Strom, A., Wang, P., Iaccarino, L., et al. (2020). Diagnostic value of plasma phosphorylated tau181 in Alzheimer's disease and frontotemporal lobar degeneration. *Nature Medicine, 26*(3), 387–397.

Thorsell, A., Bjerke, M., Gobom, J., Brunhage, E., Vanmechelen, E., Andreasen, N., et al. (2010). Neurogranin in cerebrospinal fluid as a marker of synaptic degeneration in Alzheimer's disease. *Brain Research, 1362*, 13–22.

Tomlinson, B. E. (1989). Second Dorothy S. Russell memorial. The neuropathology of Alzheimer's diseaselecture. *Neuropathology and Applied Neurobiology, 15*(6), 491–512.

Tomlinson, B. E., Blessed, G., & Roth, M. (1968). Observations on the brains of non-demented old people. *Journal of the Neurological Sciences, 7*(2), 331–356.

Tomlinson, B. E., Blessed, G., & Roth, M. (1970). Observations on the brains of demented old people. *Journal of the Neurological Sciences, 11*(3), 205–242.

Vanmechelen, E., Vanderstichele, H., Davidsson, P., Van Kerschaver, E., Van Der Perre, B., Sjogren, M., et al. (2000). Quantification of tau phosphorylated at threonine 181 in human cerebrospinal fluid: a sandwich ELISA with a synthetic phosphopeptide for standardization. *Neuroscience Letters, 285*(1), 49–52.

Vemuri, P., Lesnick, T. G., Przybelski, S. A., Knopman, D. S., Roberts, R. O., Lowe, V. J., et al. (2012). Effect of lifestyle activities on Alzheimer disease biomarkers and cognition. *Annals of Neurology, 72*(5), 730–738.

Visser, P. J., Verhey, F., Knol, D. L., Scheltens, P., Wahlund, L. O., Freund-Levi, Y., et al. (2009). Prevalence and prognostic value of CSF markers of Alzheimer's disease pathology in patients with subjective cognitive impairment or mild cognitive impairment in the DESCRIPA study: a prospective cohort study. *Lancet Neurology, 8*(7), 619–627.

Wellington, H., Paterson, R. W., Portelius, E., Tornqvist, U., Magdalinou, N., Fox, N. C., et al. (2016). Increased CSF neurogranin concentration is specific to Alzheimer disease. *Neurology, 86*(9), 829–835.

Weston, P. S. J., Poole, T., Ryan, N. S., Nair, A., Liang, Y., Macpherson, K., et al. (2017). Serum neurofilament light in familial Alzheimer disease: a marker of early neurodegeneration. *Neurology, 89*(21), 2167–2175.

Yu, J. T., Xu, W., Tan, C. C., Andrieu, S., Suckling, J., Evangelou, E., et al. (2020). Evidence-based prevention of Alzheimer's disease: systematic review and meta-analysis of 243 observational prospective studies and 153 randomised controlled trials. *Journal of Neurology, Neurosurgery, and Psychiatry, 91*(11), 1201–1209.

Zetterberg, H., Mortberg, E., Song, L., Chang, L., Provuncher, G. K., Patel, P. P., et al. (2011). Hypoxia due to cardiac arrest induces a time-dependent increase in serum amyloid beta levels in humans. *PLoS One, 6*(12), e28263.

Zou, C., Montagna, E., Shi, Y., Peters, F., Blazquez-Llorca, L., Shi, S., et al. (2015). Intraneuronal APP and extracellular Abeta independently cause dendritic spine pathology in transgenic mouse models of Alzheimer's disease. *Acta Neuropathologica, 129*(6), 909–920.

Chapter 8
The Capability Approach in Research on Ageing Well at Home for Frail Older People

Synneve Dahlin-Ivanoff, Qarin Lood, Katarina Wilhelmson, Kajsa Eklund, Emmelie Barenfeld, Greta Häggblom-Kronlöf, Theresa Westgård, and Isabelle Andersson Hammar

8.1 Introduction

Today's highly specialised health and social care is poorly adapted to the comprehensive needs of frail older people (SBU, 2014). This exposes them to avoidable risks such as loss of functional capacities accompanied by health and social care needs, as well as increased premature mortality (Morley et al., 2013). In an attempt to contribute to more equitable research and healthcare services with and for frail older people, this chapter describes the work of the Frail Elderly Support Research Group (FRESH) in relation to the capability approach as a theoretical departure. Frail older people have always been our target group because they are at risk of further deterioration if their needs are not acknowledged (Morley et al., 2013). Frailty can be defined as a state of decreased reserve resistance to stressors as a result of cumulative decline across multiple physiological systems, causing vulnerability to different outcomes, such as falls, hospitalisation, institutionalisation and mortality (Fried et al., 2004; Fried et al., 2001). The prevalence of frailty increases with age and is associated with an elevated risk of adverse health outcomes. Within Europe, the overall prevalence of frailty for people aged 65 years and older is approximately 10%, with the northern countries having lower prevalence than the southern (Clegg et al., 2013). By applying the capability approach to our

S. Dahlin-Ivanoff (✉) · Q. Lood · K. Wilhelmson · K. Eklund · E. Barenfeld
G. Häggblom-Kronlöf · T. Westgård · I. Andersson Hammar
Institute of Neuroscience and Physiology, Department of Psychiatry and Neurochemistry, Sahlgrenska Academy at the University of Gothenburg, Gothenburg, Sweden

Centre for Ageing and Health – AgeCap, University of Gothenburg, Gothenburg, Sweden
e-mail: synneve.dahlin-ivanoff@neuro.gu.se; qarin.lood@neuro.gu.se; katarina.wilhelmson@gu.se; emmelie.barenfeld@neuro.gu.se; greta.haggblom-kronlof@neuro.gu.se; theresa.westgard@neuro.gu.se; isabelle.a-h@neuro.gu.se

H. Falk Erhag et al. (eds.), *A Multidisciplinary Approach to Capability in Age and Ageing*, International Perspectives on Aging 31,
https://doi.org/10.1007/978-3-030-78063-0_8

interdisciplinary research, we aim to identify and acknowledge the values and freedoms unique to each person. There are few publications addressing how the capability approach could be applied to empirical studies with frail older people (Blasimme, 2017). Therefore, this chapter aims to utilise the capability approach as a theoretical framework for research with and for frail older people, focusing on their opportunities to realise their goal in relation to various contextual factors that may influence them.

The capability approach allows us to identify advantages and disadvantages among different groups of people, since it focuses on social justice and human development. In the context of research on ageing and health, many people are currently disadvantaged due to morbidity and disabilities associated with high age and frailty. For instance, people over 65 in need of home care or other social services face the risk of being given no, or limited, choice with regards to when to get out of bed in the morning, what and when to eat, or when to go outdoors. Such injustices can be captured by the multidimensional capability approach, which seeks to identify constraints in both choice and control based on a person's age, frailty, morbidity and/or disabilities. We work with and for people who are at risk of developing frailty, as well as those who are already frail or very frail. Applying the capability approach to qualitative and quantitative studies in empirical settings, FRESH's research programme 'Ageing well at home', referred to in this chapter, aims to find measures that can support older people to remain living in ordinary housing for as long as possible, in a way that they experience as meaningful and satisfying. We also aim to broaden our understanding of the concept of frailty in general. With its contribution to our understanding of the frailty process and how it may influence people as they age, the capability approach is a fundamental part of all projects, focusing on people's real opportunities to achieve what it is possible for them to achieve, and what they have a reason to value, in relation to the resources they have at hand. Based on mutual respect and the sharing of ideas, we as a research group also apply person-centredness to our research with and for frail older people. This means that we place a high value on human interaction, and every person involved in the research process is regarded as capable of contributing with their experience, knowledge and expertise. Every effort is made to involve a wide range of people with different backgrounds and abilities, and to avoid unjust exclusion from research participation based on assumptions about the abilities of frail older people with various linguistic and cultural backgrounds. In combination with the capability approach, person-centredness allows us to understand how to identify and support what is required for each person to age well at home. Our primary focus is to make sure that older people's voices are heard, but the voices of professionals are also important for the development of support that is feasible to implement in real life. The FRESH research group represents both junior and senior researchers who have a broad set of competences representing different disciplines such as caring science, history, medical science, occupational science and social sciences. The research group has experience of both quantitative and qualitative methods and extensive experience of conducting interprofessional and multidimensional intervention studies (RCT) with frail older people in collaboration with hospitals, primary care, and health and social care. In this chapter, we describe the key concepts of the capability approach as applied to our research, and outline a suggestion for how research can use the capability approach to assess and minimise inequalities as experienced by frail older people.

8.2 A Capability Approach to Ageing Well at Home – Key Concepts for Research

The capability approach, as described by Sen (1993), is a normative framework that builds on the belief that all people have equal rights to experience health and well-being, and that the opportunities to do so should be understood in relation to each person's capabilities (Sen, 1993). Two of the core concepts of the capability approach that are applied to FRESH's research with and for frail older people are capabilities and functionings, the latter not to be confused with functional ability. Functionings in the capability approach are described in relation to people's valuable goals, and capabilities refer to their abilities to realise valuable goals. As the name of the approach suggests, the term 'capabilities' is central to understanding the capability approach, and it is defined as a person's ability to achieve their valuable goals (Sen, 1985). Capabilities are not necessarily associated with something that people do, but refer to their ability to choose between different activities and reach their goals, given the resources and services they have to hand. And whether or not people are able to do and be what they have a reason to value is assessed by functionings, defined as what people are really achieving. We describe capabilities and functionings in more detail in relation to our previous studies below.

8.3 Capabilities

Although ageing well at home may be interpreted as an achievement in itself, it is not only influenced by the person's ability to achieve, but also by their freedom to choose from a set of alternative achievements, and that is what is meant by capabilities. According to Sen (1985), capabilities refer to the ability to achieve valuable goals, and this includes the freedom to choose or not to choose between different activities (Sen, 1985). As mentioned in the introductory example of people in need of health and social care, capabilities concern the freedom to choose when and how to go about one's everyday activities. Freedom of choice also refers to the opportunity to choose not to do certain things and, as such, capabilities refer to what people are enabled to do and be, given their circumstances. In relation to FRESH's research programme, such circumstances have been defined and measured by three distinct clinical entities that are causally related: frailty, morbidity and disability. As people age, frailty, morbidity and disability may have a negative impact upon their freedom or opportunity to choose. Each entity, individually, occurs frequently and has significant importance clinically. Additionally, old age associates strongly with frailty and, with increasing age, the risk of disability also increases (Reuben, 1998). However, it is important to distinguish between them in order to understand the factors that may affect different people across the life course (Fried et al., 2004), and to take variations in need into account. Even though old age associates strongly with each of frailty, morbidity and disability, they are three different entities that need to be separated in order to be able to identify adequate measures to support frail older people to age well at home.

Frailty is a complex geriatric syndrome, which usually manifests in weight loss, exhaustion, low physical activity, slowness and weakness. Some also advocate that the definition of frailty should be expanded to include additional aspects such as social factors, as well as the physical and social environment (Lally & Crome, 2007; Hogan et al., 2003). There is evidence, however, for the more physical definition of frailty, mentioned above, as a complex geriatric syndrome (Morley et al., 2013), and this is the definition we have used in our studies to capture the biological ageing process. The frailty indicators (weakness, fatigue, low physical activity, poor balance, slow gait speed, visual impairment and impaired cognition) have been used to identify inequalities in all the FRESH studies (Dahlin-Ivanoff et al., 2010). This information is crucial in order to capture the biological ageing process and enable older people to continue performing the daily activities they want and need to do, in their own home environment, as they age.

Morbidity is estimated using the Cumulative Illness Rating Scale for Geriatrics (CIRS-G) (Linn et al. 1968), a rating instrument of chronic medical illness burden that is used to identify inequality (heart, vascular, hematopoietic, respiratory, eyes, ear, nose, throat and larynx, upper gastrointestinal, lower gastrointestinal, liver, renal, genital-urinary, musculoskeletal, neurological, endocrine and psychiatric illness). This information is of great importance clinically. Research shows that morbidity increases with increasing age (Fabbri et al., 2015) and that susceptibility to disease increases if one is frail (Fulop et al., 2010). Morbidity and frailty thus interact with each other and as a person becomes both frail and has one or more diseases, this can eventually lead to them becoming dependent on other people to support and help them with everyday activities, or to premature death.

Disability is defined by dependence in the activities of daily living, to capture inequality in the outcome of the ability to realise valuable goals. Since the ability to realise valuable goals is the focus in the research programme 'Ageing well at home', we assess dependence in the activities of daily living (cleaning, shopping, transportation, cooking, bathing, dressing, going to the toilet, transferring and feeding (Sonn, 1996)) as the primary outcome measure in all our intervention studies. Dependence is defined as another person being involved in the activity by giving personal or directive assistance. People living with another person are assessed as independent if they can perform the activity when alone. The use of dependence in activities of daily living as the primary outcome measure is strengthened by the fact that older people have defined their health in relation to what they can expect in terms of activity and participation on the basis of the more or less inevitable symptoms and diseases that come with old age (Fänge & Dahlin-Ivanoff, 2009; Ebrahimi et al., 2015; Ebrahimi et al., 2013).

Impaired ability to perform daily activities can be a consequence of morbidity and/or frailty, but different people have different abilities and opportunities, depending on what diseases they have and how frail they are. Our knowledge, gathered from many years of research and clinical work with research on older people's abilities to perform everyday activities, shows that it is more complex than just asking how the person manages, or has managed, their everyday activities. For instance, being in the hands of others, such as home help services, can result in frail older people not being able to perform activities in the way they want to. With increasing frailty, the home may become a place for assistive devices and adaptations, and a workplace for social services and healthcare staff. Having to reorganise their home and the frequent comings and goings of professionals and other people can affect the sense of freedom expressed by frail older people (Dahlin-Ivanoff et al., 2007; Fänge & Dahlin-Ivanoff, 2009). Moreover, it is not uncommon for there to be a difference between what a person says they do and what they actually do, and between what they can do and what they actually do. In order to make a correct analysis of what the person has done, and how they have done it, we must start with a conversation that is designed as a dialogue between two equal people, who both have valuable knowledge. This means listening to what the other person is saying, and how they are saying it, by setting the person's problems, needs and priorities in the foreground. In a dialogue of this kind, the person in question must be given the opportunity to express what is important to them and how they want things to be. This means that the person is given the opportunity to be involved and self-determining in terms of health and medical care, as well as in their everyday activities.

8.4 Functionings

Functionings are described by Sen as what people actually achieve, representing the goals that each person has a reason to value (Sen 1987). Such goals are often influenced by the ageing process. For instance, maintaining engagement in daily life through performing daily activities and personal care has been described as an important goal for older people (Häggblom-Kronlöf et al., 2007; Haak et al., 2007). This performance, however, is influenced by contextual factors, such as the environment in which the older person finds themselves. People tend to create meaning and significance in the spaces and places where they live, and in a study of community-dwelling 99-year-old people (Häggblom-Kronlöf et al., 2007), the participants described seeing themselves as competent, creative and proud because they were able to manage their home-related activities. On the other hand, they also described themselves as incapable and restricted as a result of frailty, lack of accessibility to the environment and social hindrances. The participants adapted and reshaped their sense of self to the new circumstances caused by frailty or external factors in a unique way. Daily life for many frail older people thus becomes more and more focused on the home as a place for daily activities. At home, things occur on the older people's own terms, they feel secure and can maintain their self-image as an active and capable human being despite increased dependence on other people (Fänge & Dahlin-Ivanoff, 2009; Dahlin-Ivanoff et al., 2007). The home may thus influence the older person's functionings, since it represents a contextual factor that has an impact on their opportunities to realise their valuable goals.

Research has confirmed that independence in daily activities is strongly linked to older people's health and well-being because it can reinforce their sense of self (Haak et al., 2007). Independent performance of daily activities has therefore been used to define examples of valuable goals, or functionings, for frail older people in FRESH's studies. The instrument Canadian Occupational Performance Measure (COPM) identifies and prioritises people's valuable goals in everyday life in the areas of self-care, productivity and leisure. Even though it would be better to measure each person's valuable goals, or functionings, using a measure such as the COPM, the FRESH research group has decided to capture functionings in terms of the independent performance of daily activities.

Self-determination is another central concept when studying whether or not frail older people achieve the goals they want to achieve, and if they have the contextual conditions to live a life they consider to be good and worthy (Ottenvall Hammar et al., 2014b). The concept can be defined as a phenomenon which comprises having the ability, as well as enough knowledge and control over a whole process, to act/decide of one's own free will, and to have ethical/legal rights (Ekelund et al., 2014).

Self-determination in daily life can be assessed using the statements from the Impact on Participation and Autonomy-Older Persons (IPA-O). The IPA-O is based on self-assessment statements that capture older people's perceptions of their opportunities to decide in their daily life, such as, for example: 'My chances to help or support people in any way are good' (Ottenvall Hammar et al., 2014b). One cross-sectional study using the IPA-O found that reduced self-determination in daily life was prominent among older people who were dissatisfied with their physical health. Frail older people had nearly three times higher odds of perceiving reduced self-determination than people who were not frail (Ottenvall Hammar et al., 2016). Thus, frail older people need support from others in their surroundings in order to exercise self-determination and to reach their valuable goals. As older people become increasingly frail and dependent on other people, they may, however, have decreased opportunities to decide for themselves about what to do, when and how. Frail older people who are in the process of losing their ability to perform the activities of daily living independently often meet numerous healthcare professionals, both in their homes and within different healthcare organisations.

Although their right to self-determination is acknowledged both in law and by professionals, studies indicate that the exercising of this right is not fully respected (Janlöv et al., 2006; Boyle, 2004). In one study (Ottenvall Hammar et al., 2014a), older people in the early stages of developing dependence on other people when performing the activities of daily living were recruited and their experiences of self-determination were explored. The older people experienced their self-determination as a process, shifting from self-governing to being governed by other people or being governed by their ageing body. Furthermore, self-determination was experienced as a struggle against their own body, in order to continue exercising self-determination in daily life, which in turn contributed to a feeling of being able to self-govern. Depending on the relationship between the people involved in an activity, continued self-governing in daily life was possible. Thus, decision-making in daily life was relational. Furthermore, the older people experienced a need to guard their own independence in relation to homecare services and their relatives, which gave rise to a sense of control. Freedom was sometimes beyond their opportunities. Self-determination varies over time, from actually achieving valuable goals in real life towards being ruled by others in terms of everyday life decisions (Ottenvall Hammar et al., 2014a).

To understand this divergence between the legal rights of self-determination that are acknowledged by professionals, and the fact that self-determination is still not being experienced by older people themselves, we studied the concept from two different angles. Firstly, a concept analysis, including a thorough literature review, was conducted in order to clarify the concept in relation to community-dwelling frail older people (Ekelund et al., 2014). Secondly, older people with varying degrees of frailty were asked about their experiences of the concept as described above (Ottenvall Hammar et al., 2014a). In a healthcare context, self-determination has been defined as participation in decision-making without control by others, but the two studies above (Ekelund et al., 2014; Ottenvall Hammar et al., 2014a) show that self-determination among frail older people is more complex than that. Moreover, self-determination can be threatened when the ability to independently perform daily activities is affected (Ottenvall Hammar et al., 2015). This is noteworthy because it is important for older people's health and well-being that they are allowed to make and influence decisions about their own daily lives, especially if they are dependent on others.

8.5 The Capability Approach as a Theoretical Framework for Research with and for Frail Older People

Viewing FRESH's research programme 'Ageing well at home', and how we conduct research, from the perspective of the capability approach, we are focusing on user involvement in research. We study the freedom needed by frail older people to decide what, when and how to do things, and we explore whether or not involvement in research on ageing and health is a valuable goal from the perspective of the frail older people themselves. Another central aspect of our research is whether and how involvement in research could increase frail older people's opportunities to lead a life they have reason to value. An important ethical starting point is that frail older people should be treated as persons who can decide for themselves and their lives, even though they are limited by frailty, morbidity and disability and are dependent on other people's help and support. Therefore, frail older people's own free choice has always been and still is an important area within our research programme.

As a partnership-focused programme, 'Ageing well at home' is well established in the ethical values of equality and respect. This means that we as researchers strive for transparency with regard to the aim of involving frail older people in research, what the research will lead to, and how each person can contribute to the research process with their experience, knowledge and expertise. Researchers and participants respect each other and each other's roles and perspectives and, by adapting research methods and designs, we also aim to make it possible for a diversity of different people to participate in the research. By diversity, we mean differences in age, degree of frailty and cognition, socioeconomic background, linguistic preferences, national background and experiences of, and attitudes towards, research.

Conducting research projects with and for frail older people is often a complex endeavour, with regards to both design and outcome measures, and few previous attempts have been made to include very old or very frail people in research. Understanding about how and when to conduct research together with frail older people is sparse, and even though FRESH has a strong history of involving frail older people in the research process (Dahlin-Ivanoff et al., 2010; Gustafsson et al., 2015), we still need to fill the knowledge gap with regard to frail older people's needs and desires to be involved in the research project to a greater extent than participating in an interview or filling in a survey.

Frail older people may be hard to reach out to, and they are frequently excluded from participation in research. There is a general assumption that frailty, disability and morbidity have a negative impact upon a person's ability to contribute to the research process, or that participation in research would not be beneficial for frail older people (Dewar, 2005; Ferrucci et al., 2004). Consequently, frail older people, who may also experience various degrees of disability and morbidity, have been excluded from research on ageing and health, based on the assumption that they would not have the energy to participate, or that the research would not be of benefit to them (Ferrucci et al., 2004). Linguistic differences between researchers and participants have also been used to exclude older people with experience of international migration, because the use of interpreters and translators is often an endeavour demanding substantial resources (Hussain-Gambles et al., 2004). Contextual aspects such as age, frailty and linguistic background thus seem to be important for people's real opportunities to become involved in research. There is a need for research about the complexity and diversity of desires and needs among the ageing population, with regard to both health and medical needs and the need and desire to be involved in research. Involvement in research could be used as a tool for frail older people to make their voices heard and mediate their abilities and needs, and this, in turn, could be used to improve health and social care for this segment of the population. The lack of knowledge and theoretical support for when and how frail older people could and should be involved in research has led to serious limitations on their rights to make their voices heard and have their needs met.

Frail older people's participation in research has been described as a way for them to access care and medical examinations that they are not able to access in any other way. It is also described in relation to loyalty to the researcher who asks them to participate, and to the group of older people in general (Mein et al., 2012). Participation in research thus seems to be a way for older people to access health and social care from which they would otherwise be largely or entirely excluded. This motive for participation reveals inequities in the healthcare system, and raises the question of whether frail older people are the group with the worst access to health and social care, even though they are in most need (Townsend & Cox, 2013; Dahlin-Ivanoff et al., 2019). To improve access to health and social care, we must first discover what needs frail older people have and what is of most importance to them. The involvement of frail older people in research could contribute to an improved understanding of their abilities and experiences, as this would allow them to contribute to the research process with their unique perspectives on what we should prioritise and how research could become more relevant to the public as the population ages (Hanson et al., 2007). Yet, many frail older people who participate in research are treated as passive informants, and the research process is entirely controlled by the researchers (Camden et al., 2015). To distribute power over the research process more equally between researchers and participating frail older people, and to work as equal partners in a joint project, we need to know more about frail older people's real opportunities. We also need to evaluate the potential challenges and pitfalls facing such work. The goal of the user involvement approach in 'Ageing well at home' is therefore to involve a broad group of people in our research, in order to counteract negative assumptions about who is capable of being involved in research.

FRESH conducts studies with and for frail older people, as well as healthcare professionals and other researchers on ageing and health. All parties are regarded as equal partners, with competence and important roles in the co-creation of knowledge. As researchers, we are experts on the research process and scientific knowledge, frail older people are experts on their own abilities and needs, and healthcare professionals are experts on what is feasible within different organisations. We do not wish to change these roles, since the value of co-creation is based on differences in perspectives and understandings. A dilemma that could arise with time is that the co-creating partnership will lead to a weaker critical mass, which means that researchers and participants may become too similar to be able to question each other. Another dilemma is the unequal division of power, with the risk that researchers' high status within many societies may impact upon frail older people's willingness and preparedness to question them or to question research-based knowledge. This influences the power relations between the two parties in the research project, which could have a negative influence on both the relationship between the researchers and participants, and the research per se. The importance of creating a trusting, tolerant and relaxed environment is highlighted, to encourage frail older people to share their experiences and knowledge. Being together with other people in a non-judgemental and enabling environment could allow the older people to express their perspectives, and in that way to distribute the power more equitably between themselves and the researchers. There are also dilemmas associated with time and resources. Co-creation projects usually require a longer time for research because other people outside of academia are influencing the research process. This takes time and is complex. Contrasting this with the urge for quick results and publications could lead to difficulties with co-creation projects.

8.6 Conclusion

In conclusion, the purpose of this chapter was to describe how the capability approach as a theoretical framework can be applied to research on ageing well at home for frail older people. We have strived to describe the capability approach to research with and for frail older people in order to focus on the older people's opportunities to realise their goals in relation to contextual factors that may influence these opportunities. This is important because there has been criticism towards the significance of the capability approach when it comes to its application in empirical studies (Robeyns 2006), and also because knowledge regarding how the capability approach can be applied to empirical studies is sparse. Thus, instead of only assessing the health of frail older people in objective terms, the capability approach may also allow us to evaluate their opportunities to be healthy, and assess their resources to achieve their valuable goals.

To understand what is valuable and important to each person, one must start with a conversation, a dialogue, where people are seen as equal, and where everyone can contribute with knowledge that is considered valuable. This means that frail older people must be given the opportunity to express what is important to them, and how they want things to be done. It also entails that frail older people need to be given opportunities to be involved in decision-making, and to exercise self-determination in daily life when they want to. When assessing ageing well at home, the capability approach could be a possible way to focus on what older people are effectively able to do and be, when considering contextual factors as well as individual choice (Sen, 1985). Our research programme 'Ageing well at home' illustrates the need to recognise each person's capabilities, because it can mean the difference between success and failure in attaining valued goals in life. Despite there being an instrument (COPM) that identifies and prioritises valuable goals in everyday life, we have not so far assessed each person's level of valuable goals (functionings). Based on earlier qualitative research, and by assessing ADL, we do however capture functionings at a general level, even though it would be better if we measured each person's valuable goals (functionings).

In summary, the core of what we do is to promote frail older people's real opportunities to do and be what they have a reason to value. We have conducted several qualitative studies and the results have given a picture of the real opportunities people achieve. This chapter could be a stepping-stone for future researchers to consider evaluating and implementing the capability approach into their research.

References

Blasimme, A. (2017). Physical frailty, sarcopenia, and the enablement of autonomy: Philosophical issues in geriatric medicine. *Aging Clinical and Experimental Research, 29*, 59–63.

Boyle, G. (2004). Facilitating choice and control for older persons in long-term care. *Health & Social Work, 12*, 212–220.

Camden, C., Shikako-Thomas, K., Nguyen, T., Graham, E., Thomas, A., Sprung, J., Morris, C., & Russell, D. (2015). Engaging stakeholders in rehabilitation research: A scoping review of strategies used in partnerships and evaluation of impacts. *Disability and Rehabilitation, 37*, 1390–1400.

Clegg, A., Young, J., Ilie, S., Rikkert, M., & Rockwood, K. (2013). Frailty in elderly people. *Lancet, 381*, 752–762.

Dahlin-Ivanoff, S., Haak, M., Fänge, A., & Iwarsson, S. (2007). The multiple meaning of home as experienced by very old Swedish people. *Scandinavian Journal of Occupational Therapy, 14*, 25–32.

Dahlin-Ivanoff, S., Gosman-Hedström, G., Edberg, A.-K., Wilhelmson, K., Eklund, K., Duner, A., Zidén, L., Welmer, A.-K., & Landahl, S. (2010). Elderly persons in the risk zone: Design of a multidimensional, health-promoting, randomised three-armed controlled trial for 'prefrail' people of 80+ years living at home. *BMC Geriatrics, 10*, 27.

Dahlin-Ivanoff, S., Rydberg Sterner, T., Blennow, K., Skoog, I., & Falk Erhag, H. (2019). Was it worth it? Older adults' experiences of participating in a population-based cohort study: A focus group study. *BMC Geriatrics, 19*, 224.

Dewar, B. (2005). Beyond tokenistic involvement of older people in research: A framework for future development and understanding. *Journal of Clinical Neuroscience, 14*, 48–53.

Ebrahimi, Z., Wilhelmson, K., Eklund, K., Moore, C., & Jakobsson, A. (2013). Health despite frailty: Exploring influences on frail older adults' experiences of health. *Geriatric Nursing, 34*, 289–294.

Ebrahimi, Z., Dahlin-Ivanoff, S., Eklund, K., Jakobsson, A., & Wilhelmson, K. (2015). Self-rated health and health strengthens factors in community living frail elders. *Journal of Advanced Nursing, 71*, 825–836.

Ekelund, C., Dahlin-Ivanoff, S., & Eklund, K. (2014). Self-determination and older persons: A concept analysis. *Scandinavian Journal of Occupational Therapy, 21*, 116–124.

Fabbri, E., Zoli, M., Gonzalez-Freire, M., Salive, M., Studenski, S., & Ferrucci, L. (2015). Aging and multimorbidity: New tasks, priorities, and frontiers for integrated gerontological and clinical research. *Journal of the American Medical Directors Association, 16*, 640–647.

Fänge, A., & Dahlin-Ivanoff, S. (2009). The home is the hub of health in very old age: Findings from the ENABLE-AGE project. *Archives of Gerontology and Geriatrics, 48*, 340–345.

Ferrucci, L., Guralnik, J., Studenski, S., Fried, L., Cutler, G., & Walston, J. (2004). Designing randomized, controlled trials aimed at preventing or delaying functional decline and disability in frail, older persons: A consensus report. *Journal of the American Geriatrics Society, 52*, 625–634.

Fried, L., Tangen, C., Walston, J., Newman, A., Hirsch, C., Gottdiener, J., Seeman, T., Tracy, R., Kop, W., Burke, G., & McBurnie, M. (2001). Frailty in older adults: Evidence for a phenotype. *The Journals of Gerontology, 56*, M146–M156.

Fried, L., Ferrucci, L., Darer, J., Williamson, J., & Anderson, G. (2004). Untangling the concepts of disability, frailty, and comorbidity: Implications for improved targeting and care. *The Journals of Gerontology: Series A, Biology, 59*, 255–263.

Fulop, T., Larbi, A., Witkowski, J., McElhaney, J., Loeb, M., Mitnitski, A., & Pawelec, G. (2010). Aging, frailty and age-related diseases. *Biogerontology, 11*, 547–563.

Gustafsson, S., Lood, Q., Wilhelmson, K., Häggblom-Kronlöf, G., Landahl, S., & Dahlin-Ivanoff, S. (2015). A person-centred approach to health promotion for persons 70+ who have migrated to Sweden: Promoting aging migrants' capabilities implementation and RCT study protocol. *BMC Geriatrics, 15*, 10.

Haak, M., Fänge, A., Iwarsson, S., & Dahlin-Ivanoff, S. (2007). Home as a signification of independence and autonomy: Experiences among very old Swedish people. *Scandinavian Journal of Occupational Therapy, 14*, 16–24.

Häggblom-Kronlöf, G., Hultberg, J., Eriksson, B., & Sonn, U. (2007). Experiences of daily occupations at 99 years of age. *Scandinavian Journal of Occupational Therapy, 14*, 192–200.

Hanson, E., Magnusson, L., Arvidsson, H. A. K., Keady, J., & Nolan, M. (2007). Working together with persons with early stage dementia and their family members to design a user-friendly technology-based support service. *Dementia: The International Journal of Social Research and Practice, 6*, 411–434.

Hogan, D., MacKnight, C., & Bergman, H. (2003). Models, definitions, and criteria of frailty. *Aging Clinical and Experimental Research, 15*, 1–29.

Hussain-Gambles, M., Atkin, K., & Leese, B. (2004). Why ethnic minority groups are under-represented in clinical trials: A review of the literature. *Health & Social Care in the Community, 12*, 382–388.

Janlöv, A., Hallberg, I., & Petersson, K. (2006). Older persons' experience of being assessed for and receiving public home help: Do they have any influence over it? *Health & Social Care in the Community, 12*, 26–36.

Lally, F., & Crome, P. (2007). Understanding frailty. *Postgraduate Medical Journal, 83*, 16–20.

Mein, G., Seale, C., Rice, H., Johal, S., Ashcroft, R., Ellison, G., & Tinker, G. (2012). Altruism and participation in longitudinal health research? Insights from the Whitehall II study. *Social Science & Medicine, 75*, 2345–2352.

Morley, J., Vellas, B., Van Kan, G., Anker, S., Bauer, J., Bernabei, R., Cesari, M., Chumlea, W., Doehner, W., Evans, J., Fried, L., Guralnik, J., Katz, P., Malmstrom, T., McCarter, R., Guiterrez Robledo, L., Rockwood, K., Von Haehling, S., Vandewoude, M., & Walston, J. (2013). Frailty consensus: A call to action. *Journal of the American Medical Directors Association, 14*, 392–397.

Ottenvall Hammar, I., Dahlin-Ivanoff, S., Wilhelmson, K., & Eklund, K. (2014a). Shifting between self-governing and being governed: A qualitative study of older persons' self-determination. *BMC Geriatrics, 14*, 126.

Ottenvall Hammar, I., Ekelund, C., Wilhelmson, K., & Eklund, K. (2014b). Impact on participation and autonomy: Test of validity and reliability for older persons. *Health Psychology, 2*, 68–73.

Ottenvall Hammar, I., Dahlin-Ivanoff, S., Wilhelmson, K., & Eklund, K. (2015). People dependent on support in daily activities perceives reduced self-determination: A cross-sectional study with community-dwelling older persons. *Quality in Ageing, 16*, 208–221.

Ottenvall Hammar, I., Dahlin-Ivanoff, S., Wilhelmson, K., & Eklund, K. (2016). Self-determination among community-dwelling older persons: Explanatory factors. *Scandinavian Journal of Occupational Therapy, 23*, 198–206.

Reuben, D. (1998). Warning signs along the road to functional dependency. *Annals of Internal Medicine, 128*, 138–139.

SBU. (2014). *Comprehensive geriatric assessment and care of frail elderly* (SBU report no 221 (in Swedish)). SBU.

Sen, A. (1985). Well-being, agency and freedom: The Dewey lectures 1984. *Journal of Philosophy, 82*, 169–221.

Sen, A. (1993). Capability and Well-being. In M. Nussbaum & A. Sen (Eds.), *The quality of life* (pp. 1–30). Clarendon Press.

Sonn, U. (1996). Longitudinal studies of dependence in daily life activities among elderly persons. *Scandinavian Journal of Rehabilitation Medicine. Supplement, 34*, 1–35.

Townsend, A., & Cox, S. (2013). Accessing health services through the back door: A qualitative interview study investigating reasons why people participate in health research in Canada. *BMC Med Ethics, 14*(40), Web.

Chapter 9
eHealth Literacy and Capability in the Context of the Pandemic Crisis

Dimitrios Kokkinakis

9.1 Introduction

This chapter presents an approach to eHealth literacy (eHL) inspired by research that uses the concept of capability as its point of departure. It highlights the importance of paying analytical attention to a wide range of variables related to older people's everyday lives in the face of the COVID-19 pandemic. The capability approach is a broad normative framework developed during the 1980s and onwards by the Indian philosopher, economist and Nobel laureate Amartya Sen (1999), and further developed by the philosopher Martha Nussbaum (2013). Capability or Capabilities are broadly understood as 'the individual's ability to perform actions in order to reach goals he or she has reason to value'. To achieve health equality and maintain good health under rapidly changing circumstances caused by, for example, a pandemic, and particularly in later life, there is a need to improve the potential for maximising individuals' capabilities, at both the societal and individual levels. The capability approach can be operationalised differently in different contexts, allowing individuals control over their own lives by taking into account the intersections of diversity, such as age and gender. The capability approach can offer a framework for the holistic conceptualisation of the importance of language and eHealth (literacy), stressing the importance of eHealth being inclusive and that eHL receives the necessary attention in order to minimise the risk of inducing or increasing health inequalities (Thulesius, 2020). It also offers an alternative paradigm which recognises that not all individuals will or can participate or benefit from the advice and recommendations given by public health agencies, expert committees, health

D. Kokkinakis (✉)
Department of Swedish, University of Gothenburg, Gothenburg, Sweden

Centre for Ageing and Health – AgeCap, University of Gothenburg, Gothenburg, Sweden
e-mail: dimitrios.kokkinakis@svenska.gu.se

H. Falk Erhag et al. (eds.), *A Multidisciplinary Approach to Capability in Age and Ageing*, International Perspectives on Aging 31,
https://doi.org/10.1007/978-3-030-78063-0_9

managers and politicians in the same manner, nor can they generate the same or similar advantages in difficult circumstances, or life in general.

This chapter is divided into six main sections. The next section focuses on the notions of health literacy and eHL, highlighting the possible differences and commonalities and linking them to the capability framework, without going into a detailed discussion of the underlying theory. This section ends by discussing eHL in the pandemic scenario's paradoxical consequence of the infodemic, and how the scope of eHL can be enhanced in the light of experiences gained from COVID-19. Based on the three societal levels of AgeCap, i.e. micro, meso and macro, the third section explores eHealth within this research landscape, taking into consideration the application potential of eHL in this particular context. Methodological considerations and approaches that address eHL assessment and evaluation in general, and in the light of COVID-19 in particular, follow (Sect. 9.4). The chapter continues with a discussion and remarks on future perspectives on eHL within the COVID-19 pandemic scenario (Sect. 9.5), and Sect. 9.6 rounds off the chapter by presenting key take-home messages and conclusions.

9.2 Health Literacy and eHealth Literacy

9.2.1 Definitions and the Operationalisation of eHL

Although the definition of the broader term 'literacy' remains an open-ended question (Addey, 2017), health literacy has been defined in numerous overlapping and evolving ways. For instance, Mårtensson and Hensing (2012) identify two approaches to health literacy; one associated with the individual basic skills that are needed to understand health information and one that recognises a wide range of interactive skills within social and cultural contexts. In a series of papers, Sørensen (2019) and Sørensen et al. (2012, 2015) define health literacy as the knowledge, motivation and set of abilities required to access, understand, process, evaluate and use (basic) health information (and services) (from reliable sources) in order to make judgements and appropriate health decisions within the domains of healthcare, disease prevention and health promotion. All of this is in order to maintain or improve quality of life during the whole life course. Moreover, the rapid digitisation of healthcare and the wide availability of web-based and mobile health applications entail that in recent years health information has been increasingly sought through online and socially networked platforms (Dalmer, 2017). New competencies or 'literacies' are thus required in order to use such facilities properly and navigate effectively through the information space. These skills, required in additional to health literacy, are referred to as eHealth literacy (eHL) or electronic/digital health literacy. Thus, eHL is defined as 'the ability to seek, find, understand, and appraise health information from electronic sources and apply the knowledge gained to addressing or solving a health problem' (Norman & Skinner, 2006:2). Since eHL comprises both general health literacy and digital skills, the correlation between eHL and health literacy is often moderate, exemplified by the fact that the various available instruments partly measure different skills (Neter et al., 2015). Norman and Skinner (2006) proposed a model that describes eHL as a combination of six different skills that are required to optimise patients' experiences with eHealth, namely:

analytical, i.e. skills required to participate in daily informational life:
'computer literacy' (to operate and use various digital devices),
'health literacy' (to perform tasks within the healthcare environment),
'scientific literacy' (the basic understanding of science-based information and concepts)
context-specific, i.e. skills centred on specific issues, problem types and contexts:
'information literacy' (knowledge about potential resources to consult),
'media literacy' (ability to critically assess media content and its sources),
'traditional literacy and numeracy' (the basic skills of reading and comprehension).

In recent years, health researchers have been expanding their scope to examine an even broader range of (literacy) skills, such as 'communication' (Norman, 2011; Rubin, 2017). Nevertheless, Norman (2011) proclaims that, although different contexts may introduce new challenges to building eHL, the core skills that form eHL are unlikely to change. Although general health literacy is an important aspect of public health, eHL has become a fast-emerging area of concern, especially in the era of the COVID-19 pandemic crisis. The pandemic puts more emphasis on some of these skills, particularly digital literacy, and the urge to make all of our social contacts digital. This has created a digital gap, whereby people who are not confident or competent in using digital technologies have been excluded from social connections, with negative consequences. The consequences of this social isolation have made it more difficult to access support with technology that would enable older people to connect digitally with family and friends (cf. Rosenberg et al., 2020).

Moreover, eHL is not like conventional literacy because we must invest fairly regularly in hardware and software, while at the same time continuously learning new things, because applications and interfaces are constantly changing. This can easily become a barrier for older people. Olsson et al. (2019) note that access to information and communication technology and literacy are strongly associated with resources, which decline with age, so that both access and literacy become a question of age and we cannot assume that contemporary 55-year-olds will remain equally included at the age of 85 or 95. Such insights must be taken into account by policymakers because those who do not update their technology will be gradually excluded.

If one of the ideas about how to solve problems associated with an ageing population is to make more extensive use of digitalized public services and e-healthcare, then an awareness of the fact that such policies have significant limitations is essential. For a substantial proportion of older people, digitalization appears, in reality, to be a much less viable option. (Olsson et al., 2019: 68–69).

A solution could be to pay additional attention to older people's everyday practices by specifically looking into the ways in which digital media are used and how. This could be achieved by conducting more in-depth surveys and interviews among older adult populations. This is likely to yield a better understanding of how current digital health information-seeking and sharing behaviours influence health-related decision-making.

9.2.2 eHealth Literacy and Capability

The capability approach describes the quality of life and well-being that individuals are able to achieve. In order to access such determinants, we should measure the abilities to achieve those 'beings and doings' that people have reason to value in life (Sen, 1993). Thus, the capability framework consists of all those internal (not readily observable, e.g. basic abilities and competences) and external (observable actions/skills, e.g. social norms, and the physical and social environment, such as work opportunities and a tolerant and secure political, economic and legal framework for action) factors that are necessary for a specific case of doing or being something.

Language barriers and low (eHealth) literacy at several levels (e.g. computer or scientific), as well as inadequate institutional and cultural competence, such as a lack of culturally competent healthcare providers,[1] create obstacles to accessing and comprehending health information (Houwink et al., 2020). Therefore, an important internal factor affecting capability is the degree to which individuals have the capacity to obtain, process and understand basic health information and the services needed to make appropriate health-related decisions. Such information spans a broad range of important healthcare issues; for instance, by following instructions from a healthcare provider to manage the official recommendations of healthcare specialists before accepting them; or the ability to link knowledge about the potential health benefits and harms of particular behaviours and interventions for health outcomes.

More broadly, literacy has been given considerable attention in the work of Amartya Sen and Martha Nussbaum. According to Maddox (2008), Sen positions literacy within the hard core of 'basic capabilities', while Nussbaum includes literacy within her list of 'central human capabilities'; that is, internal factors that constitute a person's fundamental health (Tengland, 2020). Nowadays, a range of technology-based health tools and a range of devices for online connection and interaction permeate daily life, while the Internet has become an infrastructure for all kinds of services. With this in mind, we can stipulate that the more specific, subordinate aspects of literacy previously outlined, namely health literacy and eHealth

[1] For instance, one Swedish study showed that over 60% of newly arrived refugees had low health literacy (Wångdahl et al., 2014).

literacy, are now also important and necessary core capabilities and functioning, necessary for human well-being and attaining a good life (cf. Sen, 2003). Various studies have highlighted the fact that limited health literacy and low-level eHL has consequences for the healthcare system at a macro level and is associated with poor health at the micro, a.k.a. personal, level (Abrams & Farrell, 2011). Thus, healthcare providers and organisations need to be more active in developing and employing strategies to meet the language and literacy needs of diverse populations, including via online or other means of communication. For that matter, older adults' ability to perceive, comprehend and produce language has been an active area of interest to researchers in recent years. As such, eHL may be the means for achieving the goal of empowering people to make the right health-related decisions. According to various research studies (e.g. Jacobs et al., 2014; Geboers et al., 2016; Chesser et al., 2016), people with limited health literacy skills have less knowledge about their illness and its management. They tend to have higher rates of hospitalisation and readmission; are more likely to skip important preventive measures; enter the healthcare system when they are sicker; and make greater use of services designed to treat complications of disease and less use of services designed to prevent complications. Furthermore, the unforeseen consequences caused by the pandemic are accelerating research and development based on the importance of eHL and provoking a need to quickly and creatively re-think our modes of healthcare delivery. This includes embracing eHealth resources that connect care through the Internet and related technologies (Brøns et al., 2020). According to Fraser and Greenhalgh (2001) being capable can help an individual be adaptable, feel motivated and thus have resilience to stay through "tough times". Consequently, capability offers a 'promise for striking the delicate balance between paternalism and autonomy' (Ruger, 2010:41). In this context, paternalism is the practice of the state interfering with the choices of an individual with the justification that the individual or population will be better off or protected from harm (e.g. lockdown-imposed isolation). Autonomy, based on Sen's view, is to live one's life according to one's own reasons and motivations and to have the ability to perform actions in order to reach goals that he or she has reason to value.

9.2.3 Pandemic, Infodemic and eHealth Literacy

Variations in eHL have been attributed to multiple determinants, ranging from education and older age to socioeconomic status (Garcia-Codina et al., 2019). Likewise, such variation is expected for pandemic-related eHL.[2] The prevalence of covid-19 in socio-economically disadvantaged areas suggests that the consequences of the

[2] In Stockholm, for example, the lack of information about COVID-19 adapted for people with a foreign background has, among other things, been highlighted in the media as a contributing factor to the large number of infections in some social groups. According to the Stockholm Region, the incidence of COVID-19 cases was up to three times higher in the municipalities of Rinkeby-Kista

disease (including mortality) follow a socio-economic gradient (USA Today, 2020; ITV news, 2020). An understanding of the levels and determinants of pandemic-related eHL is essential to enable healthcare policymakers to formulate optimal strategies for the effective communication of critical medical information during the COVID-19 crisis and future pandemics. COVID-19 required targeted public information campaigns and the promotion of eHL at the population-based level for better navigation of the massively produced information space. This, in turn, created an infodemic (information epidemic), widespread false information, rumours and misleading health news on the Internet and social media platforms. According to Zarocostas (2020), the infodemic made it hard for everyone, and in particular the elderly population and suburban minority communities, to find trustworthy sources of information and reliable guidance when they needed it. The infodemic poses a significant threat to public health; for example, too much information can create confusion while at the same time vital behavioural changes need to be communicated in an understandable, transparent and consistent manner (Rubin & Wessely, 2020). Thus, eHL can play a crucial role in enabling people to navigate the COVID-19 information environments and can aid informed decision-making about ways to address and prevent COVID-19.

Low eHL, particularly among older adults, is a critical determinant for reaching good and effective health outcomes. eHL focuses on individual capability and does imply that some skills are needed (Jacobs et al., 2014). In today's information and technology-rich healthcare environments, web-based and mobile applications are important for the dissemination of critical pandemic-related information. According to the United Nations (2020), the Internet and other digital technologies have become a window to the world during lockdown, enabling people to connect with family and friends. Moreover, in order for confidence in online health information and participation to increase (Ek et al., 2013), eHL needs to be constantly improved and thoughtfully considered. Inability to follow recommendations due to language and literacy barriers and a resultant lower use of preventative care measures may lead to increased costs and poorer outcomes.

Our eHL capabilities strengthen our capacity to be well informed about risks and recommendations and, ideally, to engage in solidarity-based behaviours in order to achieve improved public health (Paakkari & Okan, 2020). Still, many older people have limited access to digital technologies and lack the necessary skills to fully exploit them. Even in developed countries, older adults living in institutions might also struggle to receive the necessary support to connect with their loved ones. Moreover, the older population is extremely diverse in many ways, from ability and age, to income and culture, and older people face numerous barriers, commonly related to language and eHL, which have been amplified during the pandemic. Therefore, using a variety of other communication formats, such as radio broadcasts and text messages, may ensure that critical information about measures to protect

---

and Tensta-Spånga (areas with a very high percentage of foreign-born population) than in the rest of Stockholm County (Tao, 2020).

themselves from COVID-19 and how to access services reaches older people. Xie et al. (2020) point out that, to be effective, digital public health campaigns need to be linguistically and culturally attuned to such populations, and they recommend a number of actions. For instance: to develop digitally delivered training and interventions to improve older adults' eHL that are scalable and can be deployed rapidly; to develop informatics tools that are operational with basic technologies like telephones and work with low or intermittent Internet availability; and to train community health workers to be brokers of information, culture and technology for socially isolated (ethnic minority) older adults. According to Sentell et al. (2020:2), eHL is urgently needed by the public to be able to 'synthesize, analyze, and appraise the vast amount of urgent, complex, and even conflicting information from virologists, epidemiologists, data modelers, doctors, nurses, health departments, and the media'. Although at the time of writing it is too early to have gold-standard instruments to evaluate pandemic-related eHL, some initiatives seem to be starting to take shape (cf. Sect. 9.4.3).

9.2.4 The Scope of eHealth Literacy in the Pandemic Scenario

The COVID-19 crisis has provided new opportunities to make eHealth sustainable and constitutes the best time to overcome cultural challenges, update regulations and improve interoperability between systems that has held back eHealth solutions and adoption for years (cf. Studzinski, 2020). COVID-19 has also created an urgent need to rapidly assess pandemic-related eHL by, for example, developing up-to-date, validated and standardised questionnaires. eHL is vital to both slowing down the spread of this virus and mitigating its impact and effects, by making informed decisions about ways to address and prevent the disease. Little research is currently available regarding the effects of older adults' social isolation, their use of the Internet and social media to locate and evaluate health information, or the factors that influence their eHL and use of electronic information sources and other digital technologies for accessing and using health information. Further research is necessary to investigate the temporal relationship between COVID-19-related psychological well-being and the impact of the pandemic on mental health, such as anxiety, depression or suicidality, and whether psychological stressors during the pandemic persist well past the end of the outbreak (Chew et al., 2020; Kivi et al., 2020). Public leaders and policymakers need to be aware of these determinants and cautious about them when formulating and updating the dissemination strategies of critical pandemic-related information and interventions. More studies are required to evaluate the outcomes associated with pandemic-related eHL, taking account of the processes of seeking health information, and understanding, judging and applying such information. As previously outlined, this can be achieved by compensating for low eHL by adapting oral and written information into plain language and providing visual support and audio/video versions of the communication, thus balancing the depth of the information provided (see Sect. 9.4.1).

9.3 eHealth Literacy and the Three Societal Levels of AgeCap

eHealth literacy is a research area relating to the three main societal levels that form the core of capability in ageing within the AgeCap framework, as indicated in accordingly in the introductory chapter of this book. To address (low) eHL, as previously discussed, we believe that there are three common-sense ways of considering the notion. Namely, (i) the macro level (with an emphasis on the organisational and policy components); (ii) the meso level (with an emphasis on technological resources) and (iii) the micro level (with an emphasis on socioeconomic factors and individual and interpersonal strengths and behaviours). These three levels overlap, and the model represents an oversimplification, but it provides a shared framework for understanding eHL.

The organisational and policy level, or the macro level. The digitisation of society at all levels affects what an individual can, should or prefers to do, and requires knowledge about how to handle, navigate and become a citizen of the digital world. For instance, how to access healthcare services and what literacy skills are required should be part of the laws and regulations to be enforced for all citizens of all ages (Zanobini et al., 2020). Political decisions, laws and regulations affect all the determinants of healthcare, including eHL. According to Brach (2017), for instance, a health-literate healthcare organisation is one that makes it easy for people to navigate, understand and use its information and services to take care of their own health. Brach also makes it clear that, even for pioneering organisations in health literacy, the opportunities for improvement are vast.

The technological resources and technological competence level, i.e. the meso level, is a necessity, acting as a 'glue' that develops, supports, enhances and promotes both (i) and (iii) (below). For instance, caring facilities and smart-home environments for older adults that support health, or the availability of suitable hardware and Internet access that can be both costly and even unavailable to older adults in many cases. In a survey of Swedish people aged 65–85, Olsson et al. (2019) showed that 80% of the respondents have some kind of device (mobile smartphone, laptop or tablet). Although the proportion of older people with access to such devices is higher in Sweden than in many other countries, Olsson et al. showed that the technological opportunities for this group are limited and dependent on various determinants, such as socioeconomic status, whereby increasing income increases the degree of access to information and communication. Their study also demonstrated that eHL is an important factor that explains sociodemographic effects such as age, education and household income on self-efficacy in utilising eHealth and frequency of eHealth information evaluation.

The individual and interpersonal level, i.e. the micro level. There is no health promotion and thus no health without eHL. Information transmission (digital or not) is not enough, other features such as cognitive functioning and the digital skills of information-seeking and decision-making need to be taught and practised. Furthermore, interventions aimed at promoting preventive health behaviours to avoid exposure to and transmission of COVID-19 must consider an individual's ability to receive, interpret and apply healthcare recommendations, according to their functional capacities, such as communication and social context. To ensure that older people understand what public health experts and politicians are saying or trying to convey poses significant challenges and the high degree of knowledge uncertainty at many levels makes COVID-19 news and official recommendations even more challenging. A major issue relates to concern about how the individual can integrate this sea of information into personal behavioural actions (Abel & McQueen, 2020). In fact, some organisational stereotype-based decisions reinforce existing social inequalities related to factors such as ageism, which can lead to frustration, isolation and hopelessness. Older adults are a diverse and heterogeneous group. Fraser et al. (2020:2) note that the ageist attitudes circulating during COVID-19 make some people think that 'the pandemic is an older person's problem'. In addition, many countries, including Sweden, chose to impose stricter restrictions on older adults, ordering them to remain at home during the pandemic.[3] These policies have often translated into patronising public communications depicting all older adults as 'vulnerable' members of society, while the fact may be that health professionals and policymakers lack eHL awareness and knowledge, since vulnerability could be just the result of limited financial resources, reduced mobility and/or social isolation.

Thus, a combination of all three levels outlined above is required in order to meet the unique needs and demands of eHL and facilitate an understanding of older people's perspectives and their capability to maintain good health, independence and well-being.

9.4 Methodological Considerations

9.4.1 Tailoring Information and Plain Language

In order to achieve better outcomes, the delivery of healthcare information needs to be tailored to meet older adults' health literacy needs and more must be invested in substantial technological and educational efforts. Also, developing or adapting computer-based instruments to screen older individuals accessing eHealth applications should be more highly prioritised. Computer-based algorithms that incorporate cultural and linguistic adaptations, for example (simplified) plain language (such as using familiar words and getting to the point quickly), and take a person's specific goals or needs into account, in addition to characteristics such as age, gender, ethnicity and reading ability, might prove efficacious. Therefore, plain language

[3] Nearly 10 months after the COVID-19 outbreak began (22 October 2020), the Swedish Public Health Agency's general advice for people aged 70 years or older was changed, and people aged 70 years or older are now covered by the general advice that applies to everyone.

is a strategy for making written (and even oral) information easier to understand the first time it is read or heard (cf. health.gov 2015). Moreover, relevant technology has become available and boosted by several factors, such as the increasing interest in the accessibility and usability of digital health information, and the need to provide equal access and equal opportunity for people with diverse disabilities. In this respect, the roles of various available assistive technologies based on artificial intelligence and natural language processing have gained considerable importance, and there has been a growing number of scientific events targeting these questions. Examples include: the International Conference on Computers Helping People with Special Needs[4] (ICCHP); Speech and Language Processing for Assistive Technologies[5] (SLPAT); the International ACM Conference on Computers and Accessibility[6] (ASSETS); and the Workshop on Natural Language Processing for COVID-19[7] (NLP-COVID). However, available language resources and tools to develop such assistive technologies for older adults are scarce, and for frail older adults, i.e. persons who are experiencing a decline in human functioning (physical, psychological and social), even scarcer.[8]

In a more timely manner, the format and language of COVID-19 information also needs to evolve in order for it to be easy for older people to find, understand and use. Plain language principles offer a useful model for creating clear and concise written and verbal content. Natural language processing can play an important role in aspects such as readability assessments and improved textual accessibility through an understanding of a system's information flows and data practices, while tailoring to different audiences with concise, relevant, actionable and plain-text information is a practice that can be supported with existing technology (Kloehn et al., 2018). Thus, improving access to (digital or written) language is a central issue and the WHO (2020) has proposed several key principles for improving the understanding of health-related content. This is the case for health-related information that should be accessible to all members of society. Older adults, for instance, may have problems with technical jargon, scientific terms or search engines that do not return suitable results, or they may not be able to discern the quality of the information presented. Techniques for automatic text simplification and normalisation are available (Saggion, 2017) and can be targeted towards eHealth applications.

[4] https://www.icchp.org/

[5] http://www.slpat.org/

[6] https://dl.acm.org/action/doSearch?AllField=International+ACM+Conference+on+Computers+and+Accessibility

[7] https://openreview.net/group?id=aclweb.org/ACL/2020/Workshop/NLP-COVID

[8] A positive example moving in this direction was the Swedish government's decision in June 2020 to give extra funds to invest in digital solutions that can prevent the social exclusion of older people. According to Rosenberg et al. (2020), this resulted in some (Swedish) nursing homes revealing a tendency towards more 'spectacular' technological solutions, such as the use of a Yetitablet, a 65-inch Android tablet that is the equivalent of a large flat screen TV. This is a device that, according to Rosenberg et al., seems to be appreciated by care home residents, but a lack of competence among staff and some technical problems resulted in only a few being able to use this assistive technology.

Thus, insufficient eHL can be reduced through increasing readability and comprehension by reducing the complexity of a text. Furthermore, developing more pictorial, audio and video content, instead of only presenting information in written format, became apparent as a complementary and efficient communication strategy to convey information about COVID-19.

9.4.2 *Training and Screening*

Screening instruments and evidence-based interventions can provide healthcare administrators and older adults with the necessary tools to reduce health disparities attributed to low eHL (Jacobs et al., 2014). Technological alternatives, such as audio-visual content (pictorial, diagrammatic, audio and video), in multilingual, interactive edutainment systems, available on a television screen or user-friendly web interfaces designed specifically for those with limited eHL, could allow older people to learn more about their conditions and how to take care of themselves.

Undoubtedly, eHL plays a crucial role in navigating the COVID-19 information environments. The importance of analytical strategies to measure the effectiveness of computer-based linguistic and culturally appropriate automated tailoring applications and eHL has already been stressed (Sentell et al., 2020). When time permits, society needs to invest more in technology education and provide continuous support, consultations and learning of best practices in the new technologies at libraries, education centres, seniors' union facilities and the like. Additional training is also required for specific older adult sub-groups to improve their digital literacy prior to eHealth interventions. Knowledge about technology can improve engagement and receptivity towards technological changes, which is crucial if digital interventions are to succeed (Mohammadyari & Singh, 2015). Innovative technologies, such as touch screens (see footnote 8), sign-language interpreting services, and easy and clearly navigable websites, could help older adults to use the Internet to access health information. The NHS, for instance, recently launched its 'Digital Apps Library', a platform designed to bring together a number of digital tools that can be used for health and care, designed in a clear and easy to navigate way so that 'people of all ages and digital ability can move around it' (NHS, 2021). Also, the largest freely available collection of tools associated with the measurement or screening of (e)health literacy is the 'Health Literacy Tool Shed' database.[9] As of this writing (mid-2020), the Tool Shed includes more than 200 tools.

Nevertheless, there will always be a segment of the population for whom information, however simplified, will still be difficult to fully comprehend and to whom tools and applications are inaccessible due to technological barriers. High-tech applications cannot completely replace face-to-face interaction for some older adults who need extra help (Bickmore et al., 2010), but technology is rapidly

[9] https://healthliteracy.bu.edu/

maturing, and with appropriate coaching this can be feasible to a certain extent. Public authorities should offer their elderly residents opportunities to improve their digital skills and also involve older people in the design of technology. Some municipalities in Sweden[10] have already taken the initiative to employ IT coaches who train and help the elderly with digital technology. These activities should be evaluated and disseminated on a much larger scale. Usability research conducted with older (frail) adults and their use of online health information resources and comprehensive and diagnostic measures of eHL are necessary. This can be accomplished by the validation of new (composite) scales and computer-based tools to assess eHL, which could evaluate older adults' familiarity with the Internet as reflected, in part, by the time spent online, and assess older adults' navigational knowledge and skills in using the Internet, specific to the use of eHealth applications (Watkins & Xie, 2014). eHL screening in healthcare settings would be a beneficial tool in the care of older adults (Collins et al., 2012). For instance, eHL could be a way to measure older people's ability to understand basic hygiene practices to protect themselves, along with basic age-appropriate facts and information, including symptoms, complications, transmission and prevention. Paying attention to older people's eHL is key to improving health outcomes and lessening the impact of a pandemic at both the individual and societal levels (Brørs et al., 2020), enabling stakeholders to tailor eHealth applications to user needs.

9.4.3 *Instruments and Measures*

Health literacy is measured through both performance and self-report (Collins et al., 2012), but there is a much smaller range of tools available for assessing consumers' levels of eHL and no consensus on the most appropriate eHL measure. Existing scales vary in terms of evaluation approach and administration time, while some require considerable amounts of technical equipment; therefore, their main use has been in exploratory research or for the validation of self-rating instruments (Quinn et al., 2017).

The eHealth Literacy Scale (eHEALS), developed by Norman and Skinner (2006), is designed to capture the six different aspects of eHL already discussed (Sect. 9.2.1). eHEALS measures perceived knowledge, skills and confidence in locating, evaluating and using electronic health information in order to make health-related decisions. However, factors such as information or operational and strategic Internet competencies are not included in this instrument (van der Vaart et al., 2011). Identified gaps are addressed by the eHealth Literacy Framework (eHLF), developed by Norgaard et al. (2015). eHLF, for instance, measures the ability to engage with digital services (e.g. navigation skills); the ability to 'feel safe and in control' (e.g. trust in the information available on the Internet); and the domain

[10] https://seniornet.se/

of digital services that suits individual needs (e.g. the language, interface, relevance of information, its quality and simplicity of language). Variations of eHEALS also include the eHealth Literacy Assessment Toolkit (eHLA) developed by Furstrand and Kayser (2015), which measures 'functional health literacy' (i.e. reading comprehension and numeracy skills in a health context); 'familiarity with technology' and 'technology confidence'. The Digital Health Literacy Instrument (DHLI) developed by van der Vaart and Drossaert (2017) uses a set of items in response to the need for more objective measures of eHL, such as 'operational skills', 'navigation skills', 'information searching skills' and 'adding self-generated content'. According to van der Vaart and Drossaert, previous eHL measurement instruments have measured only competencies related to searching for and using online health information, while DHLI was designed to pay more attention to interactivity on the Internet. The eHealth Literacy Questionnaire (eHLQ), a multidimensional tool based on the eHLF, has been used to understand and evaluate people's interactions with digital health services (Kayser et al., 2018). The eHLQ captures dimensions that describe the attributes of the users, the intersection between users and the technologies and users' experience of systems. Finally, the Transactional eHealth Literacy Instrument (TeHLI) is one of the most recent measures of eHL (Paige et al., 2019). eHL is operationalised through four literacies; namely: (1) 'functional eHL' (basic skills in reading and writing/typing about health); (2) 'communicative eHL' (the ability to collaborate, adapt and control communication about health with users in social online environments); (3) 'critical eHL' (the ability to evaluate the credibility, relevance and risks of sharing and receiving health information on the Internet); and (4) 'translational eHL' (the highest cognitive level of eHL, informed and built upon the three previous dimensions). For a review of other related tools, such as the Health Literacy Screening Question Methodologies (HLSQM) and the Brief Health Literacy Screeners (BHLS), see Pleasant et al. (2019).

Tests are not always transferable to other languages, cultures or linguistic contexts. The best thinkable scenario is the one that can facilitate comparisons and generalisations and thus use internationally developed tools that can be applied to several languages (Mantwill et al., 2018). A good example is the European Health Literacy Survey Questionnaire (HLS-EU-Q). This is an efficient instrument for measuring comprehensive health literacy. Since its original version, which contained 86 variables, shorter forms have been developed, with 47 or 16 measurable indicators; the latter being the HLS-EU-Q16, which has been adapted for use in the Swedish language.

Currently, there are no gold-standard instruments to evaluate pandemic-related eHL, only health literacy. Okan et al. (2020) proposed COVID-19-related health literacy measures and developed a tool for assessing coronavirus-related health literacy in population surveys (HLS-COVID-Q22). In a cross-sectional online survey, Okan et al. (2020) found that confusion about COVID-19 information was significantly higher among those who had lower eHL. Wolf et al. (2020) evaluated the health literacy related to COVID-19 among high-risk populations, such as the elderly, and found varying levels of pandemic-related health literacy. In their study of COVID-19 awareness and attitudes among chronic disease patients in the USA, it was particularly alarming to note that one-third of participants were unable to identify symptoms associated with COVID-19, and roughly one-quarter of participants felt that they were unlikely to be infected by the virus.

9.5 Discussion

In this brief scoping review (Munn et al., 2018), we have provided an overview of eHL and its relation to the extraordinary circumstances arising from the COVID-19 pandemic, positioning older people's empowerment and well-being at the forefront. The theoretical framework that the study has tried to assess is the capability approach to eHL, a theory that can be operationalised differently in different contexts. The study has touched upon some of the mechanisms that can be applied in this area, pinpointing the fact that the eHL challenge is a shared responsibility between the health sector, civil society and policymakers. In this respect, eHL should be at the top of the agenda in discussions about healthcare (Brørs et al., 2020) and successful implementation of e-health interventions (e.g. devices and their implementation) should be tailored to target different attitudes, needs and preferences, with a strong focus on information and support for older adults. Reiners et al. (2019) summarise these needs as follows: the eHealth devices should be personalised and tailored to the target user group; easy access to the Internet should be provided and family members should be involved in the use of the eHealth devices. Although there is a rising trend of supporting eHealth, older people, including in Sweden, describe feelings of ambivalence, raising 'concerns [about] accessibility to health care, mistrust in poor IT systems or impaired abilities to cope with technology' (Milos Nymberg et al., 2019: 50). Improving eHL at an individual and population level is therefore a priority area for research (Car et al., 2017). This is indirectly mirrored in the Swedish government's vision ('Vision e-health 2025', 2016), which states that by 2025 Sweden will be the best in the world at using the possibilities of digitalisation in order to (a) facilitate people to achieve good and equal health and welfare and (b) develop and strengthen their own resources for increased independence and participation in community life.

The older population is an incredibly diverse group, with chronological age being only loosely correlated to biological age. Healthcare providers must recognise the individual eHL capabilities of older adults and tailor their approach to meet their specific needs. COVID-19 has forced a major step-change in utilising eHealth and revealed the necessity for better navigation of information environments during the infodemic (Okan et al., 2020). However, seeking information on the Internet can be especially complex because it requires general knowledge about the topic of interest, basic knowledge of hardware and software operations, information-seeking skills (e.g., knowledge of how a web page's content is organised) and the ability to judge whether information sources are credible. It is thus of critical importance that healthcare providers take into consideration the older population's eHL skills in order to promote a higher degree of activation and support for the elderly to self-manage their own mental and physical health during a pandemic. It is also essential that policies, programmes and communications provide a differentiated, undistorted picture of the impact of the pandemic on older people and their contribution to the response to ensure they are not being stigmatised. As this chapter has highlighted, greater access to reliable health information is not necessarily achieved if it is in written form or plain language alone. Organisations should develop content in various formats, recognising that pictorial, audio and video content is easier for many people to access and absorb (United Nations, 2020). The literature points out that there is a need for more research into the intersection of the social determinants of health in the preparation for, response during and recovery from a pandemic. It is also imperative that future research is undertaken to evaluate levels of eHL among various groups of older people and to extend our knowledge about each of the relevant determinants in order to devise solutions to address the risk factors and assist decision-makers in their attempts to meet the identified needs of populations who are negatively affected by a pandemic. For instance, health authorities and policymakers should routinely conduct eHL reports to assess the preparedness of individuals and societies for any disease outbreak and to strengthen the public health environment and policies (Abdel-Latif, 2020).

Sen's theory aims to expand individual capability (Sen, 1999). It is recommended to examine how eHL is performed in large longitudinal studies after the first wave of the pandemic is over. Moreover, the terms used to describe high-risk groups are important, particularly in terms of framing vulnerability. As in the case of previous pandemics, most people prefer not to be labelled 'vulnerable' and, as O'Sullivan and Bourgoin (2010:22) emphasise, 'part of promoting resiliency is providing empowerment. Being at risk does not necessarily imply vulnerability, if appropriate supports are available.' Therefore, it is important to pay additional attention to older people's everyday practices. In-depth surveys and interviews among older adult populations are likely to yield a better understanding of how current digital health information-seeking and sharing behaviours influence health-related decision-making. Specifically, we need to look into the ways in which digital media are used (Olsson et al., 2019), using both statistical measurements and data derived from interviews and observations of the everyday lives of older people. In addition, older people should be involved early in the design of technology. Among other things, this would offer researchers the opportunity to also listen to and analyse their own reflections on what it means to grow older in a digitalising society and, particularly, in the context of a pandemic.

9.6 Conclusions

In this chapter, we have identified and described an important factor in the context of the incorporation of eHealth into social and healthcare services for older people; namely, of eHL and its relation to health-promoting behaviours among older adults within the capability approach. We have further examined some aspects and research highlighting the importance and direct correlation between eHL and quality of life for older adults in the capability context. Finally, we used the COVID-19 pandemic as a context within which to specifically and explicitly discuss the opportunities, challenges and future directions for rapidly developing, scaling up and enhancing eHealth for the benefit of older people. Previous research has identified the lack of eHL among older people as a significant barrier to the integration of informatics content into the healthcare context. The capability approach may offer a framework for the holistic conceptualisation of barriers and solutions to problems faced, regardless of whether these are language or technology dependent, and also provide mechanisms and tools for increasing the capacity of each individual in order to reach goals that he or she has reason to value. Further research on eHL is required in order to facilitate a better understanding of the information needs of older people; for instance, how they seek and use information about COVID-19. Of equal importance is the political attention that must be given to policies supporting the enhancement of eHL in order to avoid future risks and problems due to the impact of rumours and misinformation by providing easy-to-access and easy-to-use information. We also need to explore possible alternative ways to support older people in their use of the technologies they want and need to use in their everyday lives.

The limitations of this scoping review are derived from the low availability of rigorous scientific evidence on the topic of eHL within the pandemic framework, although for the time being there is an intense flow of COVID-19-related information and research in this direction. Therefore, the choice of methodology can be justified because it attempts to clarify some concepts and broaden the scope of eHL. Moreover, justification can also be established based on the growing body of various kinds of scientific literature about the lack of stable recommendations with a risk of biased information.

References

Abdel-Latif, M. (2020). The enigma of health literacy and COVID-19 pandemic. *Public Health, 185*, 95–96. https://doi.org/10.1016/j.puhe.2020.06.030

Abel, T., & McQueen, D. (2020). Critical health literacy and the COVID-19 crisis. *Health Promotion International*, 1–2. https://doi.org/10.1093/heapro/daaa040

Abrams, L., & Farrell, M. T. (2011). Language processing in normal aging. In J. Guendouzi et al. (Eds.), *The handbook of psycholinguistic and cognitive processes: Perspectives in communication disorders* (pp. 49–73). Psychology Press: Taylor and Francis.

Addey, C. (2017). Assembling literacy as global: The danger of a single story. In M. Milana et al. (Eds.), *The Palgrave international handbook on adult and lifelong education and learning* (pp. 315–335). Palgrave Macmillan.

Bickmore, T. W., Pfeifer, L. M., Byron, D., Forsythe, S., Henault, L. E., Jack, B. W., Silliman, R., & Paasche-Orlow, M. K. (2010). Usability of conversational agents by patients with inadequate health literacy: Evidence from two clinical trials. *Journal of Health Communication, 15*(2), 197–210. https://doi.org/10.1080/10810730.2010.499991

Brach, C. (2017). The journey to become a health literate organization: A snapshot of health system improvement. *Studies in Health Technology and Informatics, 240*, 203–237. https://doi.org/10.3233/978-1-61499-790-0-203

Brørs, G., Norman, C. D., & Norekvål, T. M. (2020). Accelerated importance of eHealth literacy in the COVID-19 outbreak and beyond. *European Journal of Cardiovascular Nursing, 19*, 458. https://doi.org/10.1177/1474515120941307

Car, J., Shin Tan, W., Huang, Z., Sloot, P., & Dean Franklin, B. (2017). eHealth in the future of medications management: Personalisation, monitoring and adherence. *BMC Medicine, 15*, 73. https://doi.org/10.1186/s12916-017-0838-0

Chesser, A. K., Keene Woods, N., Smothers, K., & Rogers, N. (2016). Health literacy and older adults: A systematic review. *Gerontology and Geriatric Medicine, 15*, 2. https://doi.org/10.1177/2333721416630492

Chew, Q. H., Wei, K. C., Vasoo, S., & Chua, H. C. (2020). Narrative synthesis of psychological and coping responses towards emerging infectious disease outbreaks in the general population: Practical considerations for the Covid-19 pandemic. *Singapore Medical Journal, 61*(7), 350–356. https://doi.org/10.11622/smedj.2020046

Collins, S. A., Currie, L. M., Bakken, S., Vawdrey, D. K., & Stone, P. W. (2012). Health literacy screening instruments for eHealth applications: A systematic review. *Journal of Biomedical Informatics, 45*(3), 598–607. https://doi.org/10.1016/j.jbi.2012.04.001

Dalmer, N. K. (2017). Questioning reliability assessments of health information on social media. *Journal of the Medical Library Association, 105*(1), 61–68. https://doi.org/10.5195/jmla.2017.108

Ek, S., Eriksson-Backa, K., & Niemelä, R. (2013). Use of and trust in health information on the internet: A nationwide eight-year follow-up survey. *Informatics for Health & Social Care, 38*(3), 236–245. https://doi.org/10.3109/17538157.2013.764305

Fraser, S. W., & Greenhalgh, T. (2001). Coping with complexity: Educating for capability. *BMJ, 323*(7316), 799–803. https://doi.org/10.1136/bmj.323.7316.799

Fraser, S., Lagacé, M., Bongué, B., Ndeye, N., Guyot, J., Bechard, L., Garcia, L., Taler, V., CCNA Social Inclusion and Stigma Working Group, Adam, S., Beaulieu, M., Bergeron, C. D., Boudjemadi, V., Desmette, D., Donizzetti, A. R., Éthier, S., Garon, S., Gillis, M., Levasseur, M., Lortie-Lussier, M., Marier, P., Robitaille, A., Sawchuk, K., Lafontaine, C., & Tougas, F. (2020). Ageism and COVID-19: What does our society's response say about us? *Age and Ageing, 49*, 692. afaa097. https://doi.org/10.1093/ageing/afaa097

Furstrand, D., & Kayser, L. (2015). Development of the eHealth literacy assessment toolkit, eHLA. *Studies in Health Technology and Informatics, 216*, 971.

Garcia-Codina, O., Juvinyà-Canal, D., Amil-Bujan, P., Bertran-Noguer, C., González-Mestre, M. A., Masachs-Fatjo, E., Santaeugènia, S. J., Magrinyà-Rull, P., & Saltó-Cerezuela, E. (2019). Determinants of health literacy in the general population: Results of the Catalan health survey. *BMC Public Health, 19*(1), 1122. https://doi.org/10.1186/s12889-019-7381-1

Geboers, B., Reijneveld, S. A., Jansen, C., & de Winter, A. F. (2016). Health literacy is associated with health behaviours and social factors among older adults: Results from the LifeLines cohort study. *Journal of Health Communication, 21*(2), 45–53.

health.gov – US Department of Health and Human Services, Office of Disease Prevention and Health Promotion. (2015). Health literacy online: A guide to simplifying the user experience. https://health.gov/our-work/health-literacy. Accessed 08 Aug 2020.

Houwink, E. J. F., Kasteleyn, M. J., Alpay, L., Pearce, C., Butler-Henderson, K., Meijer, E., van Kampen, S., Versluis, A., Bonten, T. N., van Dalfsen, J. H., van Peet, P. G., Koster, Y., Hierck, B. P., Jeeninga, I., van Luenen, S., van der Kleij, R. M. J. J., Chavannes, N. H., & Kramer, A. W. M. (2020). SERIES: eHealth in primary care. Part 3: eHealth education in primary care. *The European Journal of General Practice, 26*, 1. https://doi.org/10.1080/13814788.2020.1797675

ITV news. (2020). *Covid: Why ethnic minority groups have been hit hardest by coronavirus*. 14 Dec. Available at: https://www.itv.com/news/2020-12-14/covid-why-ethnic-minority-groups-have-been-hit-hardest-by-coronavirus. Accessed 21 Dec 2020.

Jacobs, R. J., Lou, J. Q., Ownby, R. L., & Caballero, J. (2014). A systematic review of eHealth interventions to improve health literacy. *Health Informatics Journal, 22*(2), 81–98. https://doi.org/10.1177/1460458214534092

Kayser, L., Karnoe, A., Furstrand, D., Batterham, R., Christensen, K. B., Elsworth, G., & Osborne, R. H. (2018). A multidimensional tool based on the eHealth literacy framework: Development and initial validity testing of the eHealth literacy questionnaire (eHLQ). *Journal of Medical Internet Research, 20*(2), e36. https://doi.org/10.2196/jmir.8371

Kivi, M., Hansson, I., & Bjälkebring, P. (2020). Up and about: Older adults' Well-being during the COVID-19 pandemic in a Swedish longitudinal study. *The Journals of Gerontology: Series B, 76*, e4. gbaa084. https://doi.org/10.1093/geronb/gbaa084

Kloehn, N., Leroy, G., Kauchak, D., Gu, Y., Colina, S., Yuan, N. P., & Revere, D. (2018). Improving consumer understanding of medical text: Development and validation of a new subsimplify algorithm to automatically generate term explanations in English and Spanish. *Journal of Medical Internet Research, 20*(8), e10779.

Maddox, B. (2008). What good is literacy? Insights and implications of the capabilities approach. *Journal of Human Development and Capabilities, 9*(2), 185–206. https://doi.org/10.1080/14649880802078736

Mantwill, S., Allam, A., Camerini, A.-L., & Schulz, P. J. (2018). Validity of three brief health literacy screeners to measure functional health literacy: Evidence from five different countries. *Journal of Health Communication, 23*(2), 153–161. https://doi.org/10.1080/10810730.2017.1417515

Mårtensson, L., & Hensing, G. (2012). Health literacy: A heterogeneous phenomenon: A literature review. *Scandinavian Journal of Caring Sciences, 26*(1), 151–160. https://doi.org/10.1111/j.1471-6712.2011.00900.x

Milos Nymberg, V., Borgström Bolmsjö, B., Wolff, M., Calling, S., Gerward, S., & Sandberg, M. (2019). 'Having to learn this so late in our lives…' Swedish elderly patients' beliefs, experiences, attitudes and expectations of e-health in primary health care. *Scandinavian Journal of Primary Health Care, 37*(1), 41–52. https://doi.org/10.1080/02813432.2019.1570612

Mohammadyari, S., & Singh, H. (2015). Understanding the effect of e-learning on individual performance: The role of digital literacy. *Computers in Education, 82*, 11–25. https://doi.org/10.1016/j.compedu.2014.10.025

Munn, Z., Peters, M. D. J., Stern, C., Tufanaru, C., McArthur, A., & Aromatari, E. (2018). Systematic review or scoping review? Guidance for authors when choosing between a systematic or scoping review approach. *BMC Medical Research Methodology, 18*, 143. https://doi.org/10.1186/s12874-018-0611-x

Neter, E., Brainin, E., & Baron-Epel, O. (2015). The dimensionality of health literacy and eHealth literacy. *European Journal of Health Psychology, 17*(6), 275–280.

NHS Digital Apps Library. (2021). https://www.nhs.uk/apps-library/. Accessed 18 Jan 2021.

Norgaard, O., Furstrand, D., Klokker, L., Karnoe, A., Batterham, R., Kayser, L., & Osborne, R. H. (2015). The e-health literacy framework: A conceptual framework for characterizing e-health users and their interaction with e-health systems. *Knowledge Management & E-Learning, 7*(4), 522–540. https://doi.org/10.34105/j.kmel.2015.07.035

Norman, C. D. (2011). eHealth literacy 2.0: Problems and opportunities with an evolving concept. *Journal of Medical Internet Research, 13*(4), e125. https://doi.org/10.2196/jmir.2035

Norman, C. D., & Skinner, H. A. (2006). eHealth literacy: Essential skills for consumer health in a networked world. *Journal of Medical Internet Research, 8*(2), e9. https://doi.org/10.2196/jmir.8.2.e9

Nussbaum, M. C. (2013). *Creating capabilities: The human development approach*. Belknap Press: An Imprint of Harvard University Press.

O'Sullivan, T., & Bourgoin, M. (2010). *Vulnerability in an influenza pandemic: Looking beyond medical risk*. Behaviour. 11:16. Available online at: https://homelesshub.ca/resource/vulnerability-influenza-pandemic-looking-beyond-medical-risk [Google Scholar]

Okan, O., Bollweg, T. M., Berens, E.-M., Hurrelmann, K., Bauer, U., & Schaeffer, D. (2020). Coronavirus-related health literacy: A cross-sectional study in adults during the COVID-19 infodemic in Germany. *International Journal of Environmental Research and Public Health, 17*, 5503. https://doi.org/10.3390/ijerph17155503

Olsson, T., Samuelsson, U., & Viscovi, D. (2019). At risk of exclusion? Degrees of ICT access and literacy among senior citizens. *Information, Communication & Society, 22*(1), 55–72. https://doi.org/10.1080/1369118X.2017.1355007

Paakkari, L., & Okan, O. (2020). COVID-19: Health literacy is an underestimated problem. *Lancet, 5*(5), e249–e250. https://doi.org/10.1016/S2468-2667(20)30086-4

Paige, S. R., Stellefson, M., Krieger, J. L., Miller, M. D., Cheong, J., & Anderson-Lewis, C. (2019). Transactional eHealth literacy: Developing and testing a multi-dimensional instrument. *Journal of Health Communication, 24*(10), 737–748. https://doi.org/10.1080/10810730.2019.1666940

Pleasant, A., Maish, C., O'Leary, C., & Carmona, R. (2019). Measuring health literacy in adults: An overview and discussion of current tools. In O. Okan, U. Bauer, D. Levin-Zamir, P. Pinheiro, & K. Sørensen (Eds.), *International handbook of health literacy* (pp. 67–81). Policy Press Imprint of Bristol University Press.

Quinn, S., Bond, R., & Nugent, C. (2017). Quantifying health literacy and eHealth literacy using existing instruments and browser-based software for tracking online health information seeking behavior. *Computers in Human Behavior, 69*, 256–267. https://doi.org/10.1016/j.chb.2016.12.032

Reiners, F., Sturm, J., Bouw, L. J. W., & Wouters, E. J. M. (2019). Sociodemographic factors influencing the use of eHealth in people with chronic diseases. *International Journal of Environmental Research and Public Health, 16*(4), 645. https://doi.org/10.3390/ijerph16040645

Rosenberg, L., Nygård, L., Josephsson, S., Walles Malinowsky, C. (2020). *Consequences of digital exclusion: Reflections from Sweden*. The 30th Alzheimer Europe Conference. P16.04.

Rubin, D. L. (2017). Listenability as a tool for advancing health literacy. *Journal of Health Communication, 17*(Suppl 3), 176–190. https://doi.org/10.1080/10810730.2012.71262

Rubin, G. J., & Wessely, S. (2020). The psychological effects of quarantining a city. *BMJ, 368*, m313. https://doi.org/10.1136/bmj.m313

Ruger, J. P. (2010). Health capability: Conceptualization and operationalization. *American Journal of Public Health, 100*(1), 41–49. https://doi.org/10.2105/AJPH.2008.143651

Saggion, H. (2017). *Automatic text simplification*. Synthesis Lectures on Human Language Technologies. Hirst G (series ed) Morgan & Claypool Publishers San Rafael.

Sen, A. K. (1993). Capability and Well-being. In M. Nussbaum & A. Sen (Eds.), *The quality of life*. Clarendon Press. https://doi.org/10.1093/0198287976.001.0001

Sen, A. K. (1999). *Development as freedom*. Oxford University Press.

Sen, A. K. (2003). Reflections on literacy. In C. Robinson (Ed.), *Literacy as freedom* (pp. 21–30). UNESCO.

Sentell, T., Vamos, S., & Okan, O. (2020). Interdisciplinary perspectives on health literacy research around the world: More important than ever in a time of COVID-19. *Journal of Environmental Research and Public Health, 17*, 3010. https://doi.org/10.3390/ijerph17093010

Sørensen, K. (2019). Defining health literacy: Exploring differences and commonalities. In O. Okan, U. Bauer, D. Levin-Zamir, P. Pinheiro, & K. Sørensen (Eds.), *International handbook of health literacy* (pp. 5–20). Policy Press Imprint of Bristol University Press.

Sørensen, K., van den Broucke, S., Fullam, J., Doyle, G., Pelikan, J., Slonska, Z., Brand, H., & (HLS-EU) Consortium Health Literacy Project European. (2012). Health literacy and public health: A systematic review and integration of definitions and models. *BMC Public Health, 12*, 80. https://doi.org/10.1186/1471-2458-12-80

Sørensen, K., Pelikan, J. M., Röthlin, F., Ganahl, K., Slonska, Z., Doyle, G., Fullam, J., Kondilis, B., Agrafiotis, D., Uiters, E., Falcon, M., Mensing, M., Tchamov, K., van den Broucke, S., Brand, H., & HLS-EU Consortium. (2015). Health literacy in Europe: Comparative results of the European health literacy survey (HLS-EU). *European Journal of Public Health, 25*(6), 1053–1058. https://doi.org/10.1093/eurpub/ckv043

Studzinski, J. (2020). *eHealth study: Non-clinical telehealth services are most prevalent, but COVID-19 accelerates new trends*. Healthcare Information and Management Systems Society, Inc (HIMSS) Available via: www.himss.org/news/ehealth-study-non-clinical-telehealth-services-are-most-prevalent-covid-19-a-new. Accessed 02 Aug 2020.

Tao, W. (2020). *Coronapandemin och socioekonomiska skillnader – En prognos om kort- och långsiktiga effecter* (Corona pandemic and socio-economic disparities: A forecast of short- and long-term effects). Center for Epidemiology and Community Medicine (In Swedish). Available at: https://www.folkhalsoguiden.se/globalassets/verksamheter/forskning-och-utveckling/centrum-for-epidemiologi-och-samhallsmedicin/folkhalsoguiden/rapporter-och-faktablad/coronapandemin-och-socioekonomiska-skillnader%2D%2D-en-prognos-om-kort%2D%2Doch-langsiktiga-effekter_.pdf. Accessed 25 Aug 2020.

Tengland, P. (2020). Health and capabilities: A conceptual clarification. *Medicine Health Care and Philosophy, 23*, 25–33. https://doi.org/10.1007/s11019-019-09902-w

Thulesius, H. (2020). Increased importance of digital medicine and eHealth during the Covid-19. *Scandinavian Journal of Primary Health Care, 38*(2), 105. https://doi.org/10.1080/02813432.2020.1770466

United Nations. (2020). *Policy brief: The impact of COVID-19 on older persons*. https://unsdg.un.org/sites/default/files/2020-05/Policy-Brief-The-Impact-of-COVID-19-on-Older-Persons.pdf. Accessed 01 Aug 2020.

USA Today. (2020). *An unbelievable chain of oppression: America's history of racism was a pre-existing condition for COVID-19*. 22 Oct. Available at: https://eu.usatoday.com/in-depth/news/nation/2020/10/12/coronavirus-deaths-reveal-systemic-racism-united-states/5770952002/. Accessed 21 Dec 2020.

van der Vaart, R., & Drossaert, C. (2017). Development of the digital health literacy instrument: Measuring a broad spectrum of health 1.0 and health 2.0 skills. *Journal of Medical Internet Research, 19*(1), e27. https://doi.org/10.2196/jmir.6709

van der Vaart, R., van Deursen, A. J., Drossaert, C. H., Taal, E., van Dijk, J. A., & van de Laar, M. A. (2011). Does the eHealth literacy scale (eHEALS) measure what it intends to measure? Validation of a Dutch version of the eHEALS in two adult populations. *Journal of Medical Internet Research, 13*(4), e86. https://doi.org/10.2196/jmir.1840

Vision e-health 2025. (2016). *Regeringskansliet*. Stockholm. Socialdepartementet (In Swedish) https://www.regeringen.se/informationsmaterial/2016/04/vision-e-halsa-2025/. Accessed 21 Aug 2020.

Wångdahl, J., Lytsy, P., Mårtensson, L., & Westerling, R. (2014). Health literacy among refugees in Sweden: A cross-sectional study. *BMC Public Health, 14*, 1030. https://doi.org/10.1186/1471-2458-14-1030

Watkins, I., & Xie, B. (2014). eHealth literacy interventions for older adults: A systematic review of the literature. *Journal of Medical Internet Research, 16*(11), e225. https://doi.org/10.2196/jmir.3318

WHO. (2020). *Tactics to apply to make your communications understandable*. https://www.who.int/about/communications/understandable. Accessed 13 Aug 2020.

Wolf, M. S., Serper, M., Opsasnick, L., O'Conor, R. M., Curtis, L. M., Benavente, J. Y., Wismer, G., Batio, S., Eifler, M., Zheng, P., Russell, A., Arvanitis, M., Ladner, D., Kwasny, M., Persell, S. D., Rowe, T., Linder, J. A., & Bailey, S. C. (2020). Awareness, attitudes, and actions related to COVID-19 among adults with chronic conditions at the onset of the US outbreak: A cross-sectional survey. *Annals of Internal Medicine, 173*, 100. https://doi.org/10.7326/m20-1239

Xie, B., Charness, N., Fingerman, K., Kaye, J., Kim, M. T., & Khurshid, A. (2020). When going digital becomes a necessity: Ensuring older adults' needs for information, services, and social inclusion during COVID-19. *Journal of Aging & Social Policy, 32*, 4–5. https://doi.org/10.1080/08959420.2020.1771237

Zanobini, P., Lorini, C., Baldasseroni, A., Dellisanti, C., & Bonaccorsi, G. (2020). A scoping review on how to make hospitals health literate healthcare organizations. *International Journal of Environmental Research and Public Health, 17*(3), 1036. https://doi.org/10.3390/ijerph17031036

Zarocostas, J. (2020). How to fight an infodemic. *Lancet, 395*, 10225. https://doi.org/10.1016/S0140-6736(20)30461-X

Chapter 10
Increasing People's Capabilities by Using Design Thinking in the Decision-Making Process

Jane Elisabeth Frisk and Lisbeth Svengren Holm

10.1 Introduction

A growing older population in countries like Sweden places new demands on the welfare system. The pandemic that swept across the world during the spring of 2020 revealed serious shortcomings, not least in Sweden. However, the criticisms of elder care, its lack of resources, lack of competence, lack of respect for older people etc., go back a long time. Voices have been raised claiming that caregiving needs to be transformed, that it should be based on older people's real needs and what they perceive as important, so that they can live an active and dignified life (Ekman, 2014). This chapter describes how *design thinking* (DT) has emerged as a field of research, in particular for developing new services in the public sector, and how DT as a concept for development can support new ways of thinking about problems, as well as increasing the capabilities of both service recipients and service providers.

J. E. Frisk (✉)
Business Administration, School of Business, Economics and Law at the University of Gothenburg, Gothenburg, Sweden

Centre for Ageing and Health – AgeCap, University of Gothenburg, Gothenburg, Sweden
e-mail: elisabeth.frisk@handels.gu.se

L. Svengren Holm
Centre for Ageing and Health – AgeCap, University of Gothenburg, Gothenburg, Sweden

Business and Design Lab, HDK-Valand at the University of Gothenburg, Gothenburg, Sweden
e-mail: lisbeth.svengren.holm@gu.se

H. Falk Erhag et al. (eds.), *A Multidisciplinary Approach to Capability in Age and Ageing*, International Perspectives on Aging 31,
https://doi.org/10.1007/978-3-030-78063-0_10

In a research programme for the Centre for Ageing and Health (AgeCap), the capability approach has been described as considering people's ability to reach goals and do things that are perceived as valuable. The *capability approach* (CA) concept was first developed by Amartya Sen (1985), winner of the Nobel Prize for Economics in 1998. Later, together with the political philosopher Martha C. Nussbaum, she developed the CA further, focusing on individual well-being, poverty and people's freedom of choice from a democratic perspective (Nussbaum & Sen, 2003). This was presented as an alternative to the dominant economic view on welfare. Sen and Nussbaum's research explored what individuals are capable of doing from a social and human perspective.

Recently, design researchers (Oosterlaken, 2009; Mink, 2016; Hansson et al., 2020) have begun to discuss the relevance of the CA for design research, especially in deprived contexts where people lack the capabilities to deal with poverty, ill health, etc. For instance, Oosterlaken (2009) argues that, instead of providing design as a solution to these kinds of complex problems in deprived contexts, the design process needs to identify and channel existing local capabilities. Hansson et al. (2020) suggest that the design process should give a voice to those whom the development concerns. Such 'capability-sensitive design' is, according to Oosterlaken (2009), central when working in 'poor' countries, such as India, where she did her research – or in Kenya where Hansson et al. have conducted their research. In principle, the CA is not only relevant in poor countries but also in Western countries where many people lack the capabilities and tools to participate in developments that affect them. When care services are being developed, the organisations that provide these services also need to employ individuals with the capabilities to develop and deliver services that make them better and more efficient from the perspectives of both the service provider and the receiver. To achieve this, both groups need to be involved in the development process.

The expectations that society, the public sector and the healthcare sector will deliver good services despite strained resources have led to demands for increased efficiency. A response to these expectations is to further develop digital services for caregiving, aimed primarily at citizens but also at employees. However, when deciding to invest in new digital solutions, decision-makers need to have a good understanding of both the citizens' and employees' capability to use digital technology. We argue that design thinking (DT) can support these demands.

DT is an approach to creative development that takes different perspectives, identifies stakeholders and involves different user groups, which can lead to new ways of thinking about the problems that are to be solved. In our studies, we have used DT as a process for achieving better care systems by considering both the service providers' and users' capabilities. The aim of our studies is thus to clarify *how the public-service sector can increase its capabilities in caregiving by the use of design thinking during the decision-making process*.

In the next section, we will briefly discuss the concept of *capabilities* from a caregiving perspective, followed by a discussion of how design as a field has moved from products to services and social innovations and the emergence of DT as a concept. We will then describe our two cases using DT as a tool to improve caregivers' understanding of older people's needs and the decision-making process regarding how to improve caregivers' capabilities in order to develop services that create value for the recipients of the services. Finally, we will present some conclusions regarding how the public sector can increase its capabilities to provide care for the growing older population.

10.2 The Concept of Capability

Capabilities have been discussed within different disciplines, such as engineering, design, economics, social development, and others. In design, the term *capability* has often been used as a contrast to *dis-ability*, i.e. in discussing how people with certain disabilities, especially functional disabilities, are physically hindered from fully using products as intended. The industrialisation of society and the development of mass production focused on the standardisation of products. Mass-produced items are based on average users, who constitute the largest market segment. Thus, people with less strength, which is often the case among older people, were not interesting as a market segment. There are several reasons for this, which are beyond the scope of this discussion. Furthermore, those who needed assistance for various disabilities from aid centres had few choices. Many of the products aimed towards this group of people functioned well but were not aesthetically pleasing. Several products were rather stigmatising, which led to reduced use, and the disability continued to cause limitations. This definition of capability as related to disability was very much taken for granted in a design context.

Recent design research in deprived contexts, for instance by Oosterlaken (2009), Mink (2016) and Hansson et al. (2020), however, has opened space for a more nuanced understanding of what is meant by capabilities. Thus, they refer to the *capability approach* as defined by Nussbaum and Sen (2003) – especially as an alternative to the dominant economic view of welfare. One aspect that suited these projects was Nussbaum's focus on the individual level, what individuals should be capable of doing from a social and human perspective as part of a sustainable and fair world. Nussbaum (2011) defines ten *capabilities* as a framework for basic human justice. These criteria have been highlighted within design research projects, even though not all ten criteria are relevant in all projects. Three capabilities that concern issues of collaboration link thinking and making, which makes them relevant in design research, where collaboration is a core issue for innovation and development. The first capability is *Senses, Imagination and Thoughts* (CC4), which refers to people's capability to 'imagine, experience, and produce works and events' (Nussbaum, 2011: 33) in a human way that is of one's own choice. Hence, they are actively part of the decision-making process. In our projects, this means that older people and employees in elder care should be capable of imagining, for example, how to use a digital solution, to understand the value of its service. The second capability, *Practical Reasoning* (CC6), concerns the capability 'to critically reflect on the work and the planning of one's life'. In our projects, this means that both older people and employees should be capable of understanding the processes of the service development. The third capability, *Affiliation* (CC7), refers to people's capabilities to engage in various social interactions, where they are treated as dignified beings. This can be related to older people's and employees' capability to raise their voices and experience respect for their needs.

It is easy to see how *capability* has been used as a contrasting word to *disability* within design research. The reason for the interest in how it is defined by Nussbaum is based on how design has changed, from a process focusing on product innovations to social innovation with a focus on services and organisations. This development also provides an understanding of why *design thinking* has become a concept that can contribute to increasing the capabilities of people with disabilities. Hence, we will describe this development of design research in the section below.

10.3 Design Research – From Products to Service

The development of design as a field of research has been a process of dialogue between research and practice. Design as a field of research grew out of the needs arising from industrial society and the physical world. As defined by Herbert Simon (1969, 1988), design is a field of research focusing on the creation of artificial things. The first generation of design researchers in the 1960s focused on the design process, developing theories for design methods to develop products, i.e. concrete objects (Lundequist, 1992). By the 1970s, the second generation of design researchers had decided that the design process should be an interaction between the designer's sketched proposals and the user's demands, with the result being a continuous process towards a greater degree of precision (ibid.).

The design consultancy firm Ergonomidesign (now McKinsey Design) was one of the new design agencies established in the 1970s, which embraced the user focus in design. It became a leading design consultancy firm for what was then called 'universal design', or 'design for all'. The idea was that, if a product is designed for the weakest person, then everyone can use it. However, an equally important value was to recognise people's aesthetics needs, so that products should be easy to use and functional, but also nice to look at. Within design research, the user perspective became one of the criteria for 'good design' and was incorporated into the design process.

As digital technology and computers became more ubiquitous during the late 1990s, Interaction Design emerged as a design subject focusing on human–computer interaction, i.e. how people are capable of understanding and handling computers (Ottersten et al., 2002). This technological development changed the focus of design, from material aspects to immaterial ones, from products to services.

10.4 Design Research in the Digital Era

With digitalisation, the material aspects of design were no longer central. Instead, the focus shifted to the design process, with further refinements of methods and tools for user studies, for the visualisation of problems from different perspectives and for prototyping, so that solutions could be tested by users. These design skills – user studies, visualisation, and prototyping – remained at the core when developing digital products and services (Holmlid, 2010), making *interaction design* a new subject, also in design education. This approach emphasised the necessity to identify the stakeholders who are affected by the change and to ensure that they are involved in the process. This includes not only the end-user but also those who provide the service. Service design research started to take a systems and process approach.

10.5 Service Design

Research with a focus on service design began in the public and healthcare sectors. This development was partly driven by design practitioners (e.g. Brown, 2008), design researchers (Sangiorgi, 2012; Wetter-Edman, 2014) and national design organisations, such as the Design Council in the UK and SVID in Sweden. In 2003, the US design consultancy IDEO Design collaborated with the healthcare firm Kaiser Permanent in the USA, a case which became widely recognised and studied as a role model for service design as a new field of design (Brown, 2008). IDEO designed the new services at a hospital so that the experience of the patients was the starting point. This had consequences for the hospital's organisation, but also for how staff interacted with their patients, which led to a new design for the rooms where interactions with patients took place. In this way, the hospital became more efficient without investing in new buildings, which was the original idea for solving inefficiencies within the organisation (Carlgren, 2013).

In 2005, the British social entrepreneur Hillary Cottam was awarded 'Designer of the Year' for her work in applying a design approach to problems like the rising burden of chronic healthcare in the UK. She became Director of the RED unit at the Design Council, and led a multidisciplinary team working with policymakers. They used the design process as a means of collaborating with users and other stakeholders in British healthcare, which resulted in better and more user-friendly care (Burns et al., 2006). In Italy, Ezio Manzini, professor of design at Politecnico di Milan, founded DESIS (Design for Social Innovation and Sustainability) in 2009 to conduct research into service design, especially aiming at social innovation and sustainability (Manzini, 2009). One research project at DESIS focused on the problem of older people's loneliness, and the result was a service that connected young students in need of low-cost housing with older people who had a room to let. The student had to provide some basic household services to support the older person. The side effect of this was that the older person had some social interaction with the young student and felt less lonely.

These streams of research focusing on the design process, creating different tools and methods in order to achieve a better understanding of needs and to create more innovative solutions, primarily in the public sector, demonstrated the importance of including all the stakeholders of the service system. The basic premises of participatory design are that 'those who are affected by a design should have a say in the design process' (Björgvinsson et al., 2012: 102). Participatory design can be defined as 'the creativity of designers and people not trained in design working together in the design development process' (Sanders & Stappers, 2008: 6). The aim is to develop new, innovative solutions that not only benefit the users but also make those providing the service more capable of understanding the users, in this case older adults. Thus, design is about creating suitable conditions for balancing effectiveness and efficiency, so that value can be created from both a user and a provider perspective.

10.6 From Service Design to Social Innovation

Social innovation emerged as a field within design research as a response to the dominant focus on market-driven and technical innovations. It provided a new way of approaching social problems through new practices within organisations such as healthcare organisations, hospitals, etc. At a general level, social innovation emphasises capabilities in terms of building organisational capacity that can lead to systemic change, often through collaborations that cut across the public, private and non-profit sectors (Emilson, 2015).

This development emerged in parallel in both practice and research. Design firms such as IDEO Design (Brown, 2008) and design scholars such as Ezio Manzini (2009, 2015) and Cottam and Leadbeater (2004) argued that, when it comes to dealing with complex societal issues, design needs to build on collaborative design, empathy and collaborative experiments. The idea of involving those who are affected by certain solutions, products, services, or systems in the design process is a long tradition of user-orientation within design practice. An important part of design research has been about developing methods and tools to achieve this, ranging from various ethnographic methods for collecting data about how users define and understand the situation and problems, to finding methods for enabling participatory design, i.e. co-designing creative and innovative solutions with those who are affected by them. Participatory design, designing things together or co-design, has become a field of its own with different approaches being taken within design research (Björgvinsson et al., 2012; Cruickshank, 2014; Storni et al., 2015). The objective is to give users a voice in the design process, so that new products, services and systems are based on users' capabilities.

Participatory design, or co-design, in both theory and practice has developed methods and tools based on the designer's skills at visualisation and making prototypes. Visualisation is a quick way to communicate and discuss ideas, to achieve an overview of different ideas. A prototype of a solution is an equally simple way to enable tests for how the solution works and is understood by users. The idea that users should be part of the design process, to achieve improved 'capabilities', has thus been emphasised within both theory and practice.

10.7 Design Process and the Emergence of Design Thinking

One of the most popular visual models of the design process is the Double Diamond (Fig. 10.1), developed by the Design Council in 2004 (Design Council, n.d.). It highlights two different phases of the process. The first of these focuses on discovering the problems, stakeholders etc., i.e. developing an increased understanding of the problems (Discover – a divergent phase). This is sometimes described as 'framing the problems' (Hookway et al., 2019).

When a number of relevant problems and stakeholders have been identified, a priority list is drawn up to decide which problem is to be solved in that particular project (Define – a convergent phase). In the next phase, the focus is to search for innovative solutions, again opening up opportunities for creating many different solutions (Develop – a divergent phase). A decision is then made about which solution to work on. In the final phase, the solution is then refined and launched (Deliver – a convergent phase).

This process should also be used by non-designers, i.e. people who are not designers by education but have received training in how designers think and work when trying to identify problems and develop solutions. Especially in-service

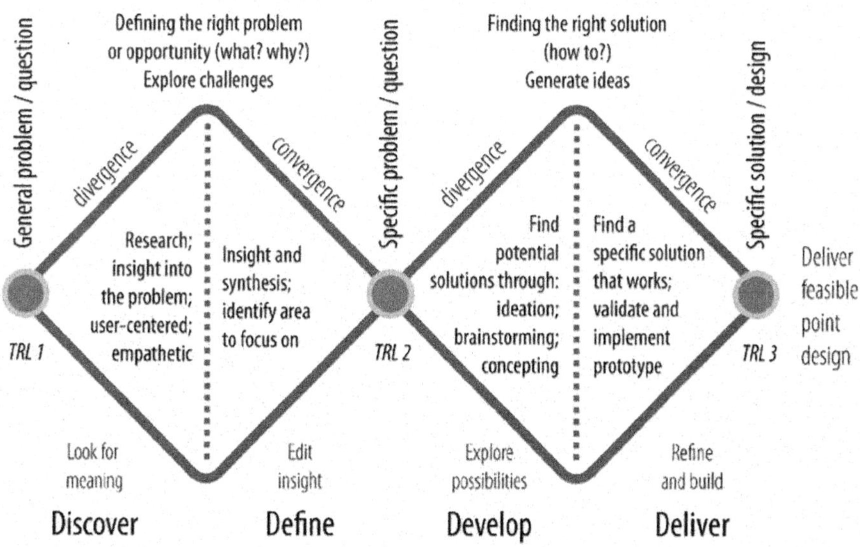

Fig. 10.1 The Double Diamond – visualisation of the design process (Design Council, n.d.)

development, this process has also become popular among those who are not professional designers by education. 'Service designer' has even become a professional title for those who have been trained, or educated, in this way of working. This is often referred to as design thinking because it embraces a process that is based on how designers think and act.

10.8 Design Thinking – Exceeding the Boundary of the Design Discipline

The notion of design thinking (DT) has been used in different ways in academia and industry and is therefore a concept that carries different meanings (Navarro Aguiar, 2017). For example, it has been described as a cognitive style (Dorst, 2011), as a method for management when it comes to innovation (Brown, 2008) and as a method for decision-making (Boland Jr. & Collopy, 2004), but also as a general theory for design (Buchanan, 2015).

Within management, DT became recognised as a concept for a new way of thinking. Having a design attitude meant using a different way to frame problems, to come up with unexpected solutions, to balance different perspectives and recognise that problems can be complex, not only complicated. This is argued as being a different way of thinking from a traditional management way of thinking, which is defined as a decision attitude (Boland Jr. & Collopy, 2004; Michlewski, 2015). Boland Jr. et al. (2008) came up with the notion of 'Managing as Designing'. According to these authors, the industrial era is now over, and it is time to solve problems from a pluralistic perspective instead of optimising.

Boland Jr. and Collopy (2004) were inspired while working with the architect Frank Gehry, who led the design of a new department building within their university. The architect tried to return to important assumptions that had gone invisible and unnoticed within the organisation. He also looked for concrete things that could be accomplished and looked beyond the residue of years of organisational habit; then he sought inspiration in other sources and suggested improvements. In order to create understanding of their work processes and what they perceived to be important, he interviewed both employees and students. The design process was described by Boland Jr. and Collopy (2004) as 'liquid and open' and involving different stakeholders affected by the change. They also refer to Herbert Simon, who in *The science of the artificial* (1969/1996) suggested that the design process should be a method for managers to utilise in their problem solving. Dunne and Martin (2006) also suggest that DT is a method for approaching managerial problems as it is a means 'to think broadly about problems, develop a deep understanding of users, and recognise the value in the contribution of others' (p. 512). This change in approach towards how to manage and make decisions is also relevant for public organisations, not least those in which human perspectives are extremely important and where problems have become increasingly complex. According to Kolko (2015), managers – regardless of whether they work within the private or public sector – need to cope with increasing complexity and they can utilise design as a way to simplify and humanise complex systems, which is what caregiving for older people is turning into.

Designers in general spend a large amount of time exploring problems, investigating the 'why', what lies behind the problem, not least in an institutional context, which broadens the space for both the problem and the solution (Johansson & Svengren Holm, 2008; Dorst, 2011; Jahnke, 2013). This use of time to understand the problem, the 'pre-study', often clashes with a decision attitude, where time is of the essence, where there is pressure to move on quickly in the decision-making process, and where the problem that should be reflected upon is decided very early on. Designers argue that the framing and re-framing of problems must be allowed to take the time that is needed (Hookway et al., 2019). The needs that can be brought to the surface are key to creativity and creative solutions (Dorst, 2011) (Fig. 10.2).

This 'design attitude' is the basis of DT. In design research, the focus is on how to enable individuals within an organisational context to increase their capability of being innovative and creative. This is related to Nussbaum's capability of *Senses, Imagination and Thoughts*, which means being capable of sensing, imagining and – in this case – trusting the process when it comes to solving increasingly complex problems in a global, digital context. Also, recognising that the work is never done but needs constant development.

In our studies, we have mainly used DT as a concept for innovation, introducing it into healthcare organisations that are about to develop new digital services. But we have also used it where the result is a method for improving the decision-making process. Instead of a *decision attitude*, we argue that it is necessary to take a *design attitude*, balancing the economic perspective with a humanistic perspective.

Fig. 10.2 Double Diamond illustrating the time aspects of the process, in particular the need to spend more time in the first phase in order to understand the problems and needs (Herzfeld & Nguyen, 2018)

However, to develop a design attitude, people need to have the capability to trust their own capabilities, as stated in Nussbaum's capability (CC4) to 'imagine, experience and produce works and events'. The design attitude can also refer to the third capability (CC7), so older clients and employees raise their voices and are accorded respect for their needs. The *decision attitude* is largely based on analytical methods, focusing on predefined content that seldom considers the contextual or humanistic need. This can be relevant when issues are complicated rather than complex and there is a need for constant changes.

10.9 Using Design Thinking as an Approach to Changing Practice

Although Scandinavia has a strong tradition of user involvement in design projects, the UK pioneered the way in user involvement in the health sector (Burns et al., 2006). Recently, projects related to elder care have also been conducted. The British Design Council ran the project *Transform Ageing* (Design Council, 2018), aimed at finding new social entrepreneurs who can come up with better and more innovative solutions for the heterogeneous group of older people. The project resulted in many ideas for which the entrepreneurs received start-up money to continue to develop their ideas into sustainable enterprises.

In the design research project *Aging Playfully*, led by Lancaster University and Age UK Lancashire (Imagination Lancaster, 2017), researchers used the methods of the design process to give people in the early stages of dementia the opportunity to co-design two-dimensional and three-dimensional images and models to stimulate and enable their physical mobility, imagination and social interaction in various workshops in a creative and playful manner. The results showed that people with dementia could be engaged and have meaningful social interactions. Thus, not only did the personnel become more capable in handling people with dementia, but also the people with dementia themselves increased their capabilities to use their imaginations.

Another project discussing the problem of caregiving in workplaces was conducted by a master's student, Kevin Dagostino, on the Business and Design Master's programme at the University of Gothenburg in 2017, with us as supervisors (Dagostino, 2017). This project focused on the stress that people experience when, in the middle of their careers, they also must simultaneously take care of both older parents and young children. Dagostino conducted several workshops at a small architectural firm, where interviews with managers and employees revealed that the managers were not aware of the stress the employees felt. It was a problem the employees did not feel comfortable to talk about, even though they realised it affected them at work. The DT process allowed these employees '… to access unspoken ideas; it also encouraged spoken ideas to occur outside of the activities, especially around the often subjective opinion of how culture should look inside of a workplace' (Dagostino, 2017: 56). The process included a co-design project in which the employees prototyped a creative solution that ultimately sparked conversations between the employees and management. This in turn contributed to a deeper dialogue associated with the challenges presented by the problem, which was considered a first step towards a more caregiver-friendly workplace (ibid.). The result was that people within the organisation, both employees and managers, became more capable of handling these kinds of sensitive matters in a constructive way, which can be referred to as the affiliation capability (CC7), the capability to raise one's voice and find respect for one's needs.

Below, we describe our two cases where we try to improve people's capabilities by using DT in research on older people's needs and caregiving organisations' decision-making processes.

10.10 Two Case Studies

10.10.1 Design Thinking as an Approach to Improving Home Services

Within the AgeCap programme, we initiated the pre-study '*Design Thinking for Ageing Capabilities*' (DTAC). This study was conducted in collaboration with Gothenburg City (GC), which had already started a programme, '*Attractive Home Services*' designed to deliver better services and organisation of home care.

The questions in our study were: 'how can DT, as a working process, contribute to an increased understanding of older people's needs?' and 'how can the Home-Care Service increase its ability to deliver good service?' In 2016, GC conducted a survey (consisting of about 200 interviews) to gain an improved understanding of the needs and the ways in which welfare technology could support this development. GC aims to introduce at least ten digital services by 2022 to support the organisation. Digital solutions and systems can streamline operations in many ways, but at the same time, they will require new skills among employees, Home-Care Services, and the older people themselves. The Home-Care Service was interested in finding new ways to understand the problems in the field.

In collaboration with personnel from GC, we organised two workshops to discuss the problems older people experience when meeting staff from Home Care, but also to find out what is more and/or less important in these meetings. The workshop involved eight older people and four employees from Home-Care Services. We recruited one designer, an expert in DT and service design, to create the visual materials needed for the activities in the workshop and also to participate in it. The two workshops were conducted 2 weeks apart. The first workshop focused on discovering what the older people experienced when meeting members of the Home-Care Service.

The older people were aged 70–90 years, with an equal number of men and women. To achieve an atmosphere in which everyone felt comfortable to talk, each person brought a special piece from home as a symbol for introducing themselves.

This so-called 'ice-breaker' created a light and fun atmosphere and generated a good starting point to getting to know each other. According to Cruickshank (2014), the start of a workshop is important to set the tone for the discussion.

During the workshops, participants were encouraged to think and tell stories about different situations, with the help of visual tools that were developed for this purpose. The stories had the themes of 'the good day' and 'the bad day'. The stories that emerged were placed on a board, which was then shared, and we all discussed and problematised the questions raised. The results provided the input for the second workshop, which focused on the meetings with home-care staff, what constitutes good and bad home care, how relations are built, and what it is important to prioritise in home-care services. In addition, stories were created, shared, and discussed.

The participants emphasised their capability to be able to activate themselves, being mobile, being able to walk outdoors and perform different physical activities, but also to interact socially with friends and family, as well as with the personnel they meet from the Home-Care Service. It further emerged just how important it is to be seen and listened to as an individual – integrity and respect for the individual were seen as central. The problems experienced were a lack of time with the personnel, causing stress and hindering them from actually talking about their needs with the person coming in from Home Care. This was further problematised by the lack of continuity of staff from the Home-Care Service.

Images from our workshop in Design Thinking for Ageing Capabilities

10.11 Design Thinking as an Approach for Improving the Decision-Making Process

The Swedish Municipalities and Regions (SKR) initiated a collaboration with the Swedish Industrial Design Foundation (SVID) to learn DT and service design and use it as a support for developing innovative solutions within the public sector. The reason behind this was a recognition, at both the national and municipal levels, that decision-making related to development issues needs to stem from the users and with an increased capability to 'think new'. A survey conducted by SKR and IVO (the Swedish Health and Care Inspectorate) showed that the public sector lacked knowledge about how to work effectively with such issues. The result was the 'Innovation Guide', which aims to gain an increased understanding of people's real needs, enabling a creative and engaging work process and developing ideas that can be tested to see if and how they work.

In 2019, five municipalities in Sweden took part in a project called '*Needs-Driven Development*'. We participated as researchers, together with different managers, coordinators, educators, a method developer, care-home staff and social secretaries, in total 30 participants. The project ran for 7 months and included five workshops. Two coaches from SKR, trained in the DT process and familiar with the Innovation Guide, led the workshops and supported the municipalities between these gatherings. Our aim was to learn more about why and how service design, with the support of the Innovation Guide, can support a municipality's decision-making regarding the development of new innovative services. The study used observations during each workshop, interviews were conducted as part of the fourth workshop in groups with participants from each municipality, and two questionnaires distributed at the fourth and fifth workshops were answered individually by the participants, except in one municipality where participants chose to do it in groups.

Overall, the participants were very satisfied with using DT as an approach for improving the decision-making process. It was perceived that decisions were now based on facts to a greater extent, i.e. that the decisions were based on information received from service users and employees, instead of being based on assumptions, as previously. Another reflection from the participants was that DT provides decision-makers with an improved understanding of the problem by framing it suitably. The case also shows that, during the first phase, when the participants perceive a growing understanding of the problem, several participants changed their assumptions about what the real problem was. When interviewing the users of healthcare services, it was evident that the initial assumptions were wrong, and the real problem turned out to be something else. Also, during the second phase, creating design solutions, participants from one organisation were surprised by how creative the end users were and what good solutions were designed.

10.12 Discussing the Results of the Two Case Studies

The results from the first DTAC study emphasise the importance of improved understanding of the issues raised by both the users of healthcare services and employees. Solutions are seldom right or wrong, but rather more or less good or bad. Improvement needs to be an ongoing process with regular assessments. It is a collaborative process in which the users of healthcare services should participate, but employees who are affected should also be involved because they are closer to the reality of daily operations and therefore have greater insight regarding prioritisations. DT can be used to support management when managing these kinds of issues and can also support strategic priorities (Frisk et al., 2018).

The results from our first case were to some extent in accordance with the results of the survey conducted by GC home services but, as reflected by the head of GC home services, required far fewer resources. The workshops can be described as using playful methods, such as the personal objects, the visual maps and brief notes, but these are also methods that encourage and trigger communication and conversations. The tools were quickly accepted, and participants thought that these tools stimulated their imaginations and memories, as well as the discussion. It helped them to realise their capability to sense and imagine (CC4).

One result was that the process of DT seems to be a method that, using few resources, can make the participants more capable of imagining situations and communicating them, which provided valuable and interesting results (Frisk et al., 2018).

The main result of the SKR study, 'Needs-Driven Development', was that the participants considered DT to be a creative process that contributes to a better decision-making process. This is because the decisions were to a greater extent based on facts instead of assumptions about what was needed. When employees investigated the problem and tested the solutions before making a decision, a better understanding of what creates value for the receiver of the service was achieved. Also, by illuminating the problem from different perspectives, the complexity of the issue can also be better identified by politicians, who can then avoid making incorrect decisions.

When employees and users were involved in a more structured way, *not only doing things right but also doing the right things* was brought up as another advantage of the process, i.e. enabling the balancing of efficiency with effectiveness. This in turn was considered to have a positive effect on the results achieved by the organisation because employees will stop doing things that are not requested and will instead focus on what is requested, and therefore create value that in fact increases the user's capabilities.

In both cases, the participants were very positive about using DT as a tool to improve the decision-making process about which services create value for citizens and increase their capabilities. The possibilities for users to increase their capabilities, i.e. to sense and understand, to critically reflect upon and collaborate on issues that concern them, will increase the likelihood that the services they want will be developed. Furthermore, both the economic and social perspectives can be better balanced in the decision-making process about what services should be offered to users because the perspectives of both the citizens and the organisation were included in the decision-making process.

10.13 Conclusions

Public organisations in Sweden are facing new and more complex challenges due to a growing older population, fewer resources and increasing demands for service quality. For instance, organisations need to cope with improving the quality of services, and being more person-centred, user-friendly, and cost-efficient, all at the same time. A consequence of this is that they need to increase both their efficiency and effectiveness. Effectiveness in this case relates to the ability to provide services that create value and improve capabilities. To accomplish this, a conclusion is therefore that new ways of thinking and making decisions are needed within these organisations.

The results from the two cases presented in this chapter show that design thinking (DT) can support such development. The use of DT as an approach for developing new services that improve capabilities can both be resource efficient and provide services that create value for the recipient. This is accomplished using the DT process, which emphasises the importance of giving more time and attention to discussing the problems from different perspectives, i.e. framing and reframing the problems. Then new solutions might emerge that were not considered initially because early definitions of which problems are suitable to work on are often too narrow. Also, both service recipients and service providers are involved in the process, enabling more relevant insights. Furthermore, the DT process also opens up opportunities for increased creativity because it creates an innovative mind-set among the people involved. This can be a valuable starting point for increasing people's capabilities, as discussed by Nussbaum (2011).

Therefore, managers who make decisions about new solutions need to abandon a traditional decision attitude, which is mostly about making choices based on financial figures. Instead, a decision-making process based on a design attitude has advantages, because it provides a better understanding of 'social facts' (rather than assumptions), when it comes to generating better insights into what creates value for users. Therefore, DT will increase the chances of solving the 'right problems' and improving capabilities.

Another conclusion is that design thinking (DT) can support the organisation to achieve this and to do more with less. The case study using DT and creative workshops, conducted in collaboration with Gothenburg City, was described as very beneficial. Compared with an earlier study conducted by Gothenburg City, in which interviews with 200 people required a lot of time and resources, the two one-day workshops, taking up far fewer resources and time, gave equally valuable results. Thus, even though DT seems to be an approach that takes a lot of time and can been seen as costly, compared to the survey conducted by Gothenburg City, it was very cost efficient.

Acknowledgments The authors would like to thank the Torsten Söderberg Foundation and the AgeCap Programme in Sweden for enabling this research study.

References

Björgvinsson, E., Ehn, P., & Hillgren, P.-A. (2012). Design things and design thinking: Contemporary participatory design challenges. *Design Issues, 28*(3), 103.

Boland, J., Jr., & Collopy, F. (2004). *Managing as designing*. Stanford University Press.

Boland, J., Jr., Collopy, F., Lyytinen, K., & Yoo, Y. (2008). Managing as designing: Lessons for organization leaders from the design practice of Frank O. *Gehry. Design Issues, 24*(1), 10–25.

Brown, T. (2008). Design thinking. *Harvard Business Review, 86*(6), 84–95.

Buchanan, R. (2015). Worlds in the making: Design, management, and the reform of organizational culture. *She Ji: The Journal of Design, Economics and Innovation, 1*(1), 5–21.

Burns, C., Cottam, H., Vanstone, C., & Winhall, J. (2006). *Red paper 02: Transformation design*. Design Council. https://www.designcouncil.org.uk/sites/default/files/asset/document/red-paper-transformation-design.pdf

Carlgren, L. (2013). *Design thinking as an enabler of innovation: Exploring the concept and its relation to building innovation capabilities*. Dissertation, Department of Technology Management and Economics. Chalmers university of Technology, Gothenburg.

Cottam, H., & Leadbeater, C. (2004). *Open welfare: Designs on the public good*. Design Council.

Cruickshank, L. (2014). *Open design and innovation: Facilitating creativity in everyone*. Routledge.

Dagostino, K. (2017). *The interplay of informal caregiver employees and small creative businesses: Co-designing towards a more care-giver friendly workplace*. Master's Thesis. Business and Design Master's Programme, Academy of Design and Crafts, University of Gothenburg.

Design Council. (2018). *Transform ageing*. https://www.designcouncil.org.uk/what-we-do/social-innovation/transform-ageing. Accessed 15 Mar 2019.

Design Council. (n.d.). *What is the framework for innovation? Design Council's evolved double diamond*. https://www.designcouncil.org.uk/news-opinion/design-process-what-double-diamond. Accessed 15 Mar 2019.

Dorst, K. (2011). The core of 'design thinking' and its application. *Design Studies, 32*, 521–532.

Dunne, D., & Martin, R. (2006). Design thinking and how it will change management education: An interview and discussion. *Academy of Management Learning and Education, 5*(4), 512–523.

Ekman, I. (Ed.) (2014). *Personcentrering inom hälso- och sjukvård: från filosofi till praktik. 1. uppl.* Liber, Stockholm. https://www.vardhandboken.se/arbetssatt-och-ansvar/bemotande-i-vard-och-omsorg/bemotande-i-vard-och-omsorg-vardegrund/personcentrerad-vard/.

Emilson, A. (2015). *Design in the space between stories: Design for social innovation and sustainability – From responding to societal challenges to preparing for societal collapse*. Doctoral thesis in interaction design, Malmö University, Department: School of Arts and Communication.

Frisk, E., Svengren Holm, L., & Hookway, S. (2018). *Design thinking som stöd vid komplexa problemställningar*. Rapport. AGECAP/HDK. Göteborgs universitet.

Hansson, H., Mwango, F., Svengren Holm, L., & Nyström Reutersvärd, M. (2020). *Creating the crafted playground through co-design*. 4D 55. SZAM 2020.

Herzfeld, L., & Nguyen, T. H. (2018). *Re-mystifying design methods: An exploratory study on creative values of design methods and their practice*. Master's Thesis, Business & Design Master's Programme, University of Gothenburg, Academy of Arts and Design.

Holmlid, S. (2010 [2009]). "Design och designledning på vägen mot väldesignade myndigheter". i Lindblad-Gidlund, Katarina (red.). *Förvaltning och medborgarskap i förändring: Etablerad praxis och kritiska perspektiv*. Studentlitteratur. ISBN 978-91-4405-562-6.

Hookway, S., Fay Johansson, M., Svensson, A., & Heiden, B. (2019). The problems with problems: Reframing and cognitive bias in healthcare innovation. *The Design Journal, 22*(1), 553–574.

Imagination Lancaster. (2017). *Ageing playfully: Co-designing interactive and playful ways to encourage dementia-friendly exercise and movement*. Lancaster University. http://148.88.47.13/html/imagination/activities/Ageing_Playfully. Accessed 15 Mar 2019.

Jahnke, M. (2013). *Meaning in the making: Introducing a hermeneutic perspective on the contribution of design practice to innovation*. ArtMonitor.

Johansson, U., & Svengren Holm, L. (2008). *Möten kring design. Om relationen mellan design, teknik och marknadsföring*. Studentlitteratur AB.

Kolko, J. (2015). Design thinking comes of age: The approach, once used primarily in product design, is now infusing corporate culture. *Harvard Business Review*, September, *7*,66–71.

Lundequist, J. (1992). Om designteorins uppkomst. *Nordisk Arkitekturforskning, 1992*(4), 7–18.

Manzini, E. (2009). Service design in the age of networks and sustainability. In S. Miettinen & M. Koivisto (Eds.), *Designing services with innovative methods* (pp. 44–59). University of Art and Design.

Manzini, E. (2015). *Design when everybody designs: An introduction to design for social innovation*. MIT Press.

Michlewski, K. (2015). *Design attitude*. Gower Publishing.

Mink, A. M. (2016). *Capability driven design: An approach for understanding users' lives in design for development*. Doctoral Thesis, Delft University of Technology.

Navarro Aguiar, U. (2017). *Negotiating the value(s) of design(ing): An organizational inquiry*. Doctoral Thesis, University of Gothenburg, School of Business, Economics and Law.

Nussbaum, M. (2011). *Creating capabilities: The human development approach*. The Belknap Press of Harvard University Press.

Nussbaum, M., & Sen, A. (Eds.). (2003 November). *Quality of life*. Oxford Scholarship Online.

Oosterlaken, I. (2009). Design for development: A capability approach. *Design Issues, 25*(4), 91–102. https://doi.org/10.1162/desi.2009.25.4.91

Ottersten, I., Berndtsson, J., & Isaksson, D. (2002). *Användbarhet i praktiken: praktiska handgrepp, grundbegrepp och tankemodeller*. Studentlitteratur. Libris 8435431. ISBN 91-44-04122-5.

Sanders, E. B-N., & Stappers, P. J. (2008). Co-creation and the new landscape of design. *Co-design international journal of cocreation and the arts, 4*(1).

Sangiorgi, D. (2012). Value co-creation in design for services. In S. Miettinen & A. Valtonen (Eds.), *Service design with theory: Discussions on change, value and methods* (pp. 95–104). Lapland University Press.

Sen, A. (1985). *Commodities and capabilities*. Elsevier Science.

Simon, H. (1969/1996). *The sciences of the artificial [3rd edn 1996]* (1st ed.). MIT Press.

Simon, H. (1988). The science of design: Creating the artificial. *Design Issues, 4*(1/2), 67–82. https://pdfs.semanticscholar.org/d494/439a347e34599924d99af0007d26f510f870.pdf.

Storni, C., Binder, T., Linde, P., & Stuedahl, D. (2015). Designing things together: Intersections of co-design and actor–network theory. *CoDesign, 11*(3/4), 149–151.

Wetter-Edman, K. (2014). *Design for service: A framework for articulating designers' contribution as interpreter of users' experience*. Dissertation, Art Monitor, University of Gothenburg.

Chapter 11
The Capability Approach in Social Work with Older People

Inger Kjellberg

11.1 Introduction

In this chapter, I will focus on how the capability approach has been used in research on social work with older people. The chapter starts with a general definition of social work, and social work with older people in particular, followed by a discussion of the merits and challenges of the use of the capability approach in social work research addressing the social care of older people.

Social work is both a practice-based profession and an academic discipline, which is mainly concerned with a large range of social problems such as poverty, homelessness, drug abuse, criminality and violence against vulnerable groups. Poverty is a primary subject of research and the social deprivation associated with it is of great concern to social workers (Payne, 2005). The capability approach as conceived by the economist Amartya Sen (1999) and developed by philosopher Martha Nussbaum (2011) offers tools for a multidimensional analysis of poverty, with a broad perspective on the different constraints that can limit people's lives. The capability approach has also been developed by Ingrid Robeyns (2005, 2006, 2017). In social work research, different theories are used, for example, as a heuristic or as a framework for analysis, and the capability approach developed by Sen (1993, 1999) is one such theory. Sen defines the capability approach as 'an intellectual discipline that gives a central role to the evaluation of a person's achievements and freedoms in terms of her actual ability to do the different things a person has reason to value doing or being' (Sen, 2009: 16). In social work research, the capability approach can be a useful tool for exploring individuals' expectations and

I. Kjellberg (✉)
Department of Social Work, University of Gothenburg, Gothenburg, Sweden

Centre for Ageing and Health – AgeCap, University of Gothenburg, Gothenburg, Sweden
e-mail: inger.kjellberg@socwork.gu.se

H. Falk Erhag et al. (eds.), *A Multidisciplinary Approach to Capability in Age and Ageing*, International Perspectives on Aging 31,
https://doi.org/10.1007/978-3-030-78063-0_11

their opportunities to realise those expectations in general. Sen (1993, 1999) argues that what people can positively achieve depends on their economic opportunities, social powers, political liberties and the enabling conditions of good health, basic education, encouragement and the cultivation of initiatives. It has been suggested that the key concepts of the capability approach are easily connected to the core of social work and that it offers directions for almost every basic social work strategy (den Braber, 2013). However, these key concepts are still said to be relatively unknown and undeveloped in social work (Babic et al., 2010).

11.2 Social Work with Older People

There are two main branches of social work with older people: care of older people and ageing (Jönson & Harnett, 2015). Social workers are engaged in the care of older people in different ways and social work education has to prepare students for working within social care. However, their tasks differ between countries. In Sweden, for example, social workers conduct need assessments for home-care services, and eligibility assessments for residential care (for people aged 65 and above); they work as care managers in residential care facilities for older people, in interdisciplinary healthcare teams and with support for informal caregivers. Social workers also meet older people in other social work areas, such as homeless centres and substance abuse clinics.

The other branch of social work focuses on social problems. Older people are not a social problem in themselves, but discriminatory practices are such a problem. Thus, the second branch of social work with older people (i.e. ageing) concerns social problems associated with old age and ageism: stereotypical categorisations and assumptions about older people as a group (Andersson, 2008; Bytheway, 2005), which interfere with social work services and ethical principles within social work. Social workers are involved in the care of older people who have complex and significant support needs or where there are other social problems, such as gender-based violence, drug abuse, poverty or social deprivation. Older people are not a homogeneous group, people with all kinds of problems grow old. Categorisation by chronological age is just one way of delimiting a group of people, but it may not be because of age-related problems that older people seek the help of social workers. Most people live their lives without having to use social services, and only a minority of older people and their informal carers are in need of social work skills (Ray & Phillips, 2012). The need for social services by older people is definitely not inevitable. However, it has been suggested that the capability approach seems to embrace the different aspects of social work with older people and that this approach offers a focus on processes and interactions that pays attention to diversity and the contextualisation of people's social constraints (Gopinath, 2018).

11.3 Main Concepts of the Capability Approach

According to Ingrid Robeyns (2006: 352), the capability approach is not a theory that can explain poverty, inequality or well-being, but it is 'a normative framework for the evaluation and assessment of individual well-being and social arrangements, the design of policies, and proposals about societal change'. Social justice is also important to social work and it is defined in the Code of Ethics for social workers as well as in the definition of what social work is (The International Federation of Social Workers [IFSW], 2014). Discussions within social work have been highlighting the need for social work to develop its own theoretical basis for social justice and suggesting that the capability approach, as developed by Sen and Nussbaum, can provide a philosophical frame of justice for teaching social work (Carlson et al., 2016). Notwithstanding, Robeyns (2006) argues that the capability approach suggests complementary insights to other approaches, and does not replace other theories. The capability approach opens up an interdisciplinary space in the study of well-being, inequality, justice and public policies.

There are several essential concepts in the capability approach. Here, I will only recapitulate the main characteristics of five main concepts. *Functionings* are described as valuable activities, various things a person values being able to do and to be, indicating individual choices. *Capabilities* are the actual opportunities people have to live the life they value and to implement their choices or achieve their *functionings*. An older person's capabilities are dependent on the opportunities he or she has, and the abilities she or he possesses. Another concept is *freedom*. In order for individuals to practise their rights and to live a life that they value, they need to use their capabilities to do the things that they value. Sen (1999) distinguishes two different kinds of freedom: substantive and instrumental. The former allows individuals to participate in a democratic community, the latter concerns individual freedom to live the life you choose. *Conversion factors* influence individuals' freedom to achieve functioning at both a personal and an environmental level. Finally, *agency* is closely related to freedom and well-being. Individual agency is a person's ability to pursue the goals they have reason to value (Deneulin, 2008; Sen, 1999). An agent may exercise agency in seeking his or her own well-being, but agency may also be pursued collectively or to reach altruistic goals. Robeyns (2017) states that not all versions of the capability approach need to endorse an account of agency, although for social workers the acting agent plays a crucial role in achieving goals in human life (den Braber, 2013).

11.4 The Capability Approach and Social Work

Several researchers have commented on the potential of the capability approach as an alternative conceptual framework for social work that can challenge the dominance of neoliberal ideology and promote human rights and social justice

(Banerjee & Canda, 2012; Gupta, 2017; Reisch & Jani, 2012). The focus of the capability framework overlaps with much of the interest in social work research, as well as in social work practice: the focus on evaluating individual levels of well-being and social institutions, policy formation and social change towards social justice. In social work, social justice is a core value of the profession, and it is defined in the Code of Ethics for Social Workers (National Association of Social Workers [NASW], 2017) as well as in the Global Definition of Social Work (IFSW, 2014). There are however competing approaches in social work research, for example different emancipatory forms of social work, which are also closely connected to the endorsement of social justice and human rights, such as empowerment (Adams, 2008) and anti-oppressive practice (Dominelli, 2002). Empowerment has been defined as 'the capacity of individuals, groups and/or communities to take control of their circumstances' (Adams, 2008: xvi) in order to maximise the quality of their lives. In correspondence with the capability approach, empowerment is also contested via differing perspectives and use (Tew, 2006); it can be used to mean individuals' ability to take control of their own lives, mutual support and collective action undertaken by marginalised groups, but it can also be defined for powerless people by professionals and politicians. Nonetheless, despite the similarities in rhetoric between certain forms of emancipatory social work and the capability approach, there are also differences. In anti-oppressive research, power relations that influence research projects have been scrutinised, encouraging critical reflexivity on the processes of power in social work research (Rogers, 2012; Strier, 2007). In anti-oppressive social work practice, social justice and human development are promoted by developing empowering forms of practice. Anti-oppressive practice is concerned with 'personal, institutional, cultural and economic issues and examines how these impinge on individuals' behaviour and opportunities to develop their full potential as persons living within collective entities' (Dominelli, 2002: 36).

Neither power relations nor anti-oppressive strategies for researching marginalised groups are particularly pronounced in the capability approach. Although there are obvious connections between the capability approach and social work, questions about whether it is sufficiently critical of social power, oppression and global injustices have been raised (Carlson et al., 2016; Dean, 2009; Deneulin, 2008). Critical social work has both a narrow and a broad definition (Gray & Webb, 2009). In the narrow sense, structural analyses of the aspects of society that are oppressive, unjust and exploitative are connected to the various circumstances experienced by social workers and service users. Such analyses often have their starting point in theories aimed at a structural level, identifying political domination, as in for example feminism, race theory and Marxism. The broad sense of critical social work is more concerned with developing 'best practice' agendas where the critical dimension is regarded as a disposition of the social workers and their capacity to reformulate or challenge existing practices (Gray & Webb, 2009).

What critical social work is, and can be, is an ongoing debate within social work, which highlights the question of what social work really is (Hugman, 2010; Olson,

2007; Payne, 2005). Olson (2007) defines social work as two distinct projects: the social justice project, which seeks to transform the conditions of human suffering, and the professional project, with its focus on achieving legitimacy within a competitive professional system. Olson argues that these two projects have different assumptions, missions and goals; however, they are conflated in social work's understanding of itself and what it does. Olson also concludes that it is the social justice project that loses out in this conflation.

Social work has also been distinguished in micro- and macro-level approaches (Hugman, 2010). The micro-level approach is concerned with individual functioning and questions of social order. Historically, the micro-level approach can be traced back to the emergence of the social work profession at the end of the nineteenth century, and more specifically to the Charity Organisation Societies (Hugman, 2010). This branch of social work has generally been regarded as politically conservative, and builds on a theory of charity recipients' ability to make the best use of the resources given to them. The macro-level perspective is based on a structural understanding of social problems whereby social change is pursued. This has been regarded as a politically radical view (Hugman, 2010; Olson, 2007). The emergence of the macro-level aspect of social work has its roots in the Settlement movement, in which well-educated and wealthy people moved to poor areas to live and work (Payne, 2005). The theory behind this movement was that the wealthy class possessed social resources that spread outward to the whole community, and thus everybody living in the area would then develop capacities to improve their own lives and resolve social problems (Hugman, 2010).

11.5 Methodological Framework

There is no comprehensive review of the literature on how the capability approach is used in social work research. Research findings relevant to social work professionals and researchers can be found in many journals from different disciplines. In order to understand how the capability approach has actually been used in social work research, a scoping review was conducted (Kjellberg & Jansson, 2020). A scoping review shares some similarities with systematic reviews, such as the use of rigorous and transparent methods to identify and analyse relevant literature regarding a well-defined topic. Scoping reviews are used when the topic has not yet been extensively reviewed and where a potentially large body of literature is available, which includes different study designs and methodologies (Pham et al., 2014). In contrast, systematic reviews often synthesise evidence from randomised controlled trials, summing up the best available research. Our scoping review followed the framework outlined by Arksey and O'Malley (2005) and used the PRISMA checklist and flow chart for scoping reviews (Tricco et al., 2018). The focus of the review was to identify and analyse how the capability approach is used in social work research, including research employing a range of different methods, and not to critically evaluate the research for best practice, as would have been the focus in a systematic review. After a two-step screening, 17 articles were included in the analysis (Kjellberg & Jansson, 2020). Only three of these articles addressed social work with older people (Horrell et al., 2015; Tanner et al., 2018; Yeung & Breheny, 2016). For the specific purposes of this chapter, the search terms were expanded to 'gerontological social work', older people and social work using three databases (Proquest Social Service, Web of Science, Scopus), the timeframe ranging from 1 January 2000 to 20 February 2018. The inclusion criteria were: (1) the capability approach was a main part of the research process, (2) the article contained empirical research specifically addressing social work with older people, and (3) social work theory or practice was explicitly addressed. The exclusion criteria were: (1) capabilities were not connected to the capability approach as outlined by Sen or Nussbaum, (2) no empirical material was presented (e.g., some of the articles contained theoretical discussions and no identified research population or method), and (3) the article did not address social work research with older people. Articles using the capability approach in research about older people amongst other professions (e.g. nursing) were also excluded. Only one more article was found that presented primary research using the capability approach with a focus on older people, in comparison with the scoping review (Kjellberg & Jansson, 2020). The selected studies were limited to English-language, peer-reviewed journals accessible from Gothenburg University Library. In all, four articles are discussed in this chapter; three studies were identified in the scoping review and one more in the extended search.

In the four studies discussed below, the research methods and findings are identified, the use of the capability approach is specified and the extent to which this approach is presented as valuable to social work with older people is considered. A scoping review is not a comprehensive evaluative method of research quality. The questions guiding the presentation and discussion of the studies are: in what way is the capability approach used in the analysis of the empirical material: What applications, merits and challenges are discussed? To what extent is the capability approach acknowledged (or not) as valuable for social work with older people, and with what kinds of arguments?

11.6 Different Uses of the Capability Approach

The uses of the capability approach in social work research were delineated into four main categories: exploring the subjective sense of well-being, addressing social inequalities at a structural level, as a tool for social workers in practice and to evaluate social work practices (Kjellberg & Jansson, 2020). The first two categories concern the level at which the empirical material was analysed. Three of the articles explored the subjective sense of well-being, and the capability approach addressed subjective experiences at an individual level (Gilroy, 2006; Horrell et al., 2015; Yeung & Breheny, 2016). Although three of the articles concerned well-being at an individual level, it was also claimed that it is not enough to be engaged with individuals and families. Critical social work also needs to be developed through engaging with the suffering of individuals in the context of political processes at the societal level. The second category includes articles mostly exploring social structures, and their influence on different groups of people. One article (Tanner et al., 2018) fell into this category. The third category deals with the specific use of the capability approach for social workers when working with people in need of support, but none of the four studies fitted this category. Finally, the fourth category has evaluative aims, where the capability approach is used as a measurement of quality of life. None of the studies fell into this category, although one article (Gilroy, 2006) used a list of quality of life, but it did not have any evaluative aims.

11.7 The Capability Approach in Social Work with Older People

The four studies addressing social work with older people reported research findings from New Zealand (some of the same authors in two studies, but different empirical material) and the UK, using both qualitative and quantitative methodology (see Table 11.1).

Table 11.1 Description of reviewed research articles by author, year of publication, researched group, country, empirical material, and objective of the studies

Author	Year	Researched group	Country	Empirical material	Objective of the study
Gilroy	2006	Older people >50	UK	10 studies from growing older, four audit commissions	To create a list of capabilities derived from older people's own voices and contribute to the empowerment of older people.
Horrell et al.	2015	Informal caregivers for older people	New Zealand	Online forum, 60 caregivers	To create a capability list specific to the values and health needs of those providing informal eldercare.
Tanner et al.	2018	Older people (aged 70–92) self-funding social care	England	Eight individual semi-structured interviews	To advance understanding of the experiences of older people living in the community who are self-funding their own social care by applying the capability approach (CA) to these experiences.
Yeung and Breheny	2016	People aged 50–87	New Zealand	NZ longitudinal study of ageing (N = 2793)	To explore the determinants of subjective Well-being among older people.

11.7.1 Exploring the Subjective Sense of Well-being

In a study from the UK, Gilroy (2006) worked out a list of capabilities derived from research within government-funded programmes that gave prominence to older people's own definitions of a life worth living. Gilroy's research included ten empirical studies from government-funded programmes. The objectives of these research programmes were to explore different aspects of quality of life in old age. The list followed Ingrid Robeyns' (2006) approach by listing factors of importance for quality of life as expressed by older people themselves, which included the following domains: Health, adequate income, mobility, a safe neighbourhood, a comfortable and secure home, social relations and support. The capability approach was described as appropriate for analysing how policy, societal attitudes and neglect constrain the freedom of older people. It was also suggested that the sum of all capabilities may not be expressed as freedom, as in Sen's view; instead, older people preferred the word independence. Moreover, the capability approach was highly recommended because it brought the older people's voices into focus and thus also contributed to their empowerment. This article is important for social work because it stresses social policies and support for older people with special needs.

One study from New Zealand (Horrell et al., 2015) examined the capabilities that are important for the health of informal caregivers of older people in New Zealand. The method used was an online forum in which 60 informal caregivers participated, and the material analysed was their discussion on the forum. The capability approach informed the qualitative inquiry, and in the thematic analysis Nussbaum's list of core capabilities was used. The results showed the interconnection between capabilities and emotions. The caregivers' freedom to choose how they lived their lives was to a high extent influenced by their emotional attachment to those for whom they cared. The caregivers valued the capability to care for loved ones. The core principle emphasised in this study was to identify capabilities through deliberative democracy, which inspired the methodology of online 'democratic dialogue' (ibid.). It was also asserted that the capability approach as delineated by Sen informed the choice of a participatory method and the use of thick descriptions (i.e., a detailed account of field experiences in which the researcher makes explicit the patterns of cultural and social relationships and places them in context). The capacity to experience emotions was important across all capabilities. The different capabilities were described as interconnected; for example, providing care for loved ones required giving up employment, leading to financial difficulties. This study is important for social work because informal caregiving and support for this group is a field of practice for social workers. Furthermore, social care and social policies were discussed in the article.

In another study from New Zealand, Yeung and Breheny (2016) used the capability approach to understand the determinants of subjective well-being among community-dwelling older people. A sample from the New Zealand Longitudinal Study of Ageing (n = 2793, aged 50–87) was used to examine the relationships between commodities, environmental factors and the capabilities of older people to achieve well-being. A specific model of the capability approach was employed which situated 'healthy ageing as a matter of social justice and in particular, an issue of inequality' (Saleeby, 2007: 296). The characteristics of commodities were distinguished as a reflection of a person's life situation, which includes environmental and personal factors as well as physical functioning. Personal factors, for example economic well-being, disability and environmental factors such as accessibility, stigma and attitude were said to facilitate or limit functionings. Additionally, a measure of living standards for older people based on Sen's capability approach (LSCAPE) was developed and included in the survey (further described in Yeung & Breheny, 2016, Appendix 2). This study aimed to explain the relationships between measured functionings, and the results showed that real opportunities increased well-being. For the oldest participants, the relationship between living standards and well-being was weak, but experiences of discrimination had a stronger effect on well-being. The need for policymakers and social workers to address aspects of discrimination, poor mental health and disability in older age was highlighted, issues that are of high priority for social work.

11.7.2 Addressing Social Inequalities at a Structural Level

Older people's experiences of self-funding social care in the UK were analysed by Tanner et al. (2018). The authors discuss both the capability approach and personalisation, arguing that these are individualised and not collective ways to conceive functionings and well-being. The authors criticise these approaches for reflecting neoliberal values, which do not sufficiently consider the influence of social structures on capabilities. By using a relational–political interpretation of the capability approach, they seek to remedy the criticism of an individual agenda and instead embrace structural factors that restrict or enhance capabilities and relationships that have an impact on well-being. The results underline networks of care, and through viewing capabilities and functionings in relational terms, older people's well-being is depicted as depending on relationships with others and not on individual purchasing power or consumer choice. This research is important for social work with older people because it addresses the complexities involved in finding, arranging and managing care, particularly for older people with multiple needs. At a general level, this research also aims to formulate more socially just policy responses to the funding of social care, which is also in line with a social work agenda.

11.8 Discussion

The aim of the scoping review was to examine how the use of the capability approach is linked to policies, practices and social justice approaches in social work research addressing older people. In general, most articles arguing that the capability approach is suitable for social work research emphasise that it is a theory that can be used to understand, and sometimes to underpin, action for social justice, human dignity and well-being, which correspond to the core principles of social work (den Braber, 2013). The history of social work, and its origins in welfare work once carried out by charity organisations or through the settlement movements, reveals two different theoretical approaches. Welfare is either something that is given to those in need, who use their individual abilities to make the best of their situation – or as functionings (knowledge, skills) that can be achieved in a democratic community where people share resources and support one another. In the best of worlds, these two different assumptions would be conflated, and it has been argued that the capability approach offers such an evaluative theoretical frame (Robeyns, 2005), which could be adopted, for example, in social work education (Carlson et al., 2016). However, Robeyns (2005) cautions against regarding the capability approach as simply a formula for interpersonal comparisons of welfare or as merely a theory of equality or social justice. She stresses that it is a broad normative framework with which it is possible to conceptualise and evaluate poverty, inequality and well-being. In the studies presented here, the capability approach was used as a measure of the relationship between different capabilities for older people. This resulted in general recommendations for policymakers and social workers to pay attention to discriminatory practices (Yeung & Breheny, 2016). The approach was also used to understand the relationship between emotions and capabilities, leading to discussions relevant to support for informal caregivers (Horrell et al., 2015), and paying attention to relational factors, such as networks of care (Tanner et al., 2018). Finally, the capability approach was used as a way of promoting empowerment through the first-hand experiences of older people, with attention directed towards policymakers and social work in general (Gilroy, 2006).

The studies all referred to Sen, Nussabaum and Robeyns. Yeung and Breheny included specific questions in a nationwide survey designed in line with Sen's capability approach. Gilroy (2006) elaborated on Robeyns' approach of deriving a list of capabilities from 'democratic processes', and Horrell et al. (2015) used Nussbaum's ten core capabilities to analyse their material. None of the studies had an evaluative aim; instead, they assessed well-being for older people and provided recommendations for policy development and social work practice. As with most research findings, the question remains as to the degree to which policymakers and social workers actually read and make use of these research results.

Capabilities help people to achieve their functionings, but there can also be barriers to capability in people's environments, such as poverty (Sen, 1999). These social constraints, inequalities and discrimination are taken into account when using the capability approach, which is important in social work. The promotion of empowerment for older people through a focus on their own voices and encouragement to live lives of independence and well-being is also in line with the social work agenda. However, different anti-oppressive and critical theories and practices are already commonly used and discussed in social work (e.g. Dominelli, 2002). The empowerment movement has a long tradition in social work (e.g. Adams, 2008). It rests on the same premises as the capability approach: social justice, anti-oppressive actions and equality. The concept of empowerment was also used in the studies analysed in this chapter. As a matter of fact, the contradictory uses (and misuses) of empowerment in social work may carry some lessons for the future implementation of the capability approach, which now seems to be dawning upon social work. Tew (2006) cautions against the different uses of empowerment in social work, where it is defined *for* powerless people *by* professionals, and it is not uncommon for this definition of empowerment to be in line with a neoliberal discourse of everybody being responsible for their own actions, coupled with a call to dismantle welfare policies. For example, not every person is equally able to make choices, an issue that has been discussed in relation to older people's difficulties in choosing to leave a nursing home if they are dissatisfied with the care (Kjellberg, 2012). A similar critique applies to anti-oppressive practices (e.g. Wilson & Beresford, 2000) and has also been raised towards the capability approach (Dean, 2009). However, as Robeyns (2006) states, the social influences on individual choice require complimentary theories in order to be adequately analysed. Nor is the capability approach a theory that can explain poverty or inequality. There may be a risk of overstating the social justice aspect of the capability approach because it corresponds to core principals in social work, just as empowerment attracts social work due to its emphasis on participatory power. However, the studies presented here did demonstrate a potential for the capability approach to be used in assessing older people's well-being. In the future, more studies concerning social care for older people with different, and more developed, ways of using the capability approach are likely to follow.

11.9 Conclusions

Promoting social justice and human rights in a global context are core values of the social work profession, and correspond with the basic principles of the capability approach. In this chapter, a sample of research discussing and using the capability approach in social work with older people has been presented. The starting point for the literature search was a scoping review of how the capability approach has been used in social work research (Kjellberg & Jansson, 2020). This revealed four main applications of the capability approach: to explore the sense of subjective well-being, to address social inequalities at a structural level, as a tool for social workers in practice (e.g. to promote strength and support individuals and disadvantaged groups to realise their capabilities) and to evaluate social practices. Only four articles addressing social work with older people were found, despite the use of an extended search strategy. These four articles explored the sense of subjective well-being of older people or their informal caregivers and one study discussed social inequalities at a structural level.

It has been argued that there is great potential for the capability approach to be applied to social work strategies, professional work and research (den Braber, 2013; Babic et al., 2010). The care of older people is of great concern for social work because many social workers are engaged in this field. Only a few studies were found in this search; however, more seems to have been done within the fields of healthcare and developmental studies. Moreover, many empirical studies concern capabilities, poverty and disadvantaged groups, but many studies do not explicitly address 'social work', and therefore they were not included in this analysis. These studies may very well be of great interest for social work research and practice. Despite these limitations, our conclusion is that the capability approach has obviously attracted some interest in social work with older people and the amount of research elaborating on the capability approach in social work in general is growing. However, when it comes to social work with older people, it seems as though this development is in its infancy, and that there is a potential in the capability approach to assess older people's well-being. It is likely that further developments of different uses of the capability approach will follow.

References

Adams, R. (2008). *Empowerment, participation and social work* (4th ed.). Palgrave Macmillan.

Andersson, L. (2008). *Ålderism* [Ageism]. Studentlitteratur.

Arksey, H., & O'Malley, L. (2005). Scoping studies: Towards a methodological framework. *International Journal of Social Research Methodology, 8*(1), 19–32. https://doi.org/10.1080/1364557032000119616

Babic, B., Graf, G., & Germes Castro, O. (2010). The capability approach as a framework for the evaluation of child and youth care. *European Journal of Social Work, 13*(3), 409–413. https://doi.org/10.1080/13691457.2010.519114

Banerjee, M., & Canda, E. (2012). Comparing Rawlsian justice and the capabilities approach to justice from a spiritually sensitive social work perspective. *Journal of Religion & Spirituality in Social Work: Social Thought, 31*(1–2), 9–31. https://doi.org/10.1080/15426432.2012.647874

Bytheway, B. (2005). Ageism and age categorization. *Journal of Social Issues, 61*(2), 361–374. https://doi.org/10.1111/j.1540-4560.2005.00410.x

Carlson, J., Nguyen, H., & Reinardy, J. (2016). Social justice and the capabilities approach: Seeking a global blueprint for the EPAS. *Journal of Social Work Education, 52*(3), 269–282. https://doi.org/10.1080/10437797.2016.1174635

Dean, H. (2009). Critiquing capabilities: The distractions of a beguiling concept. *Critical Social Policy, 29*(2), 261–278. https://doi.org/10.1177/0261018308101629

den Braber, C. (2013). The introduction of the capability approach in social work across a neoliberal Europe. *Journal of Social Intervention: Theory and Practice, 22*(4), 61–77. https://doi.org/10.18352/jsi.380

Deneulin, S. (2008). Beyond individual agency and freedom: Structures of living together in the capability approach. In S. Alkire, M. Qizilbash, & F. Comim (Eds.), *The capability approach: Concepts, measures and applications* (pp. 105–125). Cambridge University Press.

Dominelli, L. (2002). *Anti-oppressive social work theory and practice*. Palgrave Macmillan.

Gilroy, R. (2006). Taking a capabilities approach to evaluating supportive environments for older people. *Applied Research in Quality of Life, 1*(3), 343–356. https://doi.org/10.1007/s11482-007-9025-3

Gopinath, M. (2018). Thinking about later life: Insights from the capability approach. *Ageing International, 43*(2), 254–264. https://doi.org/10.1007/s12126-018-9323-0

Gray, M., & Webb, S. (2009). Critical social work. In M. Gray & S. Webb (Eds.), *Social work theories and methods* (pp. 76–85). Sage.

Gupta, A. (2017). Learning from others: An autoethnographic exploration of children and families: Social work, poverty and the capability approach. *Qualitative Social Work, 16*(4), 449–464. https://doi.org/10.1177/1473325015620946

Horrell, B., Stephens, C., Breheny, M., et al. (2015). Capability to care: Supporting the health of informal caregivers for older people. *Health Psychology, 34*(4), 339–348. https://doi.org/10.1037/hea0000144

Hugman, R. (2010). *Understanding international social work. A critical analysis*. Palgrave Macmillan.

International Federation of Social Workers/International Association of Schools of Social Work. (2014). *The global definition of social work.* http://ifsw.org/get-involved/global-definition-of-social-work/. Accessed 20 Feb 2018.

Jönson, H., & Harnett, T. (2015). *Socialt arbete med äldre* [Social work with older people]. Natur och kultur.

Kjellberg, I. (2012). *Klagomålshantering och lex Sarah-anmälningar i äldreomsorgen. En institutionell etnografisk studie* [Complaints procedures and mandatory reporting in Swedish care of older people: An institutional ethnography]. Department of Social Work, University of Gothenburg.

Kjellberg, I., & Jansson, B. (2020). The capability approach in social work research: A scoping review of research addressing practical social work. *International Social Work*. https://doi.org/10.1177/0020872819896849

National Association of Social Workers. (2017). *Code of ethics of the National Association of Social Workers*. National Association of Social Workers, Washington, DC.

Nussbaum, M. (2011). *Creating capabilities: The human development approach.* Harvard University Press.

Olson, J. (2007). Social work's professional and social justice projects: Discourses in conflict. *Journal of Progressive Human Services, 18*(1), 45–69. https://doi.org/10.1300/J059v18n01_04

Payne, M. (2005). *The origins of social work: Continuity and change*. Palgrave Macmillan.

Pham, M., Rajić, A., Greig, J., et al. (2014). A scoping review of scoping reviews: Advancing the approach and enhancing the consistency. *Research Synthesis Methods, 5*(4), 371–385. https://doi.org/10.1002/jrsm.1123

Ray, M., & Phillips, J. (2012). *Social work with older people* (5th ed.). Palgrave Macmillan.

Reisch, M., & Jani, J. (2012). The new politics of social work practice: Understanding context to promote change. *British Journal of Social Work, 42*(6), 1132–1150. https://doi.org/10.1093/bjsw/bcs072

Robeyns, I. (2005). The capability approach: A theoretical survey. *Journal of Human Development, 6*(1), 93–117. https://doi.org/10.1080/146498805200034266

Robeyns, I. (2006). The capability approach in practice. *Journal of Political Philosophy, 14*(3), 351–376. https://doi.org/10.1111/j.1467-9760.2006.00263.x

Robeyns, I. (2017). *Wellbeing, freedom and justice: The capability approach re-examined.* Open Book Publishers. https://doi.org/10.11647/OBP.0130

Rogers, J. (2012). Anti-Oppressive social work research: Reflections on power in the creation of knowledge. *Social Work Education, 31*(7):866–879. https://doi.org/10.1080/02615479.2011.602965

Saleeby, P. (2007). Applications of a capability approach to disability and the international classification of functioning, disability and health (ICF) in social work practice. *Journal of Social Work in Disability & Rehabilitation, 6*(1–2), 217–232. https://doi.org/10.1300/J198v06n01_12

Sen, A. (1993). Capability and well-being. In Nussbaum, M., & Sen, A. (Eds.) *The quality of life.* Clarendon Press.

Sen, A. (1999). The possibility of social choice. *American Economic Review, 89*(3), 349–378. https://doi.org/10.1257/aer.89.3.34

Sen, A. (2009). Capability: Reach and Limit. In *Debating Global Society: Reach and Limits of the Capability Approach.* Fondazione Giangiacomo Feltrinelli (pp. 15–28).

Strier, R. (2007). Anti-oppressive research in social work: A preliminary definition. *British Journal of Social Work, 37*(5), 857–871. https://doi.org/10.1093/bjsw/bcl062

Tanner, D., Ward, L., & Ray, M. (2018). Paying our own way: Application of the capability approach to explore older people's experiences of self-funding social care. *Critical Social Policy, 38*(2), 262–282. https://doi.org/10.1177/0261018317724344

Tew, J. (2006). Understanding power and powerlessness. *Journal of Social Work, 6*(1), 33–51. https://doi.org/10.1177/1468017306062222

Tricco, A. C., Lillie, E., Zarin, W., et al. (2018). PRISMA extension for scoping reviews (PRISMA-ScR): Checklist and explanation. *Annals of Internal Medicine, 169*(7), 467–473. https://doi.org/10.7326/M18-0850

Wilson, A., & Beresford, P. (2000). Anti-oppressive practice: Emancipation or appropriation? *British Journal of Social Work, 30*(5), 553–573. https://doi.org/10.1093/bjsw/30.5.553

Yeung, P., & Breheny, M. (2016). Using the capability approach to understand the determinants of subjective Well-being among community-dwelling older people in New Zealand. *Age and Ageing, 45*(2), 292–298. https://doi.org/10.1093/ageing/afw002

Chapter 12
A Historical Perspective on Ageing and Capability

Ulrika Lagerlöf Nilsson and Helene Castenbrandt

12.1 Introduction

> I am a soldier's widow, 60 1/2 years old, I do not enjoy any pension, but have housing until I die. By helping a bachelor with his household, I get food for myself. I receive some poor relief (1/2 cord of wood). Otherwise, I am very sick. Will I get a pension this year? How much? Do I need to pay a fee? Answers are most gratefully apprehended in your honourable newspaper's local edition. *Soldier's Widow*. (Stockholmstidningen, 5 March 1914 [This quote is translated from Swedish and the language has been adjusted to aid the readability]

This letter was posted in a Swedish newspaper when a universal pension system was being implemented in 1914, more than 100 years ago. At that time, several newspapers ran 'Questions and Answers columns' related to the new pension reform. A lot of people, like the soldier's widow in this letter, seemed to see the new law as an opportunity to improve their well-being, lifting them out of their often poverty-stricken circumstances. Moreover, this reform can be seen as a change in the functionings with which society found it reasonable to provide its citizens, marking a shift in the state's responsibility for the well-being of older people.

Historians in general are interested in studying continuity and change at the macro-, meso- and micro-levels and they ask questions such as: How has development at a societal level affected the living conditions of individuals? Are there patterns and lines that can be followed throughout history? By trying to understand

U. Lagerlöf Nilsson (✉)
Department of Historical Studies, University of Gothenburg, Gothenburg, Sweden

Centre for Ageing and Health – AgeCap, University of Gothenburg, Gothenburg, Sweden
e-mail: ulrika.lagerlof.nilsson@history.gu.se

H. Castenbrandt
Centre for Ageing and Health – AgeCap, University of Gothenburg, Gothenburg, Sweden

Department of Economic History, Lund University, Lund, Sweden
e-mail: helene.castenbrandt@ekh.lu.se

H. Falk Erhag et al. (eds.), *A Multidisciplinary Approach to Capability in Age and Ageing*, International Perspectives on Aging 31,
https://doi.org/10.1007/978-3-030-78063-0_12

how development has taken place during the past, and by focusing on continuities and changes, we gain knowledge about how these have been dealt with and how dilemmas have been resolved. One could then argue whether or not the changes throughout history should be viewed as progress or a reversion, whether they have been fast or slow, and which groups have benefited or become disadvantaged through these developments. Such changes are sometimes obvious, but at other times they are almost imperceptible, and historians seek to explain and understand the driving forces behind these developments.

The aim of this chapter is to explore the usefulness of the capability approach within historical research on age and ageing. As historians, we investigate phenomena that are important for today's society that have occurred throughout history. Studies can then explore questions such as: How have the processes of caring for older people been organised in the past? What changes can be observed over time? How have these changes been argued for? For example, how was an 'older person' defined in the past, what changes can be noted, and how can such changes be explained? What activities are seemingly embedded in human society or more governed by rapid change? These are all questions that drive historical research. In this chapter, we ask how the capability approach fits into questions involving historical transformations. The main question is thus: what does capability mean in different times and spaces? One reason for exploring the usefulness of the capability approach in our historical analyses is that it enables conversations between scientific disciplines. Using the same theoretical framework dissolves the obstacles created by the differences between our disciplines and enables us to hold a dialogue around the common goal of our research: to better understand the living conditions of older people in the past and present, and how such issues can be addressed in the future.

Since Amartya Sen framed and developed the theoretical framework around the capability approach during the 1980s and 1990s, it has been widely debated and theorised (Sen, 1979, 1985, 1989, 1999). At the political scale, Sen's work has influenced the design of the Human Development Index (HDI), in which key capabilities, such as access to health and education, are used as indicators of well-being, displaying a practical implementation of the theory (Stanton, 2007). A very tangible implementation of the HDI is the United Nations Human Development Report, which has been published annually since 1990 with the aim of increasing human well-being by shifting the focus from econometric measures to human life in itself (United Nations Development Programme, n.d.). Still, researchers have found it difficult to operationalise the theoretical framework of the capability approach into distinct methodological tools (Robeyns, 2006; Alkire, 2005). Even so, the empirical applications are increasing, and several books have been published trying to demonstrate, with empirical examples, the applications of the capability approach in several different research areas (Ibrahim & Tiwari, 2014; Kuklys, 2005; Stoecklin & Bonvin, 2014; Robeyns, 2005).

The main point of the capability approach is to analyse well-being in broad terms, taking into account a number of indicators to create a multi-dimensional approach (Robeyns, 2005; Kremakova, 2013; Ibrahim, 2014). It is also a normative framework, which incorporates distinguishing factors, such as poverty, equality and well-being for individuals in groups and society. However, as Ingrid Robeyns emphasises: 'The capability approach is not a theory that can *explain* poverty, inequality or well-being; instead, it provides concepts and a framework that can help to *conceptualize* and *evaluate* these phenomena.' (Robeyns, 2005, 2006: 353; Kremakova, 2013: 404; Zimmermann, 2006.) The rest of this chapter gives a short introduction to the usage of the capability approach in historical research, followed by examples, where we use the capability approach to explore the different, and changing, capabilities of older people during the early twentieth century in Sweden.

12.2 The Capability Approach and Historical Studies

Capability can be broadly understood as an individual's ability to achieve good well-being and live a good life. The capability approach aims to focus on material goods and services, as well as the functionings and capabilities that a person needs to live a life they value as good. What this means depends on ideas that are widespread in society, as well as the individual's own perceptions. These ideas and perceptions differ over time and space, due to society's view of certain groups (e.g. older people or children), as well as individual opportunities and limitations in terms of finances, resources and interests (Robeyns, 2005).

When we take a historical perspective to try to understand the lives people have lived, there are some basic factors we need to take into account in order to understand the past. Sweden, like most other countries, has experienced major changes to its population structure. The group of older people has increased tremendously; at the turn of the twentieth century, the number of people aged 70 or over had almost tripled since 1850, while the population as a whole had increased by around 50% during the same period (Statistiska centralbyrån, 1969, 68). This development was explosive, and the Swedish healthcare system had just begun to be publicly bureaucratically organised and institutionalised. There was still a long way to go before it was available to everyone. The groups who suffered most were older people and children (Odén, 1982: 29). Furthermore, a person's living conditions were entirely based upon who they were and where they lived. This meant that class, geographical domicile and gender were crucial factors impacting upon the life you were going to live, and had consequences for how life developed as you got older.

It has been argued that one of the weaknesses of the capability approach is handling changes over time (Srinivasan, 1994). What people value changes over time, making it difficult to evaluate and compare the well-being of different generations throughout history. However, rather than recognising it as a weakness, changes in people's abilities and what they value can be used to capture the evolving opportunities for individuals. This notion has led other scholars to state that it is this openness and breadth of the capability approach that makes it applicable to historical and sociological studies (Robeyns, 2005; Kremakova, 2013). Moreover, Ingrid Robeyns argues that the cross-disciplinary use and highly developed theoretical framework around the capability approach make it a useful theoretical approach as well as a methodological one (Robeyns, 2005, 2006). By this, Robeyns means that it is absolutely necessary to know the circumstances in which a person has been living if we are to determine which functionings that person can attain. She states:

> The capability approach takes account of human diversity in two ways: by its focus on the plurality of functionings and capabilities as the evaluative space, and by the explicit focus on personal and socio-environmental conversion factors of commodities into functionings, and on the whole social and institutional context that affects the conversion factors and also the capability set directly. (Robeyns, 2005: 99)

Thus, if a historical perspective were included, it would be possible to understand, for example, why some resources can be functionings and while others are not. Everything must be related to and understood in a wider context, not least in relation to the past. Then, using a capability approach in historical studies, combined with other perspectives and/or theories, can give a better understanding of how social structures, human sociality, collective living and the meaning of social action have developed over time and across place (Kremakova, 2013: 413).

The Swedish historian Maria Ågren has claimed that the capability approach in Sen's interpretation needs to be expressed in a way that helps people today to understand what well-being and a good society are and what 'to have capability' meant in the past. She claims that 'translation work' is needed to avoid any misunderstanding of how a good development should be characterised and understood from a historical perspective (Ågren, 2012). Ågren proposes talking about a 'good society', rather than 'good development'. It is only possible to interpret and understand what characterises a good society relative to contemporary time and space. She writes: 'Considering how central work was for people in early modern Sweden, it seems extremely relevant to ask how the possibilities and difficulties of work affected people's situation, their identity, their actions and their image of what a good society meant' (Ågren, 2012: 63).

The transition from working life to preparing oneself for old age provides an example of how historians can make use of a capability approach in order to study individual preconditions and society's expectations of its older citizens. This is an area where there has been continuous change, in the past as well as the present. Work is a phenomenon that can reflect several different functionings. Depending on the perspective of the study and the research question, work could be analysed as goods or as factors that could be explored as achieved functionings or something that enables evaluating capability (Robeyns, 2005: 101). Taking work as a starting point makes it possible to study perspectives on work and well-being, and how their *meaning* has changed over time.

With a focus on senior citizens, we have to ask ourselves: what capabilities have older people valued and what capabilities has society found it reasonable that they should have? How can we access such information about past generations? Historical information about which capabilities people, or groups of people, have valued at a certain time and place can be analysed through sources such as newspapers, biographies, diaries, letters and novels. By examining government reports, newspapers, parliamentary debates etc., it is possible to gain an understanding of the capabilities that societies have valued for older citizens over time. Moreover, it is also feasible to study how certain functionings have changed for a given group of individuals. In that sense, we can capture not only what people valued, but how they actually lived their lives, and how this has changed over time. Again, when considering older people, functionings like life expectancy, health, housing, social interactions and agency (viewed through work, living conditions and finances) would give us a sense of how the well-being of older people has changed over time, even though it cannot capture how they valued these functionings themselves.

When it comes to studies about age and ageing, it is important to be aware that 'being old' is not a definite or fixed stage in a person's life; instead, the definition of an old person differs across context, time and space (Thane, 2003: 98). In historical times, a person's ability to influence their lives depended on the social stratum of society to which they belonged. Birgitta Odén has therefore argued that the interesting historical question is how, despite their varying social and economic conditions, people tried to prepare themselves for old age, and how society, through its laws, institutions and organisational arrangements framed a person's available space to act (Odén, 1982: 28). Answers to such questions frame the functionings that society found it reasonable for older people to have, as well as what capabilities individuals valued.

12.3 Capabilities Among Older Women in the Early Twentieth Century

When historical studies are conducted to identify and evaluate the conditions that affected people's lives, a number of factors, such as gender, civil status and economic conditions, must be taken into account. Western families were in general structured around marriage, with nuclear families being the norm, even though intergenerational co-residence was fairly common (Ruggles, 2010: 15–16). There were more widows than widowers, because women often married younger and lived longer, while men more frequently remarried. These cultural and demographic structures left many widows in a difficult economic position (Blom, 1991: 192–195). Since it is well known that the history of women and their living conditions has traditionally been less thoroughly explored than that of men, we argue that it is valuable and beneficial to provide examples of the living conditions of older women in the early twentieth century. Through these examples, we aim to provide an understanding of how women in different social strata dealt with ageing, how their economic and marital status affected their opportunities, or lack thereof, and what freedoms they had to make choices as an older person.

In the first example, we introduce Selma Lagerlöf (1858–1940), who was (and still is) one of the most famous of all Swedish authors. In 1909, she was the first woman to be awarded the Nobel Prize in Literature. Lagerlöf's life and old age provide an excellent example, demonstrating how her life-story influenced her life as an old person. Selma Lagerlöf grew up in a family that had to deal with constant economic crises, and her father had alcohol problems. Early on, Lagerlöf wanted to get an education and she did receive support and encouragement, which enabled her to go to Stockholm and train at the Higher Teachers' Seminary. In this way, she was able to earn her own living. Lagerlöf had problems stemming from a hip injury sustained during childhood, and therefore had physical limitations. Her life took on completely different opportunities after she had forged a career as an author. After receiving the Nobel Prize, she was able to buy back the farm where she had grown up: Mårbacka, located in Värmland in the western part of Sweden. It had previously been sold at an executive auction due to her father's debts. She had the manor house rebuilt and modernised the farm's agriculture. She was eager to learn about how agriculture could be made more efficient and became a patron at Mårbacka (Palm, 2019). Lagerlöf was a prominent figure in the Swedish women's movement during the first decades of the twentieth century. As part of the large group of unmarried women, Lagerlöf, and many others in her situation, had to find a way of making a living on their own (Stenberg, 2018).

Selma Lagerlöf is a good example of a woman who made choices and decisions that resulted in a good life that supported her in her later years. It was far from clear what capabilities she would have as an old, unmarried woman. Her limited physical mobility, which for instance gave her a limp when walking, reduced her physical flexibility and made it difficult for her to perform hard physical work. This, in turn, meant that if she had not been financially independent due to her author status, she would have ended up either in the village's poor-house or as part of the parish's maintenance responsibility. During this time, in order to make a decent living, you had to be able to work without physical limitations. When analysing Lagerlöf's biography, we can see how the decisions she made throughout her life signify how she valued her capability. This was superior to everything else, because she had the freedom of choice due to being financially self-sufficient. She valued being independent, but to be so she had to work hard and struggle against the values and social order that were dominant at that time. Marriage was the legal order that ensured both support and financial security when a woman grew old, provided that she was part of a social group that enjoyed financial security. In contrast to Lagerlöf, we will also give some examples of women who did not have the same education or social background. These women had rather different experiences, which limited their capabilities as they reached old age.

Selma Lagerlöf had assets, both money and land, enabling her to live the life she wanted for herself as she aged. As previously mentioned, Lagerlöf was an important voice in the women's movement. She worked hard for the suffrage of women and for women to have their own rights and independence. Suffrage was at that time seen as the optimal consequence and functioning of the capability to gain the freedom to decide over one's own life. This was far from a matter of course for women at this time. The women who were active in the suffrage movement during the first decades of the twentieth century were driven to influence their own lives and to live the lives that they considered valuable for themselves. Not least, this concerned how they could continue to live as independent women even during the later years of life.

Although Selma Lagerlöf, like many women in the women's movement and Swedish suffrage movement, struggled and worked hard to achieve her life's work, she still belonged to a privileged group who had the options and freedom to think and hope for a long and healthy life. Hopefully, that would also mean a life with some economic security. But what about less fortunate women, like the soldier's widow quoted in the introduction? What could they hope for in later life, and what capabilities did they possess to aid them in their hopes? At the turn of the twentieth century, Sweden was still a poor country. Its great industrial breakthrough had just taken off, and a large part of the population still lived on the margins. Rising proletarianisation, a growing number of industrial workers, urbanisation and many people finding themselves in small, rented lodgings were all developments that made the need for some kind of pension system ever more apparent. The question had been debated in parliament for decades, but an agreement between political parties had proven difficult to achieve.

Throughout Europe, various different types of pension systems had been implemented and it was difficult to agree on what would be best for Sweden. Which groups should be included, on what grounds the pension should be granted and how it should be financed were all questions that were discussed (Elmér, 1960, 1972, 1986). Eventually, a law granting a universal pension was passed in 1913. This was made up of two parts. One part was based on individual contributions and was obtainable at the age of 67. However, this part was insignificant during the first few decades because one needed to contribute during an entire working life in order to receive the maximum amount. The second, state-funded, part was based on invalidity assessments and available to anyone over 15 years of age who could prove themselves permanently unable to work (Aldén, 1914). Even though this second part was small, and in line with the average level of poor relief, it was an important milestone in terms of self-determination and civil rights for those granted this pension. For the first time, Swedish citizens received an income transfer to poor groups that did not imply a restriction on civil rights, as poor relief did. Accessing the second part of the pension was function-dependent, because the important issue was not age, but a person's inability to perform a job. For most people, this meant that, even with the new pension system, they could not imagine themselves enjoying a time when they still had health and strength and would be able to draw an income without working. However, after a change in the law in 1935, a proper old age pension was eventually created, making both parts of the pension available to anyone over 67, regardless of invalidity status (von Schulzenheim, 1935).

When the implementation of the pension system was investigated, a survey of income and invalidity was conducted, covering everyone in Sweden over the age of 60. Questionnaires were sent to all the municipalities in Sweden asking them to fill in information on all the individuals in their area, and 93% were returned with sufficient information. This material provides information on the conditions and capabilities of unmarried women, in a way that is seldom visible in other data. The answers revealed that 60 percent of unmarried women over the age of 60 were receiving support for their livelihood in 1907. As close relatives had a dependency obligation, a majority (60%) were supported by relatives, often adult children, while the rest received municipality poor relief. Of those who received support, 95% were listed as unable to work, meaning that there was a large group of unmarried women who had to rely on support from others for their livelihood and to maintain their basic capabilities (Ålderdomsförsäkringskommittén & Lindstedt, 1912). This group of older, worn-out women did not have much choice about how to live their lives. They were fully dependent on what others could offer them, and what little help they could provide in return. For these women, the new pension reform offered a way of restoring their sense of value.

In 1913 and 1914, one of the large newspapers ran a 'Questions and Answers' column in relation to the new pension reform. It ran for nine months, and many people sent questions related to whether or not they could receive a pension (*Aftonbladet* November 1913–July 1914). Those who wrote were of all ages, and many were in some way or another unable to earn a living due to invalidity. Those of younger ages were often living with their parents. This was the case for a 47-year-old unmarried woman who had been bedbound for 3 years and was living with, and nursed by, her 73-year-old mother (*Aftonbladet* 16 January 1914). Another example is a 22-year-old woman who was partially paralysed after suffering from polio and was therefore unable to make a living, and had no one but her poor elderly parents to rely on (*Aftonbladet* 27 December 1913). The older people who sent questions were mostly poor and had no strength left to make a living. One example was a 66-year-old widow who was unable to work and for a long time had been supported by her children (*Aftonbladet* 26 February 1914). Another example is an incurably ill 64-year-old widow whose store had gone bankrupt in 1912. Since then, she had managed by renting out one or two rooms and by borrowing from friends. Having no strength left, she had no means of subsistence (*Aftonbladet* 18 December 1913). Judging by their letters, these people valued the basic security that a small pension would provide in their lives. In most cases, they had no income and no way of supporting themselves. Instead, they were dependent on the support of close relatives or municipality poor relief, and were at risk of ending up in a poor house. For them, the possibility of receiving a small, but steady, pension would gain them the opportunity, not to choose what life to live, but to be of some value to the relatives who supported them. For those who were living on poor relief, a pension might restore their pride as citizens.

As society changed, and new forms of support were needed, so it created a new structural support system that enabled those who had lost a key capability, namely the ability to support themselves through work, to uphold their sense of dignity. It no longer seemed reasonable that people who had struggled, but could no longer provide for themselves, should have to rely on stigmatising poor relief, or to be a heavy burden on their often impoverished relatives.

These examples have shown how differently the economic conditions and opportunities for women from different social groups influenced how they were able to live their lives as older people. This thus influenced their capability and how they valued their functionings.

12.4 Discussion

The aim of this chapter was to explore and discuss the usefulness of the capability approach within historical research on age and ageing. In this analysis, we have focused on gender and class, two fundamental factors influencing the capabilities that people value as they prepare for old age. These factors, along with many other parameters, are important in order to fully understand the differences in achieved capabilities and why a person values his or her life in the way that they do. The preconditions for the values of factors and goods are constantly shifting and are always dependent on context. In historical studies, it is therefore necessary to identify people's social background, the available preconditions and also society's contemporary expectations of the individual. Currently, both over recent decades and in the future, gender and class seem to be factors that (will) influence and determine the opportunities for self-determination and the ability to achieve capability. It seems that, ultimately, the practical application of legislation and regulations always becomes individual and is influenced by a person's unique conditions, assets and opportunities.

By focusing on which functionings society has been able to provide for its older citizens in different historical times and environments, it could become clear which capabilities older people value. How this is expressed may differ depending on the time and place in which the phenomenon occurs. It is also necessary to be aware of the importance of focusing on the three different societal levels: macro, meso and micro, in order to fully comprehend the opportunities to use functionings as a way to achieve a person's capability to live a good life, or at least a life that they value as good.

During each historical period, as well as today, a fundamental priority in life has been to fulfil a person's basic needs: to have food, somewhere to live and social connections with others. The authorities at different levels have the responsibility to support their citizens by removing the obstacles preventing them from fulfilling these basic needs. This in turn leads to the other factor that we have highlighted through our given examples. People, whether they are rich or poor, want to feel self-respect. They also want to have a sense of dignity and pride as citizens. Regardless of gender, financial or social status, people want to feel valued as human beings. It is clear that those impoverished women who had lost their main capability to support themselves through work welcomed the basic security and sense of value that the new universal pension could provide for them. However, the same need for human value is also clear in the example of Selma Lagerlöf, one of the many women who fought for independence and respect. The road to get there was a difficult one when the social order stipulated something else. A woman should be married and depend on her husband, be responsible for her children and take care of the home. The women who wanted to live a different life, and wanted to achieve other forms of capabilities, needed to find alternative ways to reach their goals. Sometimes their functionings, supported by society and government institutions, could help them, but at other times the support and tools were few or non-existent.

It is in these latter cases that it is interesting to examine in more detail the strategies and approaches that women used to achieve the goal that they believed constituted a dignified life.

The range and uses of the capability approach are many. It is most desirable in large collaborations when different research areas are studying the same question from different perspectives (see e.g. Alkire, 2005). The framework of the capability approach demands multidisciplinary studies, and Robeyns stresses that there is a need for 'multidimensional empirical analysis' to underpin and operationalise the capability approach (Robeyns, 2006: 371). She argues:

> To fully understand the importance of groups, the capability approach should engage more intensively in a dialogue with disciplines such as sociology, anthropology, history, and gender and cultural studies. Disciplinary boundaries and structures make this kind of dialogue difficult, but there is no inherent reason why this could not be done. (Robeyns, 2005: 109–110).

This underlines the importance of a multidisciplinary volume like this, where different scientific fields frame the use of this theoretical and methodological approach. Moreover, scholars have claimed that the capability approach is neither a theory nor a method. It has also been stated that the approach is difficult to use to make comparisons over time. There seems to be a reason why historians have not used the capability concept or even characterised their research approach as a capability approach. We want to argue that historians can benefit from using this approach. It could be used to conceptualise and evaluate phenomena that give a deeper, hopefully better, understanding of human circumstances, regardless of time and space. Capability is about interpreting different living conditions, and it illuminates continuity and change, similarities and variations. By making these patterns visible, we gain an understanding of the past, can better understand our present-day, and thus might be better able to prepare ourselves to handle the future. In this chapter, the capability approach has been demonstrated to be a good tool for visualising historical patterns, and therefore supports the claim that this approach is feasible to be used to a greater extent in historical research.

References

Aftonbladet. (November 1913–July 1914), https://tidningar.kb.se. Accessed 5 Apr 2020.

Ågren, M. (2012). Genus och arbete i det tidigmoderna Sverige. *Historisk tidskrift, 132*(1), 55–64.

Aldén, G. A. (Ed.). (1914). *Lagen om allmän folkpensionering av den 30 juni 1913* (6th ed.). Hökerberg.

Ålderdomsförsäkringskommittén, Lindstedt, A. (1912). *Ålderdomsförsäkringskommittén 2 Kostnadsberäkningar*. Stockholm.

Alkire, S. (2005). Why the capability approach? *Journal of Human Development, 6*(1), 115–135. https://doi.org/10.1080/146498805200034275

Blom, I. (1991). The history of widowhood: A bibliographic overview. *Journal of Family History, 16*(2), 191–210. https://doi.org/10.1177/036319909101600206

Elmér, Å. (1960). *Folkpensioneringen i Sverige. Med särskild hänsyn till ålderspensioneringen*. Gleerup.

Elmér, Å. (1972). *Från Fattigsverige till välfärdsstaten. Sociala förhållanden och socialpolitik i Sverige under nittonhundratalet* (5th ed.). Aldus.

Elmér, Å. (1986). *Svensk socialpolitik* (16th ed.). Liber.

Ibrahim, S. (2014). Introduction: The capability approach: From theory to practice –rationale, review and reflections. In S. Ibrahim & M. Tiwari (Eds.), *The capability approach: From theory to practice* (pp. 1–28). Palgrave Macmillan.

Ibrahim, S., & Tiwari, M. (2014). *The capability approach: From theory to practice*. Palgrave Macmillan.

Kremakova, M. (2013). Too soft for economics, too rigid for sociology, or just right? The productive ambiguities of Sen's capability approach. *European Journal of Sociology, 54*(3), 393–419. https://doi.org/10.1017/S0003975613000210

Kuklys, W. (2005). *Amartya Sen's capability approach: Theoretical insights and empirical applications*. Springer.

Odén, B. (1982). Demografi. En introduktion. In L. Tornstam, B. Odén, & A. Svanborg (Eds.), *Äldre i samhället. Förr, nu och i framtiden. D. 2, Probleminventeringar* (pp. 27–39). Liber Förlag.

Palm, A. (2019). 'Jag vill sätta världen i rörelse'. En biografi över Selma Lagerlöf. Albert Bonniers förlag.

Robeyns, I. (2005). The capability approach: A theoretical survey. *Journal of Human Development, 6*(1), 93–114. https://doi.org/10.1080/146498805200034266

Robeyns, I. (2006). The capability approach in practice. *Journal of Political Philosophy, 14*(3), 351–376.

Ruggles, S. (2010). Stem families and joint families in comparative historical perspective. *Population and Development Review, 36*(3), 563–577. https://doi.org/10.1111/j.1728-4457.2010.00346.x

Sen A (1979) *Equality of what? The Tanner Lectures on human values*. Delivered at Stanford University (Publication no. https://tannerlectures.utah.edu/_documents/a-to-z/s/sen80.pdf.) Accessed 12 Mar 2018.

Sen, A. (1985). *Commodities and capabilities*. North-Holland.

Sen, A. (1989). *Development as capability expansion*. http://www.masterhdfs.org/masterHDFS/wp-content/uploads/2014/05/Sen-development.pdf. Accessed 14 Mar 2018.

Sen, A. (1999). *Development as freedom*. Oxford University Press.

Srinivasan, T. N. (1994). Human development: A new paradigm or reinvention of the wheel? *The American Economic Review, 84*(2), 238–243. https://www.jstor.org/stable/2117836. Accessed 8 Feb 2018.

Stanton, E. (2007). *The Human Development Index: A history*. https://scholarworks.umass.edu/cgi/viewcontent.cgi?article=1101&context=peri_workingpapers. Accessed 8 Feb 2018.

Statistiska centralbyrån. (1969). *Historisk statistik för Sverige: Del 1. Befolkning* (2nd ed.).

Stenberg, L. (2018). *Selma Ottilia Lovisa Lagerlöf*. http://www.skbl.se/sv/artikel/SelmaLagerlof,Svensktkvinnobiografisktlexikon. Accessed 21 Sept 2020.

Stockholmstidningen. (1914, March 5). https://tidningar.kb.se Accessed 2 July 2020.

Stoecklin, D., & Bonvin, J. M. (2014). *Children's rights and the capability approach: Challenges and prospects*. Springer.

Thane, P. (2003). Social histories of old age and aging. *Journal of social history 37*(1), 93–111.

United Nations Development Programme. (n.d.) *About human development*. Retrieved from http://hdr.undp.org/en/humandev Accessed 8 Feb 2018.

von Schulzenheim, H. (1935). Den nya lagen om folkpensionering. In *Svensk Sjukkassekalender 1936: Uppslagsbok för sjukkassefolket* (pp. 9–19).

Zimmermann, B. (2006). Pragmatism and the capability approach: Challenges in social theory and empirical research. *European Journal of Social Theory, 9*(4), 467–484. https://doi.org/10.1177/1368431006073014

Chapter 13
The Capabilities Approach and the Concepts of Self-Determination, Legal Competence and Human Dignity in Social Services for Older People

Eva-Maria Svensson, Therese Bäckman, and Torbjörn Odlöw

13.1 Introduction

The example at the beginning of this chapter illustrates some of the complexities. According to Swedish law, it is not within the power of a legal representative to apply for special housing for a person who does not want it, even when the person's need could motivate such an application. Legal representation in the form of mentorship or administratorship in Sweden should not be used for compulsory power when it comes to questions of social services for older people and, for example, the need for special housing (Hovrätten över Skåne och Blekinge, mål nr ÖÄ 1368-07). Hence, one could argue that there is a tension between the right to self-determination and human dignity within the Swedish legal system.

Sven is 86 years old and lives alone in his apartment. He is suffering from incipient dementia and has home help services according to the Swedish Social Services Act. Sven doesn't shower for weeks at a time and the smell becomes unbearable. Some days he refuses to take his medicine. As his home conditions deteriorate, the home help staff draw attention to Sven's need for special housing. But Sven doesn't want to move, he is happy in his apartment and makes it clear to the social services officer that he will not apply for special housing. A few months pass and Sven is assigned a mentor who is supposed to support him in his decision-making. Sven is persistent, he does not want to apply for special housing. Since the need for special housing is apparent, the mentor decides to fill in an application on Sven's behalf.

E.-M. Svensson (✉) · T. Bäckman · T. Odlöw
Department of Law, School of Business, Economics and Law, University of Gothenburg, Gothenburg, Sweden

Centre for Ageing and Health – AgeCap, University of Gothenburg, Gothenburg, Sweden
e-mail: eva-maria.svensson@law.gu.se; therese.backman@law.gu.se; torbjorn.odlow@law.gu.se

H. Falk Erhag et al. (eds.), *A Multidisciplinary Approach to Capability in Age and Ageing*, International Perspectives on Aging 31,
https://doi.org/10.1007/978-3-030-78063-0_13

The law regulates most spheres of life, private as well as public, and applies to everyone. The law also sets the preconditions for people in their everyday lives. The starting point is that every human being has the competence to determine what to do with their life. But what happens when a person is not capable of doing so? The law is anchored in a belief in human dignity and solidarity, which obligates society to take care of people who are not able to take care of themselves. The law has to balance between these values, and the outcome of this balancing act is implemented with the help of institutions and resources established by the authorities or the political system within a society. How this system works and guarantees certain values, such as self-determination and human dignity, is an issue for legal scholarship. To grow old, or to age, is a condition that most people experience. Some of them are or will become dependent on others in their daily lives. How well the system, constructed in law, will work at this point is reflected upon here.

Ageing today is increasingly framed as successful (e.g. Örebro University n.d.; AgeCap at University of Gothenburg n.d.) and there is, at least in a Nordic context, an intense debate about older people's right to continue working based on better health in later life and longer life expectancy. Capability, meaning the individual's ability to perform actions in order to reach goals he or she has reason to value, as a concept and as a normative framework (the Capability or Capabilities approach) used to promote individuals' capability to convert available resources into desired functions – for example enjoying good health, being able to socially integrate and participate, and to maintain independence – can be seen in this context. The focus seems to be on the individual's ability (capability) but, as we will elaborate further in this chapter, supportive structures are equally necessary.

At the same time, older people are not only identified as active agents. They are also addressed as being in need of specific protection and, at least potentially, as vulnerable, in international and national governmental policies and legislation (see e.g. The AGE Platform Europe n.d.). Old age and stereotypical prejudices about age are also addressed as problems (Butler, 1969; Abramsson et al., 2017), not least when it comes to participation in the labour market (see e.g. The European Union Agency for Fundamental Rights n.d.). Since the beginning of the twenty-first century, age has been identified as one of the grounds protected by law against discrimination, and the protection of older people is addressed in international and national policies and legal documents, such as the United Nations Principles for Older Persons, adopted in 1991, the Recommendation (2014)02 on the promotion of human rights of older persons by the Council of Erope Parliamentary Assembly, and adopted by the Committee of Ministers on 19 February 2014. There is also a proposed United Nation Convention on the Rights of Older Persons, promoted by the Open-Ended Working Group on Ageing that was established by the General Assembly in 2010. This convention is based on other instruments with a focus on specific groups, such as the Convention on the Rights of Persons with Disabilities (CRPD) ratified by Sweden in 2008. CRPD is also relevant when it comes to older people, because disabilities increase with age.

The tension between increased capability and the need for protection among older people is also of interest regarding the specific issue of social services for older people in Sweden. Social services in Sweden aim to meet individual needs among people who are particularly vulnerable or experiencing difficulties. The objectives of the government policy are to assist older people:

> to be able to lead active lives and have influence in society and their own everyday lives, for them to be able to grow old in security and retain their independence, for them to be met with respect and to have access to good health and social services. (Prop., 2018/19:1 Utgiftsområde 9, 16)

The municipalities, which are responsible for providing social services to older people, should, according to the law, focus on creating conditions that ensure older people can lead a life of dignity and well-being.

Social services are based on the two pillars of self-determination and protection from harm (human dignity). Self-determination, a concept close to capability, seems to require what in legal terms is constructed as two separate concepts: 'to have an ability' and to have 'legal competence'. Everyone has a (potential) ability, but competence can be limited and the most obvious group having restricted competence is children. People with limited, or even no, ability to make decisions nevertheless have the right to self-determination. Consequently, self-determination cannot be synonymous with individual autonomy or the capability to make decisions. Self-determination is a fiction that is sometimes performed by someone other than the person her/himself, a representative (rules on legal representation are included in The Children and Parents Code as well as in the Guardianship Ordinance).

Self-determination in the context of social services for older people (according to the Social Services Act) means that everyone has the right to decide whether they need social services and, if so, in what way. At the same time, there is an obligation for the municipalities to ensure human dignity for everyone and a life that is in accordance with fundamental values, such as a reasonable standard of living, irrespective of the person's own wishes. This obligation could, at least hypothetically, be in conflict with the individual person's self-determination. What happens if a person does not have the physical or cognitive ability to make decisions, or if a person decides to live in a way that is not in accordance with a reasonable standard of living? The legal system provides certain tools to handle these situations. If a person does not have the ability to make a decision, she or he may be represented by someone else, through some kind of legal representation. A situation in which a person makes decisions that are contradictory to human dignity, or to some other fundamental value, is more complicated and quite controversial at a time in which self-determination and individual autonomy are increasingly emphasised.

In this chapter, we will address the tensions between self-determination on the one hand, and human dignity on the other, within the Swedish legal system regarding social services for older people, with help from the capabilities approach.[1] The

[1] The capability approach, formulated by Amartya Sen as an alternative approach to welfare economics and further elaborated by Martha C. Nussbaum (who extended the capability concept to the plural), has been predominant as a paradigm for policy debate around human development. A range of ideas that were previously excluded from (or inadequately formulated in) traditional approaches (measured by, e.g., GDP) to the economics of welfare were brought together in this approach. The capabilities approach is sensitive to inequalities and lack of resources for a part of the population, and meets the need to acknowledge distribution and, additionally, to improve the levels of quality of life (Nussbaum, 2013).

increased focus on self-determination, which has been around for some years, based on philosophical presumptions of individual autonomy and free will, together with a quest to enable increased capability for older people, might, in the context of a dismantled welfare state, turn out to be a double-edged sword, leaving the individual with self-determination but no (or insufficient) available social services to decide about. The capabilities approach, which is influential in the global human development agenda for measuring levels of quality of life and address human dignity, resonates with the responsibilities of the Nordic welfare state. It emphasises the responsibility of the State (or a similar subject) and can be used to analyse the impact of legal and political obligations imposed upon nation-states for the specific group of older persons, and to balance the somewhat one-sided quest for individual autonomy.

Even though the core focus of the capabilities approach is on the individual person's ability (or capability) to make decisions, in its broader version[2] it implies the importance of a supportive societal system or structure that enables the realisation of self-determination and individual ability, including for individuals who are not fully capable of making arrangements for themselves. The most important aspects of the broader approach are the focus on human dignity (in addition to enhancing individual freedom), normativity (a set of fundamental capabilities is identified), and the central role of the nation-state (as the political subject responsible for the achievement of minimum thresholds for all capabilities). These three aspects are all of specific relevance in the Swedish legal context when it comes to social services for older people.

13.2 The Rights to Self-determination and Protection from Harm in Social Services for Older People

Social services for older people, as for everyone, are based on the two pillars of self-determination and protection from harm (human dignity). In this matter, the relevant Swedish legislation (Social Services Act, Social Services Ordinance, Children and Parents Code and Guardianship Ordinance) is in line with EU and international human rights documents, such as the United Nations Principles for Older Persons, adopted in 1991, the Recommendation (2014)02 on the promotion of human rights of older persons of the Council of Europe Parliamentary Assembly, and the Convention on the Rights of Persons with Disabilities (CRPD), as well as with the proposed Convention on the Rights of Older Persons. Nevertheless, the two pillars might sometimes be contradictory. Protection from harm can sometimes restrict an individual's self-determination.

[2] Here represented by Martha C. Nussbaum (2006), but even more elaborated by e.g. Jonathan Wolff and Avner de-Shalit (2007).

13.2.1 Self-Determination and Legal Competence

The right to self-determination as a legal prerequisite for social services is designed to enhance individual freedom, in line with what is captured through the capability concept, but this is upon the condition that a person has the ability to perform actions in order to reach goals he or she has reason to value. Only focusing on the individual right to self-determination can obscure the dilemmas that arise when there is only limited ability. The capability concept, especially in the Capabilities approach context, carries with it a potential to balance individual self-determination and its limitations when so required in the name of concern for a person's dignity. What is also interesting is that the legal concepts corresponding to capability can be helpful in reaching a more nuanced perception of capability and also of the concept of self-determination.

Capability, or a person's ability to perform actions, is elaborated in a legal context in terms of two aspects. Every person is a legal subject who has 'legal capacity' (the Swedish legal term is rättskapacitet), meaning the potential capacity to possess rights and duties that can be upheld by law. Legal capacity does not in and of itself entail that a person also has the authority to determine something or express the determination, or, in legal terms, has 'legal competence' (rättshandlingsförmåga). To have legal competence means having the ability to act, to make decisions and agreements, and to litigate, and with such ability there follow legal consequences. Legal competence is described as the essential issue in balancing the right to autonomy and decision-making with the right to protection from harm (Mäki-Petäjä-Leinonen & Juva, 2015; Odlöw, 2005; Fridström Montoya, 2015).

Legal capacity can never be limited, in contrast to legal competence, which can be limited due to certain reasons. If a person's ability is limited, and if she has a need for legal representation, that person may be legally represented by someone else.[3] Old age as such is not a reason for limitations on a person's legal competence, but the consideration forming the basis for the law is that older people are considered to be at risk of suffering from physical or mental disorders that could motivate a query as to whether a person understands the decision at hand. A significant proportion of individuals with some sort of legal representation are older people suffering from neurocognitive disorders due to a dementia disease, such as Alzheimer's disease (SOU, 2004:112, p. 421). The risk of dementia increases significantly with age (Ds, 2003:47, p. 39).

[3] Rules regarding limitations on legal competence are expressed in the Swedish Children and Parents Code, not only for underaged persons represented by a guardian and/or a custodian (often the same person/-s), but also for adults. The individual's opinion about the selection of a representative in mentorships and administratorships shall be a determining factor for the appointing authority, if the suggested person is suitable for the assignment and accepts the appointment, Children and Parents Code, ch. 11, para. 12. There is also a possibility for a person to appoint a representative beforehand by issuing a continuing power of attorney (CPA) (Swedish: Framtidsfullmakt), see lag (2017:310) om framtidsfullmakter (Continuing Powers of Attorney Act), prop. 2016/17:30; Ds 2014:16; SOU, 2004:112.

How a person's ability or inability to make decisions is assessed, and how a limited ability is handled, varies between jurisdictions. Certain legal assumptions and considerations at the structural level establish potential limitations at the individual level. One way, as in the Swedish context, can be to establish legal representation for the person. Legal representation can be established in two forms, 'mentorship' (godmanskap) and 'administratorship' (förvaltarskap).

In Sweden, legal representation by a mentor is often described as a form of 'supported decision-making' rather than 'substituted decision-making'. Supported decision-making does not limit a person's decision-making competence[4] (i.e. the formal power to perform legal actions), while substituted decision-making does allow for significant removals of a person's right to perform legally binding acts of her own. According to the Committee on the Convention on the Rights of Persons with Disabilities (CRPD), supported decision-making is in line with a human-rights-based model of disability (UN/CPRD/C/GC/1, section I, para. 3).

Even though the establishment of legal representation is always, to a certain degree, a limitation on a person's legal competence and hence infringes their self-determination and autonomy, it is not as interventional as 'guardianship', which was used in Sweden until 1989. Sweden was one of the first countries to introduce supported decision-making, in a two-step reform, in 1975 (prop., 1974:142) and 1989 (prop., 1987/88:124). Mentorship, introduced in 1975, is a voluntary measure, hence the person concerned must give consent if this is at all possible. Administratorship, introduced in 1989 as a replacement for the former guardianship, is a more interventional arrangement and denotes certain limitations on the person's legal competence in specific, clearly identified respects.

The requirements for establishing a mentorship are that the individual: i) due to a disease, a mental disorder, a weakened state of health or a similar condition (medical requirement), ii) needs help to manage her private and/or financial affairs (functional requirement), iii) that this need cannot be met by a less restrictive measure, e.g. by assistance from relatives, granting a power of attorney or likewise (principle of minimum intervention) and iv) that the individual consents to the establishment of the mentorship (Children and Parents Code, chapter 11, para. 4).

The establishment of a mentorship does not in and of itself limit the person's decision-making competence. The mentor is considered primarily to be an assistant to the person (principal) and consequently a supportive decision-maker (prop., 1987/88:124, pp. 141f). The mentor can represent the principal in all matters covered by the assignment, provided that there is consent from the principal. However, if the decision concerns the upholding of the household, or if the principal is unable to communicate a reasonably informed opinion[5], the mentor does not need consent

---

[4] Legal competence can be further divided into 'decision-making competence' (rättshandlingsbehörighet) and 'decision-making ability' (rättslig beslutsförmåga) (Odlöw, 2005; Fridström Montoya, 2015). Fridström Montoya uses the terms saklig rättshandlingsförmåga and personlig rättshandlingsförmåga instead of rättshandlingsbehörighet and rättslig beslutsförmåga.

[5] If they are incapable of expressing any view whatsoever or, although capable of speaking and answering, clearly lack sufficient comprehension of the matter.

in order to act on their behalf. In the first case, the mentor is considered to have presumed consent. In the latter case, consent is not even needed. The mentor is not legally obliged to actively involve the principal in the decision-making process. Therefore, despite the legally constructed role of the mentor as an assistant, and despite the formal requirement of consent from the principal, it happens that in practice a mentor can misuse the role and take full control over the principal's affairs, especially in relation to financial matters (Giertz, 2018).

Administratorship is a protective measure that is taken if and when there are grave concerns regarding the individual's ability to represent herself, and if they cannot be sufficiently resolved by a mentorship. Administratorship entails the limitation of a person's legal competence, and as such constitutes substitute decision-making, although only in specified matters and to meet the individual's specific needs. Some matters can never be limited, e.g. the right to vote. This specific issue was an essential argument against plenary guardianship for adults (Odlöw, 2005). The requirements are the same as in the case of appointing a mentor, except for the functional requirement. In this case, the court has to ensure that the person concerned is not only in need of help but in fact is also incapable of managing her own financial and/or personal affairs. With regard to the principle of minimum intervention, i.e. to intervene as little as possible, the legislation explicitly states that the court is prevented from appointing an administrator if it is sufficient to appoint a mentor, or if the individual's needs can be provided for in a less restrictive way.

13.2.2 Self-Determination and Human Dignity

The responsibility that rests on the municipalities when it comes to social services for older people is twofold. The municipalities shall enable self-determination about decisions concerning social services[6], and also create conditions that ensure older people can live a life of dignity and well-being or, in other words, enjoy human dignity. Self-determination as a prerequisite for legal decisions, meaning that a person must have legal competence, is not always possible, as explained in the section above. Self-determination is therefore, in practice, promoted as far as possible.

Self-determination and individual freedom to live your life as you wish can, however, conflict with fundamental values such as a reasonable standard of living, or a life lived in human dignity and well-being. When an older person chooses not to apply for social services or is reluctant to receive such services, and as a consequence of such decisions lives in a way that is not considered decent or reasonable, it is relevant to consider whether that person is capable of making informed decisions about social services. At what level should or could the individual's decision not to receive social services be neglected and replaced with a responsibility for the municipality to secure that the person achieves some level of dignity? Where should

[6] Social Services Act, Ch. 1, section 1.

the boundary between self-determination and individual freedom and the responsibility of the state be drawn? The Social Services Act gives no compulsory power to the municipalities. Older people have the freedom not to apply for or receive social services, according to the Social Services Act. Should fundamental values, such as a reasonable standard of living, human dignity and well-being, be prioritised in cases when self-determination and individual freedom lead to non-satisfactory living conditions? Since the Social Services Act is based on self-determination, one could argue that the legal answer is simple, the act gives no compulsory powers to the municipalities. However, at some point there may be a need to protect a person from his/her own decision-making. In practice, some people might be unable to understand the meaning and/or consequences of decision-making or non-decision-making that runs contrary to their own interests or well-being.

Social services officers sometimes have difficulties in bringing about certain measures that they deem necessary in order to ensure that a person is given the opportunity to live a life that is in accordance with the fundamental values of society, such as human dignity and maintaining a reasonable standard of living (see e.g. the survey conducted by the Inquiry on Guardians and Deputies for Adults, described in the government official report SOU, 2004:112, p. 702). A crucial question here is, of course: what does it mean to 'live a life that is in accordance with the fundamental values of society'? Since there are no objective criteria for how to assess whether these fundamental values are being met in a specific case, the assessment will depend on the views expressed by the social services officers, and these might differ from the view of the person concerned.

The municipalities have an obligation to ensure fundamental values for everyone, such as a reasonable standard of living. An older person, according to the Social Services Act (Ch. 4 section 1), has a legal right to social services, for example through a home help service or special housing, if the person is unable to satisfy his/her needs by himself/herself and these needs cannot be satisfied through other means. Furthermore, the need for a home help service or special housing must be considered necessary to ensure the individual has a reasonable standard of living. A reasonable standard of living, and a life lived in dignity and well-being can therefore, from a legal point of view, be described as fundamental values and constitute certain aspects of life that older people should be guaranteed through, or with the help of, the Social Services Act.

13.2.3 Self-Determination with the Help of a Legal Representative

Since the Social Services Act is based on self-determination, social services need an application and consent from the person concerned in order to grant him/her social services. When a person lacks the ability to make decisions about social services or needs to be protected from his/her own decision-making because it is contrary to their interests or well-being, the question of legal representation is sometimes raised. If a person may need some kind of legal representation (Social Services Ordinance, Ch. 5, para. 3), social services are obliged to notify the Chief Guardian, i.e. the municipal authority responsible for the supervision of mentors and administrators. If the Chief Guardian concurs with the social services' assessment, the Chief Guardian in turn is obliged to apply to the district court for the appointment of a mentor or an administrator (Guardianship Ordinance, Para. 5). Which of these representatives is appropriate depends on the nature of the person's needs and her ability to make decisions about personal or financial matters, as pointed out above (Children and Parents Code, chapter 11, para. 4 and 7). The district court then decides whether the prerequisites for appointing a legal representative have been met and, if so, appoints someone to be a mentor or an administrator for that person. The mentor/administrator then has the power to apply for, or consent to, a measure that requires self-determination. The mentor/administrator is given the power to make legally binding decisions on behalf of her ward; hence, the mentor/administrator assumes the role of the agent aspect of the person as a legal subject (Odlöw, 2005; Fridström Montoya, 2015, 2017).

One question that arises is whether legal representation through a mentor or an administrator is equivalent to self-determination for the individual who is being represented. It could be argued that the legal system, through its rules regarding legal representation, offers a method for circumventing rules that express self-determination as a fundamental legal value. Furthermore, the legal system constitutes a view on vulnerable adults that needs to be discussed: the identification of the mentor/administrator as being, in the legal sense, the person whom she represents. The fact that a person appointed by a public authority, due to a request by another public authority (the municipality), can assume her principal's legal persona and by virtue of that power apply for or consent to social assistance that the individual themselves might explicitly reject, gives reason to question whether the criterion of self-determination is actually being met. It could be argued that this is a legal fiction that creates a chimera of self-determination, when in fact it is, or at least can be regarded as, an indirect compulsory power.

To sum up, one could argue that the legal system in Sweden does not deal with the tension of self-determination and limitations on legal competence to a sufficient extent. This is also what the CRPD Committee has expressed in its opinion specifically regarding the measure of administratorship (CRPD/C/SWE/CO/1[7]). Hence, it can be argued that the Swedish model is in fact not one of supported decision-making but rather its opposite, i.e. a substitute decision-making model. The claimed self-determination is in fact constructed and fictional.

[7] The committee recommends that 'the State party take immediate steps to replace substituted decision-making with supported decision-making and provide a wide range of measures which respect the person's autonomy, will and preferences and are in full conformity with article 12 of the Convention, including with respect to the individual's right, in his or her own capacity, to give and withdraw informed consent for medical treatment, to have access to justice, to vote, to marry and to work.' (CRPD/C/SWE/CO/1, section IIIB, para. 34)

13.3 The Capabilities Approach and the Tension Between Individual Self-Determination and State Responsibility to Ensure Human Dignity

The right to personal autonomy is recognised in law as a basic right, and the principle of respecting individual autonomy, including the freedom to make one's own choices, is expressed in all UN Human Rights Conventions, including the CRPD (Art. 3), which protects and promotes the rights and dignity of persons with disabilities. Even though some older people are disabled, this is not the case for all, or even the majority. However, in an international human rights context, older people are increasingly addressed as vulnerable and subjected to ageism, i.e. discrimination based on age. These concerns are also expressed in a resolution that was adopted by the United Nations General Assembly in October 2010 (A/RES/65/182), establishing the Open-Ended Working Group on Ageing for the purpose of strengthening the Human Rights of Older Persons (OEWGA), and in the additional resolution adopted in 2012 in the context of discussions regarding a Convention on the Rights of Older Persons (A/RES/67/139). The purpose of such an international legal instrument, supported by, among others, AGE Platform Europe, is to promote and protect the rights and dignity of older people, and also to stipulate that older people in society ought to have independence, the ability to participate in society, access to social services and healthcare, and be entitled to self-fulfilment and the full dignity of life, among other rights. As we have shown, individual autonomy is a value that is also expressed in Swedish legal rules concerning social assistance for older persons. Individual autonomy, or self-determination, however, is more complicated. Not every person has the cognitive ability to make decisions, and what is more, what if a person makes decisions that conflict with a sense of human dignity and care for others?

The quest for specific human rights for older people can be understood as a general trend in which individual rights and autonomy are strengthened. This might be understood as the promotion of freedom of will and an obstacle to interfering in individuals' lives. On the other hand, it might also be understood as acknowledging that structures enabling individuals to achieve individual rights and autonomy are required. There are reasons to believe that a human rights document is not a sufficient structure. Individual rights are not enough.

The capabilities approach in its broader version emphasises human dignity rather than enhancing individual freedom at an individual level (Nussbaum, 2009; Gluchman, 2019). The focus on human dignity that is formulated as an objective to live in dignity and to have a feeling of wellbeing, as implemented in the Swedish Social Services Act of 2010, also corresponds to the wellbeing objective of value for older people that has been agreed upon internationally. The goals of being able to live in dignity and have a feeling of wellbeing in the Swedish context were explicitly intended to clarify the fundamental, normative and ethical values for elderly care[8] and were construed as a means of steering the municipalities and their management of the social services (Wennberg, 2017: 185), and not as an infringement of individuals' self-determination. However, at some point, could the value of human dignity mean that the choices of an individual can be ignored?

The capabilities approach is clearly normative and identifies a set of fundamental capabilities. To normatively identify fundamental capabilities and not only rely, as Sen (year) does, upon individual freedom, corresponds to the Nordic welfare state context, according to which certain aspects of life are identified as aspects of a decent life. Nussbaum points out ten core capabilities that are essential for people to be able to do and be what they like. These are also familiar in a Swedish context as parts of the welfare system. According to Nussbaum (2000), a political order can only be considered decent if it secures at least a threshold level of every one of these capabilities for all inhabitants. The fundamental capabilities are (Nussbaum, 2000);

- life
- bodily health
- bodily integrity
- senses, imagination and thought
- emotions
- practical reason
- affiliation
- care of and coexistence with other species
- play
- control over one's environment in two aspects, politics and the material

This theory clearly delineates the state's responsibility to build a supportive structure. It requires active measures to build such a societal structure. The welfare system based on tax revenues is one method of resource allocation, to guarantee a certain minimum level of living conditions. The act of adopting UN conventions, such as the CPRD or the proposed Convention on the Rights of Older Persons, which appoint the state as responsible for promoting, protecting and ensuring the full and equal enjoyment of all human rights and fundamental freedoms, is in itself not a guarantee of active measures. However, in a context in which the welfare system is being challenged, a combination of a human-rights based argument with an argument based on redistribution could be strengthened by the capabilities approach, which highlights an active state. A welfare system that ensures a minimum level of human dignity requires a combination of individual rights and corresponding societal responsibilities.

Nussbaum (2013) gives the nation-state a central role as the responsible political subject for the achievement of a minimum threshold for all capabilities. These core capabilities should be supported by all democracies. To give the nation-state this central role is, according to Nussbaum, not only a handy starting point, it also has a

[8] 'Elderly care' is the official English term used in the Government Policy, see the Government Offices of Sweden webpage, https://www.government.se/articles/2017/02/security-and-presence-in-elderly-care/, accessed 04-04-2019.

moral meaning. The nation-state is a system of principles and laws which, ultimately, rely upon the people. They are important expressions of the autonomy of the people, i.e., their right to live under laws they have chosen themselves. The capabilities approach, especially in its respect for practical reasoning and political self-determination, assigns the nation-state a central role and aspires to a world in which nation-states with an acceptable level of democracy enjoy protection of their national sovereignty. In such a world, nation-states would not risk losing their power to multinational companies and global financial networks with minimal, if any, accountability. This, according to Nussbaum, is a significant risk today. Whether the nation-state is the only unit that embodies the right kind of accountability is an empirical question, she adds, but so far, no other unit has taken sufficient responsibility to guarantee the minimum level of core capabilities to all inhabitants.

To sum up, the capabilities approach might be of help in an argument that stresses the importance of balancing the, somewhat contradictory, concepts of legal competence, self-determination and human dignity in order to promote the capabilities of older people. Capability, according to such a balanced understanding, is not only a matter of individual ability to make decisions (or not), self-determination and autonomy. The global pandemic of Covid-19 in 2020 has certainly shown that there is a delicate balance to be found between care for and protection of on the one hand, and individual self-autonomy on the other hand for older people. To explore the distinction between the concepts of legal capacity and legal competence can also be of assistance in elaborating a more nuanced perception of capability. It is also a matter of care and consideration for individuals who are not in a situation where they have, or are able to have, concern for themselves. To enable and empower someone requires support, and the law is part of the structural support that forms the living conditions for individuals.

References

Official Documents

Swedish Government Bills

Prop. 1974:142 Kungl. Maj:ts proposition nr 142 år 1974 med förslag till lag om ändring i föräldrabalken, m. m.; given den 4 oktober 1974 [Bill on changes in the Children and Parents' Code]. Stockholm: Justitiedepartementet.

Prop. 1987/88:124 Regeringens proposition om god man och förvaltare [Bill on mentorship and administratorship]. Stockholm: Justitiedepartementet.

Prop. 2018/19:1 Budgetpropositionen för 2019 Förslag till statens budget för 2019, finansplan och skattefrågor, Utgiftsområde 9 [Budget Bill for 2019, Expenditure area 9]. Stockholm: Finansdepartementet.

Swedish Government Official Report Series

SOU 2004:112 Frågor om Förmyndare och ställföreträdare för vuxna: Slutbetänkande av Utredningen om förmyndare, gode män och förvaltare [Government official report on legal representation, mentorship and administratorship]. Stockholm: Fritzes Offentliga Publikationer.

SOU 2015:80 Stöd och hjälp till vuxna vid ställningstaganden till vård, omsorg och forskning: Betänkande av Utredningen om beslutsoförmögna personers ställning i vård, omsorg och forskning [Government official report on persons with limited capacity to decide on questions related to medical care, social services and research]. Stockholm: Fritzes Offentliga Publikationer.

Ds 2003:47 På väg mot en god demensvård. Samhällets insatser för personer med demenssjukdomar och deras anhöriga [Government official report on the care of persons with dementia]. Departementspromemoria. Socialdepartementet.

Swedish Acts

Förmynderskapsförordning [Guardianship Ordinance] (1995:379)

Föräldrabalk [Children and Parents Code] (1949:381)

Socialtjänstlag [Social Services Act] (2001:453)

Socialtjänstförordning [Social Services Ordinance] (2001:937)

Case

Hovrätten över Skåne och Blekinge [The Scania and Blekinge Court of Appeal in Malmö], mål nr [case nr] ÖÄ 1368-07

United Nations and EU documents

A/RES/67/139. Towards a comprehensive and integral international legal instrument to promote and protect the rights and dignity of older persons. Resolution adopted by the General Assembly on 20 December 2012. 13 February 2013. https://undocs.org/A/RES/67/139. Accessed 4 Jul 2019.

A/RES/65/182. Follow-up to the Second World Assembly on Ageing. Resolution adopted by the General Assembly on 21 December 2010. 4 Febuary 2011. https://undocs.org/A/RES/65/182. Accessed 4 Jul 2019.

Convention on the Rights of Persons with Disabilities (CRPD). https://www.un.org/disabilities/documents/convention/convention_accessible_pdf.pdf. Accessed 19 Jun 2018.

CRPD/C/SWE/CO/1. Committee on the Rights of Persons with Disabilities. Concluding observations on the initial report of Sweden. https://tbinternet.ohchr.org/_layouts/15/treatybodyexternal/Download.aspx?symbolno=CRPD%2fC%2fSWE%2fCO%2f1&Lang=en. Accessed 4 Jul 2019.

Recommendation (2014)02 on the promotion of human rights of older persons by the Council of Europe Parliamentary Assembly, and adopted by the Committee of Ministers on 19 February 2014. https://search.coe.int/cm/Pages/result_details.aspx?ObjectId=09000016805c649f. Accessed 19 Jun 2018.

United Nations Principles for Older Persons Adopted by General Assembly resolution 46/91 of 16 December 1991. https://www.ohchr.org/en/professionalinterest/pages/olderpersons.aspx. Accessed 4 Jul 2019.

Literature

Abramsson, M., Hydén, L., Motel-Klingebiel, A., & Nationella Institutet för forskning om äldre och åldrande. (2017). *Vem är den äldre? : äldrebilder i ett åldrande Sverige*. Nationella institutet för forskning om äldre och åldrande, NISAL.

Butler, R. (1969). Age-ism: Another form of bigotry. *The Gerontologist, 9*(4 Part 1), 243–246.

Fridström Montoya, T. (2015). *Leva som andra genom ställföreträdare: En rättslig och faktisk paradox*. Iustus.

Fridström Montoya, T. (2017). *Homo juridicus: Den kapabla människan i rätten* (Upplaga 1 ed.)

Giertz, L. (2018). Guardianship for adults with intellectual disabilities: Accountant, advocate or 'family' member? *Scandinavian Journal of Disability Research [elektronisk Resurs], 20*, 256–265.

Gluchman, V. (2019). Human dignity as the essence of Nussbaum's ethics of human development. *Philosophia, 47*, 1127–1140. https://doi.org/10.1007/s11406-018-0034-2

Mäki-Petäjä-Leinonen, A., & Juva, K. (2015). Of sound mind? Dementia and aspects of assessing legal capacity. *European Journal of Health Law, 22*(1), 13–37.

Nussbaum, M. (2000). *Women and human development: The capabilities approach* (The John Robert Seeley lectures, [1998]). Cambridge University Press.

Nussbaum, M. (2006). *Frontiers of justice. Disability, nationality, species membership*. Harvard University Press.

Nussbaum, M. (2009). Human dignity and political entitlements. In B. Lanigan (Ed.), *Human dignity and bioethics* (pp. 245–264). Nova Science Publication.

Nussbaum, M. (2013). *Creating capabilities: The human development approach*. Harvard University Press.

Odlöw, T. (2005). *Ställföreträdare för vuxna: Kamrer eller handledare?* (1. uppl. ed). Jure.

Wennberg, L. (2017). Wellbeing and gender equality for the elderly in Arctic Sweden. *Nordic Journal on Law and Society, 1*(1–2), 176–193.

Wolff, J., & de-Shalit, A. (2007). *Disadvantage*. Oxford University Press.

Webpages

AgeCap, Centre for Ageing and Health, University of Gothenburg, https://www.gu.se/en/agecap. Accessed 15 Oct 2020

AGE Platform Europe. http://www.age-platform.eu/press-releases/new-un-convention-needed-adequately-protect-older-persons%E2%80%99-human-rights-and-combat. Accessed 19 June 2018

Committee on the Convention on the Rights of Persons with Disabilities. https://www.ohchr.org/en/hrbodies/crpd/pages/crpdindex.aspx. Accessed 4 July 2019

Government Offices of Sweden webpage. https://www.government.se/articles/2017/02/security-and-presence-in-elderly-care/. Accessed 4 Apr 2019

The European Union Agency for Fundamental Rights. Press Release: The fundamental rights of older people need to be better protected. https://fra.europa.eu/en/press-release/2018/fundamental-rights-older-people-need-be-better-protected. Accessed 4 July 2019

Örebro University. The strategic initiative Successful ageing. https://www.oru.se/english/strategic-initiatives/successful-ageing/. Accessed 4 July 2019

Chapter 14
Invisible or Powerful? Ageing in a Mediatised Society

Annika Bergström and Maria Edström

14.1 Introduction

Freedom of expression and freedom of information are core human rights that connect the concept of capability with the role of the media in society. In order to be able to live your rights and make choices to achieve your personal goals, you need to be informed, to have a voice, to be listened to and to have the opportunity to engage in society, regardless of age. The media influences the public agenda, what we think about, and what we believe is important. Images and stories in the media about older adults affect the ideas about ageing that circulate within a society, and these affect how older people are perceived. The media also significantly involves interaction and communication with family, friends, the authorities and their services. The intersection of ageing, the media and capability can therefore be found at all levels of society, from the individual to structural levels, and is closely related to ageism.

The capabilities approach formulated by Amartya Sen (1985), and further developed by Martha Nussbaum (1997), is concerned with equality and the concepts of justice and injustice, arguing that people are entitled to a certain level of resources. The concept captures what individuals are able to do and to be, but also sets the preconditions for resources such as laws and regulations, social security, the labour market, healthcare and norms surrounding ageing. Capability includes preferences, such as what an individual values when it comes to what to have, who to be and what to do. A person should have free choice to act in order to achieve his or her

A. Bergström · M. Edström (✉)
Journalism Media and Communication (JMG), University of Gothenburg, Gothenburg, Sweden

Centre for Ageing and Health – AgeCap, University of Gothenburg, Gothenburg, Sweden
e-mail: annika.bergstrom@jmg.gu.se; maria.edstrom@gu.se

H. Falk Erhag et al. (eds.), *A Multidisciplinary Approach to Capability in Age and Ageing*, International Perspectives on Aging 31,
https://doi.org/10.1007/978-3-030-78063-0_14

goals, which in turn also means having the resources to achieve valuable goals, and the ability to understand what resources one needs to achieve them.

The most relevant aspects of capability in the context of the media relates to Nussbaum's (1997) dimensions of capability, such as using the senses and imagination, feeling love and compassion, being able to reflect critically upon life choices, affiliations with others, and the ability to laugh, enjoy and play. Most important, perhaps, is having the opportunity and ability to control one's environment, to be able to participate effectively in the political choices that govern one's life, and freedom of expression, which in turn is closely related to the resource concept of capability.

In this chapter, we address the relations between ageing, the concept of capability, and the media and communication studies from the perspectives of (1) language and representation relating to how media content is made up with regard to what is communicated, how the content is framed and who is present in the media, and (2) media use and engagement, especially on digital platforms.

14.2 Living in a Mediatised World

Most of us live in a mediatised society, where much of our time is spent with media, often in front of different screens. Using and producing media is an important part of most people's lives, and the demand on citizens to critically embrace the media and information is constantly increasing. The process of the media intertwining with people's lives and with societal functions is well captured by the theory of mediatisation. This is a theoretical framework highlighting how the media shapes, maintains and changes practices and ideas in society at large and in the domestic contexts of everyday life (Hjarvard, 2013; Lykke Christensen, 2017).

A mediatised society affects both people and society at the macro, meso and micro levels (Trappel, 2019). At the macro level, implementation processes to access the media and its content can have implications for a person's choices and life chances. Policies, subsidies and regulations impact upon the actions of organisations and individuals. At the meso level, commercialisation of the media business, global monopolies and structural inequalities affect the opportunities of individuals to raise their voices and to participate in a mediatised society. At the micro level, individual factors such as socio-economic prerequisites are important for understanding the relation between capability and the media, but also factors such as the functions of the media and individual motives to engage are crucial for understanding media use and engagement. The consequences of inequalities are expressed, for instance, as skewed news representation, digital divides and knowledge gaps, which create unequal life chances (Trappel, 2019).

Nicholas Garnham (1997) applied Sen's capability approach to communication during the 1990s, and this was recently developed by Nick Couldry (2019: 48–49) to a set of functioning that we all value in relation to the media and communication:

- Not being harmed/humiliated or misrepresented through the media
- Basic access to media resources
- Opportunity to be in some broad sense represented as a type
- If one wants to speak, the opportunity to have a voice.

Relating this to ageing and older adults, two main tracks can be pointed out: (1) the media as a set of institutions that influence the public agenda and notions of ageing and older people, and how older people are represented and perceived in society, and (2) the media as tools for communication and interaction, both within close relationships and in the public sphere. Based on the concept of mediatisation, the point of departure is that the media is being simultaneously embedded in the wider society and in the lifeworld of individuals (Hjarvard, 2017).

It is of great importance to emphasise the heterogeneity within the group of older adults. How we age in society depends on socio-economic factors as well as ethnicity, gender and spatialities (rural/urban, home/work) (Torres, 2001, 2019; Westwood, 2019). Inequalities tend to increase throughout the life course, with educational level as one key component of the ability to live a long life (Seeman et al., 2008), and intersectional perspectives are called for by many scholars (Westwood, 2019: 4). As researchers of ageing, it is important to be aware of the normative assumptions that are embedded in our minds, in the research literature and in the media. In a mediatised world, media competence then becomes crucial, regardless of who you are.

14.2.1 Media and Information Literacy in a Mediatised Society

In most societies, a broad spectrum of civic engagement is considered crucial for maintaining the democratic system (McLeod et al., 1999; Putnam, 1993; Shaker, 2014). A key function of the media is to provide people with the information they need to be free and self-governing (Kovach & Rosenstiel, 2014). In this regard, the capability concept is clearly related to the concept of media and information literacy (MIL), which takes its point of departure in the more general concept of literacy.

> It is through these skills of reading and writing that those who are literate are able to participate more fully in society, both economically and socially, and are able to understand and exert a higher degree of control over everyday events. (Nutbeam, 2008: 2072)

MIL is about the ability to read media language in a broad sense, about consciousness of the social, political, cultural and economic factors behind media business and the messages distributed by the media. Both UNESCO and the European Parliament state that MIL is a necessary key competence in the information and communication society and crucial for democracy (see also Livingstone, 2008). Fundamental literacies, as expressed in Article 19 of the Universal Declarations of Human Rights, should thus be seen as a common good (Carlsson, 2010: 15, 73; 2015; Petäjä, 2006). MIL includes all kinds of media texts: the written word, as well as audio and visual expressions distributed through channels that carry all these kinds of texts, which includes all situations where messages are communicated through any technical distribution channel (Buckingham, 2003).

Media and education scholar David Buckingham (2003) presents four different types of knowledge as a framework for media literacy:

1. Production: related to the media as produced with a certain purpose, knowledge about who owns, controls, distributes and is reached by and heard in media texts. It also includes creating and reflecting upon media content.
2. Language: the production of meaning in the media. What effects follow from certain messages with a certain style, genre etc.
3. Representation: the media constructs reality. Media texts are chosen as representatives of people, groups, events and histories. This is about understanding and is related to depictions of stereotypes.
4. Audience: how different groups in society use different media, and how they interpret media messages and the effects of this. It is also about people's ability to reach out through the media.

There are several other, somewhat similar, ways to capture the general aim of MIL, which are all related to the connection between the mediatised society and capability. Livingstone (2008) relates the concept of MIL to democracy, participation and active citizenship, and also to the ability to create an opinion and to make one's voice heard. Other researchers present this in slightly different ways (Perez Tornero & Pi, 2011; Potter, 2005), but basically researchers gather around the concepts suggested by Buckingham (2003).

In the context of capability, we would like to address two main areas drawn from Buckingham's framework. One area concerns language and representation, and relates to how media content is made up with regard to what is communicated, how the content is framed and who is present in it. The other area concerns engagement in the media from the individual's point of view: producing and using media and media content.

14.2.2 Media Research – An Emerging Field

Before turning to specific cases of media and capability, something needs to be said about media research at an overall level. Media studies derive from several different disciplines, and can be understood as a multidisciplinary field. The origins include, among others, sociology, political science, humanities, literature and organisation theory.

The media is studied from several perspectives and by means of several methods. It is common – but not necessary – to separate studies of production, content and use. Production studies include media organisations, regulations and policies and how different kinds of media and information content are created. There are, for instance, studies on news value and the roles of journalists. Content studies reveal what is actually published, what characterises different types of content from aspects such as frames and representation. Studies of media use and consumption map in different ways how the audience actually makes use of content. Here it is worth mentioning that media research is an emerging field, and older age groups have often been neglected within it.

Media studies use both quantitative and qualitative methods, sometimes mixed. The quantitatively performed studies are usually based on either survey data with editors, journalists or audience members, or on systematic content analysis measuring numbers of issues, actors or other aspects of what is published or included in different policy documents. Qualitatively based studies emphasise the individual worker or user, his or her interpretation of working conditions, storytelling or, from the user's point of view, the role of the media and content in everyday life, the actual meaning of content and the like. Qualitative content analyses are based on in-depth reading of specific content in order to reveal meaning, and sometimes to read between the lines.

We will now turn to two of the previously mentioned fields, where we find the strongest correlations between media research, the concept of capability and ageing: the presentation and representation of older adults in media content and the media as a tool for communication, interaction and engagement.

14.3 Language and Representation

Media representations have an impact on how we understand the world. News media have an agenda-setting function in the sense that they draw our attention to certain topics and areas, and therefore contribute to shaping our ideas and opinions on different topics (Weaver, 2007). If you do not have a voice and are not part of the media narratives, you become more or less invisible in society. Therefore, the symbolic power of the media is a key concern for many researchers. Media scholar Nick Couldry claims that we have a growing crisis of voice across political, economic and cultural domains (Couldry, 2010). This is not primarily an issue at the individual level, but something for groups to address. Social representation is considered an important part of democracy, especially in the political sphere. The representation and presence of older persons in the media can thus be seen as a proxy for their communication rights and political rights.

At a general level, the media is interested in what is new and what the next generation has to say. In a similar way, media research tends to focus on new media trends and the impact of technology. Media scholar John Hartley even talks about juvenation, the way in which the media communicates with youth (Hartley, 1998). Similarly, media research tends to have a focus on new trends, new media platforms and expressions. This is of course a contributing factor when thinking about why there is a void when it comes to the role of ageing and health in the field of media and communication research.

Media images of ageing mainly refer to older people in a simplified manner, depicting retired people as one homogenised group. The focus is mainly on chronological age, and media representations are often stereotyped into two polarised categories: the active golden age (advertising) or the frail, helpless older person (news). The problem with this is that the diversity among older adults becomes invisible, when in fact the expanding group of older adults contains large variations of lived experience, with regard to health, functionality, socio-economic situation and ethnic background.

As more of us live longer and remain healthier, the media and surrounding businesses have an emerging interest in older age groups. Within the advertising industry, there is a clear interest in resourceful, healthy older people, often referred to as 'golden agers' (Bai, 2014). The media interest in older age groups often derives from a consumer perspective, aiming for the 'grey market' with a focus on agelessness and successful ageing. This is in strong contrast to the news media depictions of frail older persons as voiceless and facing problems of declining health (Lundgren & Ljuslinder, 2011; Nilsson & Jönsson, 2009; Wien, 2003).

These stereotyped mediatised images of ageing have an effect on all of us and may limit our ideas about ageing and what it means to grow older. The negative attitudes and tendency to undervalue older people also exist among older people themselves, having negative effects on older individuals' self-evaluation and functioning (Coudin & Alexopoulos, 2010). Negative stereotypes of ageing seem to be very resilient (Levy et al., 2015; Gullette, 2017) and have existed for a long time (Ng et al., 2015).

It is evident that a positive self-perception of ageing tends to increase longevity (Levy et al., 2002). Stereotyped images of ageing and the lack of representation of older people in the media, on the other hand, can be seen as a hindrance to capability, since stereotypes are built on prejudice that may lead to ageism and discrimination (see Butler, 1969; Gullette, 2017; Katz, 2001; Schonfield, 1982). Ageism limits older people's capabilities and the media may confirm, enforce or challenge ageism. The lack of older people in the media can be seen as a form of *symbolic annihilation*, a term coined by sociologist Gaye Tuchman (1978) to describe the lack of women in the news. The visual patterns in the media are gendered, older women are even more invisible than older men, and the media seems to promote gendered ageism (Edström, 2018; Kokkinakis et al., 2018).

However, media effects are not easy to pin down, because there are several factors contributing to our understanding of the media and the opportunity to make individual interpretations of its symbolic meaning. For example, some studies indicate that older women are negotiating and contesting the stereotyped images of ageing by choosing to dress, act and behave more in accordance with their own life experiences (Dolan, 2015; Gullette, 2017; Lykke Christensen, 2017; Twigg, 2013; Twigg & Martin, 2015). This is just to emphasise that media effects and their impact are no magic bullet; it is a complex process depending on a web of circumstances ranging from micro to macro levels.

However, when the media coverage of ageing and older adults is too simplistic, and passive or negative images of older adults and ageing circulate widely in the news, this may lead to wider implications for society. If the media does not give older adults a voice, age discrimination in the workplace and elsewhere might seem natural. And if news media keep reporting negatively on ageing, elderly care and the situation of older adults, people might internalise these negative views with consequences such as recruitment problems in the field of geriatrics.

How we speak and think about ageing affects not only interpersonal relationships, but also policymaking and decision-making. The American organisation Frame Works Institute has produced both reports and toolkits to reframe communication on ageing and ageism (O'Neil & Haydon, 2015; Sweetland et al., 2017). The aim is to shift the mind-set so that ageing can be seen as a normal and continuing process and to address the negative attitudes towards it. This will be a long-term struggle, as the coronavirus pandemic has made even more clear. The pandemic has reinforced all kinds of inequalities, not least those based on age. We will therefore take the opportunity to reflect upon ageism in the media during Covid-19.

14.3.1 The Case of Media Ageism and Covid-19

In 2020, the world suffered from the global Covid-19 pandemic, which caused deaths, tragedies and lockdowns in many countries. It also changed how older people were treated. Since the virus has struck hard among older sections of the population, many countries started to develop a public discourse of people aged 70+ as one homogeneous group, a message that was reinforced by the media. As the first studies of the media coverage of Covid 19 emerge, it becomes more evident that the media is reinforcing ageism. A Spanish study of 501 headlines related to older adults and Covid-19 confirms the presentation of a homogeneous group associated with negative representations and death (Bravo-Segal & Villar, 2020). A study of Swedish newspapers also confirms the representation of people aged 70+ as a homogeneous group, and the manifestation of an 'us vs. them' mentality regarding older people (Häggkvist & Rosvall, 2020). During spring 2020, the hashtag #BoomerRemover was used on social media to discuss whether the purpose of Covid-19 was to remove an overload of older people from the population, a mindset that can be seen as yet another manifestation of ageism (Meisner, 2020). At the same time, others, such as the United Nations Secretary General, tried to counter age-related stigmas and the divisions between age groups that they reinforced (Meisner, 2020; United Nations, 2020).

The many ageist remarks and discussions have raised concerns among geriatrics and gerontologists that the pandemic is magnifying prejudices based on age: '… there has been a parallel outbreak of ageism' states Liat Ayalon and research colleagues in an editorial (Ayalon et al., 2020: e49). Ayalon and colleagues use examples from social media and the press in various countries to argue that the public discourse is reinforcing barriers in already age-divided societies. The authors call for other measures than chronological age to be used when assessing risks and medical care, that special measures are taken to safeguard the human rights of those who are most likely to be classified as vulnerable and to encourage solidarity between generations (Ayalon et al., 2020; Ayalon, 2020).

The Frame Works Institute has again, in the light of Covid-19, called for changes in the way we think and talk about ageing by appealing to the value of justice, addressing ageism and rating a sense of solidarity as well as urging care in the use of 'othering' terms (Kendall-Taylor et al., 2020).

The Covid-19 pandemic is just one example of where the media might reinforce certain discourses about ageing. It could of course also counter or challenge existing ideas of older people as a homogenous group that needs to have separate restrictions. It is yet to be seen whether the media will act on the ageism of which it seems to be a part. 'In the meantime, although we cannot control the year we were born, we can control how we think about, treat, respect, and empathize with each other – across generations, in solidarity – especially in a time of crisis' (Meisner, 2020: 5).

14.4 Media Use and Engagement

Engagement in the media can be understood both from the perspective of undesired differences in information and knowledge resources, and from the perspective of getting involved with people and society through media content and content production. Information differences are related to media use generally, and to news consumption habits specifically. Since the 1970s, media scholars have gathered evidence of knowledge differences between different groups in society, differences that may affect societal and political engagement. Information distributed through the media was found to have great impact on knowledge levels, and media use contributes to creating knowledge gaps (Kwak, 1999). The theoretical concept of knowledge gaps has been somewhat reformulated to include motivation to acquire information in the knowledge domain under study. Gaps arise and widen when there is a difference in motivation among population segments (Ettema et al., 1983).

There is a continuously growing amount of information and services on the Internet, and digital skills have become a vital resource in contemporary society. The majority of research in this area demonstrates that there are links between social exclusion and digital engagement. It also seems that groups with limited access to information tend to be further marginalised as computer and Internet skills become more and more important (Hargittai & Hinnant, 2008; van Deursen & van Dijk, 2014).

Just as with many other forms of media technology, the Internet was unevenly distributed from its beginnings in the early 1990s. There have been so-called digital divides between groups in societies, countries and regions ever since (Hargittai & Hinnant, 2008; Norris, 2001; Tsatsou, 2011). The significance of digital inequalities is clear across a broad range of individual-level and macro-level domains, including life course, gender and class as well as in healthcare, politics, economic activity and social capital (Robinson et al., 2015). One of the most important factors explaining inequalities in access and use is age (Bergström, 2017), and it has been proven that older adults perform less well than younger generations with regard to Internet skills (van Deursen & van Dijk, 2014).

Digital inequality affects the potential to shape one's life chances in multiple ways. Personal computers and the Internet have meant increased opportunities for communication, information-gathering and entertainment and for accessing different public and commercial services (Carpenter & Buday, 2007; Dickinson & Gregor, 2006; van Deursen & Helsper, 2015). But the issue of digital inequality extends far beyond access and skills. The continuous development of the digital society strongly and increasingly affects those who for different reasons remain outside. The Internet has become important both for personal reasons and for societal involvement. 'It has become clear that reliable Internet connection and access to computing devices is not a luxury but rather, a social need and a public utility' (Treré et al., 2020: 2).

Internet activities in such areas as financial matters, entertainment, shopping, information-gathering and news offer opportunities that could be beneficial, particularly for seniors with limited mobility (Reisenwitz et al., 2007). Using a home computer, tablet or smartphone can enable older adults to continue living independently in their own homes, and communication technologies are said to have the potential to minimise social isolation (Boulton-Lewis et al., 2007; van Deursen & Helsper, 2015). The Internet has been widely recognised as a valuable tool for acquiring healthcare information and services (Rains, 2008). Furthermore, older adults are frequently heavy users of civic services in the Nordic countries, and at the same time many service providers are digitalising their range. It is worrying that older people's lack of Internet access and skills limit their engagement with online services that are highly significant to them (Robinson et al., 2015).

The use of information and communication technologies (ICTs) have the potential to enhance quality of life by sustaining independent living and providing opportunities for greater democratic and societal engagement (Boulton-Lewis et al., 2007; Loos, 2012; Obi et al., 2013; Rains, 2008). In an interview study, older adults clearly expressed feelings of empowerment connected with media use, and being able to control media technology was also linked to social positioning and identity (Givskov, 2017). But developments in the media environment with regard to communication and interaction have posed a challenge for many older adults, who have only been confronted with digital media technologies late in their lives; hence, they are generally late adopters (Lykke Christensen, 2017).

It is evident that older adults constitute a group that could both benefit from digital content and services and to a large extent are hindered from engaging with these due to lack of access, skills and motivation to use them. Although this applies to the whole group of older adults, it is especially evident among the oldest. Public authorities and IT-related commissions have struggled with these inequality issues for decades. The problem has been visible since the mid-1990s, but there have been very few proposals for concrete measures. This is partly a result of power diffusion within the field. Many different actors have different responsibilities for digital infrastructure, tools, accessibility etc. Over time, the influence of global actors over local contexts has increased. The complicated issue of responsibility makes decision-making and accountability difficult.

The issues raised in this section have become highly topical during the Covid-19 pandemic. Most everyday activities have been restricted, and online activity has become the new reality. Information flow is one of several key factors in fighting the pandemic. The Internet also enables isolated individuals to maintain social contact remotely with family, friends and acquaintances, and provides access to different kinds of entertainment and pastimes. Being an offliner in such difficult circumstances of physical distancing could lead to a dual sense of exclusion. There is a significant risk of ageism if society focuses only on digital events as a means of social participation during the pandemic (Seifert, 2020).

A recent Israeli study of older adults during the first phase of the pandemic shows that the ability to adjust their Internet use and to make use of digital technology for coping with stress-related issues is somewhat unclear and uncertain. The older adults who participated in the survey report significant increases in Internet use during the pandemic, particularly different chat software, in a manner that resembles that of young adults. They also increased their use of applications for shopping, financial management, medical support and newspaper reading. Online activities related to recreation and wellbeing, such as playing digital games, downloading films and music, writing blogs etc., did not increase during the study (Nimrod, 2020).

14.5 Conclusions: Opportunities and Challenges Within the Intersection of Ageing, the Media and Capability

To conclude, when reflecting on the relationship between ageing, the media and capability, democracy becomes the common thread, with freedom of expression and freedom of information emerging as core human rights. In order to live your rights and be able to make choices to achieve your own goals, you need to be informed, have a voice and have the opportunity to engage in the things you find valuable. As outlined above, it is not self-evident that older age groups can raise their voices either inside or outside the media or how they can make sure that their voices are heard. Nor is it clear what implications exclusion from mediatised society will have for different groups of older adults. This final section of the chapter will reflect upon different aspects of this matter, addressing challenges and suggesting ways forward.

This review of language and representation, and of engagement with the media, clearly shows that the mediatised society affects people at the micro, meso and macro levels. Inequalities exist regarding both representation in, and engagement with, the media, and age is a significant factor. It becomes something of a paradox that a growing group of older adults, whose lives would benefit greatly from becoming mediatised, are largely neglected or left out of the media society.

At a micro level, as a person grows older within a society, the media can be a tool for enhancing their capabilities, but it can also be perceived as hindering a good life. Skewed or non-representative content, or a lack of space for expressing thoughts and opinions might make you feel incapable, and may also make others feel that you are incapable. In relation to media use, especially digital media, the question of choosing not to have or to use media becomes crucial. If technology and its applications are perceived as awkward and/or difficult to access, they become obstacles rather than useful tools. Furthermore, it is not self-evident that each individual knows what resources are needed, how to get them or how to use the available resources.

Media and information literacy (MIL) is therefore key for improving the capabilities of older adults. The framework of MIL is useful for understanding the role of the media in society as a means of enhancing capability. It has primarily been used in contexts involving younger people and is commonly related to school and education. We would suggest, however, that the MIL concept be adopted in future research within the field of ageing, the media and capability, since it combines core aspects from various fields. Several perspectives within MIL are very useful in relation to ageing and capability, not least in the field of health literacy and digital devices.

At the meso level, critical issues relate to who should be accountable for media content and the lack of older adults' voices or diverse stories about them, and the responsibility of media corporations to target and reach audiences of all ages is crucial. In our opinion, the media industry needs to take into account how media content can be more inclusive, in order to counter ageism, address issues relating to diverse conditions for ageing, and take into account that there is more to ageing than chronological age. In the case of the Swedish media context, as in many countries, this is primarily something that can be achieved by means of self-regulation measures.

Media corporations and platform providers also need to include ideas for how media technology can be developed in relation to cognitive loss or disabilities. This aspect can be considered especially important for public-service media and could be a topic for regulators and self-regulators to address. Much of the responsibility for development and change is in the hands of commercial actors in contemporary society, and this is also true for the media sector. Some tech companies, and other businesses, are very interested in the emerging so-called grey market. The question is whether and how commercial actors can be held accountable to anyone other than their shareholders. Human rights are often seen as part of corporate social responsibility, but the ageing population is seldom considered part of that equation when it comes to future strategies.

During the last few decades, society has been digitalised in most areas, and digital media have become an important part of citizenship and everyday tasks. Many of the goods and services provided online have been voluntary for people, but as more and more parts of the public sector integrate digital tools, it might become crucial to have a digitally skilled population. What demands can society place on the individual older person and what can the individual claim from society? A wider discussion about media responsibility in different areas could perhaps contribute to enhancing the capabilities of people in later life.

One crucial issue at the macro level is whether regulators can demand more from media corporations without limiting freedom of expression. Regulation versus freedom has been a balancing act for several hundred years and, in the Swedish context, freedom of expression has been highly valued and guarded. Furthermore, who has the responsibility to ensure that older citizens have the technological means to act as digital citizens is somewhat unclear. It is a challenge for policymakers to meet these demands, and to encourage media engagement. In an increasingly mediatised environment, we might see an even stronger relationship between the media, health and ageing, which in turn could emphasise the importance of the role of the media in enhancing people's capabilities.

References

Ayalon, L. (2020). There is nothing new under the sun: Ageism and intergenerational tension in the age of the COVID-19 outbreak. *International Psychogeriatrics*, 32(10), 1–4. https://doi.org/10.1017/S1041610220000575

Ayalon, L., Chasteen, A., Diehl, M., Levy, B., Neupert, S. D., Rothermund, K., Tesch-Römer, C., & Wahl, H.-W. (2020). Aging in times of the COVID-19 pandemic: Avoiding ageism and fostering intergenerational solidarity. *The Journals of Gerontology: Series B. Psychological Sciences and Social Sciences,* 76(2), e49–e52, https://doi-org.ezproxy.ub.gu.se/10.1093/geronb/gbaa051

Bai, X. (2014). Images of ageing in society: A literature review. *Journal of Population Ageing, 7*(3), 231–253. https://doi.org/10.1007/s12062-014-9103-x

Bergström, A. (2017). Digital equality and the uptake of digital applications among seniors of different age. *Nordicom Review, 38*(Special Issue 1), 79–92. https://doi.org/10.1515/nor-2017-0398

Boulton-Lewis, G. M., Buys, L., Lovie-Kitchin, J., Barnett, K., & Davis, L. N. (2007). Aging, learning, and computer technology in Australia. *Educational Gerontology, 33*(3), 253–270. https://doi-org.ezproxy.ub.gu.se/10.1080/03601270601161249

Bravo-Segal, S., & Villar, F. (2020). Older people representation on the media during COVID-19 pandemic: A reinforcement of ageism? *Revista Espanola de Geriatria y Gerontologia*. https://doi.org/10.1016/j.regg.2020.06.002

Buckingham, D. (2003). *Media education: Literacy, learning and contemporary culture*. Polity Press.

Butler, R. N. (1969). Age-ism: Another form of bigotry. *The Gerontologist, 9*(4), 243–246. https://doi-org.ezproxy.ub.gu.se/10.1093/geront/9.4_Part_1.243

Carlsson, U. (Ed.). (2010). *Barn och unga i den digitala mediekulturen*. Nordicom-Sweden, University of Gothenburg.

Carlsson, U. (2015). Media and information literacy: A crucial element in democratic development. In *Media and information literacy: A crucial element in democratic development* (pp. 73–78). UNESCO. https://unesdoc.unesco.org/ark:/48223/pf0000232923_ind.locale=en

Carpenter, B. D., & Buday, S. (2007). Computer use among older adults in a naturally occurring retirement community. *Computers in Human Behavior, 23*(6), 3012–3024. https://doi.org/10.1016/j.chb.2006.08.015

Coudin, G., & Alexopoulos, T. (2010). 'Help me! I'm old!' How negative aging stereotypes create dependency among older adults. *Aging & Mental Health, 14*(5), 516–523. https://doi-org.ezproxy.ub.gu.se/10.1080/13607861003713182

Couldry, N. (2010). *Why voice matters. Culture, politics and neo liberalism*. Sage.

Couldry, N. (2019). Capabilities for what? Developing Sen's moral theory for communication research. *Journal of Information Policy, 9*, 43–55. https://www.jstor.org/stable/10.5325/jinfopoli.9.2019.0043

Dickinson, A., & Gregor, P. (2006). Computer use has no demonstrated impact on the well-being of older adults. *International Journal of Human-Computer Studies, 64*(8), 744–753. https://doi.org/10.1016/j.ijhcs.2006.03.001

Dolan, J. (2015). Crumbling rejuvenation: Archetype, embodiment and the 'aging beauty myth'. In L. Hockley & N. Fadina (Eds.), *The happiness illusion: How the media sold us a fairytale* (pp. 75–88). Routledge.

Edström, M. (2018). Visibility patterns of gendered ageism in the media buzz: A study of the representation of gender and age over three decades. *Feminist Media Studies, 18*(1), 77–93. https://doi.org/10.1080/14680777.2018.1409989

Ettema, J. S., Brown, J. W., & Puepker, R. V. (1983). Knowledge gap effects in a health information campaign. *The Public Opinion Quarterly, 47*(4), 516–527. https://doi.org/10.1086/268809

Garnham, N. (1997). Amartya Sen's 'capabilities' approach to the evaluation of welfare: Its application to communications. *Javnost – The Public, 4*(4), 25–34. https://doi.org/10.1080/13183222.1997.11008658

Givskov, C. (2017). Growing old with mediatization: Reflexivity and sense of agency. *Nordicom Review, 38*(Special Issue 1), 79–92. https://doi.org/10.1515/nor-2017-0402

Gullette, M. M. (2017). *Ending ageism: Or, how not to shoot old people*. Rutger University Press.

Häggkvist, J., & Rosvall, J. (2020). *De äldre, vi andra och Covid-19: En kritisk diskursanalys om äldres framställan i media i samband med Covid-19 rekommendationerna under perioden 16-22 mars 2020* [The elderly, the rest of us and Covid-19: A critical discourse analysis of the portrayal of older people in the media due to the Covid-19 recommendations during the period 16–22 March 2020]. Bachelor's thesis. Ersta Sköndal.

Hargittai, E., & Hinnant, A. (2008). Digital inequality: Differences in young adults' use of the internet. *Communication Research, 35*(5), 602–621. https://doi.org/10.1177/0093650208321782

Hartley, J. (1998). Juvenation: News, girls and power. In C. Carter, G. Branston, & S. Allan (Eds.), *News, gender, and power* (pp. 47–70). Routledge.

Hjarvard, S. (2013). *The mediatization of culture and society*. Routledge.

Hjarvard, S. (2017). Mediatization. In P. Rössler (Ed.), *The international encyclopedia of media effects*. Wiley-Blackwell.

Katz, S. (2001). Growing older without aging? Positive aging, anti ageism, and anti-aging. *Generations, 25*(4), 27–32. https://search-proquest-com.ezproxy.ub.gu.se/docview/60100945?accountid=11162

Kendall-Taylor, N., Neumann, A., & Schoen, J. (2020, May 28). Advocating for age in an age of uncertainty: How the COVID-19 crisis is amplifying ageism, and how advocates can push back. *Stanford Social Innovation Review*. https://ssir.org/articles/entry/advocating_for_age_in_an_age_of_uncertainty

Kokkinakis, D., Edström, M., & Berggren, M. (2018, May 2–4). Ageism and Swedish news media. In *24th Nordic Congress of Gerontoloy (NKG)*.

Kovach, B., & Rosenstiel, T. (2014). *Elements of journalism: What newspeople should know and the public should expect* (3rd ed.). Crown.

Kwak, N. (1999). Revisiting the knowledge gap hypothesis: Education, motivation, and media use. *Communication Research, 26*(4), 385–413. https://doi.org/10.1177/009365099026004002

Levy, B. R., Slade, M. D., Kunkel, S. R., & Kasl, S. V. (2002). Longevity increased by positive self-perceptions of aging. *Journal of Personality and Social Psychology, 83*(2), 261–270. https://doi.org/10.1037/0022-3514.83.2.261

Levy, B., Slade, M. D., Chung, P. H., & Gill, T. M. (2015). Resiliency over time of elders' age stereotypes after encountering stressful events. *Journals of Gerontology Series B: Psychological Sciences and Social Sciences, 70*(6), 886–890. https://doi-org.ezproxy.ub.gu.se/10.1093/geronb/gbu082

Livingstone, S. (2008). Internet literacy: Young people's negotiation of new online opportunities. In T. MacPherson (Ed.), *Digital youth, innovations, and the unexpected.* The John D. and Catherine T. MacArthur Foundation Series on Digital Media and Learning.

Loos, E. (2012). Senior citizens: Digital immigrants in their own country? *Observatorio (OBS), 6*(1), 1–23. https://doi.org/10.15847/obsOBS612012513

Lundgren, A. S., & Ljuslinder, K. (2011). Problematic demography: Representations of population ageing in the Swedish daily press. *Population Ageing, 4*, 165–183. https://doi.org/10.1007/s12062-011-9048-2

Lykke Christensen, C. (2017). Healthy ageing and mediated health expertise. *Nordicom Review, 38*(Special Issue 1), 79–92. https://doi.org/10.1515/nor-2017-0403

McLeod, J. M., Scheufele, D. A., & Moy, P. (1999). Community, communication, and participation: The role of mass media and interpersonal discussion in local political participation. *Political Communication, 16*(3), 4–87. https://doi.org/10.1080/105846099198659

Meisner, B. A. (2020). Are you OK, Boomer? Intensification of ageism and intergenerational tensions on social media amid COVID-19. *Leisure Sciences*, 1–6. https://doi.org/10.1080/01490400.2020.1773983

Ng, R., Allore, H. G., Trentalange, M., Monin, J., & Levy, B. R. (2015). Increasing negativity of age stereotypes across 200 years: Evidence from a database of 400 million words. *PLoS One, 10*(2), E0117086. https://doi.org/10.1371/journal.pone.0117086

Nilsson, M., & Jönson, H. (2009). Äldre i massmedierna – osynliga eller förknippade med problem. In H. Jönsson (Ed.), *Åldrande, åldersordning, ålderism*. Linköpings universitet.

Nimrod, G. (2020). Changes in internet use when coping with stress: Older adults during the COVID-19 pandemic. *American Journal of Geriatric Psychiatry*. https://doi.org/10.1016/j.jagp.2020.07.010

Norris, P. (2001). *Digital divide: Civic engagement, information poverty and the internet worldwide*. Cambridge University Press.

Nussbaum, M. C. (1997). Capabilities and human rights. *Fordham Law Review, 66*(2), 273–300. https://heinonline.org/HOL/P?h=hein.journals/flr66&i=289

Nutbeam, D. (2008). The evolving concept of health literacy. *Social Science & Medicine, 67*, 2017–2078. https://doi.org/10.1016/j.socscimed.2008.09.050

O'Neil, M., & Haydon, A. (2015). *Aging, agency and attribution of responsibility: Shifting public discourse about older adults*. FrameWorks Institute. Retrieved 17 Sept 2020, from https://www.frameworksinstitute.org/publication/aging-agency-and-attribution-of-responsibility-shifting-public-discourse-about-older-adults/

Obi, T., Ishmatova, D., & Iwasaki, N. (2013). Promoting ICT innovations for the aging population in Japan. *International Journal of Medical Informatics, 82*, e47–e62. https://doi.org/10.1016/j.ijmedinf.2012.05.004

Pérez Tornero, J. M., & Pi, M. (2011). A new horizon: Media literacy assessment and children in Europe. In C. von Felitzen, U. Carlsson, & C. Bucht (Eds.), *New questions, new insight, new approaches: Contributions to the research forum at the world summit on media for children and youth 2010*. Nordicom Sweden, University of Gothenburg.

Petäjä, U. (2006). *Varför yttrandefrihet? Om rättfärdigandet av yttrandefrihet med utgångspunkt från fem centrala argument i den demokratiska idétraditioner* [Why freedom of speech? On the justification of freedom of speech on the basis of five central arguments in the democratic tradition]. Acta Wexionensia 83/2006 (Växjö University).

Potter, W. J. (2005). *Media literacy*. Sage.

Putnam, R. D. (1993). *Making democracy work: Civic traditions in modern Italy*. Princeton University Press.

Rains, S. A. (2008). Health at high speed: Broadband internet access, health communication, and the digital divide. *Communication Research, 35*(3), 283–297. https://doi.org/10.1177/0093650208315958

Reisenwitz, T., Iyer, R., Kuhlmeier, D. B., & Eastman, J. K. (2007). The elderly's internet usage: An updated look. *Journal of Consumer Marketing, 24*(7), 406–418. https://doi.org/10.1108/07363760710834825

Robinson, L., Cotton, S. R., Ono, H., Quan-Haase, A., Mesch, G., Chen, W., Schulz, J., Hale, T. M., & Stern, M. J. (2015). Digital inequalities and why they matter. *Information, Communication & Society, 18*(5), 569–582. https://doi.org/10.1080/1369118X.2015.1012532

Schonfield, D. (1982). Who is stereotyping whom and why? *Gerontologist, 22*(3), 267–272. https://doi.org/10.1093/geront/22.3.267

Seeman, T., Merkin, S., Crimmins, E., Koretz, B., Charette, S., & Karlamangla, A. (2008). Education, income and ethnic differences in cumulative biological risk profiles in a national sample of US adults: NHANES III (1988–1994). *Social Science & Medicine, 66*(1), 72–87. https://doi.org/10.1016/j.socscimed.2007.08.027

Seifert, A. (2020). The digital exclusion of older adults during the COVID-19 pandemic. *Journal of Gerontological Social Work.* https://doi.org/10.1080/01634372.2020.1764687
Sen, A. (1985). *Commodities and capabilities.* Oxford University Press.
Shaker, L. (2014). Dead newspapers and citizens' civic engagement. *Political Communication, 31*(1), 131–148. https://doi.org/10.1080/10584609.2012.762817
Sweetland, J., Volmert, A., & O'Neil, M. (2017). *Finding the frame: An empirical approach to reframing aging and ageism.* FrameWorks Institute.
Torres, S. (2001). *Understanding 'successful aging': Cultural and migratory perspectives.* Dissertation, Uppsala University.
Torres, S. (2019). *Ethnicity and old age: Expanding our imagination.* Policy Press.
Trappel, J. (2019). Inequality, (new) media and communications. In J. Trappel (Ed.), *Digital media inequalities.* Nordicom, University of Gothenburg.
Treré, E., Natale, S., Keightley, E., & Punathambekar, A. (2020). The limits and boundaries of digital disconnection. *Media, Culture & Society.* https://doi.org/10.1177/016443720922054
Tsatsou, P. (2011). *Digital divides in Europe: Culture, politics and the Western-Southern divide.* Peter Lang.
Tuchman, G. (1978). Introduction: The symbolic annihilation of women in the mass media. In G. Tuchman, A. Kaplan Daniels, & J. Benet (Eds.), *Hearth and home: Images of women in the mass media.* Oxford University Press.
Twigg, J. (2013). *Fashion and age: Dress, the body and later life.* Bloomsbury Academic.
Twigg, J., & Martin, W. (2015). *Routledge handbook of cultural gerontology.* Routledge.
United Nations. (2020). *Secretary-General's policy brief: The impact of COVID-19 on older persons.* http://www.un.org/development/desa/ageing/wp-content/uploads/sites/24/2020/05/COVID-Olderpersons
van Deursen, A. J. A. M., & Helsper, E. J. (2015). A nuanced understanding of internet use and non-use among elderly. *European Journal of Communication, 30*(2), 171–187. https://doi.org/10.1177/0267323115578059
van Deursen, A., & van Dijk, J. (2014). The digital divide shifts to differences in usage. *New Media & Society, 16*(3), 507–526. https://doi.org/10.1177/1461444813487959
Weaver, D. H. (2007). Thoughts on agenda setting, framing, and priming. *Journal of Communication, 57*(1), 142–147. https://doi.org/10.1111/j.1460-2466.2006.00333.x
Westwood, S. (2019). *Ageing, diversity and equality: Social justice perspectives* (1st ed.). Routledge.
Wien, C. (2003). *Aeldrebilledet i medierna gennem 50 år.* Syddanskt universitetsforlag.

Chapter 15
System and Life-Course Perspectives on Capability to Work and Capability Through Work

Lotta Dellve, Robin Jonsson, Marita Flisbäck, and Mattias Bengtsson

15.1 Introduction

The many dimensions of the meaning of work and the contemporary challenges related to an older workforce require interdisciplinary perspectives in order to capture the essence of capability in relation to working. The research field of work science focuses on the contexts and values of work and working conditions for both individual workers and groups of workers in society. The scientific interest in the meaning of work and how work has significance for capability has a long history and has engaged many disciplines. The occupational health perspective was already being developed in the seventeenth century, with an attempt to better understand how diseases that arose through working conditions could be prevented. In the 1920s, a focus began to emerge on the productive workforce and how to monetise and rationalise human activities at work. Examples of this can be found in Taylorism and Scientific Management. Nevertheless, this was based on a human view that does not correspond with the capability perspective. The human body was seen as a machine and the focus was to adapt humans to the demands of work in order to increase organisational efficiency – and not to adapt work to the values of individuals. Today, the work science perspective often includes a strong criticism of this

L. Dellve (✉) · R. Jonsson · M. Bengtsson
Department of sociology and work science, University of Gothenburg, Gothenburg, Sweden

Centre for Ageing and Health – AgeCap, University of Gothenburg, Gothenburg, Sweden
e-mail: lotta.dellve@socav.gu.se; robin.jonsson@gu.se; mattias.bengtsson@socav.gu.se

M. Flisbäck
Department of sociology and work science, University of Gothenburg, Gothenburg, Sweden

Centre for Ageing and Health – AgeCap, University of Gothenburg, Gothenburg, Sweden

University of Borås, Borås, Sweden
e-mail: marita.flisback@socav.gu.se

H. Falk Erhag et al. (eds.), *A Multidisciplinary Approach to Capability in Age and Ageing*, International Perspectives on Aging 31,
https://doi.org/10.1007/978-3-030-78063-0_15

view of workers, when individuals' capabilities are neglected in relation to the demands of production at work. Still, work science studies also focus on how synergies between values related to production can be balanced with the values of individuals. This requires cross-disciplinary collaborations to challenge the perspectives of balances and synergies. Our perspectives taken from work science research often shed light on working conditions that create imbalances and inequalities between working individuals and groups of workers. Such imbalances can arise across organisational levels and work systems. From this perspective, the capability approach is useful as a theoretical framework complemented with system theory.

This chapter reports findings from interdisciplinary work science studies from the sociology of work, ergonomics and occupational health, as well as organisational and leadership studies. The studies of individuals' values and their chances of a long and healthy working life include broad applications of data, including register and panel data, health data and longitudinal qualitative interviews, as well as both qualitative and quantitative analyses. The capability approach in work science is demonstrated using a system theory framework, to contribute to more holistic understandings of the capability through work (work as a function and consequences of work) and capability to work (resources and conversion factors). The system theory includes a practice perspective, describing the conversion factors that form the effective opportunities for working at older ages. This often demands integrated handling of perspectives across system levels.

The capability approach is not only relevant to gaining a better conceptual understanding of individuals' abilities and motivation to work, it can also be employed to map and explore the potential consequences that various working conditions have for people when they reach old age. More specifically, we suggest that, since individuals' health, and thus their capabilities, is affected by both current and/or previous working conditions (Nilsen et al., 2014; Dellve et al., 2003), perceived capability (or lack thereof) is also determined through work. In line with this, the capability approach can be employed to better understand various aspects of work, and the consequences thereof, at older ages: work as a defined function and an indication of being part of society (Nussbaum, 2001), work as a goal that the individual has reason to value (Sen, 2009) or factors at work that affect individuals' opportunities to achieve other goals. The chapter includes descriptions of central working-life resources for capability at all system levels. Regarding theoretical foundations, the chapter applies (a) the classical system theory approach developed by Bronfenbrenner (1999) and later modified to work science studies by Bone (2015) and complemented with perspectives of conversion factors by Dellve and Eriksson (2017), and (b) the central concepts in the AgeCap capability framework, described by Rydberg Sterner and colleagues (see Chap. 3 in this book).

To support practical applications, we suggest important conversion factors for crafting capability to work across system levels and patterns of interactions between capability to work and capability through working-life resources. Firstly, central working-life conditions as resources are defined at all system levels. Thereafter, conversion factors for crafting capability to work across system levels are described. Last but not least, we provide some examples of studies focusing on patterns of interaction between capability to work and capability through work.

15.2 Working-Life Conditions as Multi-component Resources for Capability to Work

Both system theory and the capability perspective place the individual at the centre and focus on individuals' values and preferences in life (Fig. 15.1). However, as shown in Figs. 15.1 and 15.2, this does not mean that the individual is studied in isolation; instead, she is situated within a larger context where factors operating at different system levels are assumed to continuously affect her abilities and to condition her values and preferences. System theory divides the different systems into areas, which all have their own system and make important exchanges with all other system levels, i.e. the individual level, the micro-level (the area that is directly related to the individual in the workplace and at home), the meso-level (the wider organisation beyond the direct workplace), the macro-level (the societal level) and the chrono-level (which takes the life-course and changing conditions into account). These levels, and their significance for aspects of capability, are described in the following.

The individual level includes individuals' resources for capability in terms of knowledge, demographics, work orientations, values, skills, behaviour, lifestyle, self-concept, health and general wellbeing. But the individual perspective also includes the meaning that work has for the individual. Health and wellbeing are

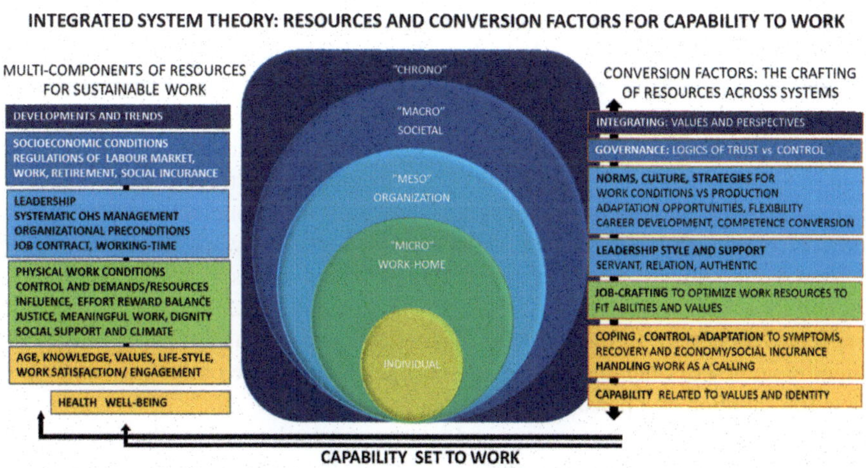

Fig. 15.1 The integrated system theory: resources and conversion factors for the capability set to work, from Dellve and Eriksson (2017)

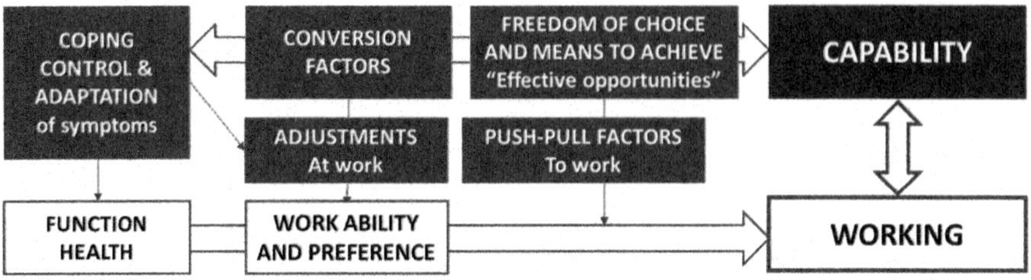

Fig. 15.2 A model of working capability process when experiencing deteriorating health

strongly connected and interlinked parts of an individual's capability. The most important resources for work-related health have been identified through several literature reviews, incorporating evidence-based knowledge, especially at the individual level and micro-level. These are also described below from each system level, and are related to the capability to work.

As part of a research tradition on the meaning of work (Bellah et al., 1985), Bengtsson and Flisbäck (2017, 2021) and Bengtsson et al. (2017) have analysed the existential dimensions of work in relation to individuals' meaning-making in the retirement process. By applying a qualitative, longitudinal design – in the form of interviews with Swedish employees both before and after retirement in order to capture the transitional nature of the retirement process – the conceptualisation of having a calling as a work orientation was foregrounded in order to capture the existential meaning dimensions of work. Bengtsson et al. (2017) outline five main components of a calling: (1) work appears as an external summons, (2) the purpose of the work activity is to serve a higher cause, (3) work is carried out using personality as a tool, (4) work involves self-sacrifice and (5) work gives rise to elevation.

In Sweden, the calling construct has previously been used mainly in relation to meeting human needs in nursing, or combatting exploitative working conditions in female-dominated jobs in the human service sector. In this type of research, work as a calling has been shown to include the risk of exhaustion and/or earlier retirement (Dellve et al., 2003). Even though Bengtsson and Flisbäck (2017) emphasise that there is a 'potential dark side of calling', such as being overworked, exploited and making sacrifices in non-work domains, their studies demonstrate that the calling can in fact be a resource for capability. To relate to, or construe, work as a calling can function as a resource because the individual positions her work within a broader existential context. Thus, this orientation towards work can be a tool for interweaving threads from various life experiences and spheres. According to Bengtsson and Flisbäck (2017, 2021) and Bengtsson et al. (2017), this seems to be especially important in the meaning making that is accentuated during the retirement process, i.e. when the individual exits occupational life on the way towards a new life situation as a pensioner.

Micro-level systems are settings and interpersonal relationships that are directly experienced by the individual workers and include the direct work environment, the workplace and the work group. Capability is directly practised at the micro-system level, and is one significant factor for maintaining health through the concepts of control over one's work and an experienced sense of coherence. In this respect, the most important psychosocial challenges to sustainable occupational health have been identified in several reviews as high job demands, lack of control, imbalance between one's effort and perceived rewards, poor support, organisational injustice (procedural and relational) and poor working climate (Dellve & Eriksson, 2017). Supportive conditions are strengthened psychosocial resources through feedback, recognition, rewards and development opportunities and closer social support, social climate and social capital (Englund et al., 2016; Rydström et al., 2017). Nevertheless, despite years of occupational and public-health research, which has identified the most important micro-level factors constituting a risk of negative health outcomes across occupations and countries, there is still a lack of knowledge about effective interventions that support resources for capability. This may be due to interacting organisational and societal resources and conversion factors.

Berglund et al. (2017) analysed *work-related* factors affecting a prolonged working life for the older workforce in Sweden. The significant effect of age is an indication of the strong values and norms associated with retiring when coming into age. This means that a job for which one is physically fit becomes less and less of a reason to stay the closer the employee gets to the upper retirement age. The study also demonstrated a retaining effect of support from workmates the older one gets. However, physical working conditions and job satisfaction 8 years earlier were the best predictors of a prolonged working life among older individuals. Feeling fit to handle the physical job demands and being satisfied with the job while in one's fifties seem to be vital to be able to continue working. From a policy perspective, it thus seems important to keep employees in their fifties satisfied with their jobs and to support them in taking care of their physical status. The dynamic nature and development of the preference to work or retire was also indicated in a survey distributed to 10,485 public sector employees of older ages (55–67 years) (Selden et al., 2020). Among the reasons for taking earlier retirement were the desire for more free time and poor health conditions, while choices to continue working at older ages appear to be motivated by perceptions of having meaningful work tasks, social cohesion and the capacity to work. These reasons were often rated in parallel, demonstrating the dynamic nature of preferences.

Meso-level systems consist of formal and informal organisational programmes, structures and company culture. In this respect, having reasonable working hours per week and an equitable employment contract are significant for individuals' sustainability in working life. Management and different kinds of organisational support are also important for decent and safe working conditions that increase work participation (Dellve & Eriksson, 2017; Dellve et al., 2008). Broader involvement in issues regarding decent working conditions are often highlighted as important for the capability to work (Dollard & McTernan, 2011).

In our questionnaire-study with 350 eldercare managers in Sweden, their quality work was successful in integrating perspectives of capability both for the employees and the eldercare recipients. This was supported by system perspectives on the conditions for a good learning climate, e.g. an organisation that supports a learning climate for operative managers, a more active learning climate in the work-group and a development-oriented leadership style. Meanwhile, managers' work overload and lack of support significantly decreased their ability to handle the multiple perspectives on values of eldercare in their organising (Dellve, 2018). Thus, capability may be achieved through the organising of service, working conditions and managerial work. Other studies have also shown the interrelated negative impact of managers' work overload and hard governance control in healthcare and eldercare for the organising of sustainable working conditions and the impact on the care provided (Larsson Fallman, 2020; Biswas et al., 2020). Thus, integrating capability perspectives (from the perspective of the users, the older workers and the managers) can have a broad impact on the sustainability of organisational improvement work.

Macro-level systems comprise the labour market structures and institutions that describe the cultural or social context. They include public policy and politics when they have an impact on work and living contexts, socioeconomic conditions and cultural ideologies. Workers may or may not be directly involved at this level, but regulations and practices shape, influence, constrain and/or strengthen the opportunities for work and work characteristics. In Sweden, policies and regulations that aim to control and support good working conditions include, for example, regulation of the social and organisational work environment, the Work Environment Act and other employment acts and regulations. The macro-system also defines the social insurance system around work-related health, which is comparatively generous in Sweden.

Despite acts and regulations, there are distinct gender and social class differences related to ill-health and capability to work among older workers in Sweden (Halleröd & Gustafsson, 2011). A majority (70%) of older workers in jobs with low educational requirements stated that they needed to continue working in order to secure sufficient future incomes (Selden et al., 2020). The results gathered by Kadefors et al. (2017) also indicate a tendency to pass on the societal costs of early labour-market exits to different economic compensation arrangements, as well as to the individuals themselves. Additionally, accumulated living/working conditions, coupled with social class/gender inequalities, tend to further increase the socioeconomic divide, worsening the situation (including morbidity and life-expectancy) for already disadvantaged groups. Thus, a key to organisational sustainability are measures at the workplace addressing health and wellbeing among disadvantaged groups.

The chrono-level encompasses the dimension of time as it relates to the work environment. Developments and changes consider personal, work-group, workplace and organisational levels. There are many factors and conditions that may facilitate trustful developments for individuals and groups. An individual's capability for development (the capability set) and the effective opportunities to live a life one values are influenced by the time in which we are living and the setting. Thus, the chrono-system's proximal processes and mechanisms for crafting resources across system levels for sustainable working life are central for capability. Below, we will highlight some of these conversion factors.

15.3 Conversion Factors – The Crafting of Resources at Work for Capability Across Systems

Despite rather good knowledge about important conditions at each level, the interactions between individual, group and organisational factors often have stronger effects than single factors. Likewise, resource conditions at several levels have stronger effects than those based on a single system level (Marmot, 2005, 2007). Therefore, conversion factors for capability need to handle interactions between conditions across different organisational levels.

Halleröd and Seldén (2013) have identified and applied multidimensional measures of capability concepts at all system levels. They found that accumulated correlations between arenas trigger vicious circles; that is, processes whereby lack of wellbeing in one specific arena cause problems in other arenas and may in the end create a situation of overall accumulated ill-health. Such problems tend to accumulate over time. Thus, suffering economic hardship is related to accumulated lack of well-being. In the following, such conversion factors are described in relation to older workers.

Individual/Micro-level Conversion Perspectives – Individuals use strategies to proactively deal with reduced resources, e.g. through adaptation, coping, recovery, selection and optimisation (Demerouti, 2015). Health is commonly viewed within the context of wellbeing as it relates to the capacity to achieve or experience a meaningful life (Nussbaum, 2001). How we respond to age-related diseases is a complex process which is based on what is already innate and how we learn to adjust to the experience.

In their studies on the retirement process, Bengtsson and Flisbäck (2017) and Bengtsson et al. (2017) argue for the need for a deeper knowledge of how existential dilemmas interact with institutional practices and political decisions. For example, an individual who embraces their calling as an existential work orientation may experience retirement as an institution in which the welfare state 'de-calls' their mission. Here, retirement seems to represents a tension, because the calling as a life task cannot easily be limited to a specific time or place. Thus, individuals have various experiences of the process: accepting and embracing the situation, relief at letting the 'dark side' of the calling go or rejection when the meaningful activities of work cannot be replaced with other types of activity. Also, Bengtsson and Flisbäck point out that the meaning of work seems to be transformed in an individualisation process, with social demands to embrace self-development as a pensioner rather than clinging to work as a calling. They identified three strategies for handling the situation of retirement, i.e., of being encouraged to pursue other types of activities than paid work, such as caring for grandchildren or self-development projects: (1) conserving work as a calling with access to temporary work; (2) learning and, in some cases, embracing the process of 'becoming a self-oriented subject'; and (3) 'redefining' the calling by transferring the work commitment to other activities. When following the first strategy, the individual can be on standby for temporary work opportunities, and thus maintain the capability developed in relation to their existential work orientation. Concerning the second strategy, the individual 'practises' socially legitimised activities that aid individual self-development, such as travelling or cultural experiences. With regard to the third strategy, sacrifices they have previously made in non-work domains, which may have followed a strong commitment to work, can be transferred to commitment to other activities. This means that the individual, as a pensioner, can listen to callings from other social domains, such as devoting substantial time to caring for grandchildren.

Micro/meso-level conversion perspectives – Leadership can be considered both an important resource and, likewise, an important conversion factor for creating resources at work. Managers' work and organising are often viewed as keys to bridging and handling the multiple components of risks and resources for individuals and groups of workers, both over and across system levels (Tengblad, 2012; Dellve & Eriksson, 2017). Some leadership approaches are more associated with employees' health and conversion of resources, e.g. servant leadership and distributed leadership to support influence and participation within the organisation (Gunnarsdottir et al., 2018). The micro−/meso-level conversion perspectives also include organisational practices related to an organisation's norms, culture, management styles and communication. For example, designing work and providing autonomy to enable individuals to proactively reduce their job demands and/or increase job resources.

From longitudinal studies of older female human service workers with chronic diseases, we identified important factors relating to their capability to work (Dellve et al., 2016; Ahlstrom et al., 2013, 2017), forming a chain of conversion factors (Fig. 15.2). When employees experience deteriorating health and work ability, it is significantly important that there are adjustment opportunities at work, as well as push and pull factors promoting work participation. From a capability perspective, there was a dynamic interactive process between capability to work and the crafting of control and adaptation to handle symptoms. In this process, the individuals' job-crafting of adjustment opportunities was important, and the effective opportunities to work (freedom of choice and means to achieve) were important for their capability. Figure 15.2 describes a model of a 'working capability process' when experiencing deteriorating health. The model is inspired by the sickness flexibility model (Johansson & Lundberg, 2004).

Meso−/Micro-/Individual-level conversion perspectives – The employer's willingness to hire and retain older workers and their active engagement at the workplace level are critical to changing retirement behaviour (Vickerstaff et al., 2003). Measures in workplaces are often included in the term 'age management', implying an explicit focus on age in human-resource policies (Ilmarinen, 2005; Naegele & Walker, 2006). Through age-conscious policies and practices, employers can offer work adjustment, training and development opportunities so that the capability and motivation of older workers can be maintained. Earlier studies indicate that European employers have few or no measures in place to recruit or retain older workers (Conen et al., 2012).

In health and eldercare, Jonsson and colleagues (2020) have described the lack of readiness and capability to retain older care workers due to factors such as line-managers' high workload, universal HR policies and the absence of age-management strategies. Thus, organisational measures and employer engagement are critical, and the Swedish Commission on Pension Age has suggested more actions at the organisational level to enable longer working lives in the general population (SOU, 2013:25). In labour market sectors experiencing labour shortages, such as eldercare, retaining older healthcare workers can mitigate some of the need for more personnel. However, the mean retirement age of workers in eldercare is strongly intertwined with the economic aspects provided through regulations for disability pensions in the social insurance system and to retirement regulations. Thus, there may be situations in which large groups of workers cannot retire due to age despite poor health. Despite changed regulations for retirement and social benefits, desired developments may be facilitated by crafting resources for sustainable conditions, through better integrating the values and perspectives of users of eldercare and older employees in eldercare. To attract and retain older workers, organisations need to develop strategies and create the right preconditions. Our questionnaire-study indicated improved organisational measures of different kinds to retain older public employees (Table 15.1). Organisational measures to strengthen resources supporting workers' freedom of choice and value-based work were most common. About half of the older workers had participated in measures to transfer competence or strengthen physical or psychological resources.

Indicated associations with preferences to continue working in older ages were seen where there existed improved resources to boost capability for freedom of choice in terms of participation and influence over decisions, as well as improved learning and competence development. In a study, Jonsson and colleagues (2021) identified the opportunities to make individual deals that match one's competence and experience as the most important for public-sector employees' retirement preferences (Jonsson et al., 2020).

Table 15.1 Organisational measures to increase resources for older workers in the public sector and the proportion of older workers who participated in the measures

Organisational measures to strengthen	Provided and participated (%)
Functional resources	
Physical resources	48%
Psychological resources	44%
Social resources, cooperation	64%
Technical development	70%
Resources for freedom of choice	
Participation and influence over decisions	66%
Career development	58%
Competence development	65%
Values at work	
Trust in work-group	65%
Value-based work	73%
Mentoring, competence transfer	48%

15.4 Interaction Between Capability to Work and Capability Through Work

Factors of central importance for decisions to continue working and not retire are: generally good health and working conditions, a meaningful job, socio-economic issues and also the organisational learning climate, measures to strengthen resource adaptation and adjustments to work as one gets older. The integrated system theory model is suggested in order to better understand the multi-component key resources for capability at work among older workers, and also the conversion factors – capability through work – at the individual, micro, meso, macro and chrono levels. A system theory of important conditions has already been developed in many other aspects, but the capability approach contributes with conversion factors and conditions to better understand the complex social practices. These acknowledge the positive effect of crafting interactions, 'bridgings', and crossing over systems boundaries.

In practice, when supporting capability and finding ways to better analyse how to manage the retirement phase, the focus must be on what individuals value, and taking a view of retirement as a process that can make visible existential meanings. Nevertheless, as seen above, Bengtsson and Flisbäck (2017) and Bengtsson et al. (2017) interweave the individual's existential concerns with forces at a macro level, what sociologists (cf. Kohli, 1986; Beck & Beck Gernsheim, 2002) have conceptualised as individualisation processes in late modernity. Welfare-state institutions do not only enable self-development, but in each life phase, even at later stages, individuals become increasingly forced to choose. This 'institutionalised individualism' does not always bring forth self-developing practices, but may be about counteracting risks, for example of an ecological, financial or health-related character. This is a social inequality issue because individuals in old age have different prerequisites to develop their life chances (Bengtsson & Flisbäck, 2017; Bengtsson et al., 2017). In other words: capability in the form of existential meaning that the individual can gain from activities relating to paid work or retirement interacts with social and economic resource structures.

Likewise, and given that most individuals spend a vast amount of time at work throughout life, it is far from surprising that working conditions, as well as differences in economic conditions generated by the labour market, contribute to disparities in living conditions between different social groups. For instance, socio-epidemiological research has repeatedly demonstrated that such differences cause inequalities in both health and longevity (Marmot, 2005, 2007; Wilkinson & Marmot, 2003). By extension, this means that they also affect individuals' capability throughout the entire lifespan. For instance, with regard to dementia, a strongly age-related neurodegenerative disorder, Hasselgren et al. (2018b) have demonstrated that occupational class could in fact moderate the effects of the apolipoprotein E (*APOE*) ε4 allele, which is currently considered the major genetic risk factor for Alzheimer's disease (Blennow et al., 2006). Likewise, Hasselgren et al. (2018a) have employed the validated Job Exposure Matrix (Johnson & Stewart, 1993) to show that control over one's work is both a potential mechanism linking occupational class differences to dementia, as well as a possible moderator of *APOE* ε4. However, in both cases, the results differ markedly between the genders. Consequently, if we are to better understand how capability is determined *through* work, it is crucial to attend to the structural determinants of differences in working conditions, e.g., social class and gender, as well as to their interrelations and interactions with lower-level factors.

In conclusion, being part of working life can be a goal in itself, but having a reasonable degree of control and influence (freedom of choice) at work can have a great impact on health and wellbeing, as well as on work ability and the capacity to work. This requires an organisation that is characterised by promoting a general learning climate and participation in decision-making, and where employees have opportunities to make individual deals that match their competence and experience. Additionally, the broader perspectives and applications of capability in working-life studies require a range of methods for critically examining how capability is formed in various contexts and from different perspectives, i.e. what aspects of capability are present, for whom, under what conditions and to what outcomes do they lead (wellbeing, power, influence, decent working conditions)?

References

Ahlstrom, L., Hagberg, M., & Dellve, L. (2013). Workplace rehabilitation and supportive conditions at work: A prospective study. *Journal of Occupational Rehabilitation, 23*(2), 248–260.

Ahlstrom, L., Dellve, L., Hagberg, M., et al. (2017). Women with neck pain on long-term sick leave: Approaches used in the return to work process: A qualitative study. *Journal of Occupational Rehabilitation, 27*(1), 92–105.

Beck, U., & Beck-Gernsheim, E. (2002). *Individualization: Institutionalized individualism and its social and political consequences*. Sage.

Bellah, R. N., Madsen, R., Sullivan, W. M., Swidler, A., & Tipton, S. M. (1985). *Habits of the heart: Individualism and commitment in American life*. University of California Press.

Bengtsson, M., & Flisbäck, M. (2017). On leaving work as a calling: Retirement as an existential imperative. *International Journal of Ageing and Later Life, 11*(1), 37–67.

Bengtsson, M., & Flisbäck, M. (2021). Illuminating existential meaning: A new approach in the study of retirement. *Qualitative Sociology Review, 17*(1), 196–214.

Bengtsson, M., Flisbäck, M., & Lund, A. (2017). *Farväl till arbetet: Sociologiska perspektiv på meningen med att gå i pension* [Farwell to work: Sociological perspectives on the meaning of retirement]. Nordic Academic Press.

Berglund, T., Selden, D., & Halleröd, B. (2017). Factors affecting prolonged working life for the older workforce: The Swedish case. *Nordic Journal of Working Life Studies, 7*(1), 19.

Biswas, U. N., Dellve, L., Bhattacharjee, A., & Wolmesjö, M. (2020). Ageing and values in the developments of home-based eldercare: Perspectives from India and Sweden. *Psychology and Developing Societies, 32*(2), 224–253.

Blennow, K., de Leon, M. J., & Zetterberg, H. (2006). Alzheimer's disease. *Lancet, 368*, 387–403.

Bone, K. D. (2015). The bioecological model: Applications in holistic workplace well-being management. *International Journal of Workplace Health Management, 8*, 256–271.

Bronfenbrenner, U. (1999). Environments in developmental perspective: Theoretical and operational models. In S. Friedman & T. Wachs (Eds.), *Measuring environment across the life span: Emerging methods and concepts* (pp. 3–28). American Psychological Association Press.
Conen, W. S., Henkens, K., & Schippers, J. (2012). Employers' attitudes and actions towards the extension of working lives in Europe. *International Journal of Manpower, 33*(6), 648–665.
Dellve. (2018). *Organizational learning climate. Importance for managers' development of value-integrated eldercare.* SGM EAWOP.
Dellve, L., & Eriksson, A. (2017). Health-promoting managerial work: A theoretical framework for a leadership program that supports knowledge and capability to craft sustainable work practices in daily practice and during organizational change. *Societies, 7*(2), 12.
Dellve, L., Lagerström, M., & Hagberg, M. (2003). Work system risk factors for disability pension among home care workers: A case-control study. *International Archives of Occupational and Environmental Health, 76*, 216–224.
Dellve, L., Skagert, K., & Eklöf, M. (2008). The impact of systematic health & safety management for occupational disorders and work ability. *Social Science & Medicine, 67*(6), 965–970.
Dellve, L., Fallman, S. L., & Ahlstrom, L. (2016). Return to work from long-term sick leave: A six-year prospective study of the importance of adjustment latitudes at work and home. *International Archives of Occupational and Environmental Health, 89*(1), 171–179.
Demerouti, E. (2015). Strategies used by individuals to prevent burnout. *European Journal of Clinical Investigation, 45*, 1106–1112.
Dollard, M. F., & McTernan, W. (2011). Psychosocial safety climate: A multilevel theory of work stress in the health and community service sector. *Epidemiology and Psychiatric Sciences, 20*(4), 287–293.
Englund, A. C., Rydström, I., Dellve, L., et al. (2016). Social support outside work and return to work among women on long-term sick leave working within human service organizations. *Applied Nursing Research, 30*, 187–193.
Gunnarsdóttir, S., Edwards, K., & Dellve, L. (2018). Improving health care organizations through servant leadership. In D. van Dierendonck (Ed.), *Practicing servant leadership* (pp. 249–273). Palgrave Macmillan.
Halleröd, B., & Gustafsson, J. E. (2011). A longitudinal analysis of the relationship between changes in socio-economic status and changes in health. *Social Science and Medicine, 72*(1), 116–123.
Halleröd, B., & Seldén, D. (2013). The multi-dimensional characteristics of wellbeing: How different aspects of wellbeing interact and do not interact with each other. *Social Indicators Research, 113*(3), 807–825.
Hasselgren, C., Dellve, L., Ekbrand, H., et al. (2018a). Socioeconomic status, gender and dementia: The influence of work environment exposures and their interactions with APOE ε4. *SSM – Population Health, 5*, 171–179.
Hasselgren, C., Ekbrand, H., Fässberg, M. M., et al. (2018b). APOE ε4 and the long arm of social inequity: Estimated effects of socio-economic status and sex on the timing of dementia onset. *Ageing & Society, 39*(9), 1951–1975.
Ilmarinen, J. (2005). *Towards a longer working life: Ageing and the quality of worklife in the European Union.* Finnish Institute of Occupational Health.
Johnson, J. V., & Stewart, W. F. (1993). Measuring work organization exposure over the life course with a job-exposure matrix. *Scandinavian Journal of Work, Environment & Health*, 21–28.
Johansson, G., & Lundberg, I. (2004). Adjustment latitude and attendance requirements as determinants of sickness absence or attendance: Empirical tests of the illness flexibility model. *Social Science & Medicine, 58*(10), 1857–1868.
Jonsson, R., Björk, L., Lindegård Andersson, A., et al. (2020). Organizational hindrances to the retention of older healthcare workers. *Nordic Journal of Working Life Studies, 10*(1), 41.
Jonsson, R., Hasselgren, C., Dellve, L., et al. (2021). Matching the pieces: The presence of idiosyncratic deals and their impact on retirement preferences among older workers. *Work Ageing and Retirement.* In press.

Kadefors, R., Nilsson, K., Rylander, L., et al. (2017). Occupation, gender and work-life exits: A Swedish population study. *Ageing & Society, 38*(7), 1332–1349.

Kohli, M. (1986). The world we forgot: A historical review of the life course. In V. W. Marshall (Ed.), *Later life: The social psychology of aging* (pp. 271–303). Sage.

Larsson Fällman, S. (2020). *Organizational flexibility in health care: Importance for health among managers and employees*. PhD thesis, KTH: Royal Institute of Technology, Stockholm.

Marmot, M. (2005). Social determinants of health inequalities. *Lancet, 365*, 1099–1104.

Marmot, M. (2007). Achieving health equity: From root causes to fair outcomes. *Lancet, 370*, 1153–1163.

Naegele, G., & Walker, A. (2006). *A guide to good practice in age management*. European Foundation for the Improvement of Living and Working Conditions.

Nilsen, C., Andel, R., Fors, S., et al. (2014). Associations between work-related stress in late midlife, educational attainment, and serious health problems in old age: A longitudinal study with over 20 years of follow-up. *BMC Public Health, 14*, 878.

Nussbaum, M. (2001). *Women and human development: The capabilities approach*. Cambridge University Press.

Rydström, I., Englund, L., Dellve, L., & Ahlstrom, L. (2017). Importance of social capital at the workplace for return to work among women with a history of long-term sick leave: A cohort study. *BMC Nursing, 16*(1), 38.

Selden, D., Hasselgren, C., Johnsson, R. & et al. (2020). *Arbete och pensionering. Uppfattningar bland medarbetare i Göteborgs Stad* [Work and retirement: Preferences and experiences among older employees in the City of Gothenburg]. Gothenburg Studies in Work Sciences, 20.

Sen, A. (2009). *The idea of justice*. Belknap Press of Harvard University Press.

SOU. (2013, 25). *Åtgärder för ett längre arbetsliv* [Measures for prolonged working-life]. Stockholm.

Tengblad, S. (2012). *The work of managers: Towards a practice theory of management*. Oxford University Press.

Vickerstaff, S., Cox, J., & Keen, L. (2003). Employers and the management of retirement. *Social Policy and Administration, 37*(3), 271–287.

Wilkinson, R., & Marmot, M. (2003). *Social determinants of health: The solid facts*. World Health Organization.

Chapter 16
Organisational Capability for Delayed Retirement

Ewa Wikström, Karin Allard, Rebecka Arman, Roy Liff, Daniel Seldén, and Roland Kadefors

16.1 Introduction

This chapter highlights the meso level in the capability approach by focusing on how organisations address problems and opportunities associated with an ageing workforce by applying various age-management measures. In order to characterise the ability of organisations to promote the delayed retirement of older workers, we turn to the concept of organisational capability.

The increasing proportion of older people in Sweden has created the need for an extended working life and delayed retirement. Three reasons are often cited for the need to delay retirement: (a) to ensure a sustainable pension system, (b) to ensure the availability of sufficient labour and the effective use of the human capital possessed by older workers and (c) to contribute to the welfare of older people. Therefore, in 2013, the Swedish Pension Age Commission of Inquiry (SOU, 2013:25) proposed a set of changes to the pension system framework aimed at increasing the incentives for older people to work longer. However, to meet and

E. Wikström (✉) · R. Arman
Department of Business Administration, University of Gothenburg, Gothenburg, Sweden

Centre for Ageing and Health – AgeCap, University of Gothenburg, Gothenburg, Sweden
e-mail: ewa.wikstrom@handels.gu.se; rebecka.arman@handels.gu.se

K. Allard · D. Seldén · R. Kadefors
Centre for Ageing and Health – AgeCap, University of Gothenburg, Gothenburg, Sweden

Department of Sociology and Work Science, University of Gothenburg, Gothenburg, Sweden
e-mail: karin.allard@gu.se; daniel.selden@socav.gu.se; roland.kadefors@socav.gu.se

R. Liff
Centre for Ageing and Health – AgeCap, University of Gothenburg, Gothenburg, Sweden

Gothenburg Research Institute, University of Gothenburg, Gothenburg, Sweden
e-mail: roy.liff@gri.gu.se

H. Falk Erhag et al. (eds.), *A Multidisciplinary Approach to Capability in Age and Ageing*, International Perspectives on Aging 31,
https://doi.org/10.1007/978-3-030-78063-0_16

participate in these changes at the policy and individual levels, changes in organisational practices are also required. Unfortunately, there is a lack of systematic knowledge about how such changes can be successfully implemented within organisations. In this chapter, we discuss this lacuna and specifically focus on organisational capability. We highlight workplace conditions and practices that may inhibit or promote the retention of workers beyond the previous norm for retirement.

The novelty of an organisational capability approach is that it highlights workplace conditions that enable older people to use their abilities to perform acts of value and to achieve a better quality of life and greater participation in society. The specific goal of this chapter is to contribute to knowledge about organisational capability and our understanding of the meso level'in the capability approach.

The workplace and the actions taken by employers have received much less attention than research on demographics, pension system financing or individual circumstances (SOU, 2013:25). Workplace resources, capabilities and functions form a dynamic pattern. Factors that influence the work abilities of older workers are related in complex interactions and not merely in the format of simple cause and effect (Ilmarinen & Ilmarinen, 2015; McDermott et al., 2010; Henkens et al., 2009; Hasselhorn & Freude, 2007; Brooke & Taylor, 2005; Henkens, 2005; Ilmarinen, 2006a, b). As several research teams have discovered, the organisation of workplaces is of central importance in addressing physical strains, psychosocial work environment, work-group norms, the division of labour, leadership and management support for older people's abilities and their preference to continue working (Furunes et al., 2011; McDermott et al., 2010; Brooke & Taylor, 2005).

16.2 Organisational Research

Organisational research addresses a wide variety of societal challenges facing today's organisations, including sustainability issues, questions pertaining to demographic challenges, the integration of a diverse workforce, diversity, equality, business case approaches, work environment and the ongoing institutional efforts to negotiate the relationship between old regimes and new beliefs. Ageing represents a global societal challenge and, in order to achieve health equality and maintain good health in the workplace and during later life, we need to focus on the potential to increase capabilities within organisations, at the societal level and at the individual level. Coordinated scientific efforts are needed to facilitate sustainable ageing within organisations and across societies. The ultimate goal is to ensure that people can experience continued overall functioning and participation in the workplace and in societal life continuing into later life.

In order to promote the organisational conditions for older workers to remain in the workforce, investments in age management practices are starting to be made (Midtsundstad, 2011). The complexity and collective practices of age management within organisations is immense; they involve the physical work environment, accommodating changes in regulations, organisational and technical changes, securing competences, creating a productive work environment for workers who are devoted to their work and, also importantly, maintaining an economically efficient organisation (Furunes et al., 2011; McDermott et al., 2010; Brooke & Taylor, 2005). At the same time, actions at the organisational level have to accommodate both macro conditions, for example changes in the retirement system, and the actual composition of the workforce; that is, individual circumstance among workers, and collective perceptions of retirement prevailing among workers. With increasing life expectancy, it has become more and more important to understand the processes which are being implemented to postpone retirement age. It is against this background that the proposed study aims to develop knowledge about what organisations already do and what more they could do in relation to older workers regarding conditions that promote and/or inhibit delayed retirement.

16.3 Applying a Capability Approach Within Organisation Studies

According to Sen (e.g., 2009), capability is the ability to perform actions in order to reach goals that the individual has reason to value. Central to Sen's idea is the notion that individuals have different conversion factors, which means that even where two individuals have access to the same resources, they do not necessarily have equal capabilities to enjoy the same functions. Because the focus of the capability approach is on the interaction between the individual's resources and preferences (micro) and the opportunity structure that exists in the workplace (meso), and is embodied in the retirement system (macro), we propose that the policies, practices and discussions concerning older people can preferably be related to the concept of organisational capability.

What employers do and communicate in relation to older workers is, of course, one significant aspect, but so are the prevailing norms in the workforce at large: the status of older workers and prevailing discourses and expectations about retirement (LaLiberte & Molke, 2009; Trethewey, 2001; Sargent et al., 2013). Organisations may hesitate to extend the tenure of older workers because measures that benefit and promote one age group over others in organisations are likely to have both positive and negative implications. Promoting later retirement may also limit jobs for new and younger workers to a certain extent, or delay their promotions. There may also be negative effects on team dynamics, if delayed retirement leads to a greater spread of age and experience; the so-called 'interrelationships between age groups' in workplaces are not always easy (Brooke & Taylor, 2005). Furthermore, if efficiency is the main driver for the implementation of organisational changes, investments are only likely to be made if they are calculated to provide the organisation with economic benefits.

In terms of economic benefits, in the human resource management literature labour economists have advocated that older workers should not be the recipients of human capital investment. This view, based on neoclassical human capital theory, has been challenged. For example, Simpson, Greller and Stroh's (2002) review distinguishes between (a) the labour economics model, and (b) the life-span career development model for human capital investment. In the labour economics model, the cost-benefit considerations are based on a comparison of the discounted net returns from education and training over the remaining years of employment before pension age. There are at least two rationales for not investing in the human capital of older workers: They are too valuable in their present job to participate in training activities, and they have too few years of work remaining to benefit the organisation.

According to advocates of the life-span development model, the payback period of training activities is generally short for any age group – perhaps of the order of 3–5 years – which tends to level out age-group differences. Moreover, older people are becoming more interested in investing in their own human capital, because they often plan to continue working up to and even beyond the official pension age (Simpson et al., 2002). So, although there is some debate on the matter, investments by organisations to keep their older workers trained and to support their continued career development can be seen as rational from a business perspective.

Irrespective of these debates, some organisations have made efforts to keep older workers longer. The term 'age management' has been used to describe organisational activities aimed at promoting a longer working life and/or balancing the interests and needs of varying age groups within an organisation (see e.g. Ilmarinen & Ilmarinen, 2015; Furunes et al., 2011; Midtsundstad, 2011; McDermott et al., 2010; Brooke & Taylor, 2005). Ilmarinen (2006a: 120) defines age management as 'taking the employee's age, and age-related factors, into account in daily work management, work planning and work organization; thus everyone – regardless of age – can achieve personal and organizational targets healthily and safely'. This way of conceiving age management places demands on both the organisation's management and workplace practices. Brooke and Taylor (2005: 418) relate age-management practices to human resource management and the interrelationships between age groups within organisations.

We propose that the management of an ageing workforce requires awareness of the realities of the interrelationships between workers of different ages, including both the intended and unintended consequences. Yet the specific content of what, in practice, should be termed 'age management' is likely to vary across contexts and organisations. As an example, in this chapter we will describe the process of creating, implementing and developing age-management practices and support through a study using the action-research approach aiming to explore organisational capability by focusing on the characteristics of age management and organisational capability, as well as the mechanisms facilitating or hindering the work ability of an ageing workforce delaying the age of retirement.

16.4 Studying Organisational Capability

This intervention and case study began with the implementation of a research consortium – a group of practitioners from eight large organisations (three private companies and five public organisations) who met and continue to meet to oversee collaborations between companies and organisations that are working with issues of postponed retirement. The aim of involving a research consortium in the study design was to enable knowledge creation by including both the practitioners and the researchers' perspectives. Accordingly, the idea of the consortium was to create a basis for sharing experiences of age management among organisations and between organisations and researchers. The consortium also had the purpose of comparing and mirroring the experiences of age management with invited researchers and practitioners from other countries.

The research consortium also formed the basis for the data collection, which has been conducted through case studies in organisational-capability research. The aim of the case-study approach has been to document and analyse age management practices as they develop. One public-sector and one private-sector organisation were selected as the primary cases for this study. The organisations both had human-resource (HR)-initiated policies and programmes that included older workers, such as mentoring and competence laboratories for knowledge sharing. The data collection involved all the relevant actors at both workplaces, including top managers, line managers, HR specialists and trade union representatives, all of whom, in different capacities, had formal responsibilities for age management. Other older and younger workers were also interviewed.

16.5 Observations of Workplace Practices: Results and Reflections

The focus on organisational capability has enabled us to observe, for example, that there are internal driving forces at the workplace level to find solutions to prolonged working life – solutions connected to labour shortages or high staff turnover and increased work-related ill health. The employers translate this situation as a need to maintain skill and knowledge retention. The employers want to keep their human capital, but also to be an attractive employer for recruiting purposes. Keeping older workers is seen as an alternative to recruiting only young people. Furthermore, in accordance with previous research (McMullin & Marshall, 2001; Snape & Redman, 2003), we found that the retaining and recruiting of older workers may be hindered by age discriminatory practices that may be based on an ageist ideology of negative stereotypes, beliefs or attitudes.

An overall observation is that age management in workplaces is often related to questions about the need for skills and a lack of labour and human capital (Wikström et al., 2018). Employers translate this situation as a need to retain competence, which is often referred to as knowledge retention or retention of know-how. However, the retention of human capital and knowledge is prevented when the focus is solely on the skills of older workers and on a view of knowledge as a 'package' (the commodification and technical packaging of knowledge which, like software, can be downloaded from a human into a computer or traded between people). Common knowledge retention methods are often unrelated to strategies based on a consideration of the silent dimension of knowledge or knowing in practice and its impact on knowledge management within an organisation. Retaining competence and know-how seems to be a constantly ongoing iterative process between older and younger workers in working life. Maintaining competence requires continuous interaction in the joint resolution of tasks between actors, where silent knowledge and know-how are important and central to the survival of the organisation and as part of its 'business case'.

Accordingly, our results highlight that the managerial response to delayed retirement and extended working life is often interpreted from a business-case perspective. The societal level meta-narrative, regarding the need to delay retirement due to demographic changes, is translated and comes into conflict with organisational narratives of efficiency, where age is seen as a predictor of declining efficiency. A business-case approach to age management addresses the employer's perspective and relates to the employer's complex calculations in trying to enable an extended working life for workers. Such managers engage in strategic HR planning with available human capital, as they try to retain organisational competence, or even a unique competence, in the form of productive workers. Our observations also reveal more multifaceted managerial responses, in which the business case is expanded. There seems to be a growing trend towards manoeuvring the mainstream discourse and practice on a business-case rationale towards a more value-driven logic, i.e. ethical values of equal opportunities for older workers as well as the societal values of sharing responsibilities for the welfare system by extending working life. By focusing on prolonged working life and delayed retirement from a capability approach, we were able to identify and problematise different attitudes and reactions to the societal norm on delayed retirement.

Another observation is that HR routines tend to prevent a prolonged working life, despite political efforts to increase the retirement age (Liff & Wikström, forthcoming). Our results show that three HR routines are central to the prevention of prolonged working life: performance reviews, salary discussions and internal recruitment. These routines seem rational and appropriate for an organisation's managers, since the requirements from a work and efficiency perspective must have priority over workers' needs. In addition, it may be considered economically rational to prioritise salary requirements for younger workers compared to older workers, as well as to stop further training for older workers. In general, it thus seems reasonable for managers to make decisions based on objective criteria such as age. Nevertheless, our results indicate that these HR routines need to be adapted if they are to support an extended working life.

Accordingly, internal organisational institutions (e.g. taken-for-granted norms and ways of thinking), which are embedded in HR routines, seem to either facilitate or hinder extended working life, creating a need for change in these institutions. HR routines take time to change, but the capability approach enables us to highlight networks of endogenous institutions and mechanisms embedded in the routines that either promote or inhibit prolonged working life. This complex interaction between different routines is considered 'institutional' because it serves to maintain existing routines or establish new routines, policies and observable material effects (e.g., prolonged working life or retirement age changes) within a specific field (the workplace). Our observations demonstrate that path-dependence can unearth the existence of strong retirement-age norms within an organisation. Managers' negative attitudes towards older workers can reinforce an early exit culture that is difficult to change. This hampers the organisational capability to delay retirement. The acknowledgement of existing age norms is a crucial first step in changing them.

Furthermore, from a life-course perspective, ageing occurs in a context that results in unique experiences. These experiences, in turn, affect people's attitudes, values and accumulated resources over time, which can be seen as positive (accumulated advantages) or negative (accumulated disadvantages). In order to change the path-dependence structure, the workplace could work with a procedural life-course perspective, i.e. ageing is seen as a process that differs between individuals. Organisations and managers thus need to be able to adapt routines and relationships in relation to this transformation – which requires a combination of a life-course perspective and an organisational analysis, such as an ongoing process.

Two different logics also appear to be of great importance for workers' retirement decisions: the logic of consequences and the logic of appropriateness. The logic of consequences, for example, describes the financial or social consequences of retirement and it has been the logic of consequences that has been given the greatest scope in research to explain individuals' retirement decisions. The results reveal that the logic of appropriateness – the logic that describes at what age it is considered appropriate to retire – has at least as much importance as the logic of consequences for the retirement decision. This may mean that employers need to work more with values and norms in relation to what is considered to be appropriate age to retire if they intend to influence workers' retirement decisions with the ambition to delay retirement.

16.6 Discussion

In order to determine why older workers choose to retire or to continue working beyond the general retirement age, we need to understand both the constraints and the possibilities, i.e., the opportunity structure, to which the individual is exposed before decisions about retirement are made. The opportunity structure is related to three different levels: macro, meso and micro. In this context, the macro level refers to laws and regulations that impact upon pensions, social security and the labour market, factors that at any given time will influence both what an individual can do and what they prefer to do. Macro-level changes are often guided by the explicit goal of changing incentives, i.e., making it more profitable to work longer, or constraining available exit options, e.g., changes to early retirement and disability benefit programmes.

The focus on organisational capability contributes to our understanding of the dynamic interactions that occur at the meso level, and we conclude that the configurations in which daily life is embedded, for example, family situation, social networks and the workplace. The way in which workplaces are organised when it comes to physical and psychosocial work environment, the organisation of work tasks and, not least, the employers' motives and interests are of central importance for older people's ability and desire to continue working. At the individual level, retirement decisions are dependent on, among other things, individual health, job satisfaction, skills and human capital, as well as retirement preferences.

When looking at retirement from the older worker's perspective, we have for example focused on the individual's capability to control the retirement process. For example, the probability that an older person will remain employed will depend partly on his or her health and human capital, and the type of job. But two seemingly similar individuals can nevertheless have very different opportunities to remain employed because their employer has implemented very different age management policies, or simply because they have different attitudes towards older workers. Since organisational capability makes it possible to focus on the interaction between the individual's resources and preferences, and the opportunity structure existing at the workplace (meso) and embodied in the retirement system (macro), much of the discussion and many of the policies and practices concerning older people can be related to the concept of capabilities.

Furthermore, the societal narratives explaining the need to address early work-life exits from the labour market have little impact on the ways in which organisations articulate their internal policies with respect to retirement issues. The managerial response to delayed retirement is related primarily to a business-case perspective, to strategic HR planning in relation to available human capital, and to the desire to retain unique competences. The absence of an ageing perspective related to operative goals when implementing HR-initiated policies and programmes, such as focusing on unique competence or mentoring, may result in a marginal or negative effect on the retirement culture and delayed retirement. Furthermore, knowledge retention is hindered by focusing solely on an explicit and commodified view of knowledge. Knowledge retention is a matter of continual interaction between actors, in which tacit knowledge and knowing are important.

Moreover, the societal policy change towards the extension of working life includes how HR strategists translate and use stories about older workers in strategic staff discussions and in their policy work (Arman et al., 2021). Employers and people with managerial responsibility see questions about age management, delayed retirement and extended working life primarily from a business-case perspective. This results in narratives at a societal level about the need to delay retirement due to demographic changes coming into conflict with organisational stories about efficiency and business case, since ageing is seen as part of a process of 'decline', during which workers' efficiency and productivity steadily reduce. In a business-case strategy for age management, employers focus on complex calculations in order to answer the question of whether delayed retirement will pay off.

Age management and delayed retirement are less often discussed on the basis of a value-driven logic, which emphasises ethical values about equal opportunities for older workers and the importance of sharing responsibility for the welfare system. By focusing on narratives of age management and retirement, this study has identified and problematised the institutional work of organisational representatives that maintains the perspectives of older workers. One conclusion is that the societal narratives explaining the need to address early retirement from the labour market have little impact on how organisations formulate their internal policies on retirement issues.

In sum, both the views on knowledge and competence, and assumptions about how older people can carry out their work, are of great importance in determining the length of their working life (Kadefors et al., 2020; Wikström et al., 2018; Wikström & Liff, 2019). These notions and assumptions, in turn, are embedded in the HR routines used by operational managers in their interactions with workers. The interaction between the chief operating officer and the employee, which occurs during the application of routines, can lead to retirement decisions being almost predetermined or predestined. Therefore, the perspective of age management needs to be broadened to include the interactions between managers and workers. The importance of examining underlying factors and assumptions has been described, and such transparency can have a major impact on how long a career will last.

16.7 Conclusion

Altogether, three types of conditions seem central to organisational capability for extended working life:

1. How older people's knowledge and skills can be seen as worth preserving within an organisation, and what organisational measures are required in order to succeed (Wikström et al., 2018). Employers and managers may need to review and redefine the view of knowledge and know-how in order for both younger and older people's knowledge and know-how to be valued within the framework of what is perceived as profitable and effective.
2. The operational managers' use of HR routines for workers' career curves and what inherent norms are embedded in these routines that need to be influenced in order for the routines to contribute to an extended working life (Liff & Wikström, 2020a, b; Wikström & Liff, 2019). One question raised by this research review concerns the obstacles that are created for older people in working life when HR routines – such as performance reviews and educational efforts – are standardised. There may be a need for operational managers to adapt such HR routines in relation to workers' life-course (Liff & Wikström, 2020a; Wikström & Liff, 2019; Kadefors, 2019).

3. The HR function for the exercise of age management (Wikström & Liff, 2019). The HR function can play a central role in strategic management as well as enabling operational line managers to integrate age management into their organisation. This is about the HR function being able to demonstrate the way in which age management can be seen as part of a value-creating process (i.e. as part of a business case); for example, by illustrating statistics about the demographics of the organisation.

A key conclusion is that there is a need to broaden the perspective and meaning of age management. Such a broader perspective focuses on how employers and managers interact with their workers through the use of different personnel management routines. Organisational conditions for an extended working life not only include changes in the workers' work organisation as well as their physical and mental work environment, but it is at least as important to consider how employers and managers interact with all workers, regardless of age.

We have highlighted the importance of how knowledge is defined within organisations and how one values the knowledge and know-how of both older and younger people within an organisation. It is also important to consider how operational managers interact with workers through their use of HR routines in recruitment, promotion and salary setting, which will affect older people's opportunities for a long, sustainable and successful career (as long as they have the capacity and willingness to remain at work). How older people can contribute with their knowledge in a workplace also plays a central role for an extended working life. An interactive perspective on age management can contribute to an in-depth knowledge and understanding of organisational capacity for delayed retirement and of the dynamic interaction patterns within the workplace, as well as the importance of an extended working life. The norm for an appropriate retirement age is also an important factor in the interaction between operational managers and workers.

The definition of an upper retirement age and a fixed retirement age appears to play a central role in the norm of an appropriate retirement age. This research highlights the need to relax such norm formations within organisations in order to enable an extended working life. However, this will probably require that societal norms and institutional frameworks are changed to modify the conditions for organisational actors – such as managers and HR – and thereby create pressure to change the norms, actions and routines of these actors. This could be achieved through a variety of measures. In the same way that changes in societal norms and institutional frameworks relating to the upper retirement age could affect the norm regarding an appropriate retirement age, tax reforms relating to the elderly could have a similar effect.

The concept of organisational capability for a longer working life thus highlights a number of complex interactions. Firstly, each individual's decision about retirement depends upon a number of composite factors, such as health, social networks, preferences and economic conditions. It has to do with the socio-economic aspects of age, and our work has highlighted the complex interplay between different factors and older workers' approach to extended working life within four categories: 'can and want to', 'can but do not want to', 'cannot but want to', and 'cannot and do

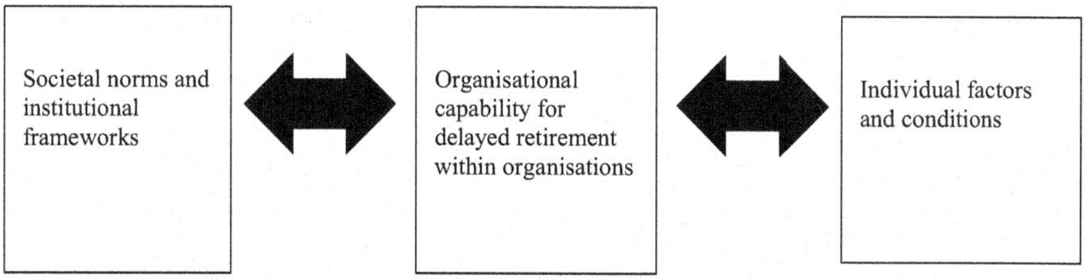

Fig. 16.1 Organisational capability for delayed retirement depends on complex institutional dynamics

not want to' (Kadefors et al., 2020). However, in this text, we have mainly focused on the interactions between different organisational conditions and prospects that affect the possibility of an extended working life. The conditions are assumed to influence both the individual's 'can' and their 'want to'.

Central societal norms and institutional frameworks include norms on appropriate retirement age, laws and regulations, as well as taxes. Significant organisational conditions are views of knowledge and skills, HR routines, notions of appropriate retirement age, HR function, flexible working conditions and organisational work environment. Individual factors include health, preference, finances and flexible conditions in the workplace. This complex interaction, which is manifested in the practice of age management, can lead either to a change in patterns of action and an extended working life or to a stabilisation of patterns of action and retirement. The interaction can be illustrated with the following image (Fig. 16.1).

References

Arman, R., Kadefors, R., & Wikström, E. (2021). We do not discuss age here. A study of organizational narratives of retirement timing. (In press). *Ageing & Society*.

Brooke, L., & Taylor, P. (2005). Older workers and employment: Managing age relations. *Ageing and Society, 25*(3), 415–429.

Furunes, T., Mykletun, R. J., & Solem, P. E. (2011). Age management in the public sector in Norway: Exploring managers' decision latitude. *The International Journal of Human Resource Management, 22*(06), 1232–1247.

Hasselhorn, H., & Freude, G. (2007). *Der Work Ability Index: Ein Leitfaden*. Wirtschaftsverlag NW.

Henkens, K. (2005). Stereotyping older workers and retirement: The managers' point of view. *Canadian Journal on Aging, 24*(4), 353–366.

Henkens, K., Van Solinge, H., & Cozijnsen, R. (2009). Let go or retain? A comparative study of the attitudes of students and managers about retirement of older workers. *Journal of Applied Social Psychology, 39*(7), 1562–1588.

Ilmarinen, J. (2006a). The ageing workforce: Challenges for occupational health. *Journal of Occupational Medicine, 56*(6), 362–364.

Ilmarinen, J. (2006b). *Towards a longer worklife: Ageing and the quality of worklife in the European Union*. The Finnish Institute of Occupational Health.

Ilmarinen, J., & Ilmarinen, V. (2015). Work ability and aging. In L. Finkelstein, D. M. Truxillo, F. Fraccaroli, & R. Frankel (Eds.), *Facing the challenges of a multi-age workforce: A use-inspired approach*. Routledge.

Kadefors, R. (2019). Att vilja och kunna arbeta längre. *Underlagsrapport till Delegationen för senior arbetskraft rapport, 9*(S 2018), 10.

Kadefors, R., Wikström, E., & Arman, R. (2020). The capability of organizations to manage delayed retirement. *Journal of Organizational Effectiveness: People and Performance, 7*(1), 38–51. https://doi-org.ezproxy.ub.gu.se/10.1108/JOEPP-06-2019-0047

LaLiberte Rudman, D. L., & Molke, D. (2009). Forever productive: The discursive shaping of later life workers in contemporary Canadian newspapers. *Work, 32*(4), 377–389.

Liff, R. & Wikström, E. (2020a). Prolonged or preserved working life? *Intraorganisational institutions embedded in human resource routines, Ageing and Society*, 1–19.

Liff, R., & Wikström, E. (2020b). An interactional perspective on age management for prolonged working life. *Nordic Journal of Welfare Research, 5*(2), 137–139.

McDermott, H. J., Kazi, A., Munir, F., & Haslam, C. (2010). Developing occupational health services for active age management. *Occupational Medicine, 60*(3), 193–204.

McMullin, J. A., & Marshall, V. W. (2001). Ageism, age relations, and garment industry work in Montreal. *The Gerontologist, 41*(1), 111–122.

Midtsundstad, T. I. (2011). Inclusive workplaces and older employees: An analysis of companies' investment in retaining senior workers. *The International Journal of Human Resource Management, 22*(6), 1277–1293.

Sargent, L. D., Lee, M. D., Martin, B., & Zikic, J. (2013). Reinventing retirement: New pathways, new arrangements, new meanings. *Human Relations, 66*(1), 3–21.

Sen, A. (2009). *The idea of justice*. Belknap Press of Harvard University Press.

Simpson, P., Greller, M., & Stroh, L. (2002). Variations in human capital investment activity by age. *Journal of Vocational Behavior, 61*, 109–113.

Snape, E., & Redman, T. (2003). Too old or too young? The impact of perceived age discrimination. *Human Resource Management Journal, 13*(1), 78–89.

SOU. (2013:25). *Slutbetänkande av pensionsåldersutredningen- Åtgärder för ett längre arbetsliv* [Measures for longer working life]. Report SOU 2013:25. Government Offices of Sweden .

Trethewey, A. (2001). Reproducing and resisting the master narrative of decline: Midlife professional women's experiences of aging. *Management Communication Quarterly, 15*(2), 183–226.

Wikström, E., & Liff, R. (2019). Chefens betydelse för ett längre arbetsliv [The importance of the manager for a longer working life]. *Underlagsrapport till Delegationen för senior arbetskraft rapport, 10*(S 2018), 10.

Wikström, E., Eriksson, E., Karamehmedovic, L., & Liff, R. (2018). Knowledge retention and age management: Senior employees' experiences in a Swedish multinational company. *Journal of Knowledge Management, 22*(7), 1510–1526.

Chapter 17
Capability and Political Participation Among Ageing Populations

Maria Solevid and Ann-Ida Scheiber Gyllenspetz

17.1 Introduction

Political science is the scientific study of politics and governance. At a general level, the discipline of political science deals with questions concerning how power is won, used and delegated; the distribution of power and values within a society; ideas and behaviours within government institutions and public authorities; and collective action and decision-making, both among individuals and within different systems of governance.

Within the subfield of political behaviour, political scientists aim to explain outcomes such as political attitudes and ideologies, as well as political participation by individuals. Political participation – 'action by ordinary citizens directed toward influencing some political outcomes' (Brady, 1999: 737) refers to activities such as voting, contacting politicians and government officials, demonstrating, signing petitions or working for political parties and action groups. Political participation is an expression of political equality; it is a fundamental principle of liberal democracy, which implies that, in general, high and equal levels of political participation across groups, especially voting, is desirable (Verba, 2003).

The societal challenges connected to population ageing, such as shrinking tax bases and the increasing costs of pensions, healthcare and elder care, are now well known and are at the top of the agenda for organisations and political bodies such as the WHO and the EU. However, less attention is being paid to the fact that a

M. Solevid (✉)
Department of Political Science, University of Gothenburg, Gothenburg, Sweden

Centre for Ageing and Health – AgeCap, University of Gothenburg, Gothenburg, Sweden
e-mail: maria.solevid@pol.gu.se

A.-I. Scheiber Gyllenspetz
Department of Political Science, University of Gothenburg, Gothenburg, Sweden
e-mail: annidagyllenspetz@hotmail.se

H. Falk Erhag et al. (eds.), *A Multidisciplinary Approach to Capability in Age and Ageing*, International Perspectives on Aging 31,
https://doi.org/10.1007/978-3-030-78063-0_17

growing ageing population also means a growing ageing electorate. Since 1973, the proportion of eligible voters aged 65 years and older in Sweden has increased from 19% to 28% (Statistics Sweden, 2013, 2018). Hence, with increased life expectancy comes a prolonged political life, during which the individual is supposed to remain active and to manifest her or his interests through voting or other political activities. At the same time, it is a well-established fact that political participation declines with old age, with the oldest old being the group who participates least (Bhatti et al., 2012; Nygård & Jakobsson, 2013).

In light of these demographic changes, it is important to highlight the *democratic* challenges that we are facing as our senior members of society become more numerous while at the same time being less inclined to vote or otherwise participate in politics compared to younger age groups. Still, we know surprisingly little about why seniors abstain from political participation, because the specific determinants as to why some older individuals are more politically active than others are rarely investigated in political science research. We argue that two main problems with previous research impair the understanding of why political participation declines with old age. Firstly, a lack of interest in the oldest old neglects how steep the decline in participation really is. This is because insufficient research methods exist to reach the oldest individuals, and also because the habit of using broad age intervals, such as age 65+ or age 80+, makes data less exact (see Bhatti & Hansen, 2012: 480 for a similar discussion). Secondly, routine and somewhat ageist assumptions that the participatory decline is natural and derives from deteriorating health, are likely to have contributed to the dismissal of further studies on why political participation declines with old age (see Burden et al., 2016 and Goerres, 2009 for similar discussions).

Against this background, the aim of our chapter is to study reasons for and conceptions of non-voting among older individuals in Sweden. We argue that asking older individuals why they do not vote is a necessary research step in order to gain a deeper understanding of why voting declines with older age and why it varies across individuals.

To achieve this aim, we present a tentative framework for studying capability and political participation among older people, in which we combine insights from previous research on age, health and political participation with the perspective of capability: what a person is effectively able to be and do (Nussbaum, 2003; Robeyns, 2005; Sen, 1980). This framework is later used as an analytical tool for understanding and categorising responses from extended interviews with eight individuals, all aged 80 years or older. The working hypothesis is that capability is a key explanation for what hinders or enables political participation among older people. Capability can refer both to available resources within the individual (internal capability/micro-level factors) and the surrounding context (external capability/meso-level factors) (Robeyns, 2005). Thus, we further assume that internal and external capability, both separately and combined, are important predictors of political participation among older people and that a negative change in capability is a core determinant of decreasing political participation.

The chapter continues with a short empirical overview of age patterns in political participation followed by a review of previous research on ageing, health and political participation. Thereafter, we briefly present the capability approach and how it adds to existing research. We then present empirical illustrations from extended interviews with eight seniors on conceptions of and reasons for non-voting in old age and how these could be understood from the capability perspective. The chapter ends with a brief discussion on the potential of a capability approach to political participation.

17.2 The Relationship Between Age and Political Participation

The relationship between age and political participation is very often described as curvilinear, with both younger and older people tending to participate less than the middle-aged. The decline in participation during old age is a well-established fact that has been observed in different countries and over time (e.g. Wolfinger & Rosenstone, 1980: 38; Bhatti & Hansen, 2012; Bhatti et al., 2012; Fieldhouse et al., 2007; Nygård & Jakobsson, 2013; Rattinger, 1992). Sweden is no exception; in the Swedish national election of 2018, the highest turnout level, 90.3%, was among voters age 65–69 and 70–74 respectively, while voters aged 80 years and older had the lowest turnout level of all age groups, at 75.1% (Statistics Sweden, 2019). Over the last 30 years, voters aged 75 years and older have consistently shown the lowest turnout levels of all age groups (see Fig. 17.1).

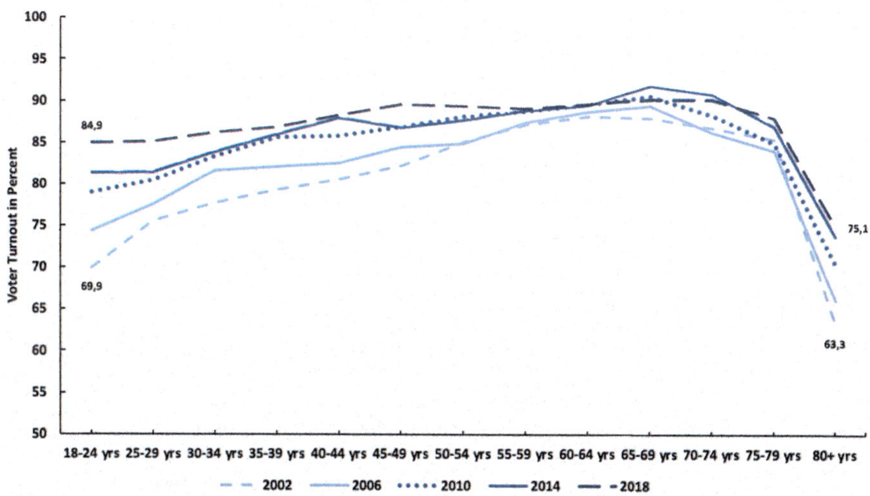

Fig. 17.1 Voter turnout by age in the Riksdag elections 2002–2018 (percent). (Source: Statistics Sweden, https://www.scb.se/hitta-statistik/statistik-efter-amne/demokrati/allmanna-val/allmanna-val-valdeltagandeundersokningen/. Last accessed 2021-02-25)

Similarly, the results for Sweden from the European Social Survey show that levels of *non-electoral* political participation, here defined as at least one political activity such as contacting politicians, signing petitions or wearing campaign badges during the previous 12 months are by and large around 70% among the young, the middle-age and the newly retired, while participation levels decrease rapidly after the age of 75 (see Fig. 17.2). Thus, what both Figs. 17.1 and 17.2 illustrate is that the relationship between age and political participation in Sweden is no longer curvilinear. Levels of participation are fairly stable across age groups until the age of 75.

However, results from the SOM Institute at the University of Gothenburg show that levels of political interest do not follow the same pattern; political interest reaches its highest levels in the oldest age groups (see Fig. 17.3). Thus, older people remain interested in politics but do not manifest this interest as frequently in either electoral or non-electoral participation. Following this, we argue that it is relevant to direct attention towards the presumed differences in political participation *within* the older age group (65 and older) and what explains these differences.

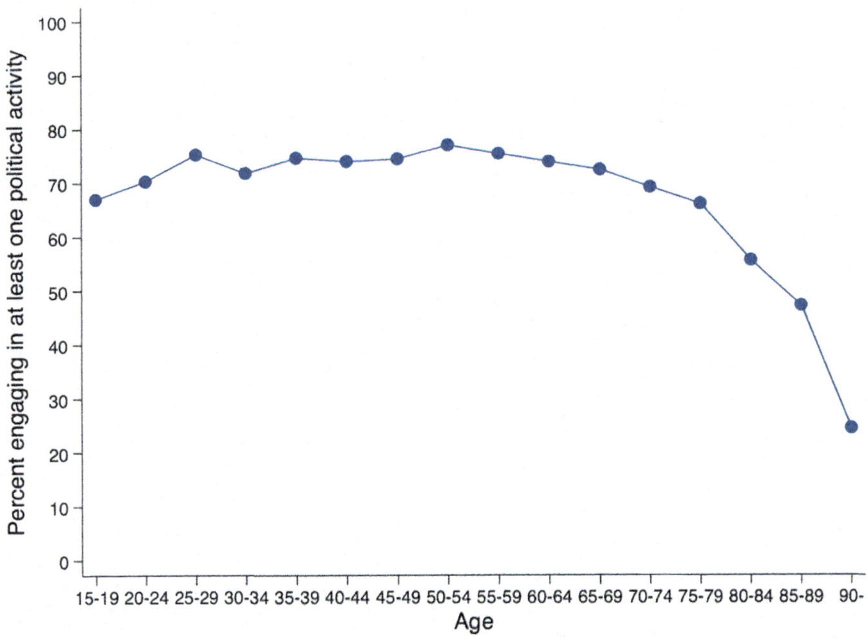

Fig. 17.2 Political participation by age, pooled data from 2002–2016 (percent). (Source: European Social Survey, pooled data for Sweden 2002, 2004, 2006, 2008, 2010, 2014 and 2016 (unweighted as sample sizes are very similar for each year). *Political participation* concerns the proportion of respondents who, during the previous 12 months, did at least one of the following activities: Contacted a politician, government or local government official, Worked in a political party or action group, Worked in another organisation or association, Wore or displayed a campaign badge/sticker, Signed a petition, Took part in a lawful public demonstration, Boycotted certain products)

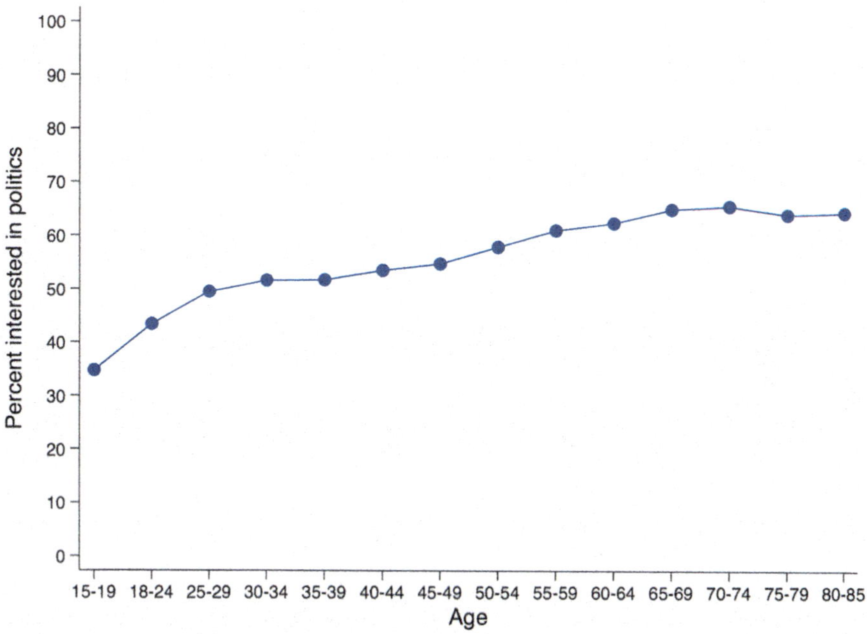

Fig. 17.3 Interest in politics by age, pooled data from 1986–2016 (percent). (Source: The Swedish National SOM Survey, pooled data 1986–2016, University of Gothenburg. Data are not weighted, which means that earlier years with smaller samples (but higher response rates) weigh equally with later years, which had larger samples but lower response rates. The overall conclusion is not altered if year-specific lines are drawn, but such a graph would also illustrate the overall increase in political interest over time in all age groups. *Political interest* concerns the proportion of respondents who have answered that they are Very or Quite interested in politics)

17.3 Ageing, Health and Political Participation

In modern political science, inequality in citizens' participation is commonly analysed using the so-called Civic Voluntarism Model, which includes three different, but intertwined, sets of variables at the individual level: socio-economic resources, such as time and skills; motivation, such as political interest and political efficacy; and recruitment, such as being part of a network. The explanations as to why some citizens report lower levels of political participation are because they cannot participate, they do not want to or no one asked (Verba et al., 1995). In short, the results show that higher education, having an interest in politics and being socially included play a significant role in explaining an individual's level of political participation, both independently and controlled for each other.

Although research focusing on political participation among seniors is scarce, there are two opposing views about how ageing potentially affects such participation. On the one hand, ageing has been both argued and shown to *increase* political participation. Ageing, and particularly retirement, increases the free time at an individual's disposal, and having time is an important resource for active participation and engagement (Verba et al., 1995). With increased time at one's disposal, there also follow increased opportunities to follow the news, which is positively associated with a high level of interest in politics (Strömbäck et al., 2013). A second factor of importance is the lifetime accumulation of political knowledge and experience, coupled with an increased sense of duty and compliance (Goerres, 2009). A third argument is the mobilisation that comes with the fact that retired or older individuals become more dependent on the state through pension systems, healthcare and eldercare. In some countries, these welfare-state benefits have mobilised strong interest groups that resist cutbacks (Campbell, 2003). Finally, the current older generation is very different from previous older generations (Goerres, 2009). Extensive research shows that living conditions, well-being and education levels have improved or increased tremendously, all important predictors of both a longer life and greater political participation. In terms of health, today's 70-year-olds are both objectively and subjectively more like the 50-year-olds of the 1970s (AgeCap, 2019).

On the other hand, ageing has also been both argued and shown to *decrease* political participation. As shown earlier, it is difficult to ignore the empirical facts that both turnout and other political activities tend to decrease after 75 years of age. The main causes behind this decline in participation are, according to one study, the disruption of social connections due to retirement and the higher probability of living alone due to loss of one's partner (Bhatti & Hansen, 2012). However, worsened general health (Burden et al., 2016; Bhatti & Hansen, 2012; Mattila et al., 2013), decreased capacity for learning, loss of memory functions and disability are also negatively associated with both social and political participation. This tendency is evident among both the population in general (Sund et al., 2017), and older people in particular (Bukow et al., 2002). Arguments have also been put forward that older people tend to focus on more inward-oriented activities (Katz, 2000). Johnson and Barer (1992) found that older people redefine themselves and readjust to a narrower social world, voluntarily or involuntarily as a way to align their functionings with the social expectations to which they are subjected. With old age, individuals become less susceptible to expectations that conflict with their capacities and shift their awareness away from the long perspective and the external, towards the present and introspection. In yet another study, it has been shown that social participation, that is participation in which one needs to share resources with others, should be seen as cumulative. People who take part in political forms of participation also engage in less demanding forms of social participation. However, with increasing age and worsening health, the oldest old refrain from political participation because it takes too much effort, and instead focus on social participation (Bukow et al., 2002). These latter studies all suggest that, for some, becoming old implies an increased feeling that politics does not matter, or, from a broader perspective, that what is going on in the outside world is of less importance than before. This would further imply that political participation is not a desirable function for everyone.

Our main point is that the degree to which ageing is associated, on the one hand, with an *increase or stability* in political participation or, on the other hand, with a *decrease* in political participation could depend on the individual's capability. We further argue that these two opposing views are a result of insufficient data, and that the more positive outlook on the relationship between ageing and political participation relies on studies conducted with the younger old. Therefore, we argue that it is important to direct attention towards the oldest old in research on ageing and political participation.

17.4 A Capability Approach to Political Participation

From the literature review above, we can conclude that the ageing process affects individuals' levels of participation differently. We argue that capability, the degree to which a person can execute valuable functionings, could serve as an overarching explanation for the ability a person has to participate in politics and that this has been overlooked in previous research.

As discussed elsewhere in this book, capabilities are functionings that make life valuable – the extent to which a person is able to function in a way that is valuable or desirable to that person (Sen, 1980). Examples of capabilities that could be seen as valuable include bodily health, bodily integrity, the senses, imagination and thought, emotions, practical reason, affiliation, play and control over one's environment (Nussbaum, 2011: 33–34). A different way to express this is that 'functionings are "being and doings", that is various states of human beings and activities that a person can undertake' (Robeyns, 2018: 112). Thus, functionings include everything from being educated, through voting to travelling and spending time with grandchildren. Every functioning has a corresponding capability, which is seen as the individual's opportunity to achieve this functioning (ibid. 2018). In addition, one ought to distinguish between internal capabilities, which are states of a person that enable him/her to exercise a specific functioning, and combined capabilities, which includes the external conditions that enable a person to exercise a specific function (see Nussbaum, 2000: 84; Robeyns, 2005: 104).

This means that capability is what a person *can do*, rather than what the person *actually does*, to achieve desirable goals. Having access to means of political influence, for example the right to vote, is often seen as an important functioning associated with well-being. In fact, it has also been pointed out that social/political participation in itself is an indicator of quality of life among older people (Bukow et al., 2002). In democratic countries, this political right is equal for everyone (one person, one vote). But not everyone has the *capability* to vote – this may be due to a lack of resources, motivation or recruiting networks, but it could also be due to not having the physical and/or mental health to be able to vote.

17.5 Study Design and Method

Even though capability is not a new concept within political science, it has not, to the best of our knowledge, been studied in relation to ageing and political participation. Studying the relationship between capability and political participation ideally requires a mixed-method approach that combines individual qualitative interviews and focus-group interviews with older individuals and elder-care professionals, along with statistical analyses of cross-sectional survey data, epidemiological population data and panel data with older people. Such a mixed-method design will remedy shortcomings identified in previous research, with earlier studies of political participation having tended not to include capability and well-being, and studies of ageing and health tending not to include political participation. Here, we will provide an empirical illustration from an interview study of how the capability approach could be used to understand conceptions of, and reasons for, non-voting among older individuals. We further argue that our study moves the field forward with its focus on the explicit conceptions of and reasons for non-voting rather than (yet) another study of who votes. The motivation for our focus on voting, rather than other forms of political participation, is that voting is the central political activity for adults in any democracy.

The population studied consists of Swedish citizens born in Sweden, who are 80 years old or older and who have good cognitive abilities and adequate hearing. The respondents were selected using the principle of maximum variation, in order to ensure, to a reasonable degree, correspondence with the general population. The factors included in the selection of respondents were explicitly chosen to increase the variety of views on conceptions and reasons for non-voting: *age, gender, voting in the 2018 election, living circumstances* and *political interest* (see Table 17.1).

Comment: Respondents from a population of Swedish citizens, born in Sweden, aged 80 or older (born in 1940 or earlier) and with sufficient hearing and no dementia disease. The assessment of political interest is a combination of the respondent's own assessment and the researcher's assessment based on answers during the interview.

The respondents were reached using a combination of snowball sampling and convenience sampling. Due to Covid-19, it was not possible to contact older people

Table 17.1 The respondents

Respondent nr.	Age (Born year)	Gender	Voted 2018	Living circumstances	Political interest
1	85 (1935)	Male	No	Own home	No interest
2	81 (1939)	Female	No	Care home	Some interest
3	82 (1938)	Female	Yes	Own home	Large interest
4	82 (1938)	Female	Yes	Own home	Large interest
5	89 (1931)	Male	Yes	Own home	Large interest
6	84 (1936)	Male	Yes	Own home	Large interest
7	86 (1934)	Female	Yes	Own home	Some interest
8	95 (1925)	Female	Yes	Care home	No interest

in person; instead, contacts were mediated through friends, family, social media posts and by contacting retirement homes. To mitigate the risk of the sample being biased towards more active and communicative individuals, the persons who mediated the contacts (e.g. relatives, friends or caretakers of respondents) were reminded that all types of individuals within the population were of interest. In total, eight respondents aged 81–95 years were interviewed by telephone between April and July 2020. Each interview took between 20 and 60 min to complete. The decision to use telephone interviews was another consequence of the ongoing Covid-19 pandemic, and the fact that all respondents were considered to belong to the high-risk group.

Conducting interviews over the telephone generally runs the risk of missing out on non-verbal communication that facilitates naturalness, comfort and trust in the interview situation. Additionally, when interviewing older people, hearing-impaired individuals can also benefit from in-person interviews (Shuy, 2001). On the other hand, telephone interviews typically generate fewer interviewer effects and facilitate less biased questions. An additional advantage is that interviews over the phone usually take less time than in-person interviews and thus reduce demanding preparations that the respondent would undertake before an in-person interview (ibid. 2001). In sum, telephone interviews were a necessary choice but nevertheless a less preferable option that does not create the same dynamic as in-person interviews would have achieved. However, our firm perception is that all respondents were comfortable in the interview situation.

The interview guide consisted of three themes: biographical and warm-up questions, questions about voting and non-voting, and questions about the social world. Each interview ended with a debriefing. All interviews were transcribed, with the consent of the respondent, and the transcripts were later analysed using the grounded theory method. This method prescribes the use of *categories*, *dimensions* and *qualities* for summarising the collected material; broad categories are identified within the empirical material, the dimensions of these categories are then determined and given specific qualities (Eneroth, 2005).

17.6 Empirical Illustration of Conceptions of and Reasons for Non-voting

Based on the interviews, conceptions and reasons for non-voting were categorised into *internal* reasons and *external* reasons, which also correspond to the two main dimensions of capability. Among the internal reasons, the dimensions: *engagement*, *health* and *efficacy* were identified. Among the external reasons, three additional dimensions were identified: *practical assistance*, *social support* and *information*. Of the six dimensions, answers related to engagement, health, practical assistance and social support all bear a close resemblance to the concept of capability; thus, these are the focus of the empirical illustration. Answers related to efficacy were strongly connected to distrust in and disappointment with politicians, while information concerned the (lack of) information provided by political parties and the election authorities. These are also well-established determinants of voter turnout in political science research (see e.g. Franklin, 2004), but will not be included in our illustration. However, all six dimensions are illustrated in Fig. 17.4 in the appendix.

17.6.1 Internal Capabilities: Engagement

R1 is an 85-year-old man who did not vote in the 2018 election and has no intention of doing so in the future. He is ‘too old’ and too frail, he says. When asked if this is a physical issue, he says:

> No, it’s not the body, it’s… One doesn’t have the strength to get familiar with the stuff. I have the strength to go out [for walks] but I don’t have the strength to take in all the political decisions in the newspapers. I can’t say ‘Oh Lord, what’s that? I have to call someone!’ – that’s over […] You see, it only has to do with age. It’s very simple: age takes its toll. I don’t have the strength to go to meetings, I don’t have the strength to get into details. I could 10–15 years ago, but… (R1)

R1 explains that it is not health issues that keep him from being engaged, which is supported by the fact that earlier in the interview he said that he is satisfied with his physical health. It is rather the effects of ageing on how much he is able to *mentally* engage with that hinder him from being engaged enough to vote.

R8, who is a 95-year-old woman who does vote, puts forward similar thoughts when she is reflecting on other people’s non-voting in old age: ‘[…] when one gets older, one doesn’t invest as much interest any more, as one would have when, for

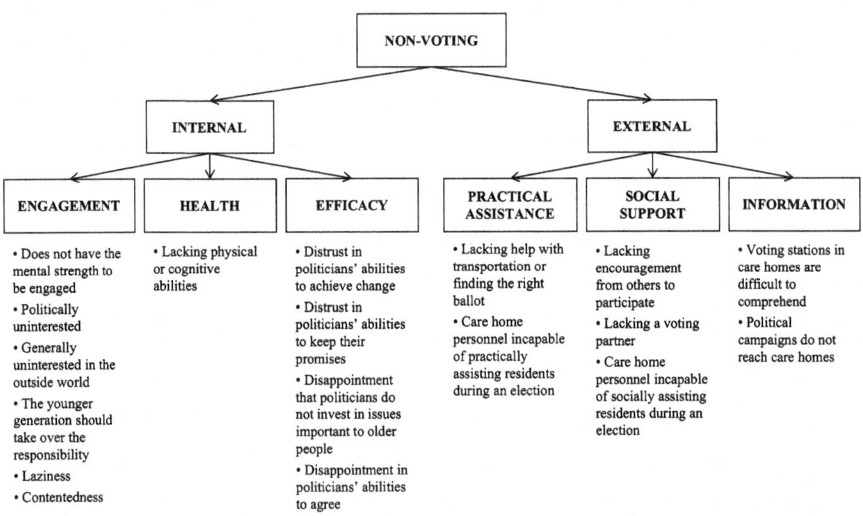

Fig. 17.4 Category schedule, conceptions of and reasons for non-voting among seniors

example, one was young. That's what I think. It just passes. "What will be will be", they think' (R8). In addition to being expressions of a lack of engagement, the answers given by R1 and R8 could also relate to a lack of the internal capabilities necessary to be able to perform the function of voting. What further unites the statements from R1 and R8 is that voting can simply be too much of an effort and that one can thus feel the need to direct one's capabilities towards other functions that are more desirable. This finding is largely in line with the work of Bukow et al. (2002).

17.6.2 Internal Capabilities: Health

The respondents also emphasise a lack of the necessary physical or cognitive abilities to be able to vote; for example, to be able to choose between different candidates, to locate the right documents and go through the procedures of voting.

R3 is an 82-year-old woman whose husband was living in a care home during the 2018 election, where she spent a lot of time with him. She puts it well when she is asked about whether she thinks the other residents in the care home were able to vote:

> No, not at all. They were too deeply immersed in their illnesses and their situation to make the excess movement – both mentally and bodily – that voting is; to go out and collect ballots, making sure that it's the right ballot, presenting their ID papers – it was too demanding. (R3)

R5 reflects on his wife's disabilities: 'She had such difficulties with mobility and with getting to the voting station, so I think her difficulties outweighed her interest' (R5). In these statements, it is evident that poor health was hindering the respondents' spouses from exercising the function of voting.

17.6.3 External Capabilities: Practical Assistance

Both the spouses of R3 and R5 had health issues that would have hindered them from being able to participate, *if* they had not received help with transportation and finding the right ballot. Thus, the external resources of their spouses were key for enabling them to vote, which can be related to the concept of combined capabilities discussed earlier.

However, it is not only family members who are a source of practical assistance for those who need it, but also professionals working close to them. R3 is displeased with the assistance that was offered her husband in his care home. She felt that the care home personnel were incapable of assisting residents with practical issues during the election; partly due to a lack of interest and partly due to low proficiency in Swedish and little civic engagement, because they were all immigrants. She says:

> […] a person who has had several strokes has difficulties with comprehending. They even have difficulties with their eyesight. They need glasses, they need assistance. And in order to read things like election material, one needs better assistance […] than what was offered at [husband's care home]. (R3)

R3's attribution of her husband's difficulties with voting to a lack of assistance rather than to his internal capabilities – his health issues – is a good example of the difference between the health dimension and the practical assistance dimension, and demonstrates once again how external conditions can either hinder or enable the function of voting.

17.6.4 External Capabilities: Social Support

The social support dimension is the external counterpart to the internal engagement dimension. While a lack of engagement is connected to internal capabilities, which can cause non-voting alone, social support can remedy the effects of low engagement. A lack of social support is therefore considered a reason for non-voting that is qualitatively different from that of low engagement. Additionally, social support is connected to external conditions that can enable a person to exercise a specific function, such as voting.

R5 cared for his wife during her final years and was not only essential for her ability to vote in terms of practical assistance, but also in terms of social encouragement. The following exchange takes place when he is asked if his wife would have been able to vote in 2018 if he had not helped her:

> No, she wouldn't have.
> **How come?**
> Well, to begin with, I don't think she was interested enough. I was probably the one who spurred her interest quite a lot […] (R5)

Verbal encouragement from others is not the only aspect of social support; the company of others can also comprise a form of support. R1 lost his wife, with whom he voted together, several years ago. Lacking a voting partner had a negative impact upon his desire to go to the voting station, which is illustrated by his answer to how voting felt after she passed away: 'Well… Then the interest in voting declined too, I guess. It's not much fun going out alone to the voting station. I guess I did it for a year or so, but then it died out' (R1). The negative effect on voting of losing a partner, as an example of a disruption of social ties, has also been established in previous research (Bhatti & Hansen, 2012; Hobbs, 2019). Thus, we can once again conclude that external capabilities, or rather the lack thereof, are important.

As previously described, R3 is displeased with the assistance that was offered to her husband in his care home and is thus also displeased with the *social* support offered. She would have wanted the staff to engage in conversation with residents about the election, but the care home staff were incapable of socially supporting residents. She describes how:

> [...] they had no social behaviour towards the residents. They made sure they were fed and clean [...] and then they disappeared into their break room where they sat, chatting with each other [...] But they had relatively recently arrived in the country, two, four years maybe. Spoke poor Swedish and weren't at all engaged in talking to the elderly. (R3)

She does not really blame the staff for their inability to assist. Holding dual citizenship herself, she understands how difficult it can be to become familiarised with the politics of another country than one's home. Thus, R3's statements include expectations of external conditions in terms of social support from eldercare professionals in order for older people to be able to exercise the functioning of voting. Whether or not this is a reasonable expectation is something we leave for future research. On the one hand, training eldercare professionals to inform their patients about elections, or to stimulate discussions about politics, could be seen as a rather large democracy project with the goal of improving political equality. On the other hand, we can also see a potential risk of biased or inadequate information and potential problems with the electoral integrity of the individual, and that such information should rather be given by trained voting aid ambassadors from the Swedish election authority.

17.7 Summing Up: The First Steps Towards a Capability Approach to Political Participation

The aim of this chapter has been to provide an integrated and empirical illustration of a capability approach to studies of political participation mong ageing populations. As emphasised by Robeyns (2005: 94), capability is not a theory per se, but rather an analytical framework that can be used for the conceptualisation and evaluation of different social arrangements and forms of well-being. Based on the combined demographic and democratic challenges posed by ageing populations, whereby the political life of individuals is prolonged, at the same time as levels of political participation in Sweden decline quite steeply after the age of 80, we used the capability approach to further understand conceptions of and reasons for non-voting among older voters.

The empirical illustration, based on interviews with eight individuals aged 80 years or older, demonstrates that the concepts of internal and combined capabilities are fruitful when understanding non-voting. For some individuals, voting is simply too much of an effort, and they need to direct their capabilities towards other, more desirable, functionings. For others, health and mobility issues hinder their ability to vote but, in some instances, both the practical and social support of close relatives enables voting participation. In sum, the reasons as to why older people abstain from voting seem to be numerous, from no longer viewing voting as important, to not having the internal and/or combined capabilities to execute this functioning.

In order to further understand and explain the differences in voting activity within the older electorate, and political participation among older individuals more generally, we need to continue to combine explanations at the macro, meso and micro levels. Although the current study has primarily focused on the individual's social context (external capability/the meso level) and socioeconomic and health-related prerequisites (internal capability/the micro level) connected to political participation, we also perceive a need to incorporate macro-level perspectives into future research. Such perspectives could be accessed via normative questions about how democratic institutions should be set up to cater to the interests of different groups, and how political participation in old age should be viewed from the perspective of political equality across generations. Additional macro-level perspectives that it would be fruitful to pursue in future research include how the design of welfare states in general, and the design and functioning of elder care, healthcare and pension systems in particular, provide different institutional constraints and opportunities for the political participation of older individuals in different countries.

Appendix

Comment: Reasons based on conceptions of non-voting among voters and non-voters, aged 80 years and older.

References

AgeCap. (2019). *H70-dagarna. Nya resultat presenteras för studiedeltagarna.* https://www.gu.se/nyheter/forbattrad-halsa-hos-dagens-70-aringar. Göteborgs universitet. Last accessed 2021-02-25.

Bhatti, Y., & Hansen, K. H. (2012). Retiring from voting: Turnout among senior voters. *Journal of Elections, Public Opinion and Parties, 22*(4), 479–500.

Bhatti, Y., Hansen, K. H., & Wass, H. (2012). The relationship between age and turnout: A roller-coaster rider. *Electoral Studies, 31*, 588–593.

Brady, H. E. (1999). Political participation. In J. P. Robinson, P. R. Shaver, & L. S. Wrightsman (Eds.), *Measures of political attitudes* (pp. 737–801). Academic.

Bukow, A., Maas, I., & Lampert, T. (2002). Social participation in very old age: Cross-sectional and longitudinal findings from BASE. *Journal of Gerontology: Psychological Sciences, 57b*(6), P510–P517.

Burden, B. C., Fletcher, J. M., Herd, P., Jones, B. M., & Moynihan, D. P. (2016). How different forms of health matter to political participation. *Journal of Politics, 79*(1), 166–178.

Campbell, A. (2003). *How policies make citizens: Senior political activism and the American welfare state.* Princeton University Press.

Eneroth, B. (2005). *Hur mäter man vackert? Grundbok i kvalitativ metod.* Natur och kultur.

Fieldhouse, E., Tranmer, M., & Russell, A. (2007). Something about young people or something about elections? Electoral participation of young people in Europe: Evidence from a multi-level analysis of the European Social Survey. *European Journal of Political Research, 46*(6), 797–822.

Franklin, M. (2004). *Voter Turnout and the Dynamics of Electoral Competition in Established Democracies Since 1945.* Cambridge University Press.

Goerres, A. (2009). *The political participation of older people in Europe: The greying of our democracies*. Palgrave Macmillan.

Hobbs, W. R. (2019). Major life events and the Age-Partisan stability association. *Political Behavior, 41*(3), 791–814.

Johnson, C., & Barer, B. (1992). Patterns of engagement and disengagement among the oldest old. *Journal of Aging Studies, 6*(4), 351–364.

Katz, S. (2000). Busy bodies: Activity, aging, and the management of everyday life. *Journal of Aging Studies, 14*(2), 135–152.

Mattila, M., Söderlund, P., Wass, H., & Rapeli, L. (2013). Healthy voting: The effect of self-reported health on turnout in 30 countries. *Electoral Studies, 32*, 886–891.

Nussbaum, M. (2000). *Women and human development: The capabilities approach*. Cambridge University Press.

Nussbaum, M. (2003). Capabilities as fundamental entitlements: Sen and social justice. *Feminist Economics, 9*(2–3), 33–59.

Nussbaum, M. (2011). *Creating capabilities: The human development approach*. Harvard University Press.

Nygård, M., & Jakobsson, G. (2013). Political participation of older adults in Scandinavia: The civic voluntarism model revisited: A multi-level analysis of three types of political participation. *International Journal of Ageing and Later Life, 8*(1), 65–96.

Rattinger, H. (1992). Demography and federal elections in Germany, 1953–1990—And beyond. *Electoral Studies, 11*(3), 223–247.

Robeyns, I. (2005). The capability approach: A theoretical survey. *Journal of Human Development, 6*(1), 93–114.

Robeyns, I. (2018). The capability approach. In S. Olsaretti (Ed.), *Oxford handbook of distributive justice*. Oxford University Press.

Sen, A. (1980). Equality of what? In S. McMurrin (Ed.), *The Tanner lectures on human values* (Vol. 1). Cambridge University Press.

Shuy, R. (2001). In-person versus telephone interviewing. In J.F. Gubrium, & J.A. Holstein (Eds.), Handbook of interview research (pp. 536–555). SAGE Publications

Statistics Sweden. (2013). *De preliminärt röstberättigade*. https://www.scb.se/Grupp/Produkter_Tjanster/Kurser/_Dokument/Demokratidagen-2013/De-preliminart-rostberattigade.pdf. Accessed 29 Jan 2019.

Statistics Sweden. (2018). *Preliminärt röstberättigade i 2018 års val till Riksdagen och kommunfullmäktige*. https://www.scb.se/hitta-statistik/statistik-efter-amne/demokrati/allmanna-val/allmanna-val-valresultat/pong/tabell-och-diagram/preliminart-rostberattigade-i-2018-ars-val-till-riksdag-och-kommunfullmaktige/. Accessed 29 Jan 2019.

Statistics Sweden. (2019). *Valdeltagande i Riksdagsvalet 2018* (Turnout in the Riksdag election 2018). https://www.scb.se/hitta-statistik/statistik-efter-amne/demokrati/allmanna-val/allmanna-val-valdeltagandeundersokningen/pong/tabell-och-diagram/valdeltagande-i-riksdagsvalet-2018/. Accessed 27 Aug 2019.

Strömbäck, J., Djerf-Pierre, M., & Shehata, A. (2013). The dynamics of political interest and news media consumption: A longitudinal perspective. *International Journal of Public Opinion Research, 25*(4), 414–435.

Sund, R., Lahtinen, H., Wass, H., Mattila, M., & Martikainen, P. (2017). How voter turnout varies between different chronic conditions? A population-based register study. *Journal of Epidemiology and Community Health, 71*(5), 475–479.

Verba, S. (2003). Would the dream of political equality turn out to be a nightmare? *Perspectives on Politics, 1*(4), 663–679.

Verba, S., Schlozman, K. L., & Brady, H. E. (1995). *Voice and equality: Civic voluntarism in American politics*. Harvard University Press.

Wolfinger, R., & Rosenstone, S. (1980). *Who votes?* Yale University Press.

Concluding Remarks

Hanna Falk Erhag, Ulrika Lagerlöf Nilsson, Therese Rydberg Sterner, and Ingmar Skoog

As mentioned in the introductory chapter, this book aims to provide its readers with diverse accounts of how capability as a concept and approach can be used in research on ageing. The authors were asked to provide answers to three questions: how do you define capability in your field of research, how do you make use of it in your research, and how do you relate your research to the micro-, meso- and macro-levels? Their answers resulted in an array of contributions that presented state-of-the-art, innovative, interdisciplinary and intradisciplinary theorising about the use of the capability approach in the study of ageing. It represents the abundance of innovative research projects and ideas that can be said to characterise AgeCap as a research centre, and, from a more universal standpoint, the concept of capability in general.

H. Falk Erhag (✉)
Neuropsychiatric Epidemiology Unit, Department of Psychiatry and Neurochemistry, Institute of Neuroscience and Physiology, Sahlgrenska Academy at the University of Gothenburg, Gothenburg, Sweden

Centre for Ageing and Health – AgeCap, University of Gothenburg, Gothenburg, Sweden

Institute of Health and Care Sciences, Sahlgrenska Academy at the University of Gothenburg, Gothenburg, Sweden
e-mail: hanna.falk@gu.se

U. Lagerlöf Nilsson
Department of Historical Studies, University of Gothenburg, Gothenburg, Sweden

Centre for Ageing and Health – AgeCap, University of Gothenburg, Gothenburg, Sweden
e-mail: ulrika.lagerlof.nilsson@history.gu.se

T. Rydberg Sterner
Neuropsychiatric Epidemiology Unit, Department of Psychiatry and Neurochemistry, Institute of Neuroscience and Physiology, Sahlgrenska Academy at the University of Gothenburg, Gothenburg, Sweden

Centre for Ageing and Health – AgeCap, University of Gothenburg, Gothenburg, Sweden
e-mail: therese.rydberg.sterner@neuro.gu.se

H. Falk Erhag et al. (eds.), *A Multidisciplinary Approach to Capability in Age and Ageing*, International Perspectives on Aging 31,
https://doi.org/10.1007/978-3-030-78063-0

Multidisciplinary research includes a multitude of challenges, ranging from differences in how to define and approach the research questions, the use of theory building, the style of writing, authorship rules and length of papers, to analytical strategies, and whether qualitative or quantitative methodologies provide the best answer to the research questions posed. On the other hand, multidisciplinary research collaborations may also lead to a deeper understanding of the phenomena being studied, and the interactions between researchers from different fields may lead to conclusions that would otherwise remain inaccessible.

When working with this book, it became clearer and clearer that the concept of capability and its conceptualisation differed greatly between disciplines. Instead of trying to combine these contrasting views into a single definition, we decided that the differences constitute the strength of this anthology, reflecting a complex reality that changes over time. Capability, per se, is a relative concept, always depending on a large number of influencing factors across all societal levels. Although multidisciplinary collaboration is a challenging task, it is crucially important for the cumulative construction of knowledge. Different ways of analysing capability are illustrated by how some chapters take their starting point in the individual perspective and individual cases, i.e. from the micro-level, while others begin with the contextual perspective, generalising findings from populations, i.e. the macro-level, or in the workplace or organisations, i.e. the meso-level. This means that some chapters contradict one another in their ways of describing capability; however, this does not imply that one chapter is more right than another. Rather, it is an expression of how different observers regard the concept from contrasting vantage points. We think that this is the right way to take on the challenge of theorising about a dynamic and multifaceted concept. It also illustrates the problem of modern science, especially the natural sciences, in which different disciplines often describe concepts in a one-dimensional way. In contrast, we argue that, by using a multidisciplinary approach, we will gain a more three-dimensional, almost kaleidoscopic, picture of capability. In a kaleidoscope, reflecting mirrors align different perspectives into a symmetrical pattern when viewed from the other end. Rotation of the kaleidoscope results in an ever-changing view being presented. The multitude of perspectives on capability in ageing presented in this book will hopefully provide its readers with a novel view of the concept and how it can be applied in research. Knowing that there is no single, definitive truth, it is up to the reader to put the pieces together and make up their own mind about how to interpret capability, and how to use its theoretical gaze when pursuing explanations that extend beyond specific empirical findings.

I. Skoog
Neuropsychiatric Epidemiology Unit, Department of Psychiatry and Neurochemistry, Institute of Neuroscience and Physiology, Sahlgrenska Academy at the University of Gothenburg, Gothenburg, Sweden

Centre for Ageing and Health – AgeCap, University of Gothenburg, Gothenburg, Sweden

Region Västra Götaland, Sahlgrenska University Hospital, Psychiatry, Cognition and Old Age Psychiatry Clinic, Gothenburg, Sweden
e-mail: ingmar.skoog@neuro.gu.se

In all of the chapters, it is emphasised that all individuals have a value, regardless of age. Some chapters focus on the aspect of capability related to justice, inequality and democracy, the normative view of older adults, and that ageism is embedded in all layers of society. Other chapters emphasise that available opportunities create factual limitations on human capital and the ability to perform or achieve certain actions or outcomes. A central tenet in some of the chapters of this book is that personal experiences, for example well-being, are key. As a concept, well-being refers to what is intrinsically valuable to someone. That is, the well-being of an older adult is the self-interest of this person, and what is ultimately good for her. Applied to human capital, being a capable human being means having a good quality of life. In line with this reasoning, being an incapable human being means having a poor quality of life and experiencing ill-being.

Another common denominator in the chapters of this book is human needs and resources. Needs are often portrayed in the shape of a pyramid, with the largest and most fundamental needs at the bottom and higher-level needs at the top. The idea behind the pyramid is that basic needs must be met in order for the person to find the motivation to meet needs higher in the hierarchical levels, such as self-actualisation. From a historical perspective, dignity for older adults was once connected to having basic needs fulfilled, such as having somewhere to live and sufficient food resources. Those unable to fulfil their basic needs were placed in the poor house, not by their own choosing. The diversity between those who were able and those who were unable to independently fulfil their basic needs were connected to where they lived. Before Swedish urbanisation, those living in urban areas had more difficulties living an independent life during old age compared to those living in rural areas, for example due to lack of food resources. During this time, dignity was to a large extent dependent on mechanical resources, social group and sex. Today, dignity for older adults may also entail a sense of self-fulfilment – being and feeling capable. Despite the fact that living conditions for older people have improved over time, there are still large discrepancies regarding the resources that need to be acquired in order to achieve a full capability set among different socio-economic groups. A resource is something from which a benefit is produced and which has some utility. Even so, a resource may be interpreted as two-fold: having it or lacking it. In some chapters, it is obvious that older people have the required resources (e.g. the knowledge and experience necessary for continuing to work beyond retirement age), while others emphasise the lack of required resources (e.g. low self-rated health or suffering from chronic diseases).

Today, an older adult who feels valuable and respected may be more likely to experience a higher capability level. However, one might wonder if this is universal and independent of historical time and place. How older adults are looked upon in society, for instance as reflected by the media, is continuously changing, it affects their societal role and is connected to societal change across time. Who is considered to be an older adult in the twenty-first century? At what time point or chronological age is an older adult no longer included in the activities and responsibilities associated with being a participant in society? Answers to questions like these affect the definition, meaning and expectations of capability in older adults. With this anthology, we would like to highlight the broad spectrum of what capability has been, is, and may become for the older adults of today, as well as the older populations to come.

Future Challenges

We believe that, in the future, the normative claims underlying the capability approach in relation to age and ageing need to be examined by multidisciplinary research projects. Freedom to achieve well-being is of primary moral importance and should be understood in terms of older adults' capabilities and valued goals. Also, capability among older adults needs to be further problematised in relation to availability. Resources and conversion factors should thus be seen in the light of factors such as socioeconomic status, gender and groups with special needs, as structural differences may occur among older adults. These may include available resources (and the ability to convert them) and the potential to achieve one's goals of value. Also, capability is related to prior experiences during the life course and expectations about one's own abilities. The conceptual content of capability is not static, but is continuously changing across generations.

In the near future, we can expect a multitude of multidisciplinary research articles presenting findings based on the capability concept in the study of ageing. We hope that the authors of these publications will address the theoretical implications of their findings and pursue explanations that extend beyond specific empirical findings. While theorising – and especially theorising across disciplines – is a challenging task, it is of crucial importance to the cumulative construction of knowledge. It is vital to be aware of each other's differences and to remain humble towards one's own and others' research paradigms. Multidisciplinary co-operation might require some sacrifices in terms of methodological choices, writing style or keeping other research traditions intact. However, by collaborating with complementary research groups, we can combine the collective expertise and achieve synergy in the field of ageing research.

The novelty of this book is its multidisciplinary and diversified display of the capability approach during ageing. Both capability and ageing are thus changing in a changing world. Being an older person is not the same as it was just a few decades ago. In addition, the surroundings of older people also change. Capability may also be influenced by sudden changes, such as the Covid-19 pandemic, which is discussed by some authors. All of this illustrates the dynamics of capability. It not only changes in relation to the discipline that is trying to conceptualise it, but also as the world transforms.